D0203012

RENEW

SUGAR ISLAND SLAVERY
IN THE AGE OF ENLIGHTENMENT

SUGAR ISLAND SLAVERY IN THE AGE OF ENLIGHTENMENT

THE POLITICAL ECONOMY OF THE CARIBBEAN WORLD

Arthur L. Stinchcombe

WITHDRAWN
UTSA LIBRARIES

PRINCETON UNIVERSITY PRESS   PRINCETON, NEW JERSEY

Copyright © 1995 by Princeton University Press
Published by Princeton University Press, 41 William Street,
Princeton, New Jersey 08540
In the United Kingdom: Princeton University Press,
Chichester, West Sussex
All Rights Reserved

Library of Congress Cataloging-in-Publication Data
Stinchcombe, Arthur L.
Sugar island slavery in the age of enlightenment : the political economy of
the Caribbean world / Arthur L. Stinchcombe.
p.   cm.
Includes bibliographical references and index.
ISBN 0–691–02995–4
1. Slavery—Caribbean Area—History. 2. Slave-trade—Caribbean Area—
History. 3. Sugar workers—Caribbean Area—History. 4. Slaves—
Emancipation—Caribbean Area—History. I. Title.
HT1072.S75   1995
306.3′62′09729—dc20   95–9227
CIP

This book has been composed in Galliard

Princeton University Press books are printed
on acid-free paper and meet the guidelines
for permanence and durability of the Committee
on Production Guidelines for Book Longevity
of the Council on Library Resources

Printed in the United States of America
by Princeton Academic Press

10 9 8 7 6 5 4 3 2 1

WITHDRAWN
UTSA LIBRARIES

Library
University of Texas
at San Antonio

Contents

Maps

Tables

Preface

> Observe that America is a rich and beautiful
> whore. The Christians say that Heaven punished
> the Indies because they adored idols, and we In-
> dians say that Heaven will punish the Christians
> because they adore the Indies.
>   (Quevado, as quoted by Ortiz Fernández)

THIS is a descriptive book. Its main purpose is to put the history of the main macroscopic social boundaries in the Caribbean (between islands, between empires, between races and ethnic groups) into a form in which it will be accessible to those who want to theorize about it, or to carry in their minds a schematic outline of the main variations. In order to do that I have used a quite a lot of social theory, some of it invented for the purpose, but most of it fairly standard modern political economy. Social theory that is not at least good description is of no use to anyone, so I make no apology for the descriptive tone of the book.

Most of the generalizations I make about the variations among islands or empires or times in history have been made before by one or more of the great synthesizers of matters Caribbean: C. R. Boxer, Philip Curtin, Tulio Halperin Donghi, Barry W. Higman, Franklin W. Knight, Jean Merrien, Sidney Mintz, Michael G. Smith, Jean Tarrade. Many of the mechanisms that I try to make into explanations of between-island or over-time variations have been suggested by one or more of the people who write about particular islands or periods: Henri Bangou, Hilary Beckles, Michael Duffy, Charles Frostin, William Green, Allan Kuethe, Manuel Moreno Fraginals, V. S. Naipaul, Orlando Patterson, Anne Pérotin-Dumon, Marcus Rediker, Rebecca Scott, Michel-Rolf Trouillot. There is a great deal of causal thinking in all narrative, but some tellers of narratives are much more reflective about that thinking than others. Being a sociologist, I am, of course, much less devoted to the art form in which the causal scaffolding is buried in subordinate clauses, or disassembled after the narrative is constructed, than the average historian. But I hope that the reader does not have to dig too hard to get the descriptive story out of my account.

To write this book I had to read a lot about the Caribbean, since I started with a *tabula* nearly *rasa*. That reading was supported by a year's leave, roughly a third supported by a Guggenheim fellowship, two-thirds by the College of Arts and Sciences of Northwestern University. It is essential to doing the sort of work in secondary sources that I do here to be able to browse in a library with a good collection. I mainly used the University of Chicago Regenstein Library for browsing, and I greatly appreciate its hospitality. Except for asking where I could find a pencil sharpener on the third floor, I made only indirect use of the staff. But the depth and richness of the collection meant that if I decided a book was stupid I could go to the one beside it; a smaller or newer collection might have had neither the bad one nor the good one. On a few of the relevant topics the Africana collection at Northwestern had the depth and richness I needed. Recent books that I wanted to look at a lot of times I usually took out from the Northwestern general collection.

It is a deep question about the nature of synthetizing scholarship in the social sciences and the humanities why one needs to read things in the library for a year to write a book someone can read in a day; no doubt some paragraphs in this book will suggest to some experts that another year might have been well spent. It seems to me that there are two aspects to the value of deep and rich collections in libraries and the practice of browsing.

The first advantage of browsing through a deep and rich collection has to do with getting context about the societies and periods one is working in, so as to select wisely what one is actually going to investigate. For that purpose one needs to read several books on a given society; the better they are the fewer one needs, of course. But to know that local government was importantly different in the Spanish and British islands, for example, one needs to happen across a book that has something about *cabildos* and something about various types of legislative bodies and councils in the British islands. Once one has a glimmering, one can then look more systematically (or perhaps better, keep one's eyes open to greater purpose) for relevant facts on the causes and consequences of the differences. But to get the glimmering one needs to read until facts that one has been running over lightly start to become interesting. Almost any good university library is good enough to get a start, but reading a book until one gets bored because nothing new is turning up is a more productive strategy in a better library, because the cost of giving up on a book is much smaller when there is another on the subject beside it.

The second reason why browsing in a good library is fruitful has to do with "keeping one's eyes open" for relevant facts. The general point is that one is looking in a sparse field, because one has by then a peculiar interest that very few people have previously concentrated on. One cannot use bibliographies because the fact that Green (1976) has a wonderful few pages on local government in the British islands does not appear as a key word in any bibliography, nor does Tulio Halperin's (1969) analysis of Latin American independence movements as in part an outgrowth of an urban-oriented colonial representation system in which rural aristocrats and planters were underrepresented. So one needs to process a lot of stuff one does not need to use, and to go back to it when it later appears that one is after all interested in urban versus rural domination of local governments. A rich library makes skimming masses of irrelevancy for the facts that gradually become relevant in the course of the research economical enough to make synthesis possible.

One will recognize from the fact that I have only one bibliography, rather than two separate ones for archives and secondary works, that there are no new facts in this book. There are, however, quite a lot of facts that most sociologists do not know, that are to be found in the Regenstein Library.

Historical literatures as well as particular historical books or articles differ in what I will define as their "archival density," the number of hours in the archives for the average page of printed text. For example, the average archival density of the literatures on the English and French islands is clearly much higher than that average for the Danish, Swedish, and Dutch islands, and for Haiti after independence; probably the average archival density for the Spanish islands is in between. A model of what I mean by high archival density is David Patrick Geggus's *Slavery, War, and Revolution: The British Occupation of Saint Domingue 1793–1798* (1982). My own guess for Geggus is about ten–fifteen hours in the archives per page. Archival density for works written during the last thirty years on the Caribbean is much higher than it was in my youth. The archival density of this book is zero.

Another measure of merit is how much one makes out of a given amount of archival material, whether found on one's own or read in a archivally dense literature, which I will call "brilliance." My model for this is V. S. Naipaul's *The Loss of El Dorado: A History* (1984 [1969]), but then he makes more out of daily life than any of the rest of us; no wonder he does it with archives, too. A more conventional historian who has a lot of it is Jean Merrien, for example, in his *La Course et la flibuste des origines à leur interdiction* (1970). It is of course easier to be brilliant but sound if one is working in a literature of high archival density, and Merrien did not pick an easy area here.

Since I have by now disclaimed the originality of having established new facts from archives, and also the originality of having a new general theory, I need a rationale for the book. I believe that one of the uses of social theory is to pack description more densely, and to make it more memorable—a plodding person's brilliance, perhaps. Whitehead somewhere said something like, "We think in generalizations, but live in details." Generalizations, written up with facts as illustrations or evidence, or mechanisms by which specific described sequences of events might have been created, give our minds two handles on the facts, two ways to get to these facts from places in our thought where they might be relevant: one through the factual context, and one through the generalization or mechanism. I hope to give the reader two or more handles on many important facts about the Caribbean late 18th and 19th centuries. And I hope to give the reader also some beautiful and some very ugly details.

Once one learns, for example, the generalization that in Cuba almost everything that was associated with either urbanism or sugar plantations increased regularly in the 18th and 19th centuries from low in the eastern province also named Cuba to Havana (Guerra y Sánchez (1972), pp. 1–11), we can remember that Havana and nearby provinces had both more slaves and more Spaniards (*peninsulares*) than the rest of Cuba, while the east had more creoles, more free colored, and fewer slaves; and we can then perhaps remember which kinds of revolutionary movements (rural populist and *caudillo* movements) tended to start in the east. So theory helps us learn the description.

This is the second time I have embarked on studying the social structure of societies that my sociological colleagues have shown little interest in. In Norway at least I was there part of the time, and Norwegians (as Carol Heimer observed, every fourth Norwegian one meets is a social scientist) are interested in Norway. I am not in the social circles where interest in the Caribbean runs high. I have consequently learned all too well from writing on the Caribbean what those who send me papers that end up on the bottom of my pile must feel like. Those colleagues who have been willing to read on societies and centuries they do not much want to know about are especially valuable: Karl Monsma, Carol Heimer, Christopher Jencks, Mindie Lazarus-Black, Frank Safford, John Markoff. By his penetrating comments on the lack of coherent generalization, and what important forces I had left out, Markoff caused Chapter 7; I hope it does him and me both credit, but I take the blame if it does not.

I have created a convention for taking account of the fact that many of the islands had different names at the time I was writing about than they do now, and that consequently historians write about them under one name, but sociologists and undergraduates know them under another. When I am writing about many islands at once, I use their modern names and put the name they had at the time in brackets, as St. Lucia [St. Lucie] for the time before the English took possession. I have usually used the name used in American English for the modern name, so that the majority of my readers will have the least trouble finding it on the map. I have usually used the name in the majority official language of the island for the one in brackets; when the majority language differed from the official language, I have used the one I found most in modern literature.

There are some ambiguities still, as when Haitians in the early 19th century called the island we know as Hispaniola Haiti, while almost everyone else called only the French part Haiti, and called the Spanish part Santo Domingo, and I have resolved these as suited my prejudices. I have similarly resolved cases where people still haven't made up their minds, as in the use of Leeward Islands (e.g., the French count their islands among the English Leewards as *du vent* or *au vent* and only Haiti as *sous le vent*). And sometimes a single source had an island named St. Christopher in some places, St. Kitts in others (or St. Barthélemy and St. Barts; Sint Maartens and St. Martin; St. Johns and St. Jans), and I have again used my prejudices. I have called the island Basse Terre that is called by some Guadeloupe writers *Guadeloupe proprement dit*, because that is what all foreigners do.

Fortunately many islands have their 18th century names preserved through changes of empire and through independence, so Trinidad kept its Spanish name (though not, of course, its Spanish pronunciation, and it is referred to in the French literature as Trinité) through a period of a majority of French-speakers, a century and a half in the English empire, and independence with a combined colored, black, and East Indian population. Only a drastic simplification of multiple conventions can make a book like this readable, and I have done the best I could.

All translations cited from a source written in another language are mine, and I have occasionally modified the translations of others (I have noted this). My native language is English, and I have varying command of the other Caribbean languages. I have had trouble understanding a few things in all the languages, including English: especially poems in dialect or patois. I spent several weeks thinking that a rich man's *hôtel particulier* took in paying guests (it is, instead, a mansion), and I'm sure there are more such errors of translation that I did not catch. I have found quite a few translation errors in the sources I have used, and have faith that I am not contributing more than my fair share of errors to the literature. But if readers want to depend on a nuance in a quotation, they should go back to the original and take their own responsibility for getting it right.

I have translated the Spanish *negro* and *moreno* and the French *noir* and *nègre* as "black," but have left the English "Negro" or "negro" as it is. I have translated the Spanish *mulato* and the French *mulâtre* as "mulatto," though the meaning seems to be more precise in those languages than in English, and have translated the Spanish *pardo* and *de color*, and rendered the British "coloured," as "colored."

In particular, the term "colored" and its equivalents in the slave period usually meant "free colored and black," and "freedmen" or *affranchis* usually meant the same group, whether they were born free or had been freed; some of that usage did not disappear when slavery was abolished (see Handler (1974), p. 5), but usually after emancipation colored came to mean "of mixed race." I have not tried to keep this straight when the original authors did not bother to, because for most purposes I want to correctly render the confusion about race of the historical subjects. It is a socially important fact that they were not geneticists.

I have called Indians and others from the Asian subcontinent East Indians, and Native Americans, Indians. I have used the word "creole" (both as a noun and an adjective) in the British West Indies sense of "born in, made in, or characteristic of the islands"; the Spanish *criollo* still has a partly racial meaning, as "pure white," rather than *mestizo*, or non-European, and in American English "creole" refers to the culture and people of French ethnicity in Louisiana, but I do not use the term in either of these senses.

There is no universal language of race and ethnicity into which the political and social connotations of Caribbean race, ethnicity, and birthplace words can be translated accurately, and American English seems to me particularly rigid, perhaps only because that's the one I have to live with. I do not intend to be taking sides in any battles of nuance (though that word in itself is an insulting diminishing of issues that can be crucial to the people involved) in cultures not my own. I do not stick very tightly to the standards I myself have chosen. There is no use in my wishing the problem of race names would all go away by no one's caring any more, but that is what I wish anyway.

I have not rendered the numerals in "the 18th century" or "the 19th century" as their written-out equivalents in the manner of copyreaders, because it would have added a couple of useless pages you would have had to pay for; I think it is a stupid convention anyway.

An earlier version of Chapter 8 was published as "Class Conflict and Diplomacy: Haitian Isolation in the 19th Century World System," in *Sociological Perspectives*, 37 (1994), 1, pp. 1–23. A version of Chapter 5 has appeared as "Freedom and Oppression of Slaves in the Eighteenth Century Caribbean," in *American Sociological Review*, 59 (December 1994), pp. 911–29. We are grateful for permission to reprint them here.

I have tried to write this preface in accord with the norms of scientific modesty, though all my friends know I have no gift for modesty. I con-

tinue with the normative disclaimer that says that all the errors that remain in this book are my responsibility. But I am always nervous at this
point that I have been too convincing in the required modesty. I remember too well the comment of my father when I described someone
as modest: "Well, he has a lot to be modest about." False modesty is the
only kind of any use in a preface.

SUGAR ISLAND SLAVERY
IN THE AGE OF ENLIGHTENMENT

1

Introduction

Purpose

The general purpose of this book is to give an analysis of the political sociology of the Caribbean islands and the seas around them from about 1750 to about 1900. The central argument is a familiar one, that plantations (especially sugar plantations) created a slave society, which created racism in politics and daily life (see, e.g., Knight (1990 [1978]), pp. 3–192). But this argument has never been carried through to the details, and has not been specified to the various historical periods in which the context gave plantations different effects, or to the variations among empires that modified those effects. It has been used as a theme to unify extended treatments of history, rather than as a theory to explain the variations among islands and between historical periods.

By a slave society I mean a society in which very many of the familial, social, political, and economic relations are shaped by the extensive and intensive deprivation of slaves of all sorts of rights to decide for themselves; the more extensively slaves are deprived of freedom in all areas of life, the more of a slave society is an island or other social formation. Of course all societies are pervaded by restrictions embedded in social relations that deprive people of the effective right to decide some things. In this sense, "slavery" is a metaphor for social life, for wage slavery, for patriarchical authoritarianism in families, for the domination of children by adults, for conscription into citizen armies, and so on.

But "slave society," as we use the term here, does not mean only the lack of anarchism, or the prevalence of restrictions of social life. Instead, it means that a pervasive purpose in many kinds of social relations between more and less powerful people is *to keep the others (slaves) from deciding or being able to decide*. Some major part of the energy of political, familial, social, and economic social relations is devoted to the purpose of restricting the freedom of slaves. Freedom of legally defined slaves to decide with whom to have children, to decide what children should be like when they grow up, to accumulate resources to buy themselves, their children, and their spouses out of slavery, and to make other familial decisions indicates less of a slave society. In the economy, restriction of the right to learn new trades, to choose for whom to work, to spend the returns from work as one wishes, to take rests at no greater cost than the value of production forgone by resting, to shape one's children for work chosen by the parents all move one from "wage slavery" as a mere metaphor to a slave society. When legislatures devote themselves to restricting the nooks and crannies in which the slave population have found things they can decide, rights they can work for, protections from others' arbitrary will they can depend on, then we have found legislatures that make an island more of a slave society.

Empirically I believe this definition of slave society usually agrees with the historically standard one of Finley (1960a), that a society "depends on" slavery, and with his main empirical indicators, that a society depends on slavery if more than about a third of its population (and their families) are slaves or that authors of the society's documents take slave ownership as a "matter of fact." I want to trace differences among islands, most of which satisfy those criteria, so I want to shape the definition of slave society so that I can locate variations along the dimension of socially organized freedom to socially organized slavery of a slave society, defined as careful deprivation of freedom for slaves, that I believe is central to both our theoretical and our moral concerns about slave societies.

The fundamental trouble with the Finley criterion is that it takes a legal dichotomy, and empirically a count of people on one or the other side of that dichotomy, instead of a variable that as a practical matter in the life of a slave varies from almost free (and perhaps soon to be freed) to extreme restriction of the right to decide about all the most elementary matters. And I will argue that that extreme restriction of freedoms in family, social, political, and economic matters tends to be produced by sugar plantations and by societies dominated, in a sense to be described, by sugar plantations.

The continued existence of plantations after emancipation helped perpetuate racism and planter control of the local political system, recreating structures similar to slavery and slave society with formal freedom. Societies on the Caribbean islands had been different before the sugar-frontier period, even if they had had slaves, than they were while a sugar slave society was being built as a speculative enterprise. Sugar islands were more different from non-sugar islands the more thoroughly sugar dominated the island's economy and politics. Sugar made society on the islands different from society on the high seas around them and from the metropolitan country.

And the decay of sugar plantations made them different again, less racist and less slave-like in labor relations, though the residue of a slave society was always there.

The larger political system, in particular, the empires holding the Caribbean islands, had specialized subparts adapted to the slave mode of

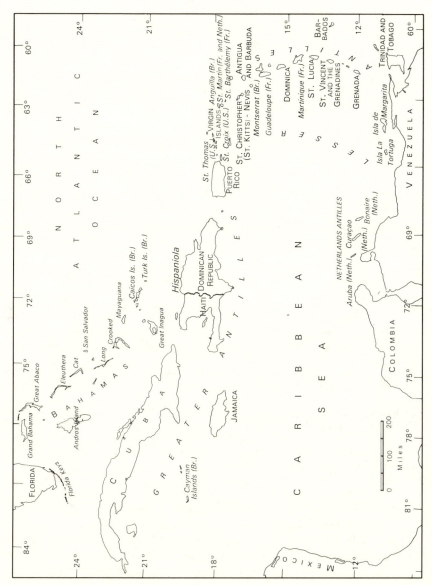

Map 1.1 The Caribbean in the 20th Century

TABLE 1.1
Size by Empire for Caribbean Islands, 1800

	Empire			
Size[a]	British	French	Spanish	Other
Small	Anegada	St. Martin		Saba (Du.)
	Antigua			Aruba
	Barbuda			Sint Maarten
	Caymans			St. Croix (Da.)
	Montserrat			St. Thomas
	St. Kitts			St. Jans
	Tobago			St. Barts (Sp.)
	Nevis			
Medium	Barbados	Martinique	Isla Margarita	Curaçao (Du.)
	Bahamas[b]	Guadeloupe		
	Dominica			
	Grenada			
	St. Lucia			
	St. Vincent			
Large	Jamaica	Haiti	Cuba	
	Trinidad[c]		Dominican Rep.[d]	
			Puerto Rico	

[a] Small means that the largest distance between shores is about 40 miles; Medium means that it is from about 40 to 80 miles; Large means that it is over about 80 miles. Trinidad is right on the border between Large and Medium, being roughly half as big as Jamaica and three times as big as Guadeloupe.

[b] The Bahamas are of many different sizes.

[c] Trinidad was Spanish up to 1800 (and so subject to the economic development policies of the Spanish empire up to that time) and became British in 1800 (and so rapidly became a sugar island after that time). It is perhaps a middle-sized island.

[d] The Dominican Republic was usually called Santo Domingo in 1800, and it was ambiguous whether it was Spanish, French, or Haitian. It had been Spanish up to 1795, and then was ceded to the French, but the French did not take charge until Toussaint L'Ouverture took it, supposedly on behalf of an unwilling Napoleon. During the following fifty years it was sometimes held by the French, the Spanish, the Haitians, and the independent Dominican Republic.

production and the slave societies it produced. Maps 1.1 and 1.2 provide a translation from the modern names of islands (Map 1.1) to the system of empires of the late 18th century (Map 1.2). The translation is fuzzy because some empire-island connections were quite unstable. Size partly determined island importance to empires. Map 1.2 communicates this visually. Table 1.1 presents a listing of islands of the empires by three size categories, which makes it easier to talk about size verbally.

The world-system politics of the seas and of military and commercial monopolies on the islands that were a part of that world system was more embedded in slave societies, the closer it got to the land of sugar

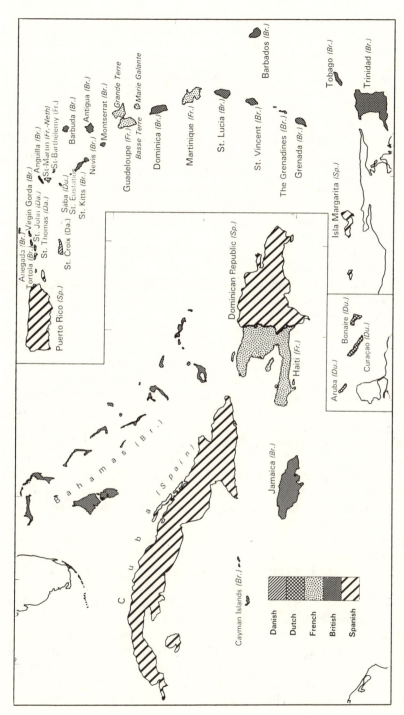

Map 1.2 Empire about 1780 for Caribbean Islands. Since Trinidad and Tobago are known as English, I have treated them as English here. Tobago was English in 1780; Trinidad was Spanish in 1780, and did not become English until around the turn of the century

islands. The main argument of the book would be extremely simple if there were not great variations among the islands in the forces producing slave societies (sugar plantations and local political autonomy). These forces, varying among the empires, produced political autonomy differently on different islands, transmitted democracy at different times and with different intensities, produced rebellion or resistance among planters to imperial power, led to management of the maritime part of the system with different kinds of market politics and administrative apparatuses, and produced environments in which slave sugar production was introduced easily or with great difficulty. And they varied over time, which produced higher degrees of entrenchment of slave societies on the early-developed islands, produced societies that had, and had not, experienced the French Revolution, and produced an environment for plantation growth in which planters would buy slaves, contract Asian labor, or hire free proletarians moving among islands, depending on the historical situation.

The nature of that larger empire's political system, as it varied among empires at a given time and within empires over time, determined in part the shape of the special adaptation of the slave subpart. All of the empires underwent a process of democratization during the 19th century, and this democratization penetrated relatively easily into the commercial, maritime, and interempire system that surrounded the islands, but with much more difficulty into the slave societies themselves. Of course, the more sugar dominated an island, and the more solidly the historical process had entrenched an autonomous slave society on the island, the more difficult the penetration of black and mulatto citizenship was. In all the empires, the slave trade was politically easier to abolish than slavery on the plantation, because maritime commerce was never part of a slave society even when it was dependent on such slave societies. People on the sea sailing for slave empires devoted little effort to depriving slaves of their freedom in the various parts of their lives, even if they profited from it.

Thus, for example, Spain itself had a weaker democratic revolution (my discussion of what I mean by "democratic" is in Chapter 7) in the metropole in the early 19th century, but had less sugar- and slave-dominated islands, and the islands were less autonomous in their internal politics. France had a very strong democratic revolution in the late 18th century and revolutions episodically in the 19th century, but its islands were very strongly dominated by slave sugar plantations, and two of them (Martinique and Guadeloupe) had thoroughly developed slave societies that were quite politically autonomous and well organized. Thus the history of the Spanish islands had produced a weak enemy for democracy to penetrate, but a democracy without much penetrating power. The history of the French islands produced the raw materials for early and recurrent social and political explosions, with episodically strong democracy and an always strong planter reaction, until the plantation system was abolished. The explosions on the French islands were timed by democratic movements in France.

Why Islands as the Units of Analysis?

But the first thing we have to establish for this argument to be fruitful is that islands were sufficiently separate as societies that they may be expected to have histories that differ, a long-run difference. Only if islands are sensible units of analysis does it make sense to say, for example, that Trinidad differed from Jamaica in having about half of its sugar-frontier period after emancipation and so importing Asian labor. That coolie labor force and the ex-slaves became free more quickly for about the last half of the frontier development (1832 to 1860) because Trinidad had a less autonomous and less well-entrenched local government, having a less socially homogeneous planter class. It had a French ethnic tradition among planters, and French planters specialized more in cocoa and other crops that produce less reactionary planters than did English planters. It is because we expect islands to remain integrally affected by causal forces of their history that we would expect these differences to produce, say, a more culturally and institutionally plural society in Trinidad than in Jamaica by the end of the 19th century.

Thus we will start our argument in Chapter 2 with an analysis of the varying geography of different islands. That analysis serves two purposes. The first is giving a solid ground for thinking that, say, Trinidad might be expected to be more different from Grenada, which is right next to it, than, say, Norfolk is different from Essex, which is right next to it, because English islands were more strongly bounded societies than English counties. And in particular the islands were very strongly bounded socially and politically from the ocean, so even though the slave and free parts of empires interacted across the docks and in the warehouses of the islands, they were not "the same" social order at all.

The second purpose is to identify variations among islands that were likely to affect the character of their development into slave societies. The most important variation is whether they were appropriate for the plantation crops. But slave society rests on coercion, and monitoring populations and bringing force to bear on them was much impeded by mountains, by dense rainforest jungles, and by the existence of many relatively unpopulated nearby islands.

Chapters 2 and 3 discuss, respectively, the geography of the islands as this affected the shape of social relations and their long-run development, and the social system of maritime commerce and naval warfare. Chapter 2 justifies treating islands as units of analysis, as things that have distinct societies, and begins to specify fundamental sources of inter-island variation in slave systems. Chapter 3 specifies why the sea link between the metropole and the islands was not such as would carry slavery back home; why that link, that maritime social system, was in fact stubbornly a source of "bourgeois democracy," with parliamentary oligarchy and free labor in the metropole, even if many of its powerful members had a strong self-interest in the slave system. Though the maritime system that connected the islands to the metropole produced defenders of slavery, it was never a slave mode of production.

Variations in Slave Societies

The sugar-frontier period, that is, the period in which much of the land and population come to be occupied in raising sugar cane and boiling sugar, greatly increased the intensity of cultivation wherever it happened. A moderately propitious environment for sugar that had been previously cultivated in other crops usually increased population by a factor of between 5 and 10 when it went over to sugar, because sugar was so much more labor intensive per acre than the other crops. Up until the 19th century this involved importing slaves on a large scale, completely swamping the population that had been there before. Significant peasant populations might persist if there was extensive mountainous land not suitable for sugar, and often some foothills near the sugar land were devoted to subsistence plots cultivated by slaves. But at least four out of five of the people on sugar land were devoted to sugar plantation work.

During the frontier period, the period between the start of the growth of sugar-exporting plantations and the stabilization of the size of the sugar labor force, the sugar workers and planters were recent immigrants, usually overwhelmingly male. Both kinds of recent immigrants died very rapidly in the Caribbean, and the sailors and the slaves died at about the same, very high rate on the Middle Passage. Adult slave, colored, and white creoles, born in the islands, died at much lower rates.

The planters who ran the plantations were the richest and most powerful people in the neighborhood. That was why a characteristic outcome on a good sugar island was a more or less completely slave society. After the good sugar land was devoted to sugar and the mills to process it for shipment were built, then except for some expansion of both the slave and the planter populations as they came to have more old people and children per worker, the population tended to stabilize. For various reasons, from then on, it was usually downhill for the planters' fortunes, but uphill in the degree of dominance of slaveholder planter interests in the society at large because the planters and local government were better organized.

To specify what sort of society one had in the late 18th century, then, we have to locate the period of the sugar frontier (I use an estimate of the midpoint of sugar extension to locate this period—the frontier periods are longer on larger, more ecologically diverse islands), and classify islands by the degree to which they eventually came to be completely demographically and economically dominated by the sugar plantation complex. That is the purpose of Chapter 4, on the economic demography of plantation societies. This economic demography also treats the social periphery on the island, which consists of two main populations: peasants and urban service workers. The main purpose of Chapter 4 is to provide estimates of the size of the race-producing sugar plantation complex on different islands at different times.

To determine island social structure, the size has to be measured against the main alternatives. Cuban sugar was big in the late 18th and early 19th centuries, but it was on a big island with a big peasant population, and that island had the main governmental and shipping center of the Spanish Caribbean on it. Thus the most substantial Spanish sugar complex during slave times was on the island with the biggest peasantry and one of the biggest urban complexes, and so did not shape the whole society. In fact it did not shape the whole slave population, since only about half or two-thirds of Cuban slaves worked on sugar plantations (Genovese (1969b), p. 66, citing estimates by Klein and Knight). Cuba was then a major force in the colonial slave system as a whole; for example, it was a major producer of sugar, comparable to the English islands, after emancipation. But that internationally dominant sugar slave enclave did not turn Cuba into a slave society like Jamaica or Haiti had been. An appendix to Chapter 5 lays out the main indicators used in Chapters 4 and 5.

The size of the causal force producing a slave society was determined by variations not only in the economic and demographic underpinning, but also in the factors that determined the power of planters. Chapter 5 is devoted to the power of planters. Obviously if planters dominated the economy, they were likely to be more powerful. But two specifically political and social factors determined how effective that implicit class power was. If the imperial constitution provided that islands had legislatures with great powers, and if the local upper class was well organized socially and politically, then the economic dominance of planters produced maximum political power of the slave system on the island. Political position multiplied economic power.

The theory as developed in Chapters 2 to 5 is mainly designed to explain variations in the slave mode of sugar production, and the production of slave societies by that mode of production, between islands. An additional test of all this apparatus is how well it explains the size and status of the free colored (see the preface on this concept) population, because it was here that the race-making and slave-society–making features of plantation societies operated without obvious connection to the mode of production. When Frank Tannenbaum, in *Slave and Citizen* (1946), wanted to show cultural effects on race relations, for example, he focused on the status of the free colored. The requirements of producing sugar in different societies may have been very similar without the consequences for race relations outside the plantation among free people being so determinate. Chapter 6 thus takes up the problem of the evolution of the status of free colored. The basic argument here is that the trends in the number and status of the free colored must be divided into three basic periods. Before the days of the sugar frontier, the free colored population grew relatively rapidly as compared to the (small) slave population and to the white population (though overall population growth was slow), and the free colored were generally not very distinct from white or Indian free people.

Where the sugar frontier never really arrived before emancipation, as in Puerto Rico, Santo Domingo, or Curaçao, the result then was a small population overall with large free colored ratio to both the slave and the white population, and very little distinction by race in the stratification system. But our argument is that this was a longer-term continuation of the same trajectory that other islands followed before the massive introduction of sugar and slaves in the sugar-frontier period.

During the sugar-frontier period, the continuing high birth rate of colored people was swamped by the massive forced immigration of slaves, so while the relative size of the free colored population compared to slaves decreased during the sugar-frontier period, there was a substantial absolute increase in that population.

Paths to Emancipation and Democratization in the 19th Century

By the end of the 19th century, all Caribbean societies had abolished slavery, and all the empires of the Caribbean had abolished slavery elsewhere under their domination. But the degree to which freedom carried with it the civil rights of free people, in the labor market, in the courts, in family law, or in freedom of migration, was very variable. And even if democratization of the metropole, in the sense of the participation of all free social groups in the selection of governments and the determination of policies, was no doubt a big cause of what happened to the islands, the best of island governments were bad democracies; the worst, really awful. I suppose I would nominate as the most "democratic" in the 19th century, by an idiosyncratic system of weighting political values, The Dominican Republic, Haiti, Puerto Rico, Martinique, and Guadeloupe. Haiti and The Dominican Republic got their political virtues (such as they were) from revolutionary independence from imperial ties; Martinique and Guadeloupe got theirs from fuller incorporation into the imperial democratic system. The racist oligarchic parliamentarism of the British islands, backed by a more or less non-governing colonial office, provided stability and some civility, but its tutelary democracy had provided more tuition than democracy, and not much of either.

While the first part of the book tried to outline how various the islands were at the end of the 18th century, the second part tries to analyze how they went different paths *in the same direction* in the 19th century. The analysis of these different paths needs to take two fundamental facts into account. The first is that all of the Caribbean islands had slavery in 1790, and none of them did in 1900. The second is that in 1790 there were no substantial movements in any of the islands[1] in the direction they were all going to go in the 19th century, while there were substantial democratic and emancipatory movements at that time in the United States, England, France, the Netherlands, Denmark, and perhaps even Spain.

The big facts of the case then indicate that probably the emancipatory motion of the islands during the 19th century was not already implicit in the slave societies of the late 18th century. For example, among the last to emancipate slaves were some with the least intense "slave society" features: Cuba, Puerto Rico, and Curaçao.

But if emancipation came ultimately from abroad, it came along channels that carried very different forces at different times and in different empires. For example, it is clear that the black and colored men of Haiti and Guadeloupe formed the main human power that emancipated them in the 1790s, but it is also clear that they were organized for that task by

---

[1] The main exceptions for blacks were maroon societies in mountains and jungles, for example, in Jamaica, Surinam and Dominica; a serious but small rebellion against the Danes on St. Johns; and blacks' joining Caribs on St. Vincent. Among whites on the islands there was minor Baptist and Wesleyan agitation, and some clerical petitioning in Spanish colonies. Anti-slavery movements in Europe were a different, and much more important, matter.

the French Revolution, though blacks recruited by the revolutionary whites used non-revolutionary networks to mobilize other blacks. And it is clear that the suppression of that emancipation on Guadeloupe was carried in the same diplomatic, administrative, and military channels that the metropolitan revolutionaries had used to organize slave and free-colored rebellion.

Similarly the autonomous local legislatures that built slave societies in the older British islands opposed emancipation, as might be expected. But they built the unfreedoms of ex-slaves of the post-emancipation period with the same autonomy that had been overridden by the parliament and the colonial office to force emancipation on them. So they built those unfreedoms slightly less effectively, and protected thereby the monopoly of a slightly more open oligarchy's power, in Trinidad, which had not had the tradition of local legislatures nullifying parliamentary laws.

But to introduce the problems with which Part II is concerned, we need to present first a very brief sketch of 19th century history in the Caribbean, because it turns out that we have said very little about what happened on a particular island when we have said that, as on all the others, emancipation took place in the 19th century.

A Sketch of Caribbean History in the 19th Century

The two big variations in fundamental geographical variables between the 18th and 19th centuries were great increases in the reliability of transportation accompanied by great decreases in cost, and the growing economic and political power of the United States. Railroads and roads made the interiors of the large islands much more accessible to commerce and to military action. The larger islands by 1900 were much more unified economies than in 1790 and their mountains were, in general, governed by the same military and political system that dominated the plains and cities. Steamships could sail year-round. Freight and commercialization costs of sugar dropped. Freight and commercialization costs had been roughly half the landed cost of sugar in England and France in the 18th century, and were much less by 1900. Navies and marines transferred imperial power to the colonies much more efficiently with steam.

Since the Unites States was so close, its economic growth and military power made it the ruling Caribbean power by 1900—other empires had their place in the Caribbean by an understanding with the United States. "So far from God, so close to the United States" applied even more to the Caribbean than to Mexico, whose president first said it.

Caribbean demography changed in three main ways. First, the tropical diseases were conquered in part by the advance of medicine, but mainly by the development of a creole black, colored, and white population whose immunities established in childhood included the main deadly diseases. Even creole whites could live moderately predictable life spans by 1900 (once they got through childhood), though invading military forces could still be defeated by disease if the island could hold out for a while. Creole blacks lived longer than either African or European immigrants had, as they had done in the 18th century. Creole whites may have lived slightly longer than creole blacks and colored, and in particular may have had lower infant mortality. The second and third demographic changes were the end of the slave trade, and then slave emancipation.

Representative and local government institutions, the other basis of 18th century planter power, were not substantially changed after emancipation in the British islands, so that local government reproduced as near to a plantation slave society as was practicable without slavery. In Barbados and Antigua the reproduction was very successful, but the labor-repressive regime decayed rapidly elsewhere into an economy with many more free peasants.

In Cuba and Puerto Rico Spanish representative institutions were modified by late 18th century Bourbon reforms of the empire, giving much more local economic and political autonomy. Further change in the same direction in colony-crown bargaining and political rhetoric was due to the independence movements in Spanish America and liberal movements in Spain. In Cuba this meant increased planter power and greater dominance of slave institutions. In Puerto Rico it mainly meant development of many foothill tree and bush crop plantations and peasant cultivation of provisions and of export crops other than sugar.

In the Dominican Republic two (or three—it depends on how one counts) conquests by revolutionary Haiti confused the political development. Independence in 1844 from Haiti's last conquest left an independent Dominican Republic without slavery, but independence was later than in most of Latin America, and both independence and all the various abolitions of slavery were earlier than in Cuba or Puerto Rico. The country's 1844 government was, roughly speaking, a counterrevolution of the urban patriciate with urban-dominated representative institutions and with strong *caudillo* tendencies from the beginning, reasonably comfortable in the brief Spanish protectorate during the American Civil War. But there were more populist *caudillo* movements in the northern valley around Santiago and the northern coast, especially in the last part of the 19th century.

Movements toward autonomy in the Spanish colonies were transformed by the increased power of the United States. For the first two-thirds of the century, American policy toward the Caribbean was shaped by the South's interest in the preservation of slavery, with Cuba, for example, being a candidate slave state, Haiti, a pariah exporting revolution, and the rest of the Caribbean and Central America, a playground for American adventurer soldiers and mercenaries.

But North American commerce with the Caribbean was still dominated by urban shippers on the East and Gulf coasts. There is a sense, for example, in which Haiti was recognized early by northern United States commerce, but by the southern-controlled State Department only after the Civil War, and then unwillingly.

After the American Civil War, the dominant U.S. political response toward the Caribbean was apathy, with aborted projects of various kinds to establish American territorial power, and with a gradual increase of "progressive imperialism" of the sort that Teddy Roosevelt came to symbolize. American Caribbean power then came to be a somewhat chaotic potential support for many different kinds of movements toward island autonomy in the Spanish islands.

The French Revolution and its early 19th century fate under Napoleon and the royalist restoration provided a template of movements to the left and back to the right that were transformed in the colonies both into racial liberation movements and into counterrevolutions. These movements, tracking revolutions in the metropole, affected especially Guadeloupe and Martinique. But they also had an influence, both on the right and on the left, in the British and Spanish islands with non-French islands French minorities. Roughly speaking, revolutions in France produced "leftward" movements in the imperial linkage system to incorporate island society into the democracy being constructed in the metropole, with equality of citizenship for the free colored and emancipation of the slaves. The dominant leaders of responsive movements in the islands were commercial and professional people in the port cities and the free colored (also mostly in cities), and quite often Republican and colored generals. The structure of island movements was some combination of military formations, with some problematic political autonomy, and urban crowds, with their councils of revolutionary government, both petitioning the metropole to become the local government of the new democracy. The planters and their power and political organization did not, of course, disappear during the revolutions. The existence of democratic movements in France during the revolutions and responsive colored, black, and city movements in the islands were by no means automatically sufficient to win full citizenship, even during the revolutions.

During the course of these French revolutions of the 19th century, democratic island institutions tended to develop a formally and sometimes militarily revolutionary wing when it turned out that a new Bonaparte or new king meant reversals of racial liberation, and a strong left-center wing when it turned out that racial liberalism could be combined with the new party of order, as after the 1870s.

One has to remember, of course, that in the 19th century both the parties of order and the parties of the revolution in France claimed the heritage of the revolution, though differently interpreted. The center and right "parties of order" emphasized more the "bourgeois" and "bonapartist" elements of the revolutionary tradition; the left, the egalitarian and anti-clerical parts. But generally speaking, this left increased its power *during* the revolutions of the 19th century, so the island illusion that the Revolution was egalitarian was not without a continuing real-life basis.

Briefly, the Great Revolution won in Haiti and confirmed that victory against the Napoleonic restoration, won in Guadeloupe and abolished slavery but lost to the Napoleonic restoration, and never really won in Martinique. The bourgeois revolution of the 1830s had very little effect on black citizenship. Then the left period of the 1848 revolution won in both Martinique and Guadeloupe, and was reincorporated with emancipation and colored equality in the restoration of Louis Bonaparte. Stable popular representation in island government and in the French parliament came in the 1870s, and the socialist movement in the last quarter of the century mainly pushed for extension to the islands of left conquests in France.

The free ports of the Danes and the Dutch faded as fairly free trade came to dominate the English empire, the Spanish made free trade concessions to their few remaining colonies, and the United States pushed for free trade insofar as it pushed at all, except for pushing the exclusion of Haiti from the diplomatic community. No one much noticed when the Danish Virgin Islands became American shortly after the end of the 19th century, partly because most of their Danes and other whites had long since gone home. Nor did anyone notice that the Dutch islands did *not* become American.

Toward the end of the century independence from England and France came to be a symbol of the political aspirations of the blacks and a possible political strategy for the colored, so the three major island political dimensions came to be quite well aligned in both empires: left to right on egalitarianism, pro-independence to pro-empire on imperialism, and black to white on race privilege. The clear alignment in the islands was reflected dimly in the colonial and racial policies of the right, center, and left in France, but colonial policy did not reliably divide England or the United States on left-to-right lines.

However the French anti-colonialist left had a strong subsection that wanted, essentially, to be incorporated into the French Revolution. There was not much such tendency in the English islands, though Catholics in Trinidad had some enthusiasm for the Irish revolution, and many blacks and colored people were incorporated into the nonconformist, especially the Baptist, part of the Anglo-American Reformation.

Independence from Spain was not nearly as linked to race or to egalitarianism, partly because independence turned out to represent attachment to the North American empire (and possibly to its southern part in particular), partly because Spanish politics was not nearly as neatly organized from left to right as French, or even English, politics, and partly because urban dominance rather than slavery was the central governmental principle in the old regime. In Spanish American revolutions rural populism and *caudillo* militarism fought urban oligarchy rather than black fighting white.

The Colonial Extensions of 19th Century Democracy

This sketch will be elaborated in considerable detail in Part II. Its purpose here is to identify the core problems of the 19th century evolution of boundaries between islands, between races and ethnicities, and between empires. The core problem of this part of the book is the transmission of the democratic movements in the metropoles to the islands, transforming the social meaning of all these boundaries. Democracy meant something different, something much more revolutionary, in a slave society than it did in a free society. Movements toward democracy in the metropole, then, threw planters into a panic in all of the slave islands (even if they were not actually terribly democratic—a definition of democracy that we would think a sham is revolutionary in a slave society), but left the Danes on St. Thomas and the Dutch almost untouched. The planters on the Spanish islands were posed with a different problem than were those on the English and French islands, because peninsular Spanish movements were not so clearly democratic, and because their island societies were not so clearly slave societies.

In particular democracy required in all the sugar islands a definition of the meaning of ethnicity, especially of race, because racial definitions were entangled with slavery and with coolie immigration and hence with democracy and political citizenship. Those sugar islands that imported new labor for developing frontiers after the end of the slave trade had to define the political meaning of East Indians and other ethnicities. Citizenship of various ethnicities was central to democracies, but was only an administrative category in immigration policy for the empires.

When a revolution was not about democracy (or better, when the saliency of democracy in a revolution was lower), the definition of the meaning of race and ethnicity was less important. Thus island race politics were most intense in the French revolutionary periods, because democratic citizenship was central to the metropolitan revolutions; they were somewhat less salient in the English parliamentary reforms of slavery because Whigs did not differ from Tories primarily in their attitude to citizenship and equality of rights; race politics were least salient in the revolutions of the Spanish empire, where most of the questions were not citizenship questions; and the saliency of race policy changed radically in the 19th century in the North American empire because the social and ideological base of American imperialism in the Caribbean changed from South to North, reactionary to "progressive," during the century.

The central task of Part II is to explain the vicissitudes of slavery, race, ethnicity, and democracy in particular islands by a combined analysis of the variations in the democratizing effect of the imperial links of the island and the responsive island social movements, especially of the free colored and of the slave and ex-slave populations.

The Chapters of Part II

Our intellectual tactics in the second part will be to discuss development within empire political systems more or less in the order that their crises of democratization came into focus, with a major temporal displacement for Cuba's (and to a much smaller degree, Puerto Rico's) development of slave sugar frontiers after the other slave systems were being dismantled, and a temporal displacement in the opposite direction for Haiti's development of a free peasantry before the other sugar islands, in isolated opposition to the imperial systems of the rest of the Caribbean.

Thus in Chapter 8 we turn to the French Revolution in Martinique, Guadeloupe, and Haiti. The revolution failed in Martinique when the British took over the island and kept emancipation and left-wing revolutionary government from developing. Then, the Revolution's having taken place in the other two main islands, the Napoleonic restoration failed in Haiti and a civil war established independence as a continuation of the Revolution. Haiti is the only region of France in which the Revolution came to power, led mainly by whites, in the early 1790s and remained in power (in a black-led revolution against Napoleon and implicitly against Napoleon's less revolutionary successors). Independence came to be very closely identified with emancipation in Haiti. The Napoleonic restoration reinstituted slavery in Guadeloupe after an experience of freedom and left-wing democratic government, with many

deaths of ex-slaves in the process. This whole complicated history also
influenced all the other islands, especially those with a French-speaking
minority.

By 1794, with the abolition of slavery and the declaration of equality
of citizenship of free people of color by the metropolitan "patriot" government, the French Revolution had clearly specified a possible relation
between French politics and racial politics on the islands. Freedom and
citizenship for slaves and free colored could be integrated with freedom
and citizenship for Frenchmen (and in the long run Frenchwomen),
though race was not central to Frenchmen's own definitions of what the
Revolution was about. That possibility was probably the central reason
that leftists in Martinique and Guadeloupe could become powerful on
these islands in the late 19th century, and the islands still remain within
the French empire. But it was also the reason why Haiti became independent by way of black and colored "continuation" of the Revolution
when Napoleon tried to cut off that possibility—the black and colored
leaders of the revolution of Haitian independence had been generals in
Napoleon's army in Saint-Domingue. Napoleon was probably following
the center of the Revolution in France, which was not very sympathetic
to the rights even of poor Frenchmen, let alone of slaves. But to put the
relatives of fairly conservative soldiers and generals, who had been slaves
or descendants of slaves, back into slavery for the sake of the Revolution
was asking a bit much.

So the French Revolution produced the first strong confrontation between a democratic anti-slavery movement in the colonies and the politics of empire. The Revolution was exported from France, as was the
reaction. The Revolution stayed in Haiti after it was mostly gone in
France; the reaction reintroduced servile labor and landlord privilege in
Guadeloupe in a way the reaction never succeeded in doing in France.
And in both islands the Revolution and its aftermath left marks on the
relation between citizenship and race for the rest of the century.

If this summary seems impossibly complex, it is because the defining
feature of revolution is that no one knows who will be the next government and on what basis they will govern. To impose a chronology of
significant turning points and to identify currents in such a period is to
impose on people's actions a view of what it all amounts to in the end,
which is precisely what *they* do not have much idea of. The chronology
in Chapter 8 tries to impose such an order, and the concept of "democratization" on whose basis the order is imposed is discussed briefly there.

Chapter 8 also deals with the development of slavery after Napoleon
in the remaining French colonies, Martinique, Guadeloupe, and a few
small islands. Slaves were emancipated in the revolution of 1848 and not
reenslaved by Louis Napoleon. A law school was established in Marti-

nique, indicating a move toward assimilation of the colonies to French citizenship. The emancipated slaves were given manhood suffrage in the revolution of the 1870s. Roughly speaking the project of the restoration after the 1870s was to incorporate the colonial governments of the islands into the "regular" French government. What was regular was still, of course, quite in dispute between the French parties of the left and the parties of order, but the long-run outcome of the reforms of 1848 was to transform the question of what to do in the West Indian colonies into one of how to govern France; the chief rationalization for treating the colonies differently, that their economy depended on slavery and hence on the political preconditions of slavery, no longer held up.

Eventually this led to the colonies' being represented by deputies in the French parliament, having a local government of the same form under the same laws as the other departments, participating in the French welfare state as Frenchmen and Frenchwomen, and fighting the political battles between the parties of the left and the parties of order along the same lines as other French citizens, as citizens of the same nation. Manhood suffrage, combined with the alignment of black and colored people with the left, resulted by the end of the century in left dominance in the politics of the islands. The last steps of this transformation were taken after World War II. The equality between mainland and island departements is still not quite convincing, but no one believes that slavery can be reintroduced into a department of France, even a *Departement d'Outre-Mer*.

Chapter 9 will treat the unique case of Haiti and its relation to the 19th century international slave system. Haiti's isolation from "the international community" (not very communal, of course) was in large measure the result of French anti-Haitian policy in the first third of the century, but of U.S. policy in the second third. Haiti represented the revolt of slaves, the destruction of sugar plantations, the exile of whites, the rejection of foreign business implanted in the island, and black rule. It was also a symbol of "bad government," of arbitrary government with military dominance and corruption rather than the rule of law. It was a symbol of anarchy and arbitrary leftism ungoverned by law, preventing rich profits from the "objective" operation of that law in the hands of planter representatives. The chapter argues that Haitian isolation from the European imperial slave system was subject to different dynamics than those of its isolation from the United States and its South American dependents.

Thus in some sense the boundaries between left and right, between African-culture-black and European-culture-white, between citizen and slave, between peasant and plantation cultivation, between metropole and colony, were drawn between Haiti and the Caribbean branch of the world system. There were class and color cultures and class and color stratification in Haiti, but they had small significance compared to the real location of the conflict: between the island and the world. The populist character and political dominance of the Haitian military, then, was a reflected version of the slave character and imperial predominance of the empires off Haiti's coasts, of the military dominance of empires whose political cultures were against peasant holdings, against black rule, against local military and political autonomy, and against citizenship for the island poor.

This was perhaps the first modern case in which a revolution set up a line in the world system between revolutionary third world countries and conservative capitalist world system rulers. The French Revolution briefly became such a symbol of a great divide in the world system in the 1790s, and of course the former Soviet Union, China, Vietnam, Cambodia, North Korea, Albania, and Iran have all, at various times, set up a mutually agreed boundary between countries representing revolution and countries against that kind of revolution. By studying how a stratification system and its conflicts can turn into a nation and its conflicts with the rest of the world, we study a common process, one of whose beginnings was in Haiti.

Chapter 10 turns to a more detailed analysis of the attempt to substitute semi-servile "free" labor for slave labor, especially in the English colonies. This took different forms in islands that were still sugar frontiers when the slave trade was abolished.

In Trinidad and Guyana only around half of the land eventually under sugar cultivation was developed by the time of emancipation. In these sugar-frontier colonies, foreigners with long-term contracts, mostly East Indians, were introduced into a society where planters dominated the political system. In particular the enforcement of labor contracts was in planter hands, so the actual conditions might be quite like slavery. But laborers were free in the sense that their servile status was formally temporary. The result was culturally distinct populations with a high level of endogamy, settled in those societies that were still sugar frontiers when the slave trade was abolished.

In Trinidad and Guyana the unfreedom of free Asian labor was achieved by semi-free contract labor relations. The development of the older colonies, which did not have such immigrants, was dominated by an attempt to make use of local government to preserve the monopolistic aspects of slavery in a free labor market mainly constituted by ex-slaves. Planters on islands having already passed their frontier period could create a rather similar semi-servile labor force among ex-slaves by restricting alternative opportunities. Various devices included legally coerced labor in "apprenticeship" systems (one was being taught to obey even though one was a free person—one was an "apprentice" to being a free person, not an apprentice to being a skilled worker), tying tenancies in houses and subsistence plots to labor contracts at a lower than market wage, keeping peasant plots scarce, making emigration in search of higher-paid work difficult, conspiring against wage competition among planters, vagrancy laws making plantation employment the alternative to jail, union busting, and the limitation of educational opportunities that would increase the ex-slaves' value in alternative employments.

Thus Chapter 10 is about planters responding to the abolition of complete monopoly over the labor power of the slave by creating other types of monopoly advantage in the free labor market. The slave society's class-conscious ideology that the alternatives to employment by the owner available to the slaves should be maintained at zero could be replaced, in islands where planters were well organized, powerful in local government, and highly class-conscious, with an opportunistic policy of collective destruction of alternative opportunities to plantation labor. This policy was carried to its highest pitch in Barbados; while it was absolutely clear that former slaves preferred freedom to slavery even when it was as restricted as in Barbados, we have difficulty seeing that small difference between slavery and the Barbados version of freedom from the distance of the 20th century. Islands with more available peasant land, more desertion of estates by bankrupt planters, less systematic planter control over enforcement of the law, or other failures of monopoly power in the labor market, did worse in maintaining low wages.

In Chapter 11 we ask what happened when a slave sugar society was established in a world in which democratic citizenship was being established, and on islands that already had creole societies and economies with temporary or absentee governors. Cuba and Puerto Rico differed from the islands studied in previous chapters both in the degree to which a creole society had developed before sugar dominance and in the degree to which the sugar economy came to dominate the island.

Puerto Rico's 19th century economic development was in some respects like Dominica's in the British islands or Venezuela's at a slightly earlier period: foothill tree crops, such as coffee and cocoa, dominated and sugar plantations on the coasts were marginal. Puerto Rico was very sparsely populated in the late 18th century. This meant that a creole peasant economy, with some subordinate exploitation of coffee by slaves who were treated more like free labor, grew in the uplands. The black slave population, mostly in sugar plantations on the coasts, never went above about an eighth of the island's total population (Dietz (1986), p. 36).

Cuba had two main exporting urban centers in 1800, Santiago de Cuba (Cuba is a province in the east as well as the name of the island) and Havana, and a number of regional market centers. Havana was cen-

tral to the defense of the sea route to and from Spain, and was a principal
provisioning and repair center for the fleet. With its suburbs, Havana
city had between a quarter and a third of the population of Cuba. Something like five-sixths of the government budget of Cuba had been supplied by a subsidy from Mexico, by far the dominant colony of Spain.
Havana, then, was a substantial urban center with a developing agricultural hinterland, serving, so to speak, as an "entrepôt with little merchant activity" for the Spanish colonies on the mainland.

The Spanish government was "strong" in the sense that there was a
good deal of military force and government bureaucracy concentrated in
the center in Havana, and in the sense that the government was the main
Cuban source of riches; its government services were the main "export
industry." Cuba's imperial tie was built up of the social materials of Havana as a "governing city," managed under the Bourbon reforming administration in the late 18th century by a sort of pact in which the creoles got substantial commercial privileges (including the export of
sugar) while the public services (as everywhere in European societies in
the 18th century, "public services" mainly consisted of military forces
and taxation bureaucracies) were largely paid for from imperial sources.
So economic development in agriculture in the Spanish colonies took
place as a sort of commercial and land development "dispensation" for
the creole upper classes, especially those represented in Havana, by a
weakened metropole. Similar Bourbon reforms were carried out in other
colonies with powerful creole upper classes, such as Mexico and Venezuela, but did not really stretch to unimportant colonies like Puerto
Rico, Trinidad, or Santo Domingo.

Havana already had a vigorous sugar frontier in the late 18th century,
and Santiago, a smaller one. These developments spread to the other
plains of Cuba. Many slaves were imported legally before Spain (reluctantly) agreed with Britain to ban the trade from Africa, imported legally
from other islands after that ban, and throughout imported illegally
from Africa. Even with vigorous development of tobacco in the foothills
in 19th century Cuba, the sugar planter slaveowners became the dominant economic interest, though still within the somewhat decrepit
framework of a strong imperial government with strong ties to the
Cuban creole urban and planter upper class. Slavery was abolished in the
1880s. While the rest of the Caribbean was moving reluctantly toward
emancipation, Cuba built and then abolished slavery and tried coolie
labor in a compressed replication of the history of the English and
French colonies. But it did this with very roughly half its society, rather
than with almost all the island, as in the main British and French colonies. The other half grew tobacco and provisions, bred cattle and draft
animals, and defended the empire.

Creole society in The Dominican Republic after 1844 was pervaded by the system of *caudillismo*, of personalistic politics based partly on informal military coteries of local leaders. The internal organization of the populist rebellions in the east of Cuba was quite similar (in fact, they recruited some generals from The Dominican Republic). And the Haitian political system after the firm establishment of independence had much of the same character, though with French words. A substantial part of this chapter consists in an analysis of what that system was and how it worked, and why newly independent Spanish colonies and the newly peasantized Haitian colony should be especially vulnerable to *caudillismo* as a system of political organization. From the point of view of the book as a whole, the central point is that *caudillismo* is not effectively planter power, so does not have slave society consequences.

Chapter 12 extracts the theory from the corpus as a whole. What we will have shown is how a capitalist world system built a slave system, and then tore it down. It built it up to different degrees and different ways in different islands, because the imperial powers differed, because the time of the sugar frontier differed, and because the islands differed.

It tore it down to different degrees and in different ways because the metropole-colony link was different in different empires, and varied over time within them. In particular it varied in the degree to which it introduced and defended elements of freedom, the degree to which it tolerated or encouraged democratization, planter resistance to democratization, and the degree to which it organized and mobilized the oppressed of different kinds. And, of course, it tore it down differently because the forces on the ground on the island were different, depending on what sort of slave system the island had had. We have therefore written the conclusion as an essay on the sociology of freedom.

A casual glance in the last two decades of the 19th century at the ramshackle competition between parties in The Dominican Republic, with colored and white *caudillos* on both sides, and the formation of mostly black and colored socialist movements oriented toward electoral politics and legal trade union bargaining in Guadeloupe and Martinique, shows that there is a lot to be explained here. The main thesis of the book is that there were two big causes at work.

The Dominican Republic had had a radically different relation than that of Guadeloupe and Martinique to the history of sugar, with very little sugar production and with slavery effectively abolished early in The Dominican Republic. The Dominican Republic got its "democratic" tradition mainly from Spain, where the politics of inequality and the connection of suffrage to that politics was not central, and the transmission of political impulses to the colony was bureaucratic and, as the Dominicans said, "*boba*," stupid.

   Guadeloupe and Martinique got their democratic tradition ultimately from the French Revolution, and immediately from a polity in which suffrage and social inequality were tightly tied together into the main axis of metropolitan politics. That tradition was transmitted effectively to the islands through links built in times of revolution, then unbuilt in times of reaction, with the same sorts of people on the same sides in each building and unbuilding, and then finally by a gradual creation of an electoral polity into which both sides were incorporated. Sugar development had not created a racist system in the Dominican Republic, and Spain's imperial link to the island did not challenge racial inequality with a strongly organized system tying together citizenship and social equality. Sugar development had produced a racist society in the French islands, and then French politics challenged that society by creating in it French citizenship tied to French democracy.

   The synthetic argument, then, will be that permutations and modifications of those two big causes, the one mainly doing its work up to the late 18th century, the other, its main work in the 19th century, produced the macrosociological and macropolitical variations in the structure of freedoms between the islands as they entered the 20th century.

Part I _____

LATE 18TH CENTURY IMPERIALISM AND
SLAVE SOCIETIES IN THE CARIBBEAN

2

Island Geography: How Tiny Islands Can Be Economic, Social, and Political Systems

Caribbean Weather

Caribbean agriculture depends on the water brought by rainfall to the islands, and on the land forms and soil materials on which that water falls. Sugar in particular needs moderately plentiful water, sun, a hot climate, and soil that has not washed away or had its nutrients leached out after the jungle has been cleared. As we will argue at the end of this chapter, in places where the weather did not provide the right conditions for sugar, the political economy of the local society was markedly different. And where the land forms were not appropriate for sugar cultivation, peasant, small planter, and rancher social structures tended to grow, and these produced a different sort of political economy.

Further, since politics is, above all, territorial, and since islands are a distinctive type of military and economic entity, the political environment of that agriculture is shaped by what kind of political unit an island is. Since the major topic of this book is the variations in the impact on the politics of different islands of a distinctive slave system of agricultural production, the sugar plantation, we need to start by understanding the human geography of the Caribbean in the 18th century. But since all the major islands were distinct units of political government, since all had complex military histories, and since politics and violence are central to slave institutions, we need to understand variations in the military character of islands as well. For example, only large islands with high mountains, very mountainous small islands, and some plantation societies on the continental coast with inaccessible jungles had separate subsocieties of runaway slaves or militarily important slave rebellions. This chapter is devoted to the land (a good general portrait of the historical human geography of the Caribbean is Watts [1987]).

The next chapter is devoted to the sea, whose human geography in the 18th century was very different from that of the land, and equally essential to understanding what an empire with slave island possessions was.

We will therefore develop in this chapter a brief amateur analysis of Caribbean weather, then of the relief of the various islands, and finally of the location of various kinds of agriculture on the islands. While the chapter is by no means intended as a contribution to geographical knowledge, it is essential background for understanding why politics in the 18th century Caribbean was so radically geographically variable, and consequently why the social and political boundaries developed in the 18th century left different legacies in different places to the emancipation of the 19th.

Broadly speaking the deserts of the world are at the latitudes of the Caribbean. The equatorial rain forest (south of this desert belt) and the equatorial "doldrums" over the oceans are a consequence of high solar heat on the surface evaporating lots of water and raising the air at the same time. As the air rises, it cools (this is because earth's air is nearly transparent to most solar energy, but fairly opaque to the infrared wavelengths that are reradiated after absorption by land or water, so it is warmer near the surface than higher up). So the humid air redeposits a large part of the water in the tropics themselves.

After losing much of its water in tropical rains, the raised air circulates at high altitude and comes down as dry air between about 15 and 30 degrees latitude, in both the southern and northern hemispheres. The Caribbean is at the same latitude as the Saharan and Middle Eastern deserts and the great deserts of northern Mexico and the southwestern United States. In the southern hemisphere, the Australian desert, the Atacama and Peruvian coastal desert, and the Kalahari deserts are at the same latitudes. So the first thing to explain is why the Caribbean is not a desert climate.

The basic answer is that the winds north of the equator blowing west across the Atlantic do, indeed, start as desert winds off Africa, and in the days of wooden ships, such desert winds dried out the wood of lifeboats of ships on their way to the West Indies so they were useless (as the Ancient Mariner says, "Water, water everywhere, and all the boards did shrink"). But as the trade winds[1] cross the Atlantic they pick up moisture from the sea, so they are reasonably damp by the time they swirl into the Caribbean from the southeast (see Couper, ed. (1983) in the "maps" section of the bibliography for maps of wind, humidity, and seasonal variations).

Incidentally, in English the "Windward" islands are windward, that is, south and east, of Guadeloupe, while the "Leewards" are small is-

---

[1] They are called northeasterly trade winds because they come from the northeast in the Atlantic—they blow mainly from the southeast in the southern border of the Caribbean between the Caribbean, the Atlantic, and the Venezuelan coast, from the east in the middle part of the Caribbean. See the maps in Couper (1983), p. 46.

lands leeward, that is, north and west, of Guadeloupe. In French and Spanish "Leeward Islands" usually refers only to the Greater Antilles to the west of both the Windwards and the Leewards small islands, since for the upper part of the Caribbean, the prevailing winds come more or less directly from the east. It took a good deal longer to go from leeward islands to windward ones than vice versa, and similarly longer to go from Mexico to Cuba than vice versa, because when going from east to west, one was sailing with the wind.

The Caribbean itself is a complex shape. Some of the continental masses around it do, some do not, have mountain barriers that guide the winds, and the narrow waist of the Atlantic near the equator mixes northern and southern hemisphere winds in odd ways. The winds' directions and their loads of moisture at particular places in the Caribbean are therefore quite confused, but broadly speaking the wind ends up exiting the Caribbean to the west over Central America and Mexico and northwards toward the Midwest of the United States with approximately the same moisture load it had when it entered. In the top corner off Florida one can catch coastal winds along the East Coast of the United States and sail with the Gulf Stream.

Toward the northern part of the Caribbean there is a Mediterranean-type seasonal rainfall variation as the boundary between the colder northern air mass and the warmer subtropical air mass moves northward in the summer and southward in the winter. This produces dry and wet seasons in different places at different times of the year.

Roughly speaking the northern hemisphere Pacific has the same structure as the northern hemisphere Atlantic, with the deserts of northern Mexico and the Southwest of the United States replacing the Sahara as the origin of dry winds. These winds get quite wet by the time they blow into the same latitudes in Luzon, Taiwan, and the South China coast. Like the Caribbean, the Philippines, Taiwan, and South China are reasonably wet and plagued with hurricanes. A comparable system in the southern hemisphere is created in the southern Indian Ocean, where the great Australian desert occupies the place of the Sahara or Baja California, and Madagascar and the sugar islands of Mauritius [île de France] and Réunion occupy the place of the Caribbean islands or Luzon and Taiwan.

In such systems of wet winds, mountain masses create vertical movement of the air, and the warm air that rises cools and releases some of its moisture as rain. The higher the mountains are, the longer the wind is kept raised by deep ranges of mountains, and the more continuous the range is in a direction perpendicular to the wind, the larger the amount of such vertical movement and the greater the total rainfall. The rainfall on almost all the Caribbean islands with higher mountains is much higher in the mountains themselves than on any of the coasts. The air that descends on the lee side of such mountains on middle-sized and larger islands is much dryer, and there is ordinarily less rain leeward.

Continuous mountain ranges in areas with a more or less steady wind direction create "rain shadows," drier areas with less total rainfall, downwind of the mountain mass. It seems likely that the near-desert conditions in coastal western Venezuela and the Netherlands Antilles may be created by the Venezuelan Sierra Nevada and coastal range to the south and southeast, and perhaps even the Guayana-Guyana highlands upwind to the southeast before that. The fact that the western zone (Cul de Sac) of Haiti around Port au Prince required irrigation (and so was developed later than the north) is probably due to the fact that the Gulf of Gonâve is surrounded on the east, north, and south by mountain ranges; the rain on those mountains is the reason it *could* be irrigated.

For the islands with their highest peaks in the interval around a kilometer or higher, therefore, there is usually one of the coasts (the leeward coast) that gets considerably less rain than the other. The south and west coasts of Cuba, Puerto Rico, Jamaica, and Hispaniola, and the west coasts of the windward islands, are usually drier. But even if such dry coasts are too dry for rain-fed cane cultivation, they can quite often be irrigated by rivers that rise in the mountains. The island ranges are not so continuous and deep as to create large mountain deserts downwind. In contrast, for example, the mountains of Baja California or the Andes of the Atacama desert do not create streams for irrigation, because the moisture has already been wrung out of the wind before it gets to those peaks.

If the winds are equally wet, then islands with higher mountains will wring more rain out of them. For example, the Bahamas are subject to fairly wet winds from the southeast or northeast according to the season. But although they have much flat land they have not been very productive plantation islands partly because they are too dry. The same likely applies to the Turks and Caicos islands, to Anegada, to Barbuda, and to the Caymans.

Barbados is not quite as flat as these, and was the earliest successful plantation island. It has the advantage of being near the tropical zone (along with Trinidad, Tobago, and Grenada), which has air of a higher average humidity, but is quite flat compared with the other windward islands. This means that (like Trinidad) it has a lot of agricultural land compared with its total area, but it gets somewhat less rainfall than its more rugged windward and leeward island neighbors stretching north.

Aruba, Curaçao, and Bonaire off the Venezuelan coast are roughly equally hilly as Barbados but are in much drier winds, and so get much less rainfall, and have never been important plantation islands. Isla Margarita has high hills but dry winds, so it has never been an important agricultural island.

Island Relief

The first and most important part of an island's relief is, of course, the place where its shores go below sea level. In the following discussion I have classified islands by size into dots, small, medium, and large (see *passim* in Rand McNally (1987) and Nelles Maps (n.d.) in the "maps" section of the bibliography for most of the data in this section; also Watts [1987]). For most of our argument, the central question is not really the total square miles of an island, but the amount of its sugar land, and the longest distance between significant subareas of the islands.

The border between dots and small islands is perhaps the size of Anguilla, which is 35 square miles (maybe 10 miles as its longest diameter—for approximately round islands the longest distance across runs about one and one half to two times the square root of the area) but had essentially no sugar cultivation and so a low population density. For many purposes this would be classified as a dot, and I was rather surprised to find out it was a country. Much larger Bahamas islands would be classified as functionally dots except for the purpose of hiding pirate ships.

Small islands range from the size of Anguilla up to about the size of Antigua, Grenada, St. Kitts, or St. Vincent. Grenada, for example, is about 133 square miles (maybe 20 miles between the farthest points) and has a fair amount of coastal plain suitable for sugar.

Middle-sized islands range up to the size of Trinidad, and include Martinique, the two main contiguous islands of Guadeloupe, Barbados, and toward the lower end Dominica, St. Lucia, St. Vincent, and Curaçao. Dominica, St. Lucia, St. Vincent, and Curaçao have the distances and therefore the military problems and problems of conquest of middle-sized islands, but are of low sugar intensity and so low population. For example, Martinique has 425 square miles and a farthest distance from coast to coast of about 40 miles, and considerable area in different parts of the island is suitable for sugar. Trinidad is about 80 miles between farthest points, and is about half the size of Jamaica or Puerto Rico, three times the size of Guadeloupe; it is classified as "medium" here mainly because that is conventional. It functions more like a large island with distinct regional centers of power and marked regional historical differentiation.

The large islands in my discussion are those usually called the Greater Antilles: Cuba, Puerto Rico, Jamaica, and Hispaniola (Haiti and the Dominican Republic). Cuba is about as big as all the rest of the Caribbean islands put together. For their longest distances they range from about 100 miles for Puerto Rico or 140 miles for Jamaica to about 700 miles for Cuba. Their regions are quite distinct and quite far from one another, able to develop separate subcultures and economies and to be the basis for substantial military and political strength separate from the capital.

The main sugar islands of the late 18th century Caribbean, such as Barbados, Grenada, Jamaica, Martinique, Haiti, Guadeloupe, Antigua, and St. Kitts, now have population densities ranging from about 400 to 800 per square mile (150–300 per square kilometer), while Dominica or Anguilla, which were not dominantly sugar islands, have densities near 200, and the Bahamas, near 50. Densities in the late 18th century of Cuba, the Dominican Republic, Puerto Rico, and Trinidad were perhaps roughly a twenty-fifth of their densities in the mid-20th century, since sugar was not yet developed and most of the land was devoted to cattle raising. Densities of Jamaica and Haiti were about a tenth of what they were around the middle of this century; those of Barbados, Antigua, Martinique, and Guadeloupe were about a half to a third of modern densities.

From the point of view of our outline of slave sugar societies in the late 18th century, this means that Jamaica, Haiti, and Trinidad were active frontiers of intensification of sugar cultivation in the late 18th century, with Jamaica's and Haiti's sugar frontiers nearing their end, and Trinidad's just starting. Barbados, Antigua, and Martinique were quite thoroughly developed sugar islands, while the Spanish islands had not really opened the sugar frontier in most parts of the islands that were to become sugar areas in the 19th century.

It is convenient to classify the ruggedness of the relief of various islands into four groups, depending on the interval within which their highest peaks fall (see Table 2.1 and Map 2.1, in which the darker islands have more rugged relief).

Three of the Greater Antilles (with four of the countries) have mountains in an interval of around 2 kilometers (or a mile and a half) and up in height. Hispaniola and both of its component countries (Haiti and the Dominican Republic) have peaks in this interval, with, roughly speaking, three parallel high ranges running the whole length of the island. Jamaica has a central range with many peaks in the 1-kilometer

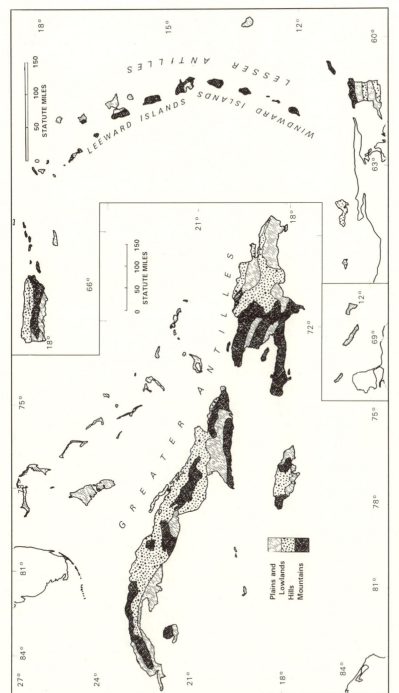

Map 2.1 Relief Map of Caribbean Islands. Based in part on James (1959).

TABLE 2.1
Size by Relief for Caribbean Islands

	Relief		
Size[a]	Mountainous[b]	Hilly, Rolling	Flat
Small[c]	Montserrat	Antigua	Barbuda
	Nevis	St. Thomas	Anegada
	Saba	St. Croix	Aruba
		St. Johns	
		Tortola	
		Tobago	
		St. Kitts	
Medium	Dominica	Barbados	Bahamas[d]
	Martinique	Grand Terre (G)	
	Basse Terre (G)	Marie Galante (G)	
	Grenada	Isla Margarita	
	St. Lucia	Curaçao	
Large	Cuba[e]	Trinidad[e]	
	Hispaniola		
	Puerto Rico		
	Jamaica		

[a] Small means up to a longest distance between shores about 40 miles; Medium longest from about 40 to 80 miles; Large over about 80 miles. Trinidad is right on the border between Large and Medium, being roughly half as big as Jamaica and three times as big as Guadeloupe.

[b] Mountainous means with peaks over about a kilometer, or 3,000 feet; Hilly means with peaks over about a quarter of a kilometer, or 1,000 feet

[c] I have exluded most of the islands that I call "dots" in the text, such as the Turks and Caicos Islands, Providencia, La Désirade, or Carriacou, and islands that are close to and dependencies of larger islands, such as Isla de Vieques, Isla de la Juventud [Isla de Pinos], Île de la Gonâve, or Île de la Tortue.

[d] The Bahamas are of many different sizes.

[e] Trinidad and Cuba both have large contiguous areas in each of the relief classifications.

interval, as well as the Blue Mountains in the 2-kilometer interval. Cuba has one range that has tall mountains, the Sierra Maestra on the southern coast in the far east. The central range running the whole length of the island mostly has peaks in the quarter-to-half-kilometer interval (these are generally called *alturas*) and has a *macizo* (in the center, near Cienfuegos) and a *sierra* (in the east, northeast of the Sierra Maestra) that have peaks in the interval of around a kilometer. Most of Cuba, then, falls in the interval of medium ruggedness, and is more favorable to more kinds of agriculture because a smaller proportion of its mountains are really high. The main difference between the islands with 2-

kilometer mountains and 1-kilometer islands discussed below is that the very high mountains are quite inaccessible and militarily hard to patrol and govern—and consequently maroon societies of runaway slaves are more likely to gain some sort of political autonomy on these islands; for most non-military analyses, though, these can be considered similar to the larger islands in the medium ruggedness (1-kilometer highest peaks) group.

Islands with peaks up to the interval around 1 kilometer (say, from 750 meters to 1,500 meters—half a mile to a mile high) include (1) one of the Greater Antilles, Puerto Rico; (2) several of the larger Lesser Antilles, more or less in their entirety: Martinique, Grenada, St. Vincent, St. Lucia, and Dominica; (3) some part of two of the other larger Lesser Antilles, though most of the plantation country in both of these is fairly far from such highlands: Trinidad, which has such highlands in the north, and the westernmost of the two major islands of Guadeloupe, Basse Terre, which has peaks in this interval; (4) three isolated volcanic peaks without much flat agricultural land attached: Saba (Netherlands), Montserrat (United Kingdom), and Nevis (now a dependency of St. Kitts [St. Christopher]).

In the third interval are islands whose highest hills are in the general region of a quarter of a kilometer to half a kilometer, often with quite a high ratio of arable plantation land to mountainous land. The larger of these are Barbados, Trinidad (except for the northern range), and Curaçao in the Netherlands Antilles off Venezuela. Smaller ones include St. Martin/Sint-Maarten (divided between France and the Netherlands), Bonaire (Dutch, off the Venezuelan coast) and St. Eustatius (Netherlands Leewards), St. Barthélemy [St. Barts] (France), Virgin Gorda and Tortola in the British Virgin Islands and St. Johns, St. Thomas, and St. Croix in the American Virgin Islands, Tobago (Trinidad), Antigua, and some of the Grenadines (Grenada).

The final group is flat islands, clearly including Anegada in the British Virgins, Anguilla, the Turks and Caicos Islands, the Cayman Islands (United Kingdom), the Bahamas, and Barbuda (Antigua), and probably including Aruba (Netherlands), and Grande Terre and Marie Galante in Guadeloupe (France), though these last have many of the features of islands with mountains in near a kilometer high because they are so near Basse Terre of Guadeloupe.

We are interested in these variations in relief for three main reasons. The first is that the highlands above about a half-kilometer (a third of a mile) and some of those between a quarter of a kilometer and half a kilometer are not easy to cultivate in sugar plantations, but at least the lower ones provide patches of ground that can be used for provision grounds for slaves. Peasant holdings to grow fruits and vegetables, coffee and cocoa plantations and coffee peasant holdings, peasant tobacco cultivation, and the like can be carried out on highlands, especially those up to about half a kilometer, and in the foothills of higher mountains.

Cattle raising on a moderately large scale was economical in some regions where the highlands provided extensive rolling land that could be systematically turned into pasture, especially in the Greater Antilles (Higman (1989), pp. 72–81).

The second important variable dependent on relief is the rainfall induced by the Atlantic damp winds being raised and cooled as they pass over an island's hills and mountains. The mountains both stimulate rainfall on the surrounding low plantation land and give rise to streams that can be used for power and irrigation; the streams' mouths create harbors for shipping. We have dealt with that variation in more detail above. In general the higher islands are very well watered, and the flat islands are moderately often too dry for plantation agriculture, though in the 18th century they were often good for building "pans" to dry salt. The exact consequences for rainfall depend on location and winds as well as the height of the islands, and in the case of Grand Terre and Marie Galante of Guadeloupe on whether there is another mountainous island (Basse Terre) nearby to create vertical movement of the winds.

The third big variable determined by the character of the relief is military vulnerability, with higher and more extensive mountains being more invulnerable. Internal groups, such as maroons, communities of runaway slaves, were more common and more likely to be sufficiently difficult to conquer so as to become in effect sovereign (e.g., to have treaties with occupying powers, or to join with invaders) on the islands with higher mountains. Such islands were also somewhat harder to conquer from the outside, for resistance could move into the mountains.

Beaches as Military Boundaries

The military character of being an island has been obviously central to the Caribbean's history, and the contact between the sea (which is the source of military intervention by great powers) and the land (which is the source of mobilization of military force on the island for the defense of the island) is therefore clearly crucial. The basic fact about beaches, harbors, etc., is that island military force has to be translated into naval force in order to be effective off the island, and naval force has to be translated into landed troops to constitute an effective government of an island. Except for Hispaniola and St. Martin/Sint Maartens, all the islands of the Caribbean have been dominated by a single government except for brief periods of invasion or longer periods of early settlement, or, on the larger islands especially, of rebellion and revolution. Apparently about three quarters of St. Martin's population was English (Bévotte (1906), p. 362), which may explain why they could remain at peace with the Dutch even when the French were at war with the Netherlands, which was sometimes in alliance with England; they could be legalistically French when the English were at war with the Netherlands. To put all this another way, the relation between empires and islands took place at harbors and across beaches. The distribution of islands of different sizes among the empires around 1800 is summarized in Table 1.1 in Chapter 1. See also Map 1.1 in Chapter 1.

The following analysis is an abstraction from a good many accounts of particular battles, and such accounts tend to be written by people not interested in abstraction and comparison. There is a great deal of random variation in the outcome of battles; outcomes are an error-full measure of the underlying strategic situation. A generalizing account of why, say, a British expedition in 1655 failed to take the Spanish colony in the Dominican Republic [Santo Domingo] but succeeded in taking the one in Jamaica is not really possible. Santo Domingo had a fort to the landward side of the main port, out of the reach of ship artillery, which was hard to "reduce," and this seems to have had something to do with it (Harding (1991), p. 155). This "accident" had dramatic consequences for differences in the later development of the two islands. Luck plays a big part in a system of many small wars on obscure islands. The following, then, are guesses about military central tendencies, based on small samples of military tests, with much noise in the details.

But we have a large central tendency to explain, that most of the very small, densely settled agricultural countries in the world have been sugar islands. Such small islands are "big" enough and their social systems have been autonomous enough that they evolved into societies that might become nations. What one needs is a theory of the military situation of such islands that is compatible with the historical outcome of two or three centuries of military accidents, namely, modern sovereignty of very small countries, and with what we know of sources of military power; but we need a theory that does not do too much violence to the historical details. What such a theory has to explain, then, is why sugar islands are defensible enough to be separate units of government when parts of the mainland of comparable size are usually not.

We must therefore analyze what it took to mobilize military forces on an island for the defense of beaches, and what it took to land a force that could conquer the island and create a government on it, to understand the nature of a beach as a military boundary. The basic interaction at the beach was shaped by the fact that island forces could be concentrated at the beach relatively quickly, and that consequently a force landed on the island had to grow quickly so as to be equal or superior to what could and would be concentrated on that beach by the island occupants.

The speed of landing was of course in general much higher in harbors, especially those created by rivers (most of the "coves" not created by rivers are at most harbors for fishermen and sports boats), and so the permanent concentrations of force by the island occupants tended to be at port cities (Harding (1991), p. 154). The "forts" were generally much stronger at port cities than at other locations in the 18th century, and it was not terribly unusual for the main town-city on an island to be named after its fort (e.g., Fort de France—earlier Fort Royal—on Martinique). If the landing was to be done elsewhere, roughly speaking, enough soldiers and equipment had to be landed "immediately" to defend the beachhead from almost all the forces on the island, taking into consideration that if the beach was within artillery range of the ships, and if those ships could be defended from attack from the sea, then a beachhead could be held with a smaller ratio of landed to island forces.

The relation between a beachhead (or a landing in a port) and the conquest of the island varied with the size of the island. On the smallest islands, roughly speaking, the minimum size of troops landed had to be big enough to defeat all the troops on the island, for these could be expected to be immediately concentrated in the battle. Once the first battle had been won, then except for "mopping up" any mountains and plantations with semi-autonomous military power, and attempting to prevent organized refugees (who might eventually come back) from leaving the island, the job was pretty much done. There might be an expensive problem taking the main fort (usually there was only one on a small island, in the main port) if there was "stubborn" (by which I mean militarily irrational) resistance from the garrison there (Harding (1991), pp. 154–56). But except for the poor sods who died in such battles, such stubbornness was not ordinarily relevant to the military problem.

For middle-sized islands, in the range of Martinique, say, the force needed to conquer the island was probably small compared to what was fairly easily mobilized by the big empires, but there were several strongpoints with their several rivers and ports, and several more or less ecologically autonomous subregions or communes, which might be separate sources of mobilization of island troops. For example, sometimes plantations were big enough to be separately militarily important. So in general there was a more complex military situation, in which it mattered how the island itself was internally organized geographically, and what the relations were among its militarily important political subparts. One crucial aspect of the complexity was that European troops and officers would start to get sick and die of their exposure to new diseases as they were kept in the Caribbean longer, so if an island could maintain even minimal strength for a while, the invading force would fade away.

The mountains on such middle-sized islands (there are really only two important ones without real highlands, and Bermuda in the Atlantic, though some of the unimportant Bahamas are quite big) presented a different military problem, because they formed a more defensible set of locations, each of which had separate routes to the various ecological centers. A conquering power may not be able to control all the mountain roads to all the relevant valleys and coastal plains. What this amounted to was that the military problem of creating a beachhead, which sufficed on a small island, was not the same as the military problem of conquering a middle-sized island so that one could create a government that monopolized force. The command of naval access to the island was more precarious until the island as a whole was conquered, because there were many places where arms and, if necessary, soldiers could be landed quickly to support the besieged population.

Of course, in the 18th century, it took a long time to organize and transport a naval military expedition with troops from Europe to save an island. Such expeditions were often militarily ineffective (from sickness, or from not getting there until the hurricane season had started because they could not leave on time), so being able to land in a cove to be welcomed by locals was valuable mainly if there was an effective force in the same empire on a nearby island.

Barbados, which does not have mountains, was attacked by a force representing the English Long Parliament, led by Sir George Ayscue, in the mid-17th century, during the English Revolution. The Royalist governor had a militia of around 5,000, as against an invading force of 860 (Beckles (1990), p. 25). Ayscue easily took some seventeen Dutch ships in the harbor, but did not dare land (for an examination of the military problem of taking a merchant ship, to see why a force this small could take them, see the following chapter). When reinforced by a force headed for Virginia to subdue royalist resistance there (which came by way of Barbados because of the way the trade winds are organized), he had 3,000 troops, and landed at Speightstown (the second-largest town, a port). He could defend the beachhead and raid plantations in the area near the town. But this was not enough to "subdue" the island, and a compromise was worked out in which both the planters who supported parliamentary power (Roundheads) and royalists were confirmed in their properties, but the royalist government was transferred to a Roundhead. Then the relevant force proceeded on to Virginia.

Thus even for islands of the size of Martinique, Guadeloupe, or Barbados, the process of conquest was in general one of stages. The capacity of the conquerors to mobilize local resources to support and extend a beachhead, then, became more important. For example, the legitimacy of the Napoleonic government of France after the Revolution for some part of the population (especially the planters and crucial generals) was probably essential for the conquest of Guadeloupe from the Patriots loyal to the Revolution, and for the Napoleonic Empire's having any chance (it turned out not to be enough of a chance) with their very substantial beachhead in Haiti [Saint Domingue]. The legitimacy of the English among the Martinique landowners early in the Revolution was apparently crucial to the English conquest and subsequent defense of that island.

So "detachments" and "strong points" and "reserves" and "living off the land" and the other stuff of large-scale warfare on land became important to the nature of a beach in middle-sized islands. The larger the island, the more it mattered what kind of social system there was that tied the island together, and that made the conquest of the center of government insufficient and, under the right conditions, left localities and mountains autonomous in the hands of resident ethnically or politically legitimate forces. Further, the ratio of local social system organization to naval and landed military organization determined the military balance more on larger islands. The better organized and unified a middle-sized island, the larger the force required to take it. The degree of organization and unity on smaller islands did not make so much difference, though the military history of early settlement of St. Kitts was affected by the military split due to the fact that part of it was St. Christopher and French.

On middle-sized islands the outcome of mobilization against conquest was determined in part by the ecological situation, such as how big the various communes were, whether there were any of substantial size that were far from the beach and commanded internal lines of communication (especially if these were mountain valleys—for example, the well-populated internal valley in the north of The Dominican Republic [Santo Domingo] made that island hard to conquer), what proportion of all "urban" folks lived in the main city of the island, etc.

Then there was the political mobilization problem, of how far regional *caudillos*, or mountain folk not entirely dominated by urban folk, such as the tobacco farmers in the hills of Cuba or in the northern valley of Santo Domingo, controlled mobilization. The more powerful such non-sugar political units, the less powerful relatively was the planter-metropole tie that was at the core of 18th century imperialism in the Caribbean. The outcome, then, was often determined by whether there was a substantial local social group with reasons to be sympathetic to the invader, or reasons and means to resist after a beachhead was established and the center of government conquered.

Defending and Supplying Naval Forces

Turning now to the military problem of naval power, the Caribbean was similar to the waters off North Africa, or off the southern coast of India, or between Indonesia and Asia, or the southern coast of the Philippines. In all these areas it was possible to have relatively small, isolated ports that were militarily defensible except to substantial attack, but port services were easily moved to another island. It was then possible to support and provision a pirate or privateer force locally that was substantial enough to be a naval threat, and sometimes strong enough to conquer more or less isolated cities for brief periods (to "sack" them).

The problem of any empire trying to wipe out the pirates or privateers would be, then, that if they conquered (say) the Tortue harbor (a privateer French base off the north coast of Haiti), they would have had to invest it and hold it for a long period of time, when it was not any good for anything except a pirate base (for an account of the various attempts by the Spanish to take and hold Tortue [Tortuga], see Esquemeling (1684 [1678]), pp. 14–22). And if they did so, they would not wipe out the pirates, but instead would just move them elsewhere (Merrien [1970]). So a minimal, but dangerous, naval force with some beachhead capabilities could be organized from a small port on a small island. A slightly more systematic case would be the Patriots' organizing privateering from Guadeloupe during the wars between France and England in the 1790s, including ship repair.

The command by the empires in Europe over their naval (and marine troop) forces in the Caribbean was quite lax. The governments could sign treaties to keep a European war out of the Caribbean, but the local forces would nevertheless try to conquer the islands of the other empire, and would fairly often succeed—usually to have the metropole give them back later.

Since these problems of control were in part that the diplomatic messages from the metropole did not get to the local forces, this must mean that material goods were also not getting to them. The provisioning difficulty was, of course, less after there were steamships, and less true of the United States as compared to the other empires. In the 18th century we have to look at other Caribbean islands, rather than at the metropole, for the provisioning and repair sources for the "invaders." Such provisioning islands formed a system of varying effectiveness for producing and supplying local naval and beachhead troop forces. An important case in the late 18th century was Cuba, which provisioned, and to some extent furnished troops for, Spanish invasions of New Orleans and Florida (Kuethe (1986)). Similarly, at various times Port Royal in Jamaica served the British, and the two main ports in Martinique served the French, in the same way. For a considerable time, a small and somewhat ungovernable force stationed on Tortuga was enough to protect the settlements of early French settlers on what later became Haiti.

The military experts and officers were generally imported to such bases from the empire, and almost all of the warships were produced in Europe. But a lot of local resources had to go into keeping a naval force in being, and imperial naval historians are usually not very specific about this (Merrien (1970) is an exception). The ratios of local to metropolitan provisions would vary with the different empires, with the different sizes of the islands, and with the income from conquest (e.g., privateering income was very important in Guadeloupe, basically paying for about 10 percent of the local government, as well as supporting itself as a military force, during the 1790s). For example Bangou ((1987a [1962]), p. 83) points out that the French fleets sent from Europe could only function for about four months in the Caribbean (rather than a theoretical eight) because France did not have ports for repair or a systematic reprovisioning administration in the Caribbean until 1784; the British had such ports and systems in Port Royal in Jamaica and English Harbor in Antigua.

Warships in the 18th century were generally taken rather than just sunk (it is very hard indeed to sink a wooden ship); those that were sunk, by running ashore during an attempted invasion or escape attempt, were sometimes refloated and refitted by the locals after they had driven off the invading force. Repair facilities on Caribbean islands were evidently to some degree equivalent to shipyards as sources of secondhand naval ships. Shipyards themselves were rare in the Caribbean.

The logistics of naval supply were as important, then, as the logistics of concentrating forces within an island for the military significance of a beach. Sophisticated Caribbean ports with ship repair facilities and access to water and provisions rendered nearby beaches vulnerable to the empire (or the pirates) who controlled them. But supply of new ships and of generals and admirals from the metropoles was crucial even for empires with local naval stations.

Size and Island Military Vulnerability

Crossing the beach and defending the beachhead were necessary and usually sufficient for conquering a small sugar island. A beachhead on a middle-sized island had to be expanded into military control of the whole island, and resistance of island forces, when mobilized, could sometimes dislodge a beachhead, with the help of malaria, yellow fever, and dysentery. Mountainous terrain increased the effective size of an island from the point of view of this generalization, so Barbados was militarily smaller than St. Vincent as military terrain.

High density and much sugar land multiplied the resources outside the main island city, so Barbados was also effectively larger than flat but larger Bahamas islands, since there is no one to mobilize for defense in the distant parts of such desert islands. Barbados was actually less vulnerable than St. Vincent because its larger population size was more important than St. Vincent's more militarily difficult terrain.

On large islands beachheads were merely one more of a set of regional political and military centers that made warfare among bounded within-island social systems possible. In the long run, however, the normal number of governments, even on the large islands, was one.

Islands of Small Value

Most of the small islands in the Caribbean that are within 25 miles (40 kilometers) of another, bigger island are governed from that island. I will take as an indication that there is something to govern the criterion that there be a town on the island big enough to be on the map in my (Rand McNally) atlas (Tortue does not now have a town that appears in the atlas, but it was so important in the 17th and 18th centuries that I include it here). Table 2.2 outlines the geographical relations of small islands to nearby large islands or to island groups governed in common from the metropole.

In the middle column are small islands (if they have towns on my map) that are dependencies of larger islands, so that in imperial times the local branch of the colonial government was on the larger island, and if they are now independent countries, the government of the independent country is normally still there. In the last column are groups of small islands governed in common (these more often include geographically large islands with small populations and small product). The table specifies the distance to the larger island or, for the groups, the longest distance from any island to the nearest one. The point of the table is that most dependent small islands are within 25 miles of the coast of the island on which they are dependent. When they are not near another island and when at least some of them are important enough to have towns on them, then they tend to be governed as a group directly from the metropole, sometimes even when they are quite far apart (as are the Dutch islands; St. Croix is quite a ways from the other Danish Virgin Islands).

In most of these cases scattered data indicate that the relatively close groups of functionally small islands have been governed together throughout much of their history, so they support the notion that some-

TABLE 2.2
Small Islands with Towns and Island Groups with Separate Governments

	Government	
Mamimum Distance[a]	*Dependencies*	*Independent or Direct Imperial Tie*[b]
Less than 25 miles	Isla de Juventud (Cuba)	Virgin Islands (Br.)
	Isla de Vieques (PR)	Bermuda (Br.)
	Isla de Culebra (PR)	Caymans (Br.)
	Marie Galante (Guadeloupe)	Turks and Caicos (Br.)
	Tobago (Trinidad)	
	Tortue (Haiti)	
	Nevis (St. Kitts)	
	Barbuda (Antigua)	
	Carriacou (Grenada)	
Over 25 miles	St. Martin (Guadeloupe)	Neth. Antilles[c] (Curaçao)
	St. Barthélemy (Guadeloupe)	Virgin Islands (Da., St. Thomas)
		Bahamas[c] (Br., Nassau)

[a] Distance from the large islands or islands that govern them, or for island groups, from the nearest island of the group.

[b] Imperial power in the 19th century is given, and for island groups that have long distances, the island on which the government was mainly located.

[c] Some of the Dutch Antilles and many of the Bahamas are geographically larger islands, but of these only Curaçao was economically or demographically substantial.

thing special is going on over sea distances of 25 miles or less. Sovereignty apparently easily stretches over 25 miles, but fades rapidly with distance over 25 miles. The most important contrary case is the Dutch Antilles. I suspect this is due to the fact that an ordinary Dutch businessman in the 18th and 19th centuries might own a "schooner" that could sail between quite distant islands within the Caribbean.

Apparently only in very exceptional circumstances did the governed small islands become militarily important. Tortue was militarily important as a base for French privateering in the 17th and early 18th centuries; St. Eustatius was important as a free port and provided big prizes when conquered by the British during the American Revolution, so it was militarily important at least as a target; Marie Galante was of occasional importance in the hands of minority political factions during the French Revolution; pirates hid (rather than having defended bases) on some of the less inhabited Bahamas, in the Turks and Caicos Islands, and in the Cayman Islands. Only one of the islands listed, St. Croix in the Danish (now American) Virgin Islands, was important as a sugar island.

The explanation of the location of governmental authority *off* the tiny or unimportant islands has to be on a different basis than the military analysis above of why small sugar islands can be autonomous. What we have to explain here is a set of mostly short-distance interisland links, at least one of whose end points was an economically and militarily unimportant island.

I propose that a stretch of sea of less than 25 miles could be traversed by the local population on boats that they could build: fishing boats, ferries, pleasure craft, and the like (e.g., from Carriacou, 23 miles from Grenada, Grenada is reached by "boats" built by one person that can be managed by three people, while other islands are reached by "schooners" built by at least two people in partnership and operated by a crew of about eight—see Smith (1962)). Such boats could land almost anywhere on both the islands they came from and the islands they were going to. This meant that it did not take a governmentally or capitalistically organized enterprise to go from one island to another. Travel could be part of the village economy, with village-level or family-level capital equipment. The "invasion" of the smaller island, then, could be a locally organized economic enterprise. Governmental authority, then, followed the "weak links" of subsistence ties or family ties from the shores to the small islands, rather than the "strong links" of economic or military interest.

These weak links carried governmental power over the 25 miles of sea *only as long as* there was no long-distance imperial tie backed by large-scale governmental and commercial power overriding it. So St. Johns in the American [Danish] Virgin Islands and Tortola in the British Virgins are only two or three miles apart, but were (and are) separated by empire lines, while St. Croix was part of the Danish Virgin Islands though it is beyond the 25-mile limit—it was obtained by the Danes from the French in a clearly interimperial deal, in which local contacts between the islands had very little importance (Mentze (1966)). Aruba is closer to Venezuela than to Curaçao. Dominica (functionally a small island—it passed from French to British hands during the late 18th century) is about 25 miles from French Martinique on one side and French Guadeloupe on the other.

Excepting such cases of imperial power intervening, small islands of no particular military or commercial importance can be incorporated into nearby islands (or coastal states) by economic forces "beneath the purview" of the world system organized by government and large-scale capitalism.

The Legal Value of Beaches

Belize and Guyana they became independent had a lot more trouble with boundaries than they had had in the imperial system. When Belize and Guyana claimed independence, they had to clarify their boundaries.

In both cases, a lot of low-density and low-value jungle territory now in those countries was claimed by Guatemalan, Honduran, and Venezuelan claimants. The low importance of the land itself was illustrated by the fact that Mexico gave up its claim that a big part of (what is now) Belize had been part of the Spanish imperial province of Quintana Roo, *unless* Guatemala made good its claim to another part—in that case Mexico wanted to reopen its claim. That is, the Mexicans did not give a damn for the land, but they did not want Guatemala to have it.

Belize and Guyana were essentially colonial islands oriented to Caribbean imperial commerce and naval military force, rather than really land possessions. The only trouble was that the "sea" on one side of these was a "trackless" jungle and, in Guyana, some almost uninhabited jungle highlands, perhaps with mineral resources (e.g., diamonds tended to wash out of them, which probably was going to amount to something someday). This meant that in the 18th century it was easy to define their centers—on the coasts—but hard to define their boundaries; the center faded away into a broad boundary region.

The only comparable areas to this "trackless jungle" in the Caribbean proper during the time of granting of independence were the small "subsistence" islands where not many people lived, and people that did not produce much of value. The Bay Islands off Honduras are an especially good example, as we will see below. In contrast Isla Margarita, which produced pearls, was firmly incorporated into the world system, was important in the politics of Venezuelan independence, and got its independence with Venezuela (on slaves in the pearl fisheries, see Acosta Saignes (1978), pp. 104, 108–11).

While in the Caribbean proper there might be competing claims to nearby islands, everyone could at least admit that the whole of the big island was included in the "center," and could be given independence as a unit. Even the boundary subsistence islands came in easily separable units; the image of "trackless" does not carry metaphorical weight even though the marine and subsistence island area was generally more sparsely settled than the jungles of Belize or Guyana.

For instance, in the case of Belize, the British had had a disputed claim to the Bahía islands, between 25 and 50 miles off Honduras, about 100 or so miles from the main Honduran Atlantic port, and much farther from Belize City. Hondurans also claimed some uninhabited islands off what is now the coast of Belize. All of these are basically dots, though the negotiation went on in a context in which subsea resources were involved in claims to otherwise valueless islands.

But since each of the islands had boundaries, and the 25-mile rule separates them into two groups, it was conceptually easy to divide up a group of islands, but much harder to divide up the jungle with Guatemala or Mexico. (However the other similarities of Belize, Guyana, French Guiana [Cayenne], and Surinam to Caribbean islands result in their being treated in many social science sources as part of the sociology or political science or history of the middle-sized and big Caribbean islands.)

The main point of this section on tiny islands is that there is a size below which the generalizations about islands creating separable economic and political systems does not apply. It applies to quite small islands if they can be intensively cultivated in sugar plantations. But dry or subsistence small islands are not parts of the core colonial system dominated by sugar plantations and slavery, and have a different relation to the boundaries created by that system. Consequently imperial and slave system boundaries leave a different historical legacy in the economic and political systems of tiny islands outside the sugar system.

The Distribution of Land Uses and Social Systems

Sugar needed to be grown on a large scale to be profitable, since the weight and volume reduction required that it be processed near the fields, before transportation to the port and before loading it onto a ship. It took about 20 tons of cane to make a ton of sugar.[2] Of course, one wanted to transport the 20 tons as short a distance as possible by transforming it into sugar near where it was grown.

But large plots of well-watered fertile flat land (actually one preferred the land to slope slightly, for drainage without erosion) were to be had in the valleys of present or ancient rivers, or in coastal plains that were either alluvial, or ancient coral reefs, around the edges of the highlands. Sugar was an intensive crop, in the sense that it used a great deal of both labor and capital per acre of land. For sugar in slave times, roughly a quarter of the capital investment was in the sugar mill, probably a quarter in the land, and half in the slaves (Dumaz (1986), p. 32).[3] Cotton

---

[2] Now it takes under 10 tons of cane per ton of sugar, largely because old mills only extracted about half the juice (Guerra y Sánchez (1940)). A general introduction to the technology and economics of the sugar mill itself and its relation to agriculture is Moreno Fraginals (1976 [1964]).

[3] Incidentally this means that whether or not the mill and slaves were included in the value of the land or as a separate part of the estate is a large determinant of the reported values per acre. The mill was usually included up to the time of the central processing plants with tenant farmers in the middle or late 19th century. But the slaves were included sometimes as part of the value of the land, sometimes not. This makes it tough for a comparative economic geographer, our role here.

One should note also that statistics on "cane land" in plantations are quite ambiguous. Schnakenbourg reports for Guadeloupe that between 25 and 50 percent of the area on sugar plantations was not ever planted to sugar, depending on the relief and soil quality,

plantations, in the United States, for example, were not on the average as large (in workers) as sugar plantations, but both crops tend to produce large, capital-intensive enterprises using gang labor on flat valley and coastal plain land.

But those lands were in some ways the hardest to prepare for cultivation, were wet and unhealthy. In the 18th century, they did not know why, but they recognized that tropical "miasmas" caused malaria and yellow fever that killed a lot of people, and that diarrhea was characteristic of the tropics. The first planting for sugar was very labor intensive. This meant that when one turned jungle into sugar plantation, one needed to import a great deal of labor, much of which would die on importation.

We will deal with the demographic impact of this frontier character of sugar plantation agriculture in a later chapter. By "frontier" we mean here that the introduction of sugar, replacing other cultivated or livestock crops, had the same demographic effect as a frontier subsituting wheat and corn cultivation in the North American Midwest that had previously been used for hunting and gathering or for cattle herding. Both situations created great waves of immigration, great increases in the capital value of land and farm or plantation installations, great rates of social mobility, and a strong tendency toward lawless "adventure capitalism."

From the point of view of this chapter it meant that the valley and coastal plain of sugar islands were very much more densely populated, and in many cases shaped the composition of the population of the whole island. It also meant that this dense strip around the edges of the island generated most of the island's wealth and most of the interest of the metropole in the island. And finally it meant that islands that still did not have sugar cultivation but had such wet valley and coastal plain, in the 18th and early 19th centuries, mainly the large Spanish islands, were seen as opportunities to get rich.

Empires and slavery came together because of sugar cultivation, and they came together most intensely on that booming frontier where new valley and coastal plain were opened rapidly to sugar by the importation

---

and that about 30 percent of the time cultivated cane land was fallow or used for subsistence crops (Schnakenbourg (1980; 1), p. 38). Unless one knows precisely what is included in the land in plantations, an estimate that roughly half of plantation land was at any given time not in cane on the flatter islands, and somewhat more was not in cane on islands with more broken relief, is a useful first approximation. In particular one does not want to compare productivities per acre between flatter colonies, such as Barbados, Antigua, Guyana, and Trinidad, with those of more mountainous islands, such as Jamaica, Martinique, or Haiti, without considerable caution.

of slave labor on a large scale. The empire created commercial access to, and controlled the allocation of, potential plantation land. It also created the political and legal requisites of slavery (or later of some other importable labor). The plantation then created slavery in the everyday life of the colony, and the political force for its maintenance. This change of the plains changed the population density and racial composition of the island and concentrated island population, wealth, and political power in small areas dominated by sugar planters.

Cocoa and coffee were and are, so to speak, reduced into concentrated shippable form by the trees themselves, so that with drying they can be moved effectively. The main capital investment required is the period of cultivation of the trees or bushes until they are ready to yield. Tobacco leaves were shipped (dried) in a form supplied directly by the plant.

Thus these crops were easily grown in piedmont or other low, hilly regions on relatively small plantations or even as family-farm ("peasant") crops (e.g., on Guadeloupe around 1900, coffee was cultivated between about 700 feet (200 meters) and 2,000 feet (600 meters) of altitude (Bévotte (1906), p. 377). The lower capital investment period of tobacco made it even more of a family-farm crop than coffee and cocoa. Thus smaller slaveholdings, more dispersed settlement, and mixtures of peasant and small plantations were all more concentrated in highlands, oftentimes away from the valley and coastal plain. Tobacco, coffee, and cocoa were often cultivated on the sides of valley and coastal plain river valleys in the interior, which sometimes had sugar on the bottomland, so the social boundaries were not necessarily as sharp as the altitude and slope boundaries.

Where whole islands had most of their agricultural land in such piedmont or foothill regions, or *alturas*, as in the windward island of Dominica and nearly all of Puerto Rico, large-scale sugar slaveholding organized in a capital-intensive fashion did not dominate the political system (this moderation of slavery in the hills was apparently only somewhat less marked on St. Lucia). On many large islands there were regions dominated by such piedmont export crops; the northern valley of the Dominican Republic, the *alturas* of Cuba, the chain of hills across northern Trinidad, and parts of Jamaica are such areas. Such "cocoa valleys" and shores also dominated the hinterland of Caracas, producing a distinctive creole aristocracy in Venezuela. For example, Simón Bolívar married into this aristocracy but easily made alliances with colored and anti-slavery forces in coastal Venezuela and Isla Margarita (Halperin Donghi (1969), pp. 99–101, 115–19). The broken terrain of the large northern valley of the Dominican Republic was also dominated by such "small planter export" crops cultivated along with subsistence crops.

In many of the areas where tree crops and tobacco were grown, high-land savannas were appropriate for cattle raising. The Jamaican "pens" were cattle-ranching operations with largely slave labor (Higman (1989)); the north of the Dominican Republic [Santo Domingo], Puerto Rico, and the Cuban *alturas* also had a good deal of *ganadería*. These savannas did not have the easy transportation access required for sugar or cotton, and they may not have been appropriate for these crops because they were not as fertile as the valley and coastal plain. The cattle-raising areas in the Caribbean were not far enough from the political and cultural centers of these societies to have all the anarchic features suggested for Latin American cattle-ranching areas by Baretta and Markoff (1978).

Ranching areas generally needed a more autonomous work force than did sugar or cotton areas, so slaves were treated more like people there, and free labor was more competitive with slave labor. Large ranching landowners were not much more interested in a repressive labor regime than their smaller coffee and cocoa neighbors. Especially on the Spanish islands, political systems with a large representation of urbanized elite ranchers gave the islands something of the flavor of Buenos Aires [Río de la Plata] or Montevideo [Banda Oriental] rather than the flavor of Barbados or Haiti: conservative and macho rather than reactionary and authoritarian, perhaps.

Many of the other export crops (e.g., arrowroot, ginger, allspice) and almost all the local food crops (e.g., manioc, plantain) and small live-stock (e.g., chickens, hogs) had no appreciable economies of scale in growing, in processing for transportation, in transportation, or in marketing. Almost everywhere in the 18th century such crops and small live-stock were most efficiently grown on small plots by a fairly independent (though generally rent-paying) peasantry.

The economies of small-scale production for these crops were, if any-thing, greater in the Caribbean than in Europe, since sugar land was more valuable than domain land on large European estates. That is, the opportunity cost of using large, fertile, flat pieces of land that could grow sugar to grow food crops and minor exports was higher than the comparable opportunity cost of using a landlord's domain land for such crops in Europe.

The statistical evidence on these crops is dominantly about the het-erogeneous residual category of "provisions" (e.g., Higman (1984), pp. 161, 167–68, 172–73, 175, 299, 325, 328, 331, 366, 382). It shows that such crops were grown more on small plots, that these small plots were scattered in areas that generally had low fertility and low economic productivity (we do not apparently have evidence whether such plots were more or less productive than subsistence cultivation by gang labor on plantations on the same islands), that when slaves worked in enter-prises growing such crops, their owner owned few slaves and evidently often worked with them, and that when free peasants got land, they mostly grew such crops.

The institutional evidence on "provision grounds" on islands that had hilly territory near sugar plantations shows the same point. When there were such plots on hills nearby, they were essentially always culti-vated by slave families working together and by individual slaves, under an incentive system that allowed them to keep both what they could eat and the proceeds of what they could sell from the provision ground. The slaveowners evidently figured that the half-day they gave the slaves off to cultivate these plots (plus perhaps Sunday work "freely" decided on by the slave) returned indirectly in added sugar production more than the crops were worth on the market, because planters had to buy fewer provisions.

It seems likely that the export crops in which there were few econo-mies of scale were cultivated much like provisions, and so provided a peasant mode of production in the interstices of the slave order, hidden away in the hills, sometimes exploited weekends by slaves, and providing a place for some of the freedmen to go where they would not be working for slavedrivers.

The Geography of Slavery

The core of slavery was the sugar plantation, so the geographical distri-bution of slavery was the distribution of sugar cultivation. By "core" we mean first of all that large and dense populations of slaves were found in sugar-cultivating areas. We further mean that the plantations there were large, creating a planter class with strong class-consciousness and the means for political organization. The maintenance of slavery as a class system, rather than as a personal relation embedded in a household with distinct incentives and privileges for different slaves, was more promi-nent in the minds of large slaveowners, as we will analyze in Chapter 5.

Finally we mean that interisland variations in the style and content of the slave system were determined by the peculiarities of sugar plantation areas on an island, and the relation of those areas to other areas. For instance, when one has said that sugar was not very prominent relative to other crops in the late 18th century in the Spanish islands (Trinidad, a Spanish island until about 1800, was already starting to be an excep-tion to this, as was a small area around Havana in Cuba) or in Dominica in the Windwards, we already know to look for signs of the laxness of slavery as a system on those islands.

When we say that sugar plantations were relatively smaller on Barbados than on other islands but completely dominated the landscape, were near one another rather than being in separate deltas of rivers separated by mountains, and had been completely settled by the mid-17th century, we are saying that slavery was entirely the dominant system on Barbados, that slaves who had married off their plantation could probably walk to sleep with their wives or husbands, and that old creole planter families would have had time by the late 18th century to develop a distinctive style of life.

This in turn means that if we want to see the politics of slave society at its purest, we should go to Barbados, though we may find some softening effect on planter class-consciousness due to small plantation size (it is not enough so I can notice, though). If, however, we want to investigate the depressing effect of infrequent cohabitation due to cross-plantation marriage on the slave birth rate, we should not go to Barbados, because slaves on neighboring plantations could probably cohabit. And if we want to see how inherited island aristocratic status systems would have worked if Jamaica in the late 18th century had not been still a sugar frontier island, we could project from the experience of Barbados.

In the late 18th century, then, we can perhaps see the impact of slavery most clearly by contrasting a full-blown sugar island of many years of societal and political development, such as Barbados, with Puerto Rico, where sugar planters and slavery were peripheral to a largely rural economy, and where planters, along with other rural elites, were dominated by a strong, urban-oriented colonial power.

On any particular island we can see how the slave system responded to particular unique events in different empires by contrasting what happened in the sugar areas as compared with elsewhere. We can then see what a slave society's reaction looks like where it is weak (in the hills), as well as where it is strong. The Cuban or Dominican Republic piedmont and *alturas* areas, or the mountains and hills of Jamaica, form a non-slave contrast to the sugar plains near the seas. The high mountains of Cuba, Haiti, the Dominican Republic, and Jamaica and the relatively impenetrable ones of Martinique, Basse Terre in Guadeloupe, and the British Windwards (except Trinidad and Barbados) form areas where runaway slaves might be moderately successful in evading capture and even creating precarious maroon societies of their own. This success can form a useful contrast to the rare and desperate riots on the sugar lowlands, always failures, except in Haiti during the French Revolution (when the rebels were allied with black and colored troops in mountain refuges). The mountains versus lowlands contrast can show what slave resistance would be like if it were not brutally and successfully repressed where the planters were strongest and where most slaves lived.

On the other hand, it is because islands were relatively tightly bounded economic and political systems, surrounded by militarily difficult boundaries from other island societies, that one can see the system dynamics. For all the mountains and cattle farms and provision grounds of Jamaica, it was an island different from the Dominican Republic [Santo Domingo] nearby. The island social system of Jamaica was one of a fairly thoroughly slave society, with a nuance here and there. Santo Domingo was a social system with a big dose of other kinds of agriculture, where an urban system dominated by peninsular Spanish faced a creole aristocracy with a hometown university, and where this urban system dominated the countryside.

What little Santo Domingo plantation slavery there was existed in an island environment that did not experience the structure of Jamaican society, some 400 miles distant. There were two harbors or two beaches to get across before one environment could affect the other, and those two shores made strong political and economic boundaries. So Jamaican *society* had a ratio of white to slave of around one to ten; the Dominican *society*, a ratio of around two whites to one slave, or around twenty times fewer slaves for each white (Santo Domingo also had many more free colored per slave). The whole environment of the relation of master and slave was shaped by those contrasting ratios, because the islands had strong political and economic boundaries.

The Dutch shipped only about a total of 5 percent of the slaves (Postma (1990), p. 302), but as Curaçao was the main competitive slave market with no monopoly restrictions on who could sell and buy, it was central to the slave system. But Curaçao did not have a slave society because it did not have sugar plantations. Its few resident slaves were domestics, or worked in the port, or raked salt in the drying ponds. The value of urban real estate on Curaçao was on the order of ten times as high as the value of all rural real estate (van Soest (1977), p. 43) in 1900, and the relation must have been very similar in the late 18th century. The large flow of slaves through the Willemstad created some moral responsibility of the Dutch for Caribbean slavery, but it did not create a slave society on the island. Dutch slave societies were created in Surinam and the other Dutch plantation colonies on the Guiana coast.

The islands that had no sugar plantations were not dominated by slavery. Their residents had an occasional slave, as Americans now have an occasional horse (though, of course, we regard the oppression of horses by being owned by different moral criteria than the oppression of slaves by being owned), if they were in an odd business that "required" slaves or if they liked to have a domestic slave about the house. This did not create the massive class-consciousness of an interest in slavery by a ruling caste dominating island culture and politics that made the Caribbean distinctive in the late 18th century. In much the same way the flat British islands that Higman (1984, pp. 64–66) calls "marginal," Anguilla, Barbuda, the Bahamas, and the Caymans, had different slave systems as wholes because they did not have sugar plantations. So the geography of slavery in its social system form, its "slave society" form, was simply the geography of sugar plantations in the 18th century.

3

Free Labor and Finance Capital on the Seas

Introduction

This chapter gives an explanation of why finance capital, corporate organization of the producing firm, and free wage labor first appeared on a large scale in long-distance shipping, long before they were applied on a large scale in industrialization. In particular, it studies late 18th century Atlantic shipping with a focus on the shipping between the Caribbean colonies and Europe. The late 18th century comes just before corporate reorganization with finance capital and wage labor of some manufacturing industries in northern England, but about three-quarters of a century after the corporate reorganization of colonial shipping and state finance in the capital markets in England (Carruthers (1989)). This corporate reorganization of colonial commerce had come earlier in the Netherlands than in England, and was just being brought about in France in the last decades of the old regime. Plantation agriculture was somewhat corporately run because it was an offshoot of European city commerce.

This chapter explains this bourgeois mode of production in shipping by the nature of the agency problems when long-distance shipping is organized with large sailing ships. It explains the importance of finance capital by the problem of commercial management of large heterogeneous capital in the ship and cargo, and the various risks of that ship and cargo that had to be managed in the light of different information. It explains corporate organization of the ship itself as the connection of the finance capital to the problem of managing a very risk-prone sailing machine. It explains proletarian wage labor, and a number of features of the contract with that labor, by the fact that the voyage required highly disciplined cooperative skilled labor that would perform the necessary prodigies in emergencies, and would stick with it until the ship came home.

The purpose of this chapter, then, is to explain why finance capital, corporate organization of the "producing" firm, and wage labor characterized Atlantic long-distance shipping in the 18th century, though I will use data from earlier when the situation seems to have been reasonably stable. These features of the bourgeois mode of production were extensive in shipping before they were found together very often in factory production or agriculture. The origin of capitalism, in the sense of extraction of surplus value from free labor by finance capital through corporate or "bureaucratic" supervision of that labor, was first found in port cities and on the high seas, and only later dominated the industrial revolution. Or to put it another way, capitalism was first a world system, and only later penetrated national economies and production within them.

Plantations, the focus of this book and of slavery in the 18th century, were, of course, also "bourgeois" or "capitalist" institutions, oriented to production in a market, involving heavy investment of other people's money. But they did not employ much proletarian wage labor. In the economy of the colonies in the late 18th century, about half of the production of the value of sugar landed in a port in Europe was the production of sugar on plantations and plantation profit; the other half was the movement of that sugar to a European port and the commercial work and profits involved in that shipping work. The shipping system also shipped slaves. So the total raw landed-sugar production system was half slave, half free.

The key to this fact is that the sea had a different institutional system than did the islands, a much more "European" system, with bourgeois government of civil laws and corporate organization. The city governments were the core regulators of this system. Banks, credit, and urban wage-labor relations were a small part of the business of 18th century European national governments, but were a matter of port city civil courts dominated by bourgeois city governments. French, British, and Dutch plantation islands were much like European port cities at the top, but their labor relations system was, of course, much different.

Shipping in the 18th century was a great deal of work, and large groups of free proletarians were recruited to do that work in all the great Atlantic commercial powers: France, England, the Netherlands, and Spain, and also in Denmark. Much of the value-added by the plantation was itself bought, after (often smaller-scale) shipment of food, clothing, timber, and slaves to and in the Caribbean and the Indian Ocean. Most staple-producing colonies were not self-sustaining (see especially Tarrade (1972), vols. 1 and 2, *passim*; Duffy (1987), ch. 1). The shipping part of commerce was cooperative physical work that added much value to the cargo.

Thus putting together the purely shipping part of the commercialization of the staple product with the shipping of inputs to the plantations, probably somewhere near half of all money paid for wholesale sugar in Europe, and somewhat less of that paid for cotton and tobacco, was ultimately paid to ship and cargo owners, and indirectly to officers and sailors, for the work of getting goods across the sea. The question of this chapter is why that half of the production of the value of colonial products in Europe was organized as a bourgeois mode of production with free labor, before the cotton-spinning factories Marx studied were thought of, and why plantations were organized as a bourgeois mode of production except for different institutions of exploitation of labor.

More precisely the question is, Why did capitalism as we now understand it come to dominate Atlantic trade even though there were alternative forms of managing ships on the Atlantic (of course, there was a slave capitalist mode in the sugar and cotton colonies, which was also theoretically an alternative). The closest alternative to the fully developed capitalism found in long-distance trade was the entrepreneurial financing and management of coastal and short-sea trade, where much of the capital in the ship, and often in the cargo, was equity of the captain. That is, smaller ships managing shorter distances and many well-known ports of call usually failed to participate much in finance capitalism, and were much less likely to be legally corporate ventures managed by captains who owned little of the ship or cargo. They did however usually have wage labor of propertyless proletarians, and extracted surplus value for the entrepreneur by exchange of wages for alienated labor. Such ships dominated the intra-Caribbean trade of the Dutch, and the trade from North America ("Boston").[1]

Other somewhat capitalist forms worked in privateering, piracy, and fishing, but they tended to have a "producers' cooperative" form of organization of the ship itself. The sailors, the captain and other officers, and the owners got shares of the returns, the shares were generally not wildly unequal, the owners rarely participated in finance markets, and they were rarely insured (see Merrien (1970); Rediker (1987); and Esquemeling (n.d. [1684, 1678])).

The Spanish managed their colonial commerce in corporatist government convoys, though some shipowners who participated were Dutch, English, and French; insurance, inspection, route of travel, the conditions of commerce, and the like were strongly regulated by the central Spanish government (Lang (1975); Pérez-Mallaína Bueno (1982); Serrano Mangas (1985); MacNeill (1985)—MacNeill has a good general comparison of the navies of the main powers). Navies paid wages to sailors but recruited some part of them by coercion ("press") rather than by

---

[1] Many of the differences between the ships are brought out clearly in the contrast in chapter 1 of Butel (1974) between European coastal trade shipping in Bordeaux and colonial shipping. The law outlined in Weber (1924 [1889]) is mostly about this situation of combined ship ownership, captaincy, and sailing management, which shows that the pressures of long distance cross-ocean trade produced much of the complexity outlined here.

contract, and governments usually owned the ships and always hired the officers that managed them (Lloyd (1970); Howarth and Howarth (1988); Merrien (1964); Duffy (1987)).

Thus the dominance of the bourgeois mode of production for long-distance shipping came about in an environment in which other forms were technically viable, politically legitimate, and prevalent in the same ports. Capitalism won out among known and viable alternatives, and the three major Atlantic powers of the 18th century, England, the Netherlands, and France (but not Spain) had dominantly finance-capitalist, corporate, wage-labor institutions in transoceanic trade.[2]

The basic explanation I will give is that the "agency problems," getting people to do the work and mangement responsibly when they were thousands of miles, and up to three months' sailing, away, were hard to solve without a capitalist incentive system (for a general analysis of this problem and of when a market is a good solution, see Williamson (1964)). In order to argue this, I will first outline the nature of the risks faced by "the adventure," the sailing of a particular ship in a particular trade with a more or less known destination with return during a particular season. This adventure was ordinarily managed by a corporate form created by a "charter party" among a shipowner, a captain (these were sometimes the same person, though the larger the ship, the rarer that was), and various merchant houses. The word "party" meant that the shares in the enterprise, and therefore any profits and losses, were to be divided (*parti*) according to the terms of the charter party.

Quite often the charter party was supplemented with separate contracts with insurers, and the merchant houses as well as the shipowner might have contracts for loans with banks or other credit institutions, obligating the merchant or shipowning firm or person to pay regardless of the outcome of the adventure. That is, the limitations of liability that made the recruitment of participation of different sorts of financial interests possible were ordinarily written into the contracts, rather than into corporate charters of limited liability corporations, as now.

I will be arguing, then, that the institutions of finance capitalism, and the creation of the corporate adventure owner with its captain and purser agents, was for the purpose of dividing and managing the risks. This had to be done in such a way as to elicit the responsibility of the person who was on the scene and had the authority to reduce losses and to exploit good luck (on this problem of locating responsibility rationally in contract systems, see Heimer (1985)). Finance capitalism and

---

[2] What was to become the United States had mostly short-sea and coastal trade managed on an entrepreneurial basis, and England dominated its long-distance trade until after the revolution.

corporate management, then, are to be explained by the special kinds of risk management problems that long-distance shipping created.

But, and this is crucial for our argument in the book as a whole about why the work force in shipping had to be free, those capitalist institutions had to reach down to discipline the workers on the ships. Sailors had first to be motivated to join the voyage at all, had to be motivated to see it through to the end, had to be motivated to work at human limits in emergencies and to cooperate quickly in teamwork. When I specified that sailors were "wage laborers" above, I did not mean that their contracts looked exactly like those one would expect to see in a modern factory, where work is usually measured in hours or in units produced, where the money value is determined in advance entirely in currency, and where the worker goes home after work. I will in fact give evidence of what capitalists were trying to motivate workers to do primarily by peculiarities of the "wage" contract. The chapter is divided into two main parts: the first explains finance capital and corporate legal form; the second explains free wage labor.

But the purpose of arguing those parts separately is that the plantation as an organization of labor was connected to the world system by that system's finance capital part, and not by its free wage labor part. In fact the successful sugar colonies (those of England, the Netherlands, and France) had a political system among the capitalist oligarchy much like that of port cities in Europe. They had often been organized in the first instance rather like corporations (or "adventures"), with oligarchic boards of directors, and their becoming territorial oligarchic council governments was based in large measure on evolution guided by city government models of European port cities.

Those urban oligarchic council governments in Europe did enforce the labor contracts with free proletarians in their civil law, but that was not their main business or the main purpose of merchant civil law. Their analogues in the sugar colonies managed both the merchant civil law part and the *slave* labor relations part.

The first part of this book as a whole explains why the slave labor relations part in the colonies was more dominant in the social system in some islands than in others. But this chapter's purpose is to explain why oligarchic council governments in the port cities of Europe, managed by the same bourgeoisie that managed the shipping part of the sugar system that produced and marketed sugar, had a similar structure at the top but a wage labor structure rather than a slave structure at the bottom.

Thus the puzzle of how governments of basically the same bourgeois form, with basically the same sorts of members of the oligarchy represented in the governing council, could manage a system that was half slave and half free has its solution in the fact that the kinds of agency problems *among capitalists* were roughly the same in the shipping and the plantation parts. But the shipping merchants had a radically different sort of agency problem in managing skilled crews of sailor labor at sea than did the sugar (and cotton) plantation part in managing gang labor in the fields.

The Risks of the Adventure for Capital

The general purpose of the next few sections is to outline the nature of the risks, and corresponding responsibilities for managing those risks, that confronted the owner structure in long-distance Atlantic shipping. We will simultaneously show how it was managed in the main institutions of the three "normal capitalist" shipping nations, England, the Netherlands, and France, and try to show that this co-occurrence of the problems and the institutions for their management constitutes an explanation of the institutions. This explains the finance capital system, and the corporate management of the ship that produced the profits of the financial system. From time to time we will specify how the corporatist forms of Spain, the entrepreneurial forms of short-sea shipping, and the producers' cooperative forms of fishing, privateering, and piracy differed from the main line, and what this means for the argument.

We divide this general problem into (1) management to secure a high total return from the voyage, or "adventure," and to minimize losses, (2) the problems of dividing up the risks into markets that specialized in the information relevant to them, (3) the problems of managing "credit," the fact that the return from that adventure would come at the end of the season (when the ship got back to Europe), while many of the expenses had to be paid in advance, and (4) the problems of managing the fact that the government to enforce contracts was not very accessible in the middle of the Atlantic, so continuity of the contracts was not automatic, and that this presented gross problems of "opportunism," or "moral hazard." (See Heimer (1985); Williamson (1964).) After that we turn to the problem of wage labor in shipping.

Corporate Equity Capital and Its Agents on the Ship

Let us take up first the problem of dealing with collective uncertainties for the owner(s), and the corollary definition of the role of the captain and purser ("bursar" is the same word in a form more familiar to American professors) at sea as agents of the owner group. In general, besides the cost of the ship, long-distance trade required that the owner lay out a good deal of voyage-specific capital, capital for the "adventure" of a particular planned trip. These costs included any advances required by the officers and crew, repair of the hull and rigging, insurance for the loss of the hull, the total costs of the provisions for the outward-bound trip (including stopover and resupplying of ships picking up slaves in Africa), and the cost of the outbound cargo and of its insurance. In the Spanish fleets (Carrera de Indias), in addition to all these problems, the crown required credit from the relevant merchants in order to finance the warships that were to protect the fleet, and credit for the fleet as a whole was somewhat separate from the credit for each ship and was organized by the Consulado de Comercio of Sevilla (Pérez-Mallaína Bueno (1982), pp. 289–91 and 302–17.)

Quite often, of course, the ship was owned and fitted out by someone or some partnership other than the owner(s) of the cargo, and various arrangements could be made about who was going to invest in operating costs for the voyage. Some of the risks (such as sinking, or being taken by a privateer or pirate) were risks equally to the ship, or "hull," and the cargo, while others were allocated separately to varying degrees (e.g., damage to the rigging in a storm to the hull owner, damage due to an unfavorable movement of prices in the destination to the cargo owner).

Various provisions in the charter party and in the insurance contract(s) for the hull and cargo would distribute these risks differently among various "owners" and risk bearers, and between them and the captain.[3] But the situation was of sufficient complexity that the central mission of the captain of the ship was in some sense as a legal officer, the manager of a court that was supposed to keep the claims and risks straight, and to make sure that decisions taken on behalf of the whole adventure in the face of various kinds of risks would not sacrifice one kind of interest of some of the owners to those of another, except as provided in the contracts.

An example, that gives the flavor of the instructions by the owners to a captain sailing from Nantes to Guadeloupe, started with a wide-ranging delegation of discretion: "[W]e approve in advance all the measures that your attachment to our interests will dictate to you for the best good of the enterprise" (Buffon (1972), pp. 26–27 [citing Meyer, *L'Armement nantaise* pp. 220–21]). In case of an accident involving damages to the ship or cargo, the captain became an agent of the insur-

---

[3] And in Spain between these and the collegial authorities in Sevilla. For contrasts between the situation described here for the merchant marine and the charter parties of pirates and privateers, see the charter party from Esquemeling quoted by Merrien (1970), pp. 117–121; see also the citations in Rediker (1987), p. 261.

ers responsible for minimizing the loss (e.g., repairing the ship before setting off again, disposing of the damaged cargo).

The captain was in turn often monitored by a person more or less in the role of an auditor, a purser, or, in Spanish, *maestre*, often recruited from a different social class than the captain was (and often aiming to become a land merchant rather than a mariner-merchant, as the captain was), who reported to the owners rather than to the captain. The purser, for instance, was supposed to check that the food bought for the crew was fed to the crew rather than sold by the captain. In Spain the *maestre* was also the main point of contact between the ship as an enterprise and the collegial bureaucracy in Sevilla that managed the fleet as a whole (Pérez-Mallaína Bueno (1982), pp. 285–89).

This meant in turn that in some sense the captain did not have to be a mariner, and that the *maîtres*, or mates, who commanded the crew in the adjustment of the sails and the loading and movement of the cargo on the ship, and the timber carpenters, who supervised repairs, were not really the captain's subordinates.

The navigator, or pilot, likewise was not going to be overruled by the captain on any technical navigational matter; he was, for example, the only person among the officers who had to be examined as a mariner by an official body in the French navy (Merrien (1964)). The captain might legally overrule the pilot, of course, but it would be an unusual relationship between their competences if he actually thought he should. Much of the knowledge involved in navigation was in the nature of craft lore, such as drawings by someone who had been there of what this or that island looked like, so that when one ended up near it, one would know where one was (Esquemeling (n.d. [1664, 1678]) has some examples of such drawings).

The captain's incentives were in general specified in the charter party. The captain's contract quite often involved some investment in the enterprise and some share (above that earned by the investment and pertaining to the role of captain as such) in the returns of the adventure. That is, the captain's incentives were aligned with those of other equity owners by his being an owner himself, and his share was modified to take account of his contribution of labor, authority, and liability for certain kinds of mistakes. The auditor therefore was not under as much pressure to make sure he was trying to maximize the collective return in, say, selling the goods.

It was mainly when the captain had an opportunity to account something as a cost and then make a personal profit by reducing that cost—by feeding the crew more biscuit and less meat, for example—that the auditor had to do any more than ensure reasonably accurate accounting for the returns from well-known cargo quantities and reasonably well-known prices in the market of destination. The merchants in Europe, of course, had to collect information from multiple sources about the reigning prices in the market of destination, so as to monitor all their agents in foreign ports, including the captain.

The captains quite often then were recruited from governing classes rather than from commercial classes when these were distinct (they were much more distinct in France and England than in the Netherlands, for example). But there were strong pressures to set up the incentive system to make the captain into a trusted agent of all the owners, and to make him have a large stake in the navigational, military, and commercial success of the adventure.

In general the smaller the ship, the more unified was ship ownership and captaincy, so that one did not have to create such a complicated coalition of different sorts of capital to get a smaller ship to sea—the captain-owner might also own a large share of the cargo. Since smaller ships, smaller cargoes, and shorter trips were characteristic of coastal trade in Europe (see note 5), in intra-Caribbean trade, and in fishing, the unification of captain and purser with owner and the lack of a complex charter party were more characteristic in these settings.

In addition the captain of a small ship was not so often from the governing or merchant classes, and quite often was an experienced mariner who had moved up to entrepreneur. So the distinction between the mariners and the captain as judge was not nearly as likely to occur in the coastal trade, *kleine vaart* (as the Dutch called intra-Caribbean trade), or in fishing, and the unified entrepreneurial structure of owner as captain, pilot, and chief mariner governing the crew was much more common in those trades.

The officers on the larger long-distance ships were divided into those in charge of the commercial, legal, and moral system of the ship, who ate with the captain, and those in charge of the ship as a technical system: the *maîtres*, or boatswains and mates, the timber carpenter, and sometimes the military noncoms. The navigators, or pilots, were somewhere in between.

The complete complement of commercial and moral officers included, besides the captain and purser, the surgeon, the priest, sometimes an admiral in charge of the whole fleet, and sometimes one or more officers of the soldiers on board. As a whole, they were "responsible to" the captain, more or less the way the 18th century government apparatus was responsible to the king. They had their separate responsibilities of caring for the sick, saying mass and performing burials, preparing for international encounters (which were, of course, more common at sea than in the land interior of countries), and the like, but these purposes were subject to the ultimate "jurisdiction" of the captain as supreme judge on board and as administrative agent of the owners.

Naturally the complement of moral and political officers was smaller on smaller ships sailing in smaller fleets, and the captains of smaller ships often served as fleet admiral, priest, military leader, and surgeon, as well as the roles specified above.

Dividing Risks among Equals

The "owner group" in the European port of origin was divided along three main dimensions: between insurers and owners; between hull (owners and insurers) and cargo (owners and insurers); and between (European) shore (bourgeois) and sea-and-foreign-port (officers). Thus, for example, after an accident the insurer became in some senses the "owner" of the ship and its cargo, and the captain became responsible to the insurer rather than the owner, since the insurer was going to pay all the losses and needed to control the captain so as to minimize those (see Heimer (1985), pp. 25, 121–23, 202). So within the European port the owner's authority passed from the shipowner to the insurer. After that point, the main agent of the owners on board ship or in the foreign port, the captain, served the insurer, because the insurer in Europe could not do anything about (say) disposing of damaged cargo in Jamaica without the captain.

The partitions among members of the owning group were managed by contracts or by the organization of often temporary corporate groups (contracts versus "societies" or "partnerships" were not, in general, strongly distinct in shipping). The insurance contract specified, of course, the relation between the hull owner or the cargo owner and the insurer, but also (in the "sue and labour" clause) the relation of the insurer to the agents on board in case of accident.

Broadly speaking, these contracts and societies tried to elicit "responsible" behavior by the various members of the owner group. Thus, for example, the insurer required of the hull owner that the ship be "seaworthy" (see Heimer (1985), pp. 103–5), meaning that the owner and the owner's agents had exercised reasonable care in making sure that the ship was ready to sail, whatever reasonable care might require in the circumstances.

Similarly, when cargo had to be thrown overboard to save the ship, the captain should not have a stronger interest in saving some of the cargo (that on which he would collect the profits) rather than other parts, so that he would responsibly try to save the most valuable cargo and throw over the least valuable. The contracts generally specified that the losses should be borne as a proportion of the total value of the separately owned bundles of cargo ("general average").

Similarly, the charter party between the owner of the ship and merchants that created the adventure would arrange the responsibilities, costs, and rewards so that the shipowner did not benefit from providing a ship in poor shape and the captain was not benefited by failing to maintain it during the voyage and make necessary repairs abroad.

That is, broadly speaking, these contracts or partnerships or societies set up an incentive system in such a way that the separable incentives of different participants in the ownership group, under various contingencies, did not undermine the total return to the group. But these collective arrangements arranged that when something could best be done by one of the partners, he (or the relevant partnership or society) should bear the cost of mistakes. For example, only under the conditions of accident did a decrease in the value of goods in a part of the cargo become the collective responsibility of all. If a cargo owner had made the mistake of shipping coals to Newcastle, he should take the loss, not the collectivity of cargo owners or the shipowner.

Similarly, it should be insurers who judged how long a ship would last in prime condition before it should be charged a higher premium. Wooden ships deteriorate quite fast, especially when exposed to dry conditions, as on the trip west to the Caribbean using the trade winds going west at the latitude of the Sahara. This variability of responsible behavior with contingencies, variability of who was responsible for what contingencies with differences in expertise, and need for responsibility because it was hard to specify rules to govern that behavior all tended to produce legal contracts or societies among equals as the main intrabourgeois formal relations. One must shape the incentives to elicit wisdom, effort, and discretion on the scene, rather than give commands from afar that do not fit.

Markets with Information about Different Risks

The hard kernel of the owner system was that the profits were due to the successful sailing of a ship with a valuable cargo from a place where the cargo was less valuable to a place where it was more valuable, to return with one that was more valuable yet. The ship with which that was done was an irreducible unity that was very expensive to build and to staff for a trip. Most of the contingencies in dividing an adventure's costs and returns were generated by variations in the value of the cargo, variations in the contingencies of sailing (weather, accidents, military attack, etc.), and variations in the costs of running the ship as an enterprise.

The kinds of information required to solve these various problems, and to bear the risks, were different, so "responsibility" as well as the expertise to meet the responsibility were to be defined differently. The merchant needed information from abroad to know where cargoes of what goods needed to be moved, packing and stowing information relevant to the preservation of the value of the cargo during sailing, and the information needed to minimize the total cost of the ship in transit.

The insurer and the mariners needed technical and experience information to minimize the risks of sailing, to maximize speed and accuracy of arriving where the ship was headed, to anticipate probable military contingencies. Because the information needs of insurers and mariners to know whether a ship was safe were similar, insurers often hired former mariners to make ship inspections and kept track of the experience of captains.[4]

But the captain, the purser, and the mates did the actual minimization of costs on board the ship, the actual preservation of cargoes, and the actual avoidance of accidents and conquests, so they needed the concrete and short-term versions of the long-term information that the merchants and insurers needed, information specified to their particular ship in a hurricane off Martinique. The mariners and the captain needed various kinds of information about costs and skill of the crew, and some facility with the government of a ship's social system.

Thus the agency problem of running a shipping enterprise was a complex web rather than a hierarchy, and tended to produce in the long run institutions of contractual equality among capitalists rather than hierarchy. Shipping cities tended to oligarchic government by councils, to exchange of information and goods at "exchanges" (Pred (1987)) with equal participants, to setting prices by auctions on the docks with equal standing of the bidders, and in other ways to a system of "equality and mutual responsibility among the rich." But this equality of standing might disappear at any particular time under the contract, depending on what contingency had come up. When there was an accident (but only then) the insurer lost and the merchant or hull owner got losses reimbursed. Authority worked in counterpoint, rather than like a soloist with accompaniment.

This equality among participants bearing different risks in its turn created more or less separate markets within which property rights subject to those risks were traded, because only with comparable information

---

[4] In Spain the inspections were multiple, often had to be repeated when the fleet was delayed, and were carried out by the Casa de Contratación of Sevilla, which had many other functions as well as safety inspections—see Pérez-Mallaína Bueno (1982), p. 281.

exchanged in that market was a market possible. But the risk-bearing property rights were intimately bound up with the deep problem of credit in long-distance shipping. The property rights were rights to income streams subject to different kinds of risks until some future time, and the delay before the income from a voyage would be available pervaded them all.

Capital as Payment in Advance: "Credit" in Long Distance Shipping

Banking, equity "markets," and insurance grew up first as institutions of trade rather than of investment in manufacturing, presumably because of the big fact that a ship's returns were not available until after the trip. Organizations that lent money (or lent things in kind valued in money) in return for larger future returns of money grew up in commercial cities. The credit demands created by the seasonality of long-distance seaborne commerce were solved by private agreements among capitalists. The institutions of private finance capital largely grew up in port cities engaged in long-distance trade. Such institutions were soon extended to the finance of wars (Carruthers (1989); Tilly (1990)), somewhat later to investment in putting out industry ("protoindustrialization"), later yet to investment by way of extension of credit by merchants in monocrop or colonial agriculture, and only finally to industrial capital equipment and factory buildings. The name "factory" itself was mostly used in early capitalism for the building belonging to a commission merchant, a "factor."

Credit has an even more obvious relation to the future than does the rationality of everyday life, and consequently more relation to risk and uncertainty. The essential legal components of the growth of financial markets therefore had to do with the segregation of risks (and responsibilities), both for the principal invested and for the profits.

As a general institutional matter, then as now, insurers bore highly specified risks, and risked their general reserves rather than anything invested in each ship or cargo. For example the "names" that underwrote marine insurance at Lloyds had unlimited liability for losses of the syndicates that they joined. Insurers were paid the premium in advance and did not share at all in the commercial risks or profits of a voyage. So although they facilitated other kinds of financial markets by segregating some sorts of risk from them (and sometimes by investment of their reserves), they were not really involved in credit except distantly.

Banks of the time might be defined in general by the fact that they tried to run only "credit risks" for both the principal they lent and interest, and did not in general participate in profits above the interest. A credit risk was one in which the total estate of the borrower (or sometimes first specified assets, as in a mortgage, then the total estate if that did not suffice) was security to the bank for both the principal and interest. Therefore risks were not connected with particular trips or ships, but rather with the general stocks and flows of assets and liabilities of the person or firm loaned to.

Equities were (then as now) forms of claims against the profits in return for investments, and varied with the profitability of the enterprise or adventure. It was important in 18th century shipping to distinguish those forms of equity ownership that represented a firm that was continuous over time, a "house," and forms that were organized around particular trips of particular ships, "adventures." These two main varieties of equity organization had different forms of participation in the risks and profits of the firm or the adventure, different kinds of partners or shareholders with different risks and different claims on the profits.

The changing business situation and strategy of the house (e.g., the amount it had borrowed, the degree of "leveraging") would change each participant's risk and opportunities for profit. In general, then, equity owners needed to be involved in firm government to one degree or another. Their investments were less "liquid," in the sense of more bound up with the current situation of the firm. They were marketable with more difficulty, and at a less predictable price, than were the forms of property created by indebtedness to a bank.

This is not the place to go into the immense variety of forms of ownership and debt that grew up in maritime cities. Max Weber's monograph (1924 [1889]) gives a sense of the immense variety of these forms, because in explaining the developments, he uses all the names invented by Italian businessmen and lawyers out of the materials of Latin law. The number of distinct Latin names in the monograph is thus an index of the complexity of the contractual field from which shipping participants selected a particular property and contract structure. The structure had got even more complex by the late 18th century.

The market in these loans, insurance liabilities, and equities of different kinds and the knowledge to assess the risks involved and the possible profits to be made were highly dependent on continuous communication among members of the merchant and capitalist class. Such businessmen would spend a lot of time in coffeehouses (e.g., Lloyds was originally a coffeehouse for insurers in London) or at "The Exchange" (whatever it was called; see Pred (1987), p. 66), where they might meet bankers and insurers as well as other capitalists. The legal cases of that merchant class quite often turned on what information it was obligatory to communicate in the course of transferring equities or commodities (see Scheppele (1988), pp. 269–98).

The key thing from our point of view here is that by the late 18th century, long-distance commerce rested on sophisticated financial institutions to manage its credit problems. Different sorts of risks were segregated, and different markets existed for the property rights that involved those different risks. One met in a different place to distribute shares of the insurance risk of a ship or a cargo than to trade partnership rights or other equity rights and to form temporary societies to participate in a voyage of a particular ship, and in a different place yet to trade mortgages or other debt-created claims on a merchant house's assets (though these were at that time less traded than held).

Only with such segregation of risks, and a corresponding segregation of responsibilities for responding to different sorts of information about those risks, could one get people to advance money to organize a voyage, at least in the Netherlands, France, and England in the late 18th century. To some degree the Spanish solution to the whole set of problems was to try to insure the whole fleet that sailed twice a year, then once a year, and then every other year, by a large contribution for military protection, to ensure against commercial risks by government control of competition and administered prices for international trade, and often to loan to the relevant commercial houses out of the government income and to confiscate private returns when the fisc got into trouble (Pérez-Mallaína Bueno (1982)).

Interloping trade (trade that is legitimate in the place of origin, such as Curaçao, St. Eustatius, St. Thomas, or Boston, but illegal "smuggling" at its destination) and privateering by the English (especially North American colonial ships), Dutch, Danish, and French had almost made the mercantilist monopoly of the *consulado* and the crown irrelevant by the late 18th century (Lang (1975), pp. 47–68; Goslinga and van Yperen (1985); Tuchman (1988)).

But in the commercially successful empires, people had a very different attitude toward risking their investment in a ship in a voyage if a storm could completely wipe them out than if insurers took that risk. Similarly, banks needed to know different things to lend to a merchant firm that had been doing business in a French port for decades than to buy bales of cotton cloth for a particular ship headed for Martinique— for example, one did not need to know a merchant one could trust in Martinique.

Correspondingly, the captain was chosen by the society or partnership organizing the voyage and had commercial as well as marine responsibilities in that voyage, so one had to trust him as a commercial agent. The insurers only kept a list of captains with information bearing on whether each maintained ships properly and avoided accidents, and combined that with information from an inspection of the ship, often by an ex-captain. The insurer had to know whether the captain knew enough to avoid accidents, but did not have to choose captains, or to trust them to bring home profits from an uncertain environment, only to bring home the ships.

The main point of all this is that long-distance merchants as a group had to be in charge of their own civil law in order to segregate risks, had to organize that law so as to locate responsibility where the corresponding risks were borne, and had to trust one another to bring home profits or to stay solvent in an uncertain environment. The government of credit formation (or "investment" if we include credit and insurance as investment), then, required civil law and enforcement of contracts, rather than government "regulation." And this in turn apparently required oligarchy and autocephaly (with respect at least to commercial matters) in port cities. It also required a relatively free flow of relevant information among independent actors in that oligarchy, so that one would know what risks one was running even if it would be to the advantage of someone else if one did not know them all.

Law and Government on the High Seas

We have discussed above the arrangements of the relationship between the captain and purser of a ship and the owners, and how under various contingencies the responsibility of the captain passed from one member of the owner group (e.g., the society organizing the adventure) to another (e.g., the insurer). The general point of this section, however, is that neither these owners nor any legal authorities who might interpret the labor contract nor any representatives of another government that had taken one's ship were in general available at sea. So while the ship was embedded in a complex system of commercial law and capitalist labor law, that law was available on shipboard only through the captain and the purser or through comparable authorities on a hostile privateer ship or military vessel.

This isolation from review, however, was not only a deprivation for the crew or lower officers, who had no appeal against a brutal, exploitative, careless, stupid, or otherwise unjust and ineffective captain. It was also a deprivation for the ownership system, which would have liked its victualing money spent on crew food, its labor relations sufficiently successful so that sailors would not desert in the Caribbean, its ship kept shipshape so that it would have fewer accidents, and its cargo sold in the most strategic markets. If absolute power corrupts absolutely, then one must set up the relation between the captain's powers and incentives at the beginning, again abroad in the port of destination, and again on the return so that the lack of shipboard appeal from the captain's final authority did not create destructive withdrawal from civilized commercial life. The agency contract for the captain (and for the purser, and for their mutual relations) should be so set up as to restrict the captain's power, under conditions of detachment at sea, to its commercially sound, technically effective, and lawful purposes and means.

We have talked about the incentive part of this, and some of the monitoring part, above. What is crucial here is that this government problem, too, depended on the creation of relations of legal certainty, of trust, and of exchange of information between the home ports and the ports in which the major intermediate monitoring could take place. From a commercial point of view, information about prices abroad had to flow back by some means other than the captain's report (an interesting variant on this problem was the desperate attempt by Guadeloupe authorities during the Revolution to get reliable inventories and prices for ships and cargoes taken by their privateers and sold in allied ports, described by Pérotin-Dumon (1988)). From a ship maintenance point of view, inspectors who knew about ships had to be ready to inspect for classification societies in all the major ports of the world, and to transmit those judgments back to London, Amsterdam, or Antwerp.[5] From a labor relations point of view, information on how many sailors would desert in the Caribbean, who would have to be replaced at New World wage rates, had to get back to Europe in such a fashion as to predict future wage costs of an excessively brutal captain. Only if the captain was embedded in an international commercial oligarchy with multiple channels of information back to the port that sent him out could adequate monitoring of captain behavior take place; but it always helped to have the purser as the first and main channel.

The English insurers, at least, kept formal lists of captains with the accumulated information on their trustworthiness from an insurer's point of view. The other participants in the business must have kept their monitoring information in many ways, but they might have been less formal because not as many people had to participate in a particular adventure as had to participate in the syndicate insuring a particular risk to spread it effectively. In the extreme, for example, the whole set of relations talked about above in an adventure could be concentrated in

---

[5] The French Bureau Veritas was first located in Antwerp. Classification societies class (inspect and evaluate) the ships for marine insurers, determining premium rates.

an owner-captain trading in his own cargo in both the port of origin and the port of destination; concentrating insurance risks of a voyage on a single person is bad insurance policy.

Agency and Capitalism

By our examination of the problems of the distribution of investment, of incentives, of responsibility, of ability to deal with risks, and of their interrelation, we argue that we have shown why finance capitalism organized in port cities was connected to corporate management of the work crew and its capital equipment, the ship. We claim also to have suggested why the Spanish system that was organized by corporatist "regulatory" control, rather than by contracts and negotiated corporate groups among finance capitalists of various sorts, was tending to go under in the 18th century; the king of Spain seems to have sometimes lost money shipping his own gold and silver back from Mexico in the 18th century, because the value of the metal in Europe was not enough to cover his shipping costs. This is also an implicit argument about why the navies of the main commercial countries were not fitted for carrying out long-distance trade.

Entrepreneurial capitalism was evidently fitted for trade across the seas, but there was a strong relation between the length of the trading voyage and the size of the ship and cargo that it was economical to send. Short-sea trade prospers with many small, frequent shipments in smaller ships serving only the two ports on each end; long-distance trade prospers with large ships making less frequent voyages with more ports of call on each end.[6] But organizing the concentration of capital for such larger ships and longer trips requires dispersing different sorts of risks to different sorts of investors willing to run those risks.

The management of the large risks, long time periods, and large investments in each adventure, then, requires a complex of contracts or a government to set up the enterprises, rather than a large number of small entrepreneurs. Since governments of the time apparently did not work very well in such commerce (at least the Spanish one, and the na-

---

[6] Cf. Butel (1974), p. 18, for Bordeaux. Even now, ships trading in the Mediterranean tend to be intermediate in size between smaller ships trading between ports on the North Sea and larger ships trading across the Atlantic, for example. See also, for example the description of the differences between Atlantic and Baltic traders in France in Tarrade (1972; 1), p. 241, and of *kleine vaart* or *cabotage* (interisland and coastal trade) in the Caribbean in Goslinga and van Yperen (1985). Smith (1962) has an account of peasants' at a much later time becoming interisland traders by building their own boats, without benefit of finance capital.

vies of England and France, did not), the inadequacy of entrepreneurial capitalism required finance capitalism. The management of risks at sea and in foreign ports required corporate control over the ship itself, through its agent, the captain, and through his monitor, the purser.

But it is not obvious that such a set of financial deals, of contracts dividing risks and responsibilities, could actually manage a crew of people changing sails, patching holes in the sides, pumping out the water to stay afloat, or moving the cargo so that it would not be soaked and yet would not tip the ship over. The management of this set of risks by means of sailor labor virtually required free wage labor, and many of the aspects of the labor contract show the functions the contract served.

Risks and Incentives of the Crew

The mate or *maître* or *stuurmann* was the main first-line supervisor of the sailors. Such men were the top of the set of people recruited among the proletariat of the ports. They were professional mariners, often recruited from careers as sailors, and, like the ship timber carpenter, they learned their trade by apprenticeship. They had direct charge of supervising the work of the sailors, the management of the sails and other matters of navigation, the loading, placement, and securing of the cargo, and generally keeping the ship "in trim."

The empirical knowledge of how much sail was usable in different types of wind, or how to stow cargo so that the ship would be stable even though the motive force was being applied high above the deck, was learned by practice. The captain and other marine officers also learned by practice, and could often supervise or replace the first mate if necessary. But the organization of such work was not really their business. Similarly, the carpenter's knowledge of what sort of patch would hold water out was craft empiricism. The captain of a large ship generally did not have such practice, or much experience managing a crew of skilled timber workers. The mates and carpenters were in charge of the morale and skill of the sailors. They managed the ship as a structure and as a machine with wind as its motive force. The mates usually recruited the sailors, divided up the work among them, and sailed the ship under the direction of the pilots.

The pilots required a great deal of empirical knowledge to try to combine running knowledge of what direction the ship was going at what speed with latitude (and later perhaps longitude, if the ship's clock was accurate enough) from the stars and sun. They thus required some scientific training and a good deal of lore, because the science was not much good when the stars were not visible or the sun could not be observed at noon, and because without reliable clocks, longitude was mainly estimated by keeping track of speeds and directions.

Winds were inherently unpredictable, but one knew what direction they generally blew from lore, corrected by compass bearings, and how hard they were blowing from the waves. One could sometimes estimate the speed of a current to adjust speed for the current, and one could check up on where one had got to only by recognizing the shape of the land.[7]

The pilots could not be recruited from people whose only skill was governing, but they also could not be recruited from in the working-class milieux of port cities. They had to be professional mariners, to have an urban education emphasizing mathematics and "science," and to have been introduced to the lore of navigation by apprenticeship. But they did not mainly earn their living by managing the work force, as the *maître*, or mate, did, or by maintaining secure commercial government over a detached social system, as the captain did.

The sailors were recruited from the male working classes of port districts each season by the mates, or directly by the captains on small ships. Like the pilot, mates, and carpenters, they were basically salaried workers for the sailing season. Wages (or salaries, which is nearer the modern equivalent) were also unequal, so a beginning sailor might be paid half or two-thirds as much as an experienced sailor, who in turn might be paid half as much as a timber carpenter, who in turn might be paid about half as much as the first mate.[8] So the range of inequality among the crew was about eight to one from first mate to unskilled sailor and four to one from first mate to ordinary sailor.

They had to be recruited with advances, because otherwise their families (if they had them) could not live while they were gone, and because they had to be assured that they would get something out of the trip even if it were not a commercial success. For most of the collective risks due to the weather and seamanship, the "natural incentives," namely, the fact that people could not survive in the middle of the ocean without a ship, would keep the sailors and mates working. This community of fate would make them pump hard when there was a leak, and would

[7] For an example of such lore, see Tuchman's (1988), pp. 221–22, account of the map of the Gulf Stream by Benjamin Franklin's cousin, Timothy Folger, with the indications vessels could use to tell where the current was—temperature measurements, speed of surface bubbles, color of the water. Franklin himself tested out these indications on a voyage in 1776. Tuchman seems to have the current going the wrong way in some passages.

[8] Merrien (1964), p. 64, for France; for the British navy, which probably approximates the British merchant marine, Lloyd (1970 [c. 1968]), esp. pp. 49, 69, also pp. 24, 48, 91, 248–54, 271; for the Dutch navy and merchant marine, Boxer (1988 [1965]), pp. 337–40.

make them adjust the sails to the winds. Captains sometimes sailed with smaller crews than were really required, or substituted extra pumping for expensive repairs, but this tended to create problems of desertion rather than refusal to keep the ship afloat.

But there were three big contingencies where it was very problematic whether the incentives of the crew and mates would be aligned with those of the owners: military risks, desertion in a foreign port, or running away with the advance before the ship sailed.

The most important collective risk in the late 18th century requiring crew incentive alignment with capitalists was in case a privateer (or a naval ship), usually operating near a coast where ship traffic was concentrated (Peterson (1975); Merrien (1970)), attempted to board the ship. For sailors, continuing to fight would naturally risk life and limb. Surrendering would not risk the advance already made, would usually save their lives (because they would be put off on shore—colored and black crew from French revolutionary corsairs were sometimes sold into slavery, which presumably made them harder to take), and would only cost them the incentives that they would earn on successful completion of the voyage. Thus the larger the ratio of the sailors' advance to the total earnings, and the more likely it was that they could find a ship to work passage home on, the less the incentive to fight.

The second most important alignment problem was that the sailors might desert at the overseas destination, to stay as immigrants or prospectors, to sign onto another ship, or to join a privateer (sometimes the one that had taken the ship) near the new shores. The coercive apparatus available on shipboard or in the home country to enforce the labor contract was not as easily available in foreign ports. The incentive system for sailors after reaching the foreign port was radically different from that when they were still at sea. "Desertion," or the notion that they were in a free labor market abroad as well as at home, was a continuing problem for merchant shippers.

The third most important alignment problem was that after accepting the advance in a European port, a sailor might sign onto another ship or otherwise skip out with the advance money; this was the same as desertion except that the sailor had not yet worked enough to pay for the advance.

The incentives for merchant crews to resist a privateer or pirate tended to change drastically depending on whether the attacking ship was near enough to board. The main military advantage of a privateer or pirate was a much larger crew, often running about three times the normal merchantman crew (Merrien (1970)), and even the small coastal boats that were the first corsairs in revolutionary Guadeloupe carried

forty or fifty men (Pérotin-Dumon (1988), p. 291, quoting Victor
Hugues). The ratio of French crew size for merchantmen to that of the
English and Dutch was apparently also about three to one, for reasons
I do not understand, so the fight between a French merchant ship and
a privateer might have been more equal.

This in turn meant that the privateer and merchant ships *as ships* were
likely to be roughly militarily equal, and roughly equal as sailing machines, but that in conditions of boarding the merchant ship would be
greatly outnumbered. So as long as a ship could run, fight with cannon,
and the like, it was usually to the merchant crew's advantage to complete
the trip and to do what was necessary to get away or to fight the attacker
off. But as soon as the advantage of the attacker became overwhelming,
at the moment of boarding, it was sensible to surrender.

The incentives in case of privateer attack were quite different for the
owners and the captain than for the crew, especially since most of the
owners were back in Europe, but also because the owners and captain
would collect more of the profits and pay more of the losses. The sailors'
decision was made in the heat of battle, so the whole thing was quite
problematic until it became obvious that the attacker was overwhelmingly superior. Nevertheless, most ships, even in naval engagements, surrendered rather than being sunk. The privateers and pirates had a strong
motive to make it to the advantage of the crew to surrender rather than
to fight, by respecting the "laws of war." The owners wanted to make
sure that the incentives to complete the voyage were substantial.

Owners in the *Croisic* addressed a complaint to the *Parlement de Bre-
tagne* in 1655 which read in part:

> But the malice of the sailors has come to such a great extremity that instead
> of recognizing, by their obedience and loyalty, the goodness of the bour-
> geois who risk such large properties to give them the means of making a liv-
> ing, they have caused, by their cowardice, the loss of 3 of the biggest and best
> vessels of the above mentioned fleet, which were taken last September by
> some Spanish frigates considerably worse armed and manned than those 3
> vessels.
>
> The cause of the fault . . . is to be discovered by the words of some of the
> sailors of the vessels, who declared that those in charge of the cannons and
> most of their companions refused to give battle . . . because they would be
> mad to risk their lives . . . to preserve the goods of those big bourgeois who
> sleep entirely at ease in their beds; and for themselves, they were happy and
> did not lose anything, since they had taken the . . . advance and that their
> share [at the end] would not be worth much. . . . So the petitioners humbly
> request that the Parlement forbid sailors to take as an advance more than a
> third of the value of their pay, say 50 *livres*, and to oblige them to obey their
> commander on penalty of their lives. (Merrien (1964), pp. 86–87)

The best study of "desertion" in foreign ports that I have found is Marcus Rediker, *Between the Devil and the Deep Blue Sea* ((1987), pp. 100–115 and *passim* under "Desertion" in his index). The contract between the captain and the bourgeois in Europe partially separated the captain's incentives for reducing labor costs from the bourgeois' incentives to set up a profitable voyage at the going wages. This created strong incentives for a captain to cut costs, mainly by saving on rations or wages after the ship was under weigh. This situation sometimes led to the captain trying to shed labor in the foreign port. The captain might, for example, try to get some of the sailors, preferably the most recalcitrant, to go over to royal navy ships or other merchantmen at the foreign port.

Further, since the captain was the ultimate source of legal authority while at sea, and since the mate was hired by the captain but the captain often had little experience in managing labor, an oppressive captain or an oppressive mate and a weak captain made the labor bargain worse than had been contracted for.

Finally, to some degree, extra work by the crew at sea (especially pumping) could be substituted for capital expenditure on ship repairs, and if that extra labor could be extracted from the same crew, it was a clear saving for the owner-captain complex. Further, a captain might get news of a commercial opportunity in an unhealthy place (disease, a "hot press" by the royal navy, or warfare all could make a place unhealthy), and change the destination in a way that exposed the crew to greater risks and costs for the same wages.

Thus a dictatorial authority system was subject both to the risks of personal tyranny by sadistic or authoritarian personalities and to the captain's incentive to extract more labor for the same or lesser wages and rations. Desertion, or "free labor" mobility, was therefore a protection against having the terms of the labor bargain changed to the workers' disadvantage; with little voice on the ship, exit was the main protection.

But, conversely, the ship very often gave the sailors passage to a labor market with higher wages. Rediker quotes a song about desertion:

O, the times are hard and the wages low
Leave her, John-ny, leave her
I'll pack my bag and go below;
It's time for us to leave her.

(Rediker (1987), p. 100)

The version I have heard sung by Pete Seeger has the lines describing the time after the trip:

The Rocky Mountains is my home,
Across the Western Ocean.

Rediker notes that sometimes by giving up the two or three months' wages owed to them for the round trip, sailors could make up to two or three times as much on the return trip. This was especially true when they were healthy in a port in which much European labor was not "seasoned"[9] and so was sick (Rediker (1987), pp. 103–4). As the second version of the song suggests, the rich opportunities behind the port cities of the Americas were an additional determinant of the higher wages for the return trip.

Aside from the incentive to rebargain the labor contract created by bad faith by shipboard authorities, then, there was the additional incentive to rebargain ("to desert") created by the fact that the higher wages of colonial labor markets were protected from immigration of cheaper European labor by the high cost of passage between Europe and the Americas. This meant that the sailor's labor contract signed in London (or elsewhere in Europe) created added value in the sailor's labor, by transporting him to a high-wage market. And if the sailor did not die in the process, his experience in tropical voyages made him a "climatically" seasoned European laborer who was especially valuable in colonies with slavery or in the slave trade itself.

Such incentive difficulties of the bourgeois faced with the risk of desertion would be partly solved if the proportion of the sailor's wages for the round trip that was *not* advanced were higher, if the captain were better controlled by the purser in the disbursement of rations and by the carpenter in seeing to the repairs needed, and if the legal system of the colonies could be made to enforce the labor contracts of deserters. We discussed above attempts to decrease the amount of the advance by regulations in the originating European port. It is also true that sometimes captains apparently managed to have the purser thrown overboard when he insisted that the crew get all their rations, indicating that owners were conscious that captains could create desertion problems and had designated the purser as responsible for seeing to it that the captain spent the ration money on food for the crew. This did not always save the purser.

Rediker uses as his sources the trials carried out in North American ports in which shipowners (through their agents in America, of course) tried to collect damages from or to punish deserters, showing that the extension of civil law abroad helped align errant sailor and bourgeois behavior.

The problem of skipping out after the advance but before the voyage

---

[9] "Seasoned" described the effects of the exposure to tropical diseases on the immune system, so seasoned workers, soldiers, and slaves did not get sick as much in the Caribbean or on slave ships. Planters presumably were seasoned the same way, but I have not seen it used to describe them, perhaps because they are not means of production but owners.

actually started was much the same as the problem of desertion, except that its solution depended on giving the sailor an incentive to get to the foreign port. A Dutch solution to this problem was to *require* the sailor to put his own chest of goods, to be traded on his own account at the destination, onto the ship when he got his advance. Then if the sailor skipped out with his advance, he lost immediately the European value of the goods left on board and eventually the value those goods would have in the port of destination.

In general the legal system of the home port city where skipping out with the advance took place was much more accessible to the owners than the legal system of foreign ports because they lived there, so regulations were much more effective in preventing deserting with the advance than deserting in the foreign port. And, of course, the market price for the labor in the European port where the sailor skipped out was in theory the same as that negotiated in the original contract, so there was no special motive to renegotiate the contract by desertion. In general, desertion at this stage was either outright fraud (e.g., signing up with two ships but sailing on only one) or simple nonperformance.[10]

Shares of salvage and shares in the commercial success (by selling the contents of their own trunks of goods) of the voyage were also part of the incentive system of the crews of merchant ships. The shares were unequal, but not as unequal as the inequality between owners and nonowners. The crew usually carried goods to trade for themselves, and apparently had different amounts of space to store these in, so they shared in the commercial success of the voyage proportionally to their rank.

Courts of admiralty divided the salvage value of a ship saved more equally between crews and owners in the days when the bravery and hard work of the crews were more important than special equipment and extra motive power in saving a ship in trouble (e.g., more equally in the 18th century than in the 20th), evidently because they wanted to motivate people strongly to help even when helping was dangerous (Heimer (1985), pp.122–27). The shares to the crew for salvage were also unequal by rank.

The crew were divided up into couples who occupied the same hammock on the two alternating watches and served the same work function. In case of the death of one of them, the other took charge of selling his box of trade goods, of delivering his pay and commercial returns to his wife or other relatives, and generally of winding up his affairs. Since they had common work, they were obvious possible substitutes for each other in cases of sickness.

[10] Merrien (1964), pp. 88–89, gives some examples of stories told to judges by sailors who were not on board when their ship sailed.

Crew Credit

The main structure of the credit situation of the sailors has been out-lined above. At the beginning of the voyage the capitalist advanced an amount that might be roughly a third of the total wage (including the profits from the sailor's private trade), and guaranteed subsistence (not counted as part of wages, but obviously crucial to the sailors, as many mutinies on questions of rations show) during the voyage. By the end of the voyage back in Europe, the sailor had typically advanced, again very roughly, half to two-thirds of his wage for a season to his employer (he might have been paid some of it at the destination). The amount ad-vanced by both parties would probably have been larger in voyages to the Far East, since they were typically two years long.

The employers' advances of wages and provisions were financed by the system described above; we do not know much about the household budgets for sailors' families while the sailors were at sea, but there was probably a large subsistence farming element, and perhaps some rural manufacturing work by wives and children, in those budgets. That is, sailor wages were implicitly advanced partly by subsistence agricultural enterprises to which they would come back. Quite often the sailors were single men, and we might imagine they might inherit a peasant holding, into which they might invest some of the returns from sailing at the end of the voyage. We are quite sure sailors did not have access to the credit institutions of finance capitalism to borrow against the wages collectible at the end of the season.

What we find, then, is that the credit system was arranged just as agency theory would predict: that the sailor was required to advance much of his season's wages to the owners, and did not collect until the voyage had been brought successfully to an end. Even though he was paid an advance at the beginning to help tide his family over for the season, it was much less than his full wages, and some of it was some-times required to be invested in trade goods to sell in the colonies on his own behalf. Of course, the bourgeois advanced the sailor's own subsis-tence until the end of the voyage.

But a surprisingly large share of the "credit" used to run long-dis-tance shipping was borrowing against the wages of the workers until the profit was available. The capital was taken from the sailor with his con-sent and with promise of repayment, so it was not quite like what Marx describes as "primitive accumulation": stealing the peasant's plot from him, simultaneously creating a proletariat and capital to exploit it with. But it had some of the same tone.

Crew Government

The core of crew government on the ship was the person called the master in French (*maître*), the mate or boatswain in English (the captain was sometimes called the master in English), the *stuurman* in Dutch (the Dutch word was also sometimes used for the pilot, and sometimes for the helmsman, and this may be because the roles were not very distinct), and the person holding the same position on the alternate watch. He supervised deck work, rigging work, the movement of cargo, and generally keeping the ship "in trim," as mentioned above. The main point of relevance here is that this involved governing everyone on deck in considerable detail and fairly continuously. The fate of the whole enterprise depended on making these decisions right, and seeing to it that the sailors in fact executed them. There was a lot of authority in these roles, and the role occupants managed the main relations of the whole crew to the authority system, as the most important technical marine agents of the captain. Some supervisors of skilled work other than deck and rigging, such as the timber carpenter or the supervisors of soldiers or gunners, had a comparable kind of authority, though not as much.

This part of ship government was not reflected in the legal documentation, and the people were trained for authority by apprenticeship rather than by instruction out of textbooks, so it is very hard to figure out how it all worked. It was probably very important that the immediate supervisors of the crew were recruited out of working-class milieux, making them responsive to their "peers" when in port.

It seems that non-lethal violence was an important part of the governance, since Merrien reports a tradition about sailors getting away from the *maître* to the rigging of the sail on the bow of the ship, where any pursuit would be likely to be fatal to one or the other of the fighters (Merrien (1964)); the point is both that the sailors apparently had to get away, and that putting oneself in a place where violence was likely to be lethal created a haven.

By and large we know very little about the creation of authority of first-line supervisors over workers in preindustrial times, I suppose because we imagine that the employers themselves did the supervision. When the employer was in Europe, and when the employer's representative on the ship was not necessarily a skilled mariner, the employer did not do the supervision.

The main point here is that although coercive labor relations could apparently create such ship governments over the same proletarians in the wartime navy, even there they paid wages and recruited free experienced sailors. In the merchant navy it is clear that mates or boatswains at the top of the workers had to have incentives to select and govern free sailors well. But it is also true that a high level of skilled performance in dangerous tasks was being required of young men whom the authorities could not afford to kill before the voyage's end, so coercion could not work well. Moderate consent had to be motivated reliably for eighty-four hours a week, a normal watch)—for more if many of the crew were sick or dead, and for overwork in emergencies.

Slaves do not make good elite troops (unless promised freedom—if not promised freedom, they often have taken over the government, as in various places in the Ottoman Empire), or good factory workers, or good housewives, or good sailors. Wherever tight cooperative coordination, responsibility out of the sight of authorities, learning a skilled trade and getting better at it over time, extra effort in emergencies, and turning over one's work in good shape to the worker who comes on for the other watch, all are required in a work role, unfree consent without rewards for good performance will not work. Such work is nowadays very often rewarded in a system with salaries rather than hourly wages, with much of the reward coming on successful completion of the tasks, with promotions to more skilled positions and ultimately to supervisory authority with experience, with a continuing bond between the authorities and the workers, and with the bond often supported by financial advances on both sides. And it was so rewarded among sailors in 18th century long-distance shipping.

The Origin of Capitalism and of Slave Society

The same people in the same cities of Europe ran the shipping system and sold the products of slave plantations. The merchants of Bordeaux or Nantes or Amsterdam or London or Liverpool were not, by and large, people who had an ideological comitment to free labor, and not really to finance capital. They were comfortable, at least for a long time, selling cotton and sugar that had been produced by slaves. They would not have built the financial capitalism and free labor system, as they did to run their shipping, unless it worked. Many of them knew from the experience of colleagues who sailed in the Carrera that the Spanish system did not work, and they had little difficulty persuading their sailors to prefer working on merchant ships rather than on navy ships. I have tried to explain how and why it worked above.

A close comparison of what I have said with what Weber (1924 [1889]) said about the Italian and Catalonian late Middle Ages shows that the system described here had been growing from seeds recognizable several centuries earlier. Something quite like it had apparently worked in the north of Italy then. It grew in much the same way in three rather different major trading countries in the 18th century; and where it did not grow that way, in Spain, it did not work.

A detailed examination of the contracts that made the web in which a ship operated suggests that the system worked because it solved a series of very difficult agent-motivating and agent-monitoring problems entailed in getting big sailing ships across the ocean and back at a profit. So first of all, the origin of capitalism was apparently located in the difficulty of making money through agents in the most world-system, shipping, part of the early capitalist world system. And second, capitalism grew first in the places, port cities, in the feudal and absolutist regime that had problems most similar to those of great industrial and commercial enterprises in modern economies, namely, the problems of long-distance shipping. Capitalism grew to manage the most modern problems of economic social organization, those most like those of industrialism, in late medieval and early modern Europe.

But if capitalism and its early modern governmental form as a city with an oligarchic council originated in port cities, then colonies organized to supply goods to such cities would be influenced by that form. The early colonies of the Netherlands, France, and England were indeed governed dominantly by "civil law," basically the law of port cities. Civil law is distinguished from criminal and administrative law mainly by providing state power to force compliance with contracts voluntarily entered into, and its main mechanism is that one of the parties voluntarily calls on the courts for that enforcement. It was contracts, together with the organization of corporations, after the fashion of European cities, that constituted the central governmental forms of early colonies.

Colonies in their very first beginnings had constitutions rather like "ships that happen to be on land." Later they came to have a structure more like corporate subsidiaries of the great colonial merchant companies, but with local boards of directors and chief executive officers. Then, without changing much about their core governmental organization, they became territorial governments of the colonies of empires. (But note that this does not describe how Spanish colonial government evolved.)

When these colonies became slave societies with the growth of sugar plantations, they preserved more or less conventional capitalist city government forms at the top, but changed the purpose and direction of that part of the law governing labor relations with slaves, the possibility of slave rebellion, and the citizenship status of the free colored. That is, the historical origins of Caribbean slave societies were exactly "bourgeois democracy." But bourgeois democracy in its early modern city form rests fundamentally on the definition of citizenship in the city—of who is a member of the city and its government and who just happens to live there.

The proletarians on the ships happened to live in or near the cities out of which they sailed, but were not citizens except that they were subject to the civil law "of free men." On the islands the slaves were excluded not only from politics, but from the civil law as well. Thus, contrary to Orlando Patterson's argument about Western civilization as a whole, (Patterson (1991;1)), Caribbean slave societies grew out of "freedom of the city," and in contrast to it. "A British Tar is a soaring soul / As free as a mountain bird," as Arthur S. Sullivan put it. And a British slave was defined in contrast to British sailors, not vice versa.

The two systems, slave and free, were joined by similarity at the top. When the Barbados courts claimed jurisdiction over bankruptcies of planters against the courts of London, the legal consequences of that were perfectly clear by the civil law tradition of the cities. But the social consequences were that bankrupt plantations would not be broken up into peasant holdings, even though peasant holdings were more valuable per acre, because that would undermine slave labor relations. No such labor relations consequences flowed from any such claim of jurisdiction within London or Liverpool. Civil law, not labor law, tied Barbados to Liverpool and London.

Many aspects of the regime of the sea were incompatible with the use of slave labor. Sailing was skilled work, and the initiative and responsibility required to get it done right were difficult to obtain by coercion. A certain amount of loyalty in combat with privateers combined with reasonableness when defeat was certain were hard to elicit from slaves, because at the time loyalty was most needed, coercion was weakest. The web of contracts among people responsible for different risks had an elective affinity with government by consent, at least consent of those with property. Extension of that web to the sailors was not only conceptually and legally easy; it also solved a number of problems of sustaining cooperative sailor motivation throughout the trip.

The maintenance of slavery tended to require the transformation of the whole social and political system of a slave island into one devoted to maintaining coercive class relations. It would have been very difficult to move such a system into all the different ports a long-distance ship was likely to have to visit. Slave galleys historically had to dock in a military port, where oarsmen could be confined effectively until the galley sailed again; when the Viking oarsmen had to go ashore to sack towns where there were no Norse forts, they had to have consented to the enterprise and their role in it.

The beach of a Caribbean island, or perhaps better, the docks in the harbors of that island, drew a boundary between a capitalist system with free labor and planter slave capitalism. Our purpose has been to explain why the advantages of the slave system were not advantages that caused it to grow over that boundary and create a slave regime on the seas, even though some elements of coercion (e.g., impressment for the navy, authoritarian work crew supervision on the ship, noncitizenship for most workers) characterized the "free" system.

The slave and port city shipping sugar system, then, was a monster joined at the head, by common forms of oligarchic council government and a common civil law. That law reigned in European cities, even when it did not govern the countryside in some countries. And it reigned in the colonies, for both plantation owners and merchants. But the free labor of urban civil law at the bottom of the city system, getting sailing machines across the seas by skilled manual labor, had different feet than the slave system.

This similar capitalist system with different labor law eventually will serve us in the explanation of how the capitalist system in the metropole was only a precarious ally of planter capitalism—for example, why in England it was dominantly Whigs, the more capitalist party, rather than the more agrarian Tories, who opposed the slave trade and proposed abolition of slavery, or why the bourgeois Revolution in France abolished slavery in its democratic phase and then took the abolition back in its Napoleonic phase.[11] The abolitionist movement was never very strong

---

[11] The "left" in all the imperial countries was divided on abolition of the slave trade and emancipation, and the colonial white left tended to be like the populist racists of the American South, supporting racism and slavery, but wanting to be more in on the government. Abolition tended to be somewhat more supported the more "democratic" the constitutional theory of a political movement: for example, more congregationalist churches, and parliamentary districts in England with broader suffrage, were more abolitionist. Abolition of the slave trade and of slavery were more *constitutionally* left positions than left positions in a class or economic interest sense. Populist currents, in favor of the "common man" but without developed constitutional theory, tended to be indifferent on slavery questions. If one ranged European movements from right to left in the usual way in, say, 1820, the aristocratic royalist right was probably usually about 80 percent pro-slavery; the popular urban revolutionary and trade union movements, about 60 percent anti-slavery (of those who had an opinion) but mostly apathetic (these numbers are guesses). The religious left (including Congregationalists and to some degree atheists) was far more anti-slavery than the class left. Our point about bourgeois democracy is twofold, then. First, as a governmental elite, bourgeois democrats were not as pro-slavery as the aristocratic and royalist right in the old regime and during restoration periods, and second, they were more open to participatory forms of government that did not suppress anti-slavery movements with as much enthusiasm as did royalists and aristocrats. Of bourgeois democrats, Napoleon was not the most anti-slavery and pro-participation that might be found. See Drescher (1990a, 1990b, 1991, 1994a, 1994b) and Pérotin-Dumon (1988, 1989).

in the islands, and always won first as a metropolitan "bourgeois" movement (though probably better supported by artisan petty bourgeois than
by the merchant and industrial capitalists of Marxist theory). It was then
transmitted to the islands as imperial policy. The difficulty of reimposing
slavery in Haiti after it was abolished, however, had to do with the post-
revolutionary strength of abolitionism among the ex-slaves and colored
people of the island, rather than anything about bourgeois democracy in
France.

The boundary between bourgeois oligarchic city government and
bourgeois free labor law that we have just been examining, then, explains why there was a place in imperial slave capitalism for an abolitionist "bourgeois" movement to grow.

4

The Economic Demography of Plantation Islands

The Main Components of Caribbean Economic Demography

The contribution of this chapter to the argument of the book as a whole is to provide measures of the relative size of the sugar plantation complex on an island. The book's argument is that this size measures the main causal complex that produced and maintained slave societies, societies in which the main public good to be produced (for the upper classes) was reliable repression of all rights of slaves, a racist ideology to support that repression (an ideology that was also applied to non-slave and African black and colored people), and constraints on the rest of the society deemed necessary to the security of the slave regime. It is this force, so we argue, that resulted in a society that could hardly bother to produce any public goods other than repression of slaves during the sugar-frontier period, and that, during the resident planter period after the sugar frontier had been developed, produced other public goods of civilized life only because slavery was secure. Further, it was that same force that after emancipation used control over the government to produce publicly enforced monopolies for planters in the "free labor market."

Our purpose, then, is to measure the size of the sugar plantation as a mode of production, producing a slave society superstructure, relative to the main other modes of production prevalent on the islands: peasant and smallholding cultivation (and in some places, livestock ranching) and urban commercial and government services. The most convenient metric for arguments in political economy in the Caribbean is the working person. Thus a sugar plantation with two hundred slaves and a few white managers will be considered roughly ten times the economic and political weight of a coffee or cocoa plantation in the foothills with twenty slaves and an owner family that manages, and one hundred times the weight of a peasant holding cultivated by a father with a grown son, with marketing work done weekends by the mother.

We will not pretend that we can give comparable figures for all the times we will argue about. But we can start with the observation that sugar cultivation was somewhere between five and ten times as labor in-

tensive as other crops per acre, so an acre in sugar produced roughly five
to ten times as much political and economic power as an acre in tree
crops or provisions. Sugar was perhaps twenty-five to one hundred times
as intensive as raising cattle or work animals, so a *latifundium* of 200
acres in sugar had the approximate political weight of a *hato latifundium*
raising livestock of 10 to 40 square miles.

The general purpose of this chapter, then, is to outline the economic
demography of Caribbean plantation islands, by which I mean the relative rates of growth of three main populations: plantation labor, "peasant" families, and the urban trade and service working class.

A first basic fact about this demography is that throughout the history
of the Caribbean, plantations that had to import their labor from elsewhere have much preferred male laborers. The sex ratio of slaves was
much more male on Caribbean sugar plantations, especially during the
sugar-frontier period, than on, for example, cotton plantations in the
United States, and this skewed sex ratio has been characteristic of the
plantation labor forces recruited by interisland or international migration since the abolition of slavery (Curtin (1990)).

This skewed sex ratio, combined with a high death rate of slaves, especially in their first few years in the islands, generally resulted in the
plantation labor force's having a low total reproduction rate, though apparently about the same fertility of women as was characteristic of North
American slaves (Mintz (1974b), (1974 [1961])).

The total fertility of the black population in the United States was
about the same (i.e., quite high) as the fertility of the white population.
The death rate of slave populations in the Caribbean, especially of newly
"immigrated" slaves, was apparently higher than in the United States.[1]

So the more rapidly the plantations in a particular area were growing,
the lower their slaves' fertility (because of lack of women and the lower
rate of formation of family groups in which the male guarantees to help
support the children). Therefore the higher the proportion of all slaves
who were newly imported, the higher the death rate and the lower the
birth rate, and so the higher the proportion of the next generation that
would have to be imported.

In general this has meant that Caribbean plantations, especially where
they grew rapidly, always depended on breaking up families somewhere
so that the men could move to become plantation labor forces. Up to

---

[1] Curtin (1990). See also for lower estimates of Caribbean death rates compared to
North American ones, Mintz (1974a), and in considerably more detail those (for the British islands in the 19th century only) of Higman (1984); the best epidemiological analysis
I know of for whites is Geggus's analysis of the British troops in Geggus (1982), pp. 347–
72; it is clear that Europeans died more rapidly in their first few years in the Caribbean than
did Africans, which undermines many theories of the high slave death rates.

the end of the 19th century, some sort of coercion was generally involved in breaking up the families. For a short period after emancipation the recruitment was, theoretically at least, the voluntary contract signed somewhere in Asia (especially India, but also Indonesia, or southern China and occasionally Africa) for servitude of limited length. That contract then turned out to be more coercive in the Caribbean than the contract's words in Asia had implied. More commonly, immigration contracts were explicitly coercive. But like slave importation, the immigration was disproportionately male, had few families, died at a higher rate than seasoned labor, and so did not reproduce itself.

This coerciveness of the indenture contract was probably related to the fact that shipping the labor for long distances was much slower and more expensive with more primitive sea transport, so a longer period of labor was required to pay it off. By the 20th century there were unemployed or underemployed people on other islands in the Caribbean who could be recruited for seasonal or other short-period work with smaller transport costs.

The second basic fact that makes the demography of plantation societies distinctive is that the development of a plantation involved a drastic increase in the labor intensity of cultivation. For example, in the parish of Léogane (the town of Léogane is 33 kilometers from Port au Prince) in Haiti the transformation between 1692 and 1730 is described by Charles Frostin:

> In 1692 this parish, besides its plantations of tobacco, had 54 indigo plantations and one single sugar plantation, and had a population of 973 whites and only 625 slaves; by 1713 tobacco had practically disappeared, indigo remained the same, but the number of sugar plantations went to 42, the number of slaves to 4959, while there were only 480 whites; finally in 1730 there were more sugar than indigo plantations by 59 to 31; the number of Blacks reached 7646, that of whites was only 706. (Frostin (1975), p. 55)

That is, the total population, taking no account of the fact that more of the imported slaves were workers than was true of the whites and the creole slaves, increased by a factor of about 5, while the ratio of slaves to whites went from about 0.6 to 1 to about 11 to 1.

The classic rule of thumb in the 18th century was one slave for one acre of cane for one ton of sugar per year (Curtin (1990), p. 4). This was approximately the same labor intensity per acre as truck gardening of vegetables, and much more intensive than the cattle, grain, root crop, or tobacco that had generally preceded sugar. In fact, sugar was sometimes grown on swampy land that was drained only when the plantation started, and so had only supported hunting and gathering densities before the plantation; in that case, the sugar frontier had to import even more labor, both for the upper class and for the slaves for the work in the fields.

This is why plantation owners and managers (especially in newer colonies) were constantly worried about recruiting labor, about their capacity to apply coercion to break up families, about the potential draining away of their labor supply by peasant agriculture, and about the rate of manumission of slaves. Since the profits of metropolitan merchants and returns to the tax authorities were not increased (or at least not much increased) by peasants up in the hills getting fatter by subsistence agriculture than they would have been on plantations, the metropolitan government generally listened sympathetically to the labor recruitment needs of the planters.

The main other population groups in the Caribbean islands were "peasant" smallholders and urban populations, and both of these tended to be free populations of normal or female-skewed sex ratios. The demography was at least self-sustaining. Since it was these populations that eventually dominated the islands, I will develop arguments about the determinants of the long-run rates of growth of those populations. Where the sugar plantation complex was small, as in the Spanish islands up to about 1800, these non-sugar plantation labor forces were the human substance of the politically and economically dominant modes of production.

By "peasant" populations I mean those in which a family runs a small holding as an agricultural enterprise, in which the tenure on the plot does not depend on slave or semi-servile work on a plantation, and in which some large share of their caloric intake ("subsistence") was raised by family labor (Mintz (1974b), p. 132; for an excellent definitional discussion, see Trouillot (1988), pp. 1–23).

Some part of the produce of such peasant farms (including the "provision ground" plots as well) has usually been marketed in the Caribbean. The marketed products tend to be more truck farm products (fruits, vegetables, chickens, and pigs) for local consumption or provisioning of ships and plantations, rather than items of international trade, such as sugar, tobacco, cotton, etc. Caribbean plantations, towns, cities, and ships have all depended to a considerable extent on local provisioning, mainly supplied by peasant farms or provision grounds cultivated by slaves for their own subsistence and a small amount of marketing. Occasionally provisions for plantations were raised by supervised work in large arable plots on sugar plantations, but the rule of thumb used by plantation owners was that it took five acres of arable land devoted to provisions to yield the revenue of one acre devoted to sugar.

A variant form of peasant cultivation combined with hunting and gathering was practiced by maroon (*cimarron*, bush Negro) populations of runaway slaves, who, being recruited from the most aggressive and newly imported parts of a dominantly male population, tended not to have as many families in which the father lived with the mother and children, tended not to have as many women to bear children, and so were not demographically similar to other peasants.

Many of the tenures on which small holdings have been held in the Caribbean have been legally precarious, and often there have been mortgages, shares, or rents to pay even when they were more legally secure. The more planters were in control (see Chapter 5 for an analysis of varying degrees of planter control), the more precarious were peasant tenures, since secure tenures raised the "reservation wage" of free peasants in the free labor market, and provided a comparison point for slaves before emancipation.

The main things that have to be supplied for peasant populations to grow are, of course, families supplying labor and plots of land that have sufficient practical security of tenure to make it worthwhile to plant. The people occupying the plots were dominantly creole populations, which tended to have balanced sex ratios, either from freed parts of the subordinate (black or Asian) population or from white settlers (especially in the Spanish islands). Small plots in the highlands, failed plantations when the planters could not keep them from being sold in pieces (Marshall (1972), pp. 32–33; see also Beckford (1972)), or expropriated plantations, as well as foothill plots in Haiti after the revolution, were the main sources of land.

For the urban populations we need to locate the sources of work in urban areas. Roughly one-third of the urban working population are usually the city's economic base, whose activities earned money through commerce, taxation, or rents in the larger interurban or international system or from serving or exploiting nearby farmers. The other two-thirds usually serve that one-third. We turn first to the growth of plantation labor, then to the growth of peasant populations, and then to city populations

The Determinants of the Growth Rate of Plantations

Plantations tended to grow more rapidly in areas where the land and transportation were appropriate. By and large, this meant that they grew in areas where there were large, flat, well-watered fields near water transportation, as we have analyzed in Chapter 2.

We can take as an estimate of the size of the niche of sugar in the French and most of the important English islands the number of slaves an island had toward the end of the 18th century (as we implied in

Chapter 2, this would not be a good measure in the Spanish islands, which had just started their growth in the late 18th century). Then from general experience of growth processes we might project that when the slave population had reached about half that size, the sugar production of the island should be in its most rapid period of growth.

Most growth processes to fill a niche have a flattened S shape, in which at first the growth is slow down near zero as the niche is first explored and adaptations to it (and of it—for sugar, the most important adaptation of the niche was often irrigation) are made, then accelerates as the base from which the growth develops gets larger, and then slows down again as the carrying capacity of the niche gets nearer. At the point at halfway to the carrying capacity, that population should have been growing from a relatively large base but not yet have started to reach the limits of the niche.

As a first estimate we can take figures from Charles Frostin ((1975), pp. 28–31; see also Watts (1987), *passim*), who gives some comparative populations of whites, freedmen, and slaves for various islands in the late 17th and 18th centuries.[2] The decade in which these colonies had around 50 percent as many slaves as they did in the 1780s was for Barbados, before 1673 (Frostin's earliest date); for Antigua and Martinique, around 1720;[3] for Guadeloupe and Jamaica, the 1750s; and for Haiti [Saint-Domingue], the 1770s.

Probably Grenada and Tobago may have been at the height of their boom at about the same time as Haiti, while St. Vincent, Guyana [Demerara-Essequibo, Berbice], and Trinidad had later dates of most rapid expansion than did Haiti, as inferred from the proportion African by age (as shown in the graphs given by Higman (1984), pp. 140–41). The midpoint of the growth of slave populations, and so our estimate of the time of most rapid development of the sugar frontier, of Cuba and Puerto Rico was probably in the mid-19th century. The Dominican Republic never had substantial slavery.[4]

Our estimates of the size of the niche of sugar growing and process-

[2] Besides islands for which he does not give data—he gives no figures for Puerto Rico, the British Lesser Antilles, or the Dutch and Danish islands—I also exclude in the text The Dominican Republic [Santo Domingo], Cuba, and the United States, for all of which he gives only one figure. Table 4.1 gives estimates on a different basis for many other islands. In the integrated analysis of how the data for Chapters 4 and 5 were generated in the appendix to Chapter 5, alternative indicators of the timing of the frontier and sources for many of the islands missing from the text are given.

[3] See Frostin (1975), p. 142, rather than the table for this dating. For an excellent summary of the economic demography of the French islands in the late 18th century, see Tarrade (1972; 1), pp. 43–63—his comments support the dating here.

[4] Slavery in Santo Domingo was abolished by the Haitians by conquest two or three times, once or twice during the French Revolution and the Haitian war of independence, and again in 1822, each time before slavery got well started.

ing relative to other occupations and the time of most rapid growth of slave or other plantation labor populations are given in Table 4.1. Map 4.1 is a graphical representation of Table 4.1.

The Composition of the Plantation Complex

For dates around 1789 we have for approximate ratios of slave to white: Barbados, 4 to 1; Antigua, 14 to 1; Martinique, 8 to 1; Guadeloupe, 6.5 to 1; Jamaica, 11 to 1; Haiti [Saint Domingue] 15 to 1; Cuba, 0.5 to 1 (that is half as many slaves as whites); The Dominican Republic [Santo

TABLE 4.1
Period of Sugar Frontier by Degree of Dominance of Sugar for Caribbean Islands.

	Period of Frontier[a]		
Sugar Dominance[b]	Before 1750	1750–1800	After 1800
80% or more	Barbados Antigua Martinique	St. Croix (Da.) Tortola (Br.) Guadeloupe	Tobago
50 to 80%	St. Kitts	Jamaica[c] Haiti Grenada	Trinidad
50% or less	Nevis	St. Vincent St. Lucia	Cuba Puerto Rico Santo Domingo (Dominican Rep.)

Never really sugar islands: (British in 1800s) Caymans, Bahamas, Dominica, Montserrat, Anegada, Barbuda; (Dutch in 1800s) Saba, Curaçao, Aruba, St. Eustatius; (Spanish and Venezuelan in 1800s) Isla Margarita; (Danish in 1800s) St. Thomas, St. Johns; (Swedish and French in 1800s) St. Bartélemy.

[a] The best measure of the peak of the sugar-frontier period is the date at which the number of slaves equaled half of what it reached when African slaves or indentured immigrants stopped being imported faster than the net loss by natural births and deaths. All the elements of this estimate are rarely available. In such cases I have guessed from slave populations, 19th century immigration figures, land clearing, sex ratios of the white population, percent African of slaves, or other indicators.

[b] By sugar dominance, I mean the proportion of the labor force occupied in sugar after the period when this labor force stopped growing rapidly. Being lower in the table means either that there were other major agricultural crops, that there were relatively large urban populations, or that nothing much would grow on the island. The estimates are guesses based on scattered export data, agricultural land use, etc. Since sugar used from five to ten times as much labor as other crops, acreage has to be adjusted to estimate labor force composition.

[c] Jamaica had considerable coffee and livestock, and may belong in the "50% and less" category.

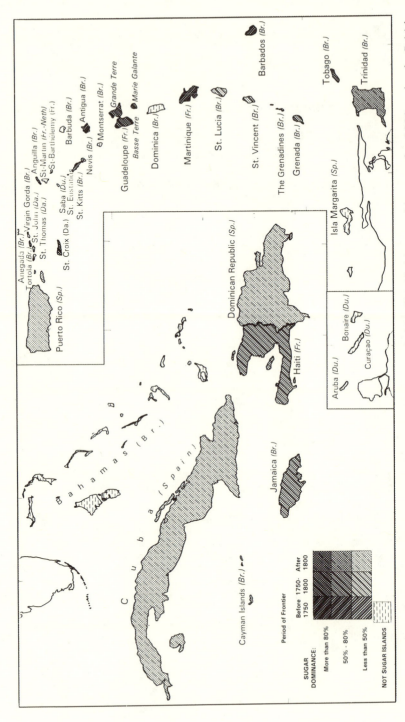

Map 4.1 Social and Economic Dominance of Sugar Planters around 1780. Trinidad is treated here as after 1800 under the British; Isla Margarita is treated as not having its own government.

Anegada (Br.)
Tortola (Br.) — Virgin Gorda (Br.)
St. John (Da.) — Anguilla (Br.)
St. Thomas (Da.) — St-Martin (Fr.-Neth)
St-Barthélemy (Fr.)

Puerto Rico (Sp.)

St. Croix (Da.)
Saba (Du.)
St. Eustatius (Du.)
St. Kitts (Br.)
Nevis (Br.)
Barbuda (Br.)
Antigua (Br.)
Montserrat (Br.)
Grande Terre
Guadeloupe (Fr.)
Basse Terre — Marie Galante
Dominica (Br.)

Martinique (Fr.)

St. Lucia (Br.)

St. Vincent (Br.)
The Grenadines (Br.)
Grenada (Br.)

Barbados (Br.)

Isla Margarita (Sp.)

Tobago (Br.)

Trinidad (Br.)

Aruba (Du.)
Bonaire (Du.)
Curaçao (Du.)

Dominican Republic (Sp.)

Haiti (Fr.)

B a h a m a s (Br.)

C u b a (S p a i n)

Jamaica (Br.)

Cayman Islands (Br.)

Period of Frontier

Before   1750-   After
1750   1800   1800

SUGAR
DOMINANCE:

More than 80%

50% - 80%

Less than 50%

NOT SUGAR ISLANDS

Domingo], 0.5 to 1; the United States, 0.25 to 1. Very roughly speaking, then, the later-developing sugar islands, in both the French and British empires, had higher slave-to-white ratios (i.e., smaller minorities of whites). The English islands (but not the English-speaking United States) may have had higher ratios (fewer whites per slave) than did the French ones; and certainly the Spanish islands had lower ratios of slaves to whites than did either French or English ones at the end of the 18th century.

The proportion of the population of African ancestry who were free was a rough measure of the average number of generations an African-ancestry family had been in the islands.[5] It can, then, serve as a demographic measure of "creolization" of the African-origin population. We would therefore expect the proportion free to rise (slowly) if there was not much importation of new African slaves (e.g., in the period before the development of the sugar frontier). We would expect the proportion free to decline with the development of the sugar frontier, for the immigration cohorts of new Africans would be a large ratio to the small creole black and colored generations, whose families had to have immigrated when sugar was not very prevalent. Then we would expect the proportion free to rise again as the old sugar island creole cohorts, especially many-generation creole cohorts, come to dominate sugar islands after the frontier period, when the slave population was not being renewed.

For the 1780s, calculations from Frostin (1975) show the ratios of freedmen to slaves were: for Haiti, 0.059; for Guadeloupe, 0.034; for Martinique, 0.063; for Barbados, 0.035; for Antigua, 0.033; for Jamaica, 0.016; for Cuba, 0.696; and for Santo Domingo, 5.33 (this last is based on what are clearly Frostin's rough estimates).

The general pattern in the French islands, where Frostin has the longest series, was that the ratio of freedmen to slaves ran between 5 and 10 percent before sugar was introduced, went down to between 1 and 3 percent during the time of great increases in the slave population, averaging perhaps 2 percent at the minimum, and then headed back upward toward around 6 percent in the late 18th and early 19th centuries. We analyze the pattern of growth and status definition of the free colored population in more detail in Chapter 6.

[5] Because in every generation there was a probability that a given family line (on the woman's side) would become free, and these remained free. As those probabilities cumulate they will produce an approximately negative exponential curve of the proportion slave of African female lineages (i.e., of one minus the proportion free), declining rapidly at first, and slowing down as the proportion slave approaches zero. Since the probability of manumission is not the same among empires or across time, with a discontinuity at emancipation, as we will discuss in the next two chapters, this expectation is rough. Nevertheless rapid importation of new slaves introduced a large proportion of the population that had a zero probability of being free at first, a small one in the second generation, etc.

The Geographical Distribution of the
Sugar Plantation Complex

The rapid growth of population with the growth of plantation agriculture mostly created a coastal lowland population. The populations on the larger islands, which had a substantial white creole population, or mountainous smaller islands (especially the Spanish islands, but also Haiti, Jamaica, Montserrat, and the Windward Islands), tended to be considerably more African in the coastal lowlands, more white and colored in the hills and mountains. The slave and imported indentured and coolie labor force was usually fairly isolated from white European peasant populations of the hillier interiors of the larger islands.

The growth rate of plantations in those late-developing sugar islands that had small areas suitable for sugar, such as Dominica and St. Lucia, was much lower than in Trinidad, Guyana, or even Jamaica in the late 18th and early 19th centuries, so there was smaller African influx. This produced on newly conquered non-sugar islands demographic behavior in the early 19th century much like that on the older, non-growing settlements.[6] Quite generally there had been no peasant population on the potential sugar plantation land, and at the least it was not very dense, so the land was "cheap but fertile." It is characteristic of frontier land, land that because of technical or economic development has recently become capable of much more intense exploitation, that it is "cheap but fertile." It was not, of course, cheap relative to its economic productivity under the old regime, but only relative to its possibilities for intensification by sugar production.

Much of the labor in sugar was the cutting, transport, crushing, and boiling down of the cane. This meant that the more fertile the land was, the more labor per acre there was. The fertility of cane land before modern fertilizers tended to decrease fairly rapidly over time (Watts (1974)), as the minerals and decayed organic matter that had created the original fertility[7] became depleted. This meant that the demand for new labor from Africa on a plantation decreased over time, both because the sex

[6] Higman (1984), p. 142. See also his graphs for Dominica and St. Lucia on p. 140, which look similar to those on p. 139 for old colonies and different from others on p. 140 for Trinidad and Guyana and other new colonies.

[7] The mechanism here is that tropical and semi-tropical rains and sun create a dense natural vegetation cover that rapidly reabsorbs minerals, and the rain leaches minerals in the soil rapidly. Most of the minerals and organic matter in the natural "jungle" are therefore concentrated in the vegetation itself, rather than in the soil, and does not leach out rapidly or wash away because it is inside the plants. When the vegetation is cleared for cultivation and the vegetation is burned, the land is therefore very fertile, but rapid leaching and erosion of friable soil decrease the soil's load of minerals and vegetable matter quite

ratio tended to equalize as more slaves were creole, and so the labor force would more nearly reproduce itself, and because less total labor would be required for a given size of plantation. Of course the total plantation slave population on a plantation might increase for a given amount of labor required, since the slave dependency ratio, the proportion of slaves too old or too young to work, would increase. Similarly as planters came to have stable families and to stay in the islands when they were old, the total white population per planter probably increased as well. This was perhaps clearest in Barbados.

Increasing the intensity of cultivation to compensate for soil exhaustion was apparently tried on Barbados during the 19th century, resulting in a very great density of labor of relatively low productivity—this was apparently only possible after emancipation by discouraging emigration (Green (1976), pp. 257–59), maintaining wage rates that were much lower than on neighboring islands.

The general point here is that the more fertile the land was, the larger was the increase in intensity of cultivation that a plantation brought, and so the greater the labor demand. Each slave or other worker would produce more sugar on more fertile land, and since much of plantation labor was processing sugar rather than cultivation as such, labor intensity per acre of cane tended to be a bit higher. So the desire to recruit more labor would be greater on more fertile land, and the money to pay for slaves would be more available. There were enough imperfections in the market for slaves so that prices of slaves were higher on more fertile, newly developed islands, especially during the highest rate of growth in the frontier period.

Thus aside from the general fact that plantation development created a frontier (defined here as the invasion of a mode of land use that was much more labor and capital intensive and more productive than the land use previously there) and so created pressure to move people there, the more fertile the land was, the more intense that frontier pressure.

For example, in the 19th century, when Cuban potential plantations were being rapidly developed, there was more pressure to recruit plantation labor in Cuba than in the English and French islands that had been developed in the previous centuries. It was harder to abolish the slave trade to Cuba than to the English or French islands, both because Cuban plantations were more fertile and so more profitable and because the plantation frontier had "already been settled" on the older islands.

---

rapidly, making it infertile. Sugar cane is a "bare ground" crop in which this leaching and erosion tend to be high. One purpose of "holing" in planting cane (each hill of cane is in a hole with small dikes around it) is to decrease the rate of erosion.

Market Factors in the Size of the Sugar Complex

If the price of sugar (or other plantation crops, such as cotton) was high, progressively less fertile land became the basis of economically viable plantations. The investment of clearing land, building irrigation and sugar-refining machinery, and buying slaves was more likely to pay off. Conversely, in the crisis of competition with beet sugar and new plantation areas (e.g., in tropical Asia and African islands in the Indian Ocean) in the late 19th century, or in the crises of freer trade in the empires, when artificially supported metropolitan prices were reduced (e.g., Mintz, 1974 [1960], p. 193; Green (1976), pp. 229–60), land devoted to plantations tended to decrease, especially in islands with a longer history of sugar cultivation.

The ratio between the cost of production and the market price was what counted, so Cuban plantations, where that ratio was low, were not much affected by the late 19th and early 20th century market bust. Nor was Trinidad, also a new frontier, much affected by the introduction of free trade within the British empire, with a consequent decline in prices. Some of the English islands and the Danish Virgin Islands, where the ratio of costs to price was high, were deserted by whites and left to peasant creole blacks and colored during the same crises.

Plantation growth was, of course, faster when the means of coercion for breaking up families to get the labor to increase the intensity of cultivation were legally available and cheap. This had two contrary effects on the growth of slave populations. In the Spanish islands during their sugar-frontier period, especially Cuba and Puerto Rico, there were settled white populations subject to authoritarian ("feudal") government. The means of coercion against "vagrants" (mostly peasants who did not "own" the land that supported them) were roughly as available to the planters as was access to the slave market. Britain interfered seriously with slave trading during the time of rapid growth of plantations in Cuba and Puerto Rico. So white and colored families on these islands could be broken up (or at least moved to plantation areas) coercively about as easily as African families. There was some advantage to this in that such laborers could support themselves back in the hills in the off-seasons.

Plantations in the 17th and 18th centuries also could grow faster as the slave-trading stations ("factories") got better established on the west coast of Africa, and as the sporadic warfare between African state peoples and tribal peoples became a regularized and more "efficient" slave-capturing enterprise.

Finally, plantations grew faster when it was easy and cheap to supply minimal food to the slave or proletarian population. Since plantations had to have access to water transportation to sell their goods (because sugar was of low value per ton, planters needed easy access to the sea), and since water transportation can bring in salt cod (which sounds a lot worse than lox, but probably was not), slave subsistence was often a matter of buying salted fish or beef and grain or flour in the international market, from New England or New Orleans or Ireland or Argentina, for example.

Where there was little hilly interior unsuitable for cane cultivation, as in Barbados, St. Kitts, or Antigua, dependence on such commerce was severe because slave plots to raise provisions were scarce. The Dutch and Danish "free ports" of Curaçao, St. Eustatius, and St. Thomas (where the free port was named Charlotte Amalie) had a good deal of what the Dutch called "*kleine vaart*," small (both small-ship and short-distance) trade, which was heavily involved in supplying food for slaves. These ports were much frequented by North American shippers, for example, of salt fish from New England, who except for the fact that they themselves did not actually usually cross into the islands of the other empires might have been called "smugglers." Since most of the 18th century empires besides the Dutch and Danish ones had fairly severe mercantilistic policies restricting trade with foreign suppliers (except for "emergencies"), much of this trade in subsistence goods for slaves was at some part of its journey formally illegal. Tarrade (1972; 1,2) gives a good portrait of the battle over the legality of this trade in the French empire.

Where there was a larger peasant population in extensive uplands, as on the Spanish islands, where there were large-scale ranches (also upland) raising livestock, as on Jamaica (Higman (1989), pp. 61–86), or where there was extensive and easily available hilly land near plantations for "provision grounds" for slaves (e.g., Jamaica and Martinique), there was less dependence on international trade and smuggling.

Emigration of planters with their slaves from islands that were mostly creole (i.e., where plantations were not growing, and where the black population more or less reproduced itself and the white population had stabilized) became important in Barbados starting around 1650, and in the French Windwards somewhat later. The effect was generally to decrease the number of men relative to the number of women slaves being left behind. This decrease of the sex ratio on the island of emigration was balanced by a contribution to the increase of the sex ratio on the island to which they immigrated.[8]

When there was a good deal of fertile land suitable for sugar, then the rate of growth of the plantation population, and consequently of the slave population and the adventurer planter population (to be discussed

---

[8] Or the continent—Barbados planters immigrated to coastal South Carolina, bringing their already matured slave code there, in the 1690s. See Jordan (1969 [1968]), pp. 63, 84–85; and Sirmans (1962).

in Chapter 5), was more rapid. It was rapid, however, only after the frontier of sugar land was opened up, and its growth was probably greatest when about half of the potential sugar land was occupied by sugar plantations. In such rapidly growing plantation islands, the sex ratio tended to be high (that is, there were too few women) for both the white and the slave population—the colored population, which was essentially all creole, had a normal sex ratio.

In rapidly growing sugar areas, the death rates of both slaves and whites were high (the rate was somewhat higher among the whites, which presumably was not a reflection of higher levels of oppression of whites), and neither population reproduced itself.

The birth rate of the sugar-frontier slave population was low, in part because of the high sex ratio, but also because fewer African women lived in families and fewer had children. Consequently the slave population on such rapidly growing islands did not reproduce itself. At the same time that more labor had to be imported for growth, labor also had to be imported to make up the deficit. The white planter population also grew by immigration, and immigration also had to make up the deficit, except in the Spanish islands that had a creole white population with a fairly well-balanced sex ratio when their sugar boom started.

As the niche of sugar came to be filled, the rate of importation of slaves was much reduced, the sex ratio of slaves tended to become more normal among the mostly creole slave population, the slave death rate was reduced,[9] and the slave birth rate increased.

Roughly the same thing tended to happen to the white population, so the sex ratio became more normal, the natural increase rate of that population approached the growth rate in Europe, and the ratio of immigrants with high death rates to adult creoles with low death rates decreased. The reason adult creoles had low death rates was that many deaths of immigrants were caused by exposure to Caribbean diseases among immigrant planters, soldiers, and slaves, to which creoles were more immune. The adult immigrant deaths occurred soon after immigration; the deaths of creoles from those same diseases occurred in childhood instead, and as adults they were already likely to be immune.

The data on comparative death rates of European and creole soldiers in the Caribbean, for example, those given by Geggus for Haiti ((1982), pp. 347–72), do not compare lifetime death rates between creoles and immigrants, and these were probably not very different. Instead they compare adult death rates when the Europeans were making up for the deaths from Caribbean diseases they and their still-living brothers and

---

[9] The death rate was lower especially among creole adults; since there were more children in self-reproducing populations and child mortality was much higher than adult mortality, the overall slave death rate may not have gone down.

sisters in Europe had not died of in their youth, while the creoles, whose brothers and sisters had died from Caribbean diseases they all had had as children, were immune.

All this analysis of the sugar growth of slave and planter populations was virtually irrelevant to the Spanish islands until the late 18th century, when they started turning their lands to sugar. But they started with a much larger "peasant" white population and a much larger population of freedmen and free colored, so the slave population never outnumbered the free population. In the Dominican Republic the whole process of sugar planting with slave growth was aborted by the events of the early 19th century.

Determinants of Growth Rates of Peasant Populations

The growth rates of peasant populations in the Caribbean were determined broadly by the availability of small plots of non-plantation land on a tenure that could be obtained by a family, and the growth of free populations that could form families to exploit such plots. The size of peasant populations on sugar islands measured the size of the interstices in the plantation system, since both the land and the population had to be unclaimed by that system (cf. Mintz (1974 [1961]), p. 146). For most of their history, the English and French islands [10] have been ruled by planters or by metropolitan governments that generally supported the planters; that comes down to saying that for peasant populations to grow, there had to be land and population that the planters did not need or could not effectively claim for other reasons.

But it would be a mistake to claim that the growth rate of peasant populations was strictly inverse to the health of the plantation system on an island. For example, both Cuba and Puerto Rico had relatively large white peasant populations at the time of their most vigorous plantation development. Barbados, in contrast, kept land in plantations even when (1897) plantation land that was broken up into peasant plots sold for 50 percent to 200 percent more than land sold as estates (Barrow (1983), p. 94), severely restricting the development of peasant alternatives for ex-slaves to working on plantations.

In Trinidad the Spanish and French settlers and the colored "refugee" migration from plantation islands and the Windwards during the wars in the late 18th century left behind for the British a relatively large free black and colored peasantry. This peasantry mostly cultivated provi-

[10] With some exceptions, such as the Bahamas after about 1800 (cf. Johnson (1988), p. 181); more generally, see the analysis in Chapter 5 for islands in which planter power was stronger versus weaker.

sions (especially for the Port of Spain in the foothills to the northeast of the city) and cocoa (Higman (1984), pp. 58–60). The size in Trinidad of the interstices in the plantation structure was not measured strictly by the inverse of the size of the plantations, because there was a great deal of unused land, and a large free population to occupy it.

Broadly speaking, the availability of practical peasant tenures depended on four factors: (1) the effective distance of arable plots from plantations, as determined by mountainous terrain or distance from the sea—the farther away the plots were, the more available they were to peasants; (2) the financial health of the island plantation economy, for example, as determined by the price of sugar, or the depletion or nonexistence of adequate soil fertility or rainfall, or by an island too small or too poorly supplied with ports to make shipping from it cheap and easy (e.g., Marie Galante, the third island of Guadeloupe), or by imperial Spanish provisions before the Bourbon reforms that made sugar plantations almost impossible—the worse off plantations were, the more land was available for peasant populations; (3) the existence or nonexistence of a vigorous market for provisions, for example, at Havana, as the last Spanish harbor before the trip to Spain, at Tortuga, off the Haitian coast, as a militarily defensible base for French privateers, and at Port Royal for much the same reason (Merrien (1970); Mintz (1974 [1960]), p. 196)—the more market there was for peasant produce, the more rapidly peasant populations grew; and (4) the Haitian revolution—the more revolution, the more peasants.

Distance from plantation areas increased the expense of coercion, by police or by citizens mobilized by justice-of-the-peace planters, to deny peasant tenures. Throughout most of the colonial period on most of the sugar islands, the formal government policy was to prevent peasant cultivation in the highlands, especially on unused plantation land ("ruinate"), since that provided a peasant alternative to plantation labor for freedmen. Also throughout most of that history up to emancipation, plots on the highlands immediately adjacent to plantations (on islands that had highlands near plantations)[11] were claimed by the plantations for provision grounds to be cultivated by the slaves for subsistence.

The inaccessibility of the mountainous interior of some of the middle-sized islands (e.g., Martinique, Basse Terre island in Guadeloupe, St. Vincent, and Grenada) and of the Greater Antilles and Trinidad made policing there very expensive. This meant that the runaway slaves (maroons, marrons, cimarrones, bush Negroes) could exist at least for a while in these interiors, as they did in jungle interiors of coastal sugar colonies.

---

[11] For example, Jamaica, Grenada, St. Vincent, Martinique, Montserrat, Basse Terre in Guadeloupe. Mintz (1974 [1960]), pp. 181, 192; Lewis (1929); Père Labat (1722).

In these conditions, squatting by whites and free blacks was difficult to control. For example 17th and 18th century French privateers and *boucaniers* (the latter harvested wild cattle and dried the meat for ship provisions—they often became privateers when an expedition was organized) could subsist for long periods in the part of Hispaniola that later became French, without much interference from the Spanish authorities.

Small islands near plantation islands, such as some of the Grenadines, off Grenada, and St. Vincent, or The Saintes, Desirade, and Marie Galante, off Guadeloupe, or Saba and Aruba, in the Dutch Antilles, sometimes had farmers and fishermen with a peasant mode of production. Other such islands, such as Isla de Juventud [Isla de Pinos], off Cuba, or Barbuda, off Antigua, had livestock ranching. Part of this peasant and ranch cultivation was due to the cost of extending coercion to deny peasant tenures reliably to such islands.

The capacity of the government or the plantation elite to apply coercion was, then, strongly inversely related to altitude and to distance from the coast, and to distance across the seas. Even when island government policy was against peasant tenures in the interior, peasants could effectively claim highland plots. Even when free colored or free blacks could get land in the plantation lowlands, they often preferred plots in the highlands of the interior in order to get away from the oppression of racist planters (Dupuy (1989), p. 27).

Conversely, islands like Barbados, St. Kitts, and Antigua were relatively flat, and had almost all their cultivable land in sugar plantations. They did not develop peasantries as much during slave times, and after emancipation the supply of labor on plantations was not so much undermined by peasant development (Barrow (1983), p. 85; Mintz (1974 [1960]), p. 181).

When plantations failed, especially after emancipation created a great many more potential peasants, they were sometimes broken up into small plots and sold. Sometimes this breakup was systematically organized by Protestant sects, as in Jamaica (cf. Mintz (1974 [1958]) for a general summary and a case study of a Baptist-missionary-organized village).

In areas where plantations were not very practical, as in Marie Galante in Guadeloupe in earlier times or in some of the Virgin Islands at later times, or where plantations had not got started on Spanish islands because of restrictions on trade, there was less social system pressure to deny peasants tenures. The suitability of land on narrow coastal plains for sugar tended to decrease when the economical size of sugar refineries became larger in the latter part of the 19th century, so, for example, peasant cultivation took over many plantation areas in Basse Terre in Guadeloupe (Dumaz (1986)). Where the value of plantation land became relatively small because of exhaustion or competition with more efficient producers, plantations were sometimes deserted and in effect turned over to squatters; this was more likely to happen when in addition to bankruptcy of the plantations there was a bit of civil disorder to encourage whites to leave (Harrigan and Varlack (1991), p. 24).

By and large, then, tenures from former plantation lands were more available in older plantation areas, where the land was less fertile, and on smaller islands (or coves distant from the main ports on larger islands), where the shipping expenses were higher.

In almost all societies the size in acres of agricultural holdings decreases near big cities. The size measured in value of product is often quite high for small agricultural holdings near cities. Truck farm intensive cultivation with careful tending of a wide variety of plants, or intensive livestock care, as for dairy cattle, was not very well organized by plantations or on the domain land of large-scale feudal establishments, so small holdings have usually tended to dominate.

The fragmentation of holdings for such truck farms sometimes has happened through the bourgeoisie's buying up land near the city (or landowners near the city becoming in effect bourgeois), and then renting out the land in small plots to truck gardeners or dairy farmers. Potential peasants could also afford higher prices, either as a price or as a rent, for land for provisions and truck garden products because the city market was so vigorous.

And finally, fragmentation near cities happened partly because urban political authorities had more interest than authorities in plantation areas in being able to provision the boats that used their harbors so that they would not lose ship chandlery trade to another port.

In the extreme, at Havana the Spanish imperial government up to the early 19th century was more interested in the function of the harbor as a provisioning, ship chandlery, and ship repair center than in anything Cuba could export from large-scale agriculture. The fact that in general fresh provisions cannot be efficiently supplied by large-scale agriculture gave the Spanish government in Cuba a good reason to develop a local peasant-bourgeois agriculture near Havana. Thus coastal agriculture in the Caribbean had (and has) two main forms, the plantation form on alluvial and coastal plain land far from the main ports, and the peasant truck farmer form on part of the alluvial land near the main ports.

Obviously, in general this sort of truck farm tenure was more market oriented than the squatter tenures in the interior. But it still probably ought to be called a "peasant" structure from the point of view of demography, since the same population groups tended to staff this structure organized as family enterprises, and probably a goodly proportion of the calories eaten by the suburban farm family were produced by the same agricultural procedures that produced provisions for the city and the ships. Although for farmers as well as for urban people, the proportion of homegrown food in the diet decreases with income, this is less true for farms that raise a variety of luxury fresh foods.

The Haitian revolution quite abruptly abolished the plantation system in Haiti and stopped the recruitment of slaves, made it possible for former slaves to claim tenure in a small plot, and created a large population of former slaves and an increased formerly free creole black and mulatto population who were potential peasants. This transition to peasant tenures took place in spite of strong attempts by the revolutionary government to preserve plantations after emancipation, with the potential planters being officers of the army or civil servants.

The Haitian transition was of the same general sort that happened in France during the Revolution (a short description is Dupuy (1989), pp. 91–92). In France, too, a small peasantry with no unfree or "feudally burdened" tenures was created by social revolution. But the depth of the social transformation involved was greater in Haiti, because the degree of coercion by the upper class and the poverty and lack of independent agricultural experience of the lower class in the old regime had been so much greater in Haiti. The revolutionary terror against white, and sometimes against colored, Haitians was more intense than anything organized by the French lower classes.

We can recognize these Caribbean peasant populations before emancipation by the following demographic signs in rural areas: a higher ratio of whites to blacks and mulattos (except, of course, in Haiti); a higher ratio of free mulattos (and sometimes of free blacks) both to slaves and to whites; a sex ratio that was fairly normal; a total fertility rate considerably higher than that of plantation areas, and usually somewhat higher than that of urban areas; and consequently a more normal ratio of children to adults (about 50–50, normal for premodern populations).

After emancipation, peasant areas of all types were quite often characterized by a good deal of seasonal migration to plantation areas of the males (encouraged by planter policies that restricted tenures on small plots), some migration of young women to the cities, and some considerable "commuting" of (mostly female) "higglers," who carried peasant and craft products to urban markets for sale on a small scale. Depending on the exact situation, the sex ratio might be skewed one way or the other by seasonal migrations out of peasant areas, and fertility might be somewhat lower because absent women and women with absent husbands do not conceive as often.

The rate of growth of the potential peasant population was most deeply determined by the ratio of the free creole white and free colored population to immigrant whites and to slaves. Very few immigrants from Europe came to the Caribbean with the aspiration to become peasants, though this may be less true of Spanish migration (especially that from the Canaries). The more the plantation system ruled a given island, and the less coerced migration there was from the metropole (this was higher in Spanish islands), the less European whites came to be peasants. Some of the islands started to have an absolute decline of the white population when the plantation system was introduced, and this decline seems to have been especially in white farmers raising foodstuffs for local consumption, who went back to Europe or elsewhere in the Americas.

This lack of whites being recruited to the peasantry on plantation islands in turn meant that manumission and emancipation were the big determinants of the rate of growth of the potential peasant population. It seems that manumission was more often given to young women and to old men (see Chapter 6 for an analysis of manumission), so the growth of the free population by manumission would not have had as strong an effect as general emancipation in creating potential peasant families, even for an equal number of people freed.

The greatest case for the argument that freedom creates peasantries was, of course, the Haitian revolution, which was real emancipation[12] all at once. But even the reluctant and precarious emancipations of such places as Jamaica or Cuba or Barbados increased the potential peasant population. High prices for plots carved from bankrupt plantations in Barbados show that Barbados had produced potential peasants, even though island conditions and government policy were both against it.

The Urban Service Working Class

Most of the free colored population in the Caribbean lived in towns and cities. The sex ratios of both the slave and the free colored populations of most Caribbean cities before emancipation seem to have been disproportionately female.[13]

---

[12] That is, there was very little "informal" coercion of "free" blacks to continue working on plantations, as there was after emancipation in the English, other French, and Spanish islands. See, for example, Chapter 9. Haitian "informal culture" was very much against any kind of coercion of blacks by whites.

[13] For the United States, see data given in the collection edited by Miller and Genovese (1974), e.g., by Robert C. Reinders [1962] for New Orleans, p. 368, William L. Richter [1969] for Baton Rouge, p. 395, Terry L. Seip [1969] for Alexandria, pp. 402, 409; for Tobago see Marshall (1982), pp. 8–9; N.A.T. Hall (1983) [quoting P. L. Oxholm (1797)] gives the sex ratio (males over females) for Christiansted and Frederiksted on St. Croix (the sugar island among the Danish Virgin Islands) in 1797 as 83.1 and 83.0, as compared with 116.2 for St. Croix rural; for Charlotte Amalie it was 68.6, compared with St. Thomas rural 108.7.

Domestics tended to be disproportionately female on plantations as well as in the cities. The female character of domestic populations partly accounts for the high proportion of females among urban slaves, because white family establishments and the residences of widows were more likely to be in cities than on the land. An occasional errant datum suggests that the male free colored were disproportionately old men beyond working age, while the proportion of free women in the working (and reproductive) years was more similar to that of the slave or white population. It further seems that the sex ratio was more in favor of women when recent manumissions were the main source of the free colored population, coming more nearly into balance among the colored population that had been born free.

Three major hypotheses suggest themselves to explain the pattern, if it was indeed there: (1) that women, like older men, were not as valuable to plantations—(lower prices for women slaves were characteristic of the whole history of the slave trade, and this would not be true unless the buyers on the average regarded them as less valuable), so they were more likely to be manumitted; (2) that intimate contact with whites bred moral obligations and exchange relationships that were likely to lead to manumission for women; and (3) that free black and mulatto men were more likely to be incorporated as farmers into peasant communities, while free colored women were more likely to be recruited into trade in peasant-produced goods and into services provided to the white upper and middle classes of cities.

The manumission patterns involved in (1) and (2) are analyzed in Chapter 6, but here we are interested in the explanation of why the service free colored population in cities was disproportionately female, rather than why the free colored population as a whole was disproportionately female. The manumission pattern translates into the urban pattern if women could not form peasant families by themselves and did not want to stay in plantation areas, which left the city as a place to make a living.

If the main source of recruitment of the free population was from the field labor force of plantations (this tended to be more the case where a planter frontier population was recruiting many Africans to a small creole slave population), then the lower value for field work and in crushing cane of women and older men would result in a pattern of paying off those of less use to the plantation in freedom rather than in subsistence. We might expect that times of economic troubles in the plantation sector might create waves of emancipations (or of slack enforcement of slave obligations, creating "informally free" populations) that would increase the rate of growth of the free colored older male and older female populations.

But if the free colored population of cities was disproportionately composed of the female and retired branches of free peasant families, the urban concentration of women might instead have reflected the usual Caribbean pattern of peasant agriculture: the cultivation was disproportionately done by the males; the marketing and some part of the craft work, by the females. In that case the working-age women were in the cities because some large part of their work was there and because contacts developed by young women in service work in the cities would be valuable resources in their small trading businesses. The older men may have been there because they had retired from cultivation. The men who formed families that became distinguished among the free colored seem to have been especially in the building trades and some artisanal parts of retail trade, such as shoemakers, tailors, butchers (Hayot (1971)).

The overall size of the urban population must have responded to three main facts. The first was that the trade in sugar was itself not a complex one, and therefore did not create terribly much commercial work in a colonial port city. The second was that the trade in provisions and craft goods, mainly from peasant production, and in imported manufactures from Europe, providing a great many different goods to make up the consumption bundle of consumers, was in general a labor-intensive enterprise, and tended to grow with average income level. Combined, these two facts meant that commercial work in the cities was disproportionately in providing consumption goods and services to the local population, rather than managing the wholesale trade. With the exception of the Dutch and Danish free ports, Kingston-Port-Royal, Havana, and St. Pierre on Martinique, there was not much complex wholesaling in Caribbean cities. Women were disproportionately occupied in provisions and consumption goods retailing, and men, in long-distance wholesale trade, so the relative lack of complex wholesaling would tend to produce jobs for women, but not terribly many total urban jobs.

The third factor producing urban jobs was that up to about the end of the 18th century, the main urban consumers of services, especially of household help, luxury crafts, and luxury trade, were the political, wholesale, and plantation upper classes. The Caribbean colonial upper classes tended to live in the metropolitan countries or on their estates, especially during the adventurer planter period of rapid plantation growth. Probably more planters maintained establishments in the cities as they became settler planters, and those planters who participated in politics probably were more likely to live in cities and "visit" their plantations. Creole political upper classes, and tourist upper classes of later times, have tended to create more urban service employment than adventurer planters did.

The flow of shipload bulk goods did not (and does not now) create nearly as much commercial work as did a flow of manufactured goods and food products in a complex mix, such as might enter into a household consumption bundle. Further, much of the work that sugar shipping did create was in the European port, where financing, breaking bulk, wholesaling, shipbuilding, and transatlantic and coastal shipping were organized.

The value of the return flow of goods from Europe did not in general balance the value of the flow of sugar and other plantation products, because the profits from plantations and some wages tended to be repatriated for planter and employee retirement in Europe. There was therefore less commercial work in the more labor-intensive import trade in manufactured goods than would otherwise have been expected. Many of what commercial transactions there were were carried out by the plantation itself, which borrowed money, received payment, bought supplies in bulk from metropolitan merchants, and generally had direct ties with the metropole (see, e.g., the evidence of direct ties with European merchants in Cauna (1987), p. 261).

The result, then, was that the trade of the colonies did not create much metropolitan development, the way it did in Europe. While Bordeaux and Nantes grew in the 18th century in large measure on the basis of colonial trade, Point à Pitre, St. Pierre, Le Cap, and Port au Prince remained small towns. The same could be said of the impact of colonial trade on Liverpool versus Bridgetown in Barbados. Most of the colonial towns' function was actually more as market towns for the surrounding countryside and for the local elite than as a population that did work to accomplish the sugar trade.

The entrepôt ports of Charlotte Amalie in the Danish Virgin Islands, St. Eustatius and Curaçao in the Dutch Antilles, and Havana, and St. Pierre had a labor force that looked more like those of European cities. They also were a larger part of the populations of their islands than was true of cities on islands without entrepôt ports.

The trade in peasant products (provisions and crafts) was much more labor intensive than trade in sugar. During the plantation period much of that trade was carried on by part-time traders, occupied either on the plantations or on peasant holdings. To some extent the smaller towns existed only on weekends when the slaves were free to trade. In larger towns there might be a continuous market or bazaar and some few firms continuously involved in retail trade and maintaining an inventory. "Firms" however were more likely to trade with the main kind of "institutional" market of those days, the provisioning of the military and of the shipping industry. In either case local trade and services for the urban population occupied a large part of the female labor force of the cities.

Ship repair in the larger towns (and sometimes building of ships) was carried on by a distinctive set of enterprises, often with a close relation with the government, and with continuous ties with forestry enterprises and craft enterprises that worked on the components of ships. The same applies to specialized work on the flow of colonial goods, such as warehousing, longshoring, packaging, and the like. Male slaves born in Africa who were manumitted were disproportionately men working in these urban port trades, as we will analyze in Chapter 6; here what is important is that when manumitted, they often continued to live in the cities.

Finally the population servicing the luxury needs of the upper classes could amount to as much as about a quarter in the 18th century capitals of the metropolitan countries: tailors, goldsmiths, specialized building craftsmen, such as masons or stoneworkers, and, of course, household servants of all kinds and levels. The size of this body of urban luxury workers depended on the size of the upper classes and their concentration in cities. As compared to Europe at the end of the 18th century, a much smaller proportion of the rich population of the islands lived in the island cities rather than on the estates.

But a much larger proportion of the island landowning upper class resided outside the island, especially apparently on the English islands. The ratio of members of the white upper classes to black slaves on the plantations themselves was extraordinarily low. The total white population of plantation areas was quite often 10 percent or less of the total population, with most of the rest being slaves. Further, that landed upper class living in the colonies and their local administrators tended to be disproportionately males without wives or with wives left in the metropolitan country. The ratio of household slaves to field slaves tended to go up dramatically when the landowner, especially a landowner and his wife, settled on the plantation after being absentee, as we will analyze in Chapter 5. But the landowner was more likely to build an impressive house with impressive contents and a stable of riding horses and hounds in England than in Jamaica.

It seems that the plantation upper classes on the Spanish islands (what few there were in the late 18th century, mainly near Havana in Cuba) were more likely to be locally resident, and perhaps more likely to concentrate their residences (for at least part of the year) in the seat of government. This may possibly be explained by the greater relative strength of commercial law, as compared with Spanish government regulation and monopoly administration of commerce, in the government of English and French islands. When civil law dominates government regulation, there was less advantage for a planter to live in the city. But this may be an illusion generated by the smaller importance of plantations during most of the history of the Spanish islands, for plantations there tended to have a more sex-balanced and more creole upper class than did government, which was itself populated largely by "bachelor adventurers."

Clearly, from all this reasoning we would expect the proportion of the working class working in cities to increase after emancipation, when there would be more peasant production and more discretion over consumption by free workers and peasants. We would expect the proportion of that urban population serving the luxury trades to have declined as plantations got less important, but to have increased again with the increase in government "services."[14]

Insofar as the sex imbalance in the cities of slave societies was created by differential manumission, we would expect the sex ratio of the urban population to increase after emancipation so that there would be more nearly a normal number of men, though the continuing disproportion of men working in the plantation sector and in cultivation in the peasant sector would decrease that effect.

Overall, then, the urban working class was much more composed of free people than the plantation population. It was much more composed of female free colored people and female domestic slaves. The heavy component of local marketing and services in that population was mainly done by free colored women. That urban service population was smaller than one would ordinarily find in European commercialized agricultural areas in the 18th century, because many of the island upper classes lived, consumed, and hired domestic labor in Europe, because export shipping from the islands was commercially simple and imports did not balance them in value, because many of the women who did the work were not married or living in family units, and because plantations were quite self-sufficient in supplying many of their own services.

The Long-Run Value of a Plantation

The Physical Productivity of Sugar Plantations

Our purpose in this part of the chapter is to understand the decline of the economic power of the plantation complex in islands where it was well established. The common analysis of this problem is that as plantations got more complex, slaves became less valuable, so free labor was preferable on more modern plantations. There are many indications that

---

[14] See Green (1976), pp. 183–84, for increases in government services in English islands after emancipation. Especially police "services" to the black and colored population were moved from the plantation to the city after emancipation.

slave plantations were in trouble in the older sugar islands, but my analysis here will suggest that it was not the slaves that produced that trouble. It would be closer to the truth to say that planters caused the trouble by not adapting to new technical and market conditions.

But my argument will be that the fundamental difficulty was that the cost of production of plantations tended to go up with age, while the price of sugar historically tended to go down with abolition or relaxation of tariffs, with new sugar frontiers being opened up, and with technical advance. I will argue, for example, that no one could really get rich on a Jamaican or Virgin Islands plantation after 1830, no matter what policy their government followed and no matter how technically advanced they were.

In the 17th to the 19th centuries, the productive value of a plantation in sugar production increased sharply as it was prepared for sugar planting and processing, with the full value "frontier development capital gain" pretty much realized by the time the third crop was planted, the crushing mill and boiling plant were working, and transport to export ships was arranged. The land's inherent productivity was never higher than at that point, because thenceforth the fertility of the land decreased from "soil exhaustion." For example, in the 1850s and 1860s, sugar plantations in Trinidad, which was opened as a sugar frontier in the last two decades of the 18th century and whose frontier period was very stretched out, were prosperous, with a wage rate 40 percent higher than that of Jamaica (which had had an earlier frontier), where many plantations were nevertheless failing (Green (1976), p. 252). Modern fertilizers have eliminated much of this decline in productivity, but most of this improvement came after the 19th century.

The amount of frontier capital gain varied with features that determined the long-run productivity of the land: in particular, fertility and slope of the land, reliability of rainfall or irrigation water, access to the sea (the bigger the ships that could dock at the plantation, the greater the productivity), nearby highlands that might provide water for power for the mill and for irrigation and might supply provision grounds for the slaves, peace, the price of sugar (which in turn depended on the tariff regime), and the like. The great fortunes in sugar planting mostly represented frontier capital gain, and they went to those planters who developed plantations in the most favorable locations.

To realize such capital gain by greatly increasing the intensity of cultivation and on-site processing required large investments. It was dangerous work to cut down and remove large trees, and new labor was moved into lowland tropics, where both European and African diseases were endemic. So both laborers and planters died from both accidents and disease (Curtin (1990); Higman (1984)). Labor was not in general locally available, and planters had to pay for it to be moved to the islands (generally, of course, by the slave trade). The dams, canals, and water wheels (or alternatively the cattle) and the crushing mills they ran, were expensive in labor and money. Political sponsorship or private armies were often necessary to get large tracts of land, and colonial politics was often expensive.

With some capital and good luck (not least, good luck with one's own health), about a decade of executive work and some investment could produce very large gains. For example, in Haiti (Cauna (1987), pp. 57–59), Aimé-Benjamin Fleuriau "travaille en pionnier" from 1743 to 1755, and then (ibid., pp., 59–64) turned the plantation over to "régisseurs, procureurs, et gérants" and went back to La Rochelle. This infusion of capital and income reestablished his family's fortune after his father's bankruptcy. He had, however, prepared himself for this pioneering work by fifteen years' apprenticeship in Haiti near the Cap, in an older region.

The right to pursue frontier capital gains was given by colonial authorities, theoretically in order to develop the colony. In order to retain the right to undeveloped land, a planter generally had to show that he (apparently the pioneers were practically never women; heirs sometimes were) was occupying it. The speculative value of such permission to develop is shown by a footnote to a 1733 ordinance of the administrators of Saint Domingue.

> [I]t is said that some planters, having several land grants and not being able "*les établer tous*," get by by placing on them some sick Blacks to retain possession. Then these lands serve as a refuge for maroons; it is prescribed to put there at least one white or a free mulatto. (Moreau de Saint-Méry [compilation of the laws] III, 369, 21 août 1733, quoted in Peytraud (1897), p. 355)

An island's frontier capital gains would, then, tend to be greatest in the aggregate in the period around the time when the slave population was about half as much as would finally fill the niche. That is, we would expect capital gains to be highest for Barbados in the earlier 17th century, for Martinique and Antigua around the 1720s, for Guadeloupe and Jamaica around the 1750s, for Haiti, Grenada, and Tobago around the 1770s, and for Trinidad, St. Vincent, and the various colonies that eventually made up Guyana around the 1790s or later. The periods of high capital gains in Cuba were likely around the middle of the 19th century; probably those in Puerto Rico and certainly those in the Dominican Republic were after slavery was abolished. Spanish growth of sugar plantations cannot be traced over time by the slave population.

A rough division into three main waves of sugar development is represented in the horizontal dimension of Table 4.1. This should, then, be a rough division by when the capital gains and the establishment of rich family fortunes by sugar-frontier development were most prevalent.

Such a fortune established by pioneering development work would tend to decline in value over time as the land got more exhausted. It apparently declined faster when left in the hands of agents in the islands, who usually worked on percentage commission. The agents then had less interest in maintaining the long-run value than in exploiting the resources in the short run. And for a plantation in Haiti, the fortune declined a great deal in a short time when the French Revolution and then the Haitian one made labor and land unexploitable.

Intensity of Cultivation

Once a plantation was running, there was a very direct relationship between the land's productivity and the amount of labor invested. Cane can be grown from the roots left from the previous year's crop (called "ratoons"), but the second crop produces considerably less sugar per acre than the first (about half as much), and the third, less than the second. The most intensive part of the work was "holing" the cane for new planting, which involves digging 4- to 5-foot squares about 6 to 9 inches deep and planting the cane in the middle. Slaves worked at a rate of about eighty holes a day (Higman (1984), p. 162, gives this estimate); this means each slave moved about 40 cubic yards, or six to eight dump truck loads, of dirt a day. Taking there to be about two thousand holes per acre (or about five thousand per hectare), this means that it took about twenty-five person-days per acre (sixty-two per hectare) to make a first planting. Depending on the fertility of the soil and rotting due to too much rain, one might have to replant every year, or every third year, or in a few places very rarely.

A common pattern was to plant about a third of the cane land each year, and to harvest the second and third ratoons in the following two harvest seasons. More ratooning could be done on well-drained land where the roots did not rot, while more planting had to be done where the soil was heavy or the rainfall excessive. For example, "ratooning" estates tended to be on the southern side of Jamaica, while "planting" estates dominated the north and the interior valleys (Higman (1984), p. 163); in Jamaica the heavy fall and spring rains tend to come from the North.

But in general more frequent planting with a very large labor input would increase productivity of the land. Thus it was technically simple to substitute labor for land; one simply planted more often and harvested ratoons less, and could get the same productivity out of less land, or more productivity out of a given amount of land. Thus the cheaper labor was, the more productive the plantation was. The planter had a very good idea of exactly what he or she would do with the extra labor that the estate could afford at the lower rate.

Barbados apparently had the usual high sugar island death rate of slaves, but a much higher birth rate than the other islands.[15] With the large population of creole slaves, Barbados actually increased production of sugar in spite of declining fertility of the "exhausted" land. At emancipation in the 1830s, Barbados had more slaves than did Trinidad, a much larger island with higher fertility per acre of land in sugar.

Efficiency of Factories

Processing of cane into sugar required a factory to grind and boil the sugar nearby, and such factories increased productivity over time by technical innovations. Because cane itself was very heavy for its value, while sugar was only about a twentieth as heavy and was much reduced in volume, cane had to be processed near where it was grown, as we discussed above. Transportation improvements on plantations and between nearby plantations could increase the size of the factory, or "central," where cane was processed into sugar, and as usual in heat-intensive productive processes, there were great economies of scale. So technical innovation in transportation and the resultant increase in factory scale improved processing efficiency. This improvement took place mainly in the late 19th and early 20th centuries

Vacuum pans in the long run decreased the amount of heat (and time in the boilers—in a vacuum, the syrup boils at a lower temperature, and the air mixed with water vapor does not have to be heated as well to keep the water from recondensing) required to separate the sugar from the cane juice, and began to be extensively introduced in the 19th century. Earlier, the "Jamaica train," which allowed kettles at different levels of concentration to be heated by the same furnace, had reduced the total heat requirement somewhat. The crucial reason for reducing heat requirements was that with low requirements, the bagasse, or fibrous waste, of the cane could provide sufficient fuel, so that access to forests for firewood became less important.

Animal power for the cane-grinding mills was always much more ex-

---

[15] Higman (1984), pp. 308–10, but given Higman's estimating procedure, a higher birth rate will produce a higher death rate. Populations with more babies did have higher death rates because babies had very high death rates before modern times. So age-unadjusted mortality was not a good measure of the condition of slaves when fertility varied, as it did in the early 19th century to which Higman's data apply.

pensive than water power if that was available, and with improvements in the reliability and efficiency of steam engines in the 19th century, steam became first more efficient than animal power, and then more efficient (because more reliable) than water power. Roads and railroads between plantations and shipping points decreased the labor of shipping the sugar, molasses, and rum. Roads and private railroads on the plantations, or connecting the plantations to a (perhaps separately owned) central processing plant, also increased efficiency.

Combined, these facts mean that the efficiency of the processing of cane, once grown, depended primarily on technical advances and (for transportation) on geographical details. Since innovation generally required liquid capital and considerable costly and closely supervised experimentation to get the bugs out of new systems, it was hard to do it from a distance through agents who were running several plantations, it was hard to do it in bad times, and it may have been harder to do it when the same people supervised the mill and the agricultural process. Necessity is the mother only of cheap inventions, not of expensive and complex ones. And attorneys or *gérants,* who managed plantations for absentee owners, oriented to this year's crop, do not want to mess with a steam engine that does not work.

But since innovation was expensive and risky, it was easier to carry out on prosperous plantations on fertile land. Innovation, however, was easier when there was more solidarity among planters, so that they could develop an agrarian expert culture among themselves, and could help one another with information, suggestions, and trained workers for repairs. It seems, for example, that in the 19th century there was a good deal of voluntary association for scientific agriculture in Barbados, and apparently groups of local planters organized to modernize sugar processing in Martinique, while in Guadeloupe modernization was managed by corporations in France (Blerald (1986), pp. 138–47).

The overall result was that the value of an estate varied with the technical efficiency of transporting, milling, and boiling down the sugar cane into sugar, and to some degree with the efficiency of further refining (e.g., the older plantation areas of the north of Haiti shipped more refined sugar than did the newer central and southern ones (Frostin (1975), pp. 32–33). But making a plantation more efficient by improving its factory and transportation system was a risky enterprise, and a great many plantations apparently went bankrupt trying to improve. Looking at the innovative history of large, successful plantations at any given time is observing a censored distribution, trimmed by the failures of those that innovated unsuccessfully as well as the failures of those that did not innovate.

The Price of Sugar

At any given time, the price of sugar was determined by the taxation (especially customs protection) and competitive situation in a given empire. This price determined where, in the ranking that led from the most efficient to the least efficient plantations, the usual marginal cost of production was above the market price; it determined how many plantations would go bankrupt because they were inherently unprofitable. Thus at a given sugar price, plantations in older colonies would be on the average worse off (nearer bankruptcy) than plantations in newer colonies because of soil exhaustion; plantations with less fertile land, with higher transportation costs, with worse access to provision grounds, or far from water power, would be worse off within a given colony than those better situated; plantations in colonies with a creole slave population reproducing itself would do better (especially after the abolition of the slave trade) than would colonies still importing slaves, because of high death rates of imported slaves and low imported-slave birth rates. Of course, rapid importation of African slaves, with its associated high death rates, was more characteristic of new sugar colonies, and so the high fertility of new land there generally compensated for the higher cost of slave or imported coolie labor.

The price of sugar within a given protected market would then tend to be determined by the proportion of all sugar land within the protected boundaries (which in the usual case meant within the empire) that was newly developed on fertile islands with many harbors, with high-technology sugar factories, and with cheaper local labor. The more highly productive plantations there were within a given empire, then, the lower the price of sugar in that empire would likely be, and so the more productive a given plantation would have to be to stay profitable. Thus Aimé-Benjamin Fleurieau was pioneering a new plantation in Haiti, a generally fertile island, with access to water from a large river, near one of the main ports (Cauna, (1987)). His plantation was in an empire in which the other main sugar islands, Martinique and Guadeloupe, had been planted for some time. Although Haiti's slave death rate was high and the birth rate low and many slaves were African-born, making slave labor expensive, on net balance it was the right time and place to be a pioneer. But it was wise of the family to collect some of the capital value so created to reinvest it in France (Cauna, (1987), p. 51).

Since the empires moved gradually toward free trade in sugar, the price of sugar in the very long run (the long run was very short in the

Netherlands, short in England, and very long indeed in the United States, which started its Caribbean empire in Cuba, Puerto Rico, and the Dominican Republic late) went down to the level required by the marginal producers in the world as a whole. Then the price went down further in the late 19th century, when beet sugar producers in the metropolitan countries got protection from competition.

For example, with the development of Haiti as a sugar producer to about the 1730s, French "white" sugar (not as white as modern white sugar) was about 25 to 40 percent cheaper in European countries than English sugar, so that "in 1740, of 80,000 barrels of sugar introduced into the ports of Europe other than those of France and England, 70,000 were of French origin" (Frostin (1975), p. 143). Because protection for sugar planters was being destroyed over time, in most empires the efficiency of the marginal producer required by the competition went up, so that the capital value of many plantations below the marginal revenue in the world as a whole was destroyed.

Conversely when free *intra-empire* trade was introduced into the Spanish colonies in the late 18th century (Halperin Donghi (1969), pp. 18–19), this greatly increased the value of all agricultural products from Cuba and the Dominican Republic, and the value of sugar in particular was increased further by the shattering of Haitian production during and after the French Revolution. These products had previously been developed primarily for Mexican markets (especially cattle and work animals) by extensive cultivation with few cattle ranch workers on higher rolling land, or smaller-scale tobacco cultivation in the foothills. The first response to opening of colonial markets under the Bourbon monarchs was therefore not exceptionally rapid growth of sugar plantations.

In Cuba, for example, from 1774 to 1817 the slave population increased in percentage terms from 25 percent to 36 percent. But the total population grew from around 170,000 inhabitants to around 550,000 (Marrero (1983; 9), pp. 174–79). In other words, although the slave population (mainly in sugar cane cultivation) grew by about 3.4 percent per year during the period, that of the whites and free colored grew by about 2.6 percent per year. The immigrating whites and growing free colored population mainly grew tobacco, provisions, truck farm products, and livestock. Of course many immigrating whites were added to the administrative and shipping elites and workers in Havana.

For comparison, the population of Haiti [Saint-Dominigue] went from about 166,000 to 524,000 in the thirty-eight years from 1751 to 1789 (Frostin (1975), p. 28). At the beginning it had about 90 percent slaves; at the end 89 percent. The slave population grew at a rate of about 3.0 percent per year. The free population grew at about 3.3 percent per year. In Haiti the free colored population grew from about a quarter to about a half of the free population in the period; in Cuba it grew from about a quarter to about a third.

In both Cuba and Haiti the sex ratio of both the white and slave populations showed the male dominance characteristic of sugar frontiers, but in Haiti the white ratio of males to females was about the same as or a little higher than the black one, while in Cuba 42 and 46 percent in 1751 and 1789 respectively of the whites were women, while 35 and 36 percent of the slaves were (Marrero (1983; 9), pp. 176, 181). That is, the sex ratio of whites in Cuba indicates that they were much more nearly a self-reproducing population than the blacks were; the sex ratios in Haiti indicate that both populations had to be replenished partly by immigration.

The free populations in Cuba and Haiti, then, were growing about three times as fast as was the white population of the period in Europe; the slave populations of both were also growing at about three times the European rate. The slave population grew largely, of course, by importation of slaves; the free population of Cuba had nearly twice as many children under 15 proportionally as did the slave population (Marrero (1983; 9), p. 178).

But, and this is the crucial difference in the pattern of growth of racial groups, the *gross* size of the addition to the white and free colored population of Cuba was much larger than in Haiti, because its base at the beginning was much larger; more of the Cuban growth came from the natural increase of the creole white and creole free colored population.

Such a growth of Cuba's large free population indicates rapid development of crops other than sugar, cultivated largely on hilly small plots or large ranches The growth of the slave population largely indicates the growth of plantation crops on the lowlands. And while the white immigration to Cuba was clearly more dominantly male than the creole population was, a great many of the immigrants must have eventually created families, in some measure with creole whites or free colored, but also in some measure with immigrant women.

Roughly the same development must have taken place in the late 18th century in the Dominican Republic, with the cattle-raising areas of the north increasing their production of tobacco, cocoa, and food crops for Caribbean markets in the large inland valley. Large increases of the white and free colored populations must have been needed for this. The sugar areas of the south grew, probably more slowly than Cuba's, by importation of blacks. In Puerto Rico the development of sugar cultivation was much slower, and coffee grown in the interior on small plots usually dominated exports (Dietz (1986), pp. 19–20 (exports), 36 (slaves)).

Capital Value and Its Uncertainty

But it was difficult for owners or creditors at the time to tell when the capital value had been destroyed by the overall evolution of the world economy. The politics of protection were not very predictable. There were large fluctuations in the price of sugar due to warfare and world supply conditions. There were large fluctuations in the costs per ton on particular plantations, due to drought, sickness of slaves, changes in the price of slaves, and the like. Thus any particular year's net revenue from a given plantation was not a very good predictor of long-run revenue, and hence of capital value. And people who own a business they work in are more likely to be optimistic than stockholders or creditors in a business are, so they do not see the unpleasant truth among the cost and price noise.

The network of merchants who bought from and supplied a particular plantation (see, e.g., the list of buyers for Aimé-Benjamin Fleuriau's plantation in Cauna (1987), p. 261) very often extended credit, often secured by either the crop or the land. Then, of course, there were financial institutions that loaned on mortgages or other measures of capital value. Creditors in Europe were in an even worse position to judge the capital value of a plantation than the planters or their agents, and very often ended up owning plantations whose capital value they had overestimated on the basis of past trade with them. They often had trouble finding anyone willing to buy them.

In general even plantations that had gone bankrupt were worth less to merchants in Europe than to the planters, because the merchants were all absentee owners, and normally had even more trouble getting reliable agents in the colonies to run them than did former pioneers and their heirs, whether resident or absentee. The casual comments of travelers and administrators of the time attributed the large amount of absentee ownership in the islands to the desire of planters to go back to the metropole when they had got rich. Many also went back when they got poor, and this, too, produced absentee ownership by merchants or other capitalists in the metropole.

People's perceptions of mobility processes are in general worthless as evidence, and this is even more true in rapidly growing or declining economies, where observed aggregate growth or decline (say, of absentee ownership) are casually put together with a few conversations with planters passing through the capital to get on board ships.

The overall result was that the value of a plantation increased very sharply during the first few years of frontier investment, and then declined slowly and irregularly with soil exhaustion, increasing costs of slaves, and decreasing sugar prices due to freer trade. But wars, droughts, epidemics, hurricanes, mistaken investments, failed or successful innovations all caused variations in both costs and returns that made it very difficult to estimate the value of a plantation at any particular time. Naturally the pervasive impression from the historical record is that plantations were always failing, because that was news: it created legal documents, complaints to the colonial office, and shifts in the fates of empires in commercial competition. The uncertainty of whether a white immigrant lived long enough to make or marry her or his fortune tended to disappear in the historical record as well, because if he or she did not make a fortune, someone else made the same one in roughly the same place.

Declines in plantation value tended to be caused by the opening of lucrative frontiers elsewhere, or increases in lucrativeness of frontiers that were within the same empire's tariff wall. Uncertainty roughly as often made people's fortunes as it caused their bankruptcy. Overall, people kept making fortunes on slavery, but it was disproportionately those who were buying slaves to open a frontier rather than those who owned them and had owned them for generations.

Social mobility disappeared from the records of civilized life (e.g., in Barbados) because social mobility happened disproportionately where civilization was just being established (e.g., in Guyana). Establishment of a frontier killed prospective white planters somewhat faster than it killed slaves, because the planters were less immune to African diseases than Africans were to European ones. But the whites who lasted tended to get rich, and so to appear in the records when there first came to be good records. But the civilized records virtually always recorded a declining society, because in the Caribbean civilization occurred in declining islands.

Shabby-Genteel Planter Aristocrats

Fortunes made in sugar plantations thus had five main sources of long-run decline. First, the value of plantations declined over time from declining productivity due to the exhaustion of the soil and the competition of new sugar colonies. Second, rises in the cost of labor made the main obvious source of increased productivity, namely, frequent replanting, more expensive, so labor could not in the long run be substituted for exhausted land (with the possible exception of Barbados).

Third, technical change in the efficiency of the factory part of the establishment required new investment to compete with the most efficient producers in new colonies, and such modernization of plant required capital that was hard for planters with poor soil to borrow. And, of course, keeping up with the state of the art is never as easy as it sounds, and is as much a matter of luck as of a gutsy entrepreneurial character; many planters "kept up" by buying or building unreliable technology and going broke.

Fourth, the decline of mercantilist policies of metropolitan governments meant that planters had to compete with the whole world rather than merely with new colonies within the empire, and the situation was sometimes even worse because of protection of metropolitan beet sugar producers with superior political clout.

Finally, since the return in a given year was not a good measure of long-run competitive position, planters often mistook their fundamental bankruptcy for a temporary embarrassment, poured further assets into the plantation, and got their merchant network to do the same. A good solid network meant they went down together.

The stability of most aristocracies is usually much overestimated, and even when based on more stable productive enterprises less exposed to market forces, aristocratic families often have too many sons going into government or the arts instead of making money, or too many wastrels, or they fail to reproduce in one or another generation.

For sugar plantation fortunes, the English aristocratic fashion of talking about the size of an estate as, say, "10,000 pounds a year" is even more inappropriate than it was in England. Some rich families remain rich, active in government (either in the metropole or in the colonies) and in setting fashions, over long periods of time in sugar aristocracies. But if one were going to create another House of Lords, one would not start with a sugar planter aristocracy.

5

Planter Power, Freedom, and Oppression of Slaves in the 18th Century Caribbean

> In countries where slavery is established, the
> leading principle on which the government is
> supported is fear: or a sense of that absolute coer-
> cive necessity which, leaving no choice of action,
> supersedes all questions of right.
> (Bryan Edwards)

Introduction

Sociologists have had great trouble developing a sociology of freedom (or of closely related concepts, such as civil society, pluralism, liberty) and of its opposite, slavery (or of related concepts, such as totalitarianism, populist authoritarianism, the iron hand of bureaucracy). This study follows the lead of Orlando Patterson by starting with the sociology of slavery (1967), and developing freedom as its opposite (1991, 1). We will also follow Patterson in starting our investigations in the Caribbean at the height of slave society[1] in the late 18th century, before "amelioration" or "emancipation" (both concepts deserve the quotation marks).

But we will not follow the intellectual strategy of Patterson's mature work (1991, 1), that of showing how the history of the idea of freedom was shaped by the social and normative experience of its opposite, slavery. Instead we will treat freedom or liberty as the high end of an empirical variable in the 18th century Caribbean, a variable whose low end is slavery in the ideal-typical sense. In particular we will study how the restriction of the possibilities among which slaves could choose was greater in some slave islands than in others, and greater among slaves serving some functions than others.

---

[1] Goveia (1980 [1965]), p. vii, defined this term in a way slightly different from mine, but the main island she studied, Antigua, was one of the most "slave society" islands in the late 18th century by the definition I am using here. See the more detailed discussion of the way I use this concept in Chapter 1. The original use was by Finley (1960a [1959]).

We define freedom as a set of liberties. As the argument develops, it will be clear that many of the decisions slaves in fact took freely were not protected by law, as, for example, freedom of speech is protected in the U.S. Constitution. John R. Commons's ((1924), pp. 92–100; 11–46) definition of liberties enables us to conceive of freedom of slaves as a variable made up of the liberties they in fact enjoy, whether or not they are defended in the law.

By a liberty, Commons means a decision that someone can take even if the consequences damage or help others, so that the decision may mean a loss to one other, but a gain to a third person. For example, Spanish law provided that if slaves of different owners married, one or the other owner had to sell the slave so that the marriage could exist. This created a legal liberty, but in fact there was often no practical possibility for such unions to be created (e.g., owners tended to import more males) and no real way for slaves to call on the law. The legal fact shows that more legal liberties existed at the time in Spanish than in British colonies, but the practical fact meant that on sugar plantations in Cuba slaves were too dominated to marry, while in Trinidad they could marry.

The reason the social structural answer to the practical existence of liberties disagrees with the legal answer depends on Commons's observation that a liberty creates an *exposure* of others to the different consequences of different choices by the free person. When the person exposed to the consequences likes them (or can contract to get the right decision for a price), all goes well. But when a practical slave liberty damages masters, law may be tightened, or informal sanctions within the liberty of slaveowners may be brought to bear, or African male slaves may be imported without women.

Freedom, then, is here defined as a latent, usually unobservable, conceptual variable describing the sum of practical liberties of a slave life, decisions that slaves can in fact take, rather than the sum of legally defended slave liberties (which were very minimal indeed). Then we can look for its indicators, for its legal and social causes, interpret the motives of slaves to seek more freedom by means other than laws, and perhaps ultimately reconstruct the life experience of the difference between legal slavery and legal freedom when slaves were manumitted or emancipated. The definition, then, is a sum of practically available liberties, including in particular the social capacity to get others to suffer the consequences of practical slave freedom to decide.

The conception of slavery as a dichotomous legal status represented in laws, and contrasted to a status of freedom, is of course irrelevant to our purpose of describing and explaining variations among slave islands and between slaves within islands. But most comparative work on slavery uses this approach, so it behooves us to analyze in more detail our differences with it. When this strategy is extended to comparative study, as Tannenbaum (1946), Klein (1967), Goveia (1980 [1965]), and Patterson (1991) have done, one treats the *elements* of slavery as dichotomies in the law, a list of various things that are not permitted or forbidden to slaves or masters that are not permitted or forbidden to free men and their superiors (or to proletarians, serfs, subfeudatories, freeholders, nobles, free women, or whoever is the contrast case analyzed). The dichotomy between slave and free is then constituted by its subdichotomies of legal freedoms or constraints, and slave systems can then be analyzed by comparing the components that constitute their overall contrast between slave and free.

As Patterson points out in his magnum opus (1991,1), such a pattern of contrasts between slaves (of various kinds) and free people (of various kinds) constitutes one society's definition of freedom, as what all non-slaves hold in common. A particularly crucial aspect of freedom so conceived is the right to call upon courts or other authorities, more or less separate from one's owner or superior, to defend one's rights, or to defend oneself by using other more or less legal liberties, such as emigration, rebellion, or the right to duel.

The dispute between Tannenbaum and Klein on the one hand and Moreno Fraginals (1976 [1964]) on the other, for example, provides a contrast in approaches between such a conception of how to analyze slavery, legal dichotomies versus daily practice. The central question Moreno Fraginals asks is how far variations in legal rights between Spanish and English colonies influenced the realization of slavery found on the Cuban *ingenios* (Spaniards called plantations "mills," *ingenios*; the English called them by their planted fields. In all colonies in the 18th century, they contained both plantations and mills) so as to make it different from that in Virginia. Moreno Fraginals argues that the probability of concrete oppression is better predicted by the demands of sugar plantations and the drive for cheap labor through legal and illegal coercion of slaves (cf. Williams (1967), 6–7—Williams argued that free labor was cheaper, because more efficient, if already there, but more expensive to move to the Caribbean) than by differences in legal freedoms or in the possibility of appeal to the church authorities. Broadly our approach agrees with that of Moreno Fraginals, that economic dominance of sugar and planter power determine the degree of oppression of slavery. But we argue that this gives a different prediction for late 18th century Cuba as a whole than he finds on the 19th century *ingenios* (these had less than half of Cuban slaves in the 19th century, and even less in the late 18th).

Our conception of the degree of unfreedom of slaves is *the probability of coercive limitation in daily life* of many rights *less often interfered with* among free men. Differences in the probability of coercive limitation of rights in everyday life defines for us the difference between slave and free, and those probability differences can be larger or smaller in different societies. Free women of the 18th century, by this definition, were less free than free men, but more free than slave men or women. There were many more decisions about daily life that, on the average, free women could make without coercive interference than slaves could.

One main argument here is that the degree to which law and political authority ferret out incipient slave liberties, patches of freedom, to relentlessly invent law to suppress them, was itself shaped by the determinants of planter power. Thus in some sense the effectiveness of the law in depriving slaves of liberty on a daily basis is another effect of the same cause as frequent intervention by the planter in slave daily life within that law. This is because slave law is a dynamic achievement of planter power, just as the concrete elimination of choice and appeal to the courts or police for slaves is. Sugar plantations of long duration on more self-governing islands cause both legal and daily life dynamics, and so slaves are less free on sugar islands.

Deliberate institutional action to restrict choices varied among island governments. For example, the Spanish colonial governments of Santo Domingo (now the Dominican Republic) and Puerto Rico and the Dutch government of Curaçao spent almost no effort to make sure slaves had no choices, no liberties, and relatively much effort to restrict the liberties of planters. The government of Barbados, in contrast, did almost nothing else but to make sure slaves could choose almost nothing, and that planters could choose all aspects of slaves' lives. We will call Barbados in the 18th century "more of a slave society" than Puerto Rico, Santo Domingo, and Curaçao, because though the latter had slaves, they did not spend much governmental effort making sure the slaves could not choose anything. Thus the first dimension we will use to discuss the variable from slave to free *among slaves* is the degree to which the island government devoted itself to their unfreedom.

But even in Barbados, some slaveowners gave some (very few) of their slaves their freedom. The enthusiasm of slaves for being free rather than slave, even though there were many restrictions on the possibilities of the "free colored" Barbadians, shows that they thought free was better than slave. And there is every sort of evidence that slaves *in the categories most often freed* (e.g., domestic servants, soldiers, skilled workers, mistresses) were treated more like free people. The owner, as well as the society, could restrict or expand the possibilities among which slaves could choose. And the way they expanded them in daily life in Barbados, or failed to restrict them in Curaçao, formed regular social patterns that we can explain.

This informal system of slaveowners providing some slaves rights to choose, even ultimately sometimes formal legal freedom, is thus another form of variation from slave to free among formal slaves. If we concentrate too much on the worst case, an owner's slave mistress in Spanish colonies could be tortured (a wonderful description of an awful case is Naipaul's "Apply the Torture" (1984 [1969]), pp. 182–221). And the extreme case for labor was for the slave to work to the limits of endurance in holing for the young sugar plant under the whip. But in fact owners' mistresses and their children tended to end up free, and moderately often rich (e.g., Cauna (1987), pp. 53–56); and in fact some slaves in Spanish colonies were paid wages (e.g., Boin and Serrule Ramúe (1985 [1979]), pp. 61, 63). The right to inherit freedom from one's slave mother and part of the estate from one's planter father is surely a step toward freedom for a person born a slave, and the right to spend one's own wages is generally taken as a test of free labor. So the worst case under the law is sometimes not the average.

The main work with a comparable intellectual strategy to this one is Holt's (1992) study of the emancipation of slaves in Jamaica. He shows that a large part of the political process of emancipation was to restrict the choices of ex-slaves so that they would freely work for planters for low wages. In part this required taking away the rights to houses and subsistence plots they had built and broken ground for in their "free time" as slaves, so that they would have to earn them back by working on the plantation. But there was no agitation among blacks to recreate slavery so they could claim houses and subsistence plots. That is, Holt studied one island as it changed from a slave society of upper-middle intensity to a "free society ruled by a planter legislature"; Holt's main point is that this latter is not very free.

Here we study instead cross-island variation between about 1750 and 1790. The intensity of government concern to preserve the unfreedom of slaves varied from one island to another. In many ways blacks on Dutch Curaçao or Aruba were freer under slavery in the mid-19th century than were the emancipated slaves in Jamaica that Holt studied. A commercial aristocracy did not need gang labor in the fields, but needed agents to help them run their businesses and their homes. They did not devote their government to slave unfreedom, nor did they devote their daily personal dealings with their slaves to the restriction of slave choice.

By first specifying the causes of variations between islands in the degree to which planter power could create a slave society, we describe one main force that restricted the choices of slaves. By specifying when masters found it to their advantage to leave some freedom in the hands of individual slaves, and sometimes to manumit them, when that is slaveowners did not find it wise to push slave lack of freedom to its utmost, we describe informal transactions that reduced or increased the size of the space of possibilities among which slaves could choose.

I will argue that this tack toward understanding variations in freedom within slavery helps get us out of the box of defining freedom, or slavery, by its essence. Defining things by their essences is always troublesome in an explanatory science. So defining slavery by its uttermost extremity, by the fact, for example, that rape of slaves by their owners could not usually be punished, does not explain why mistresses of white men were disproportionately colored, were fairly frequently given their freedom, and sometimes got part of the estate of their lover.

Nor does the extremity of hard work under the lash in holing a field to plant sugar cane explain why skilled workers on plantations or dock workers in towns were more often given their freedom, more often made contracts for their services with people other than their owners, sometimes rented houses from urban landlords, and bought their own food. Worst-case scenarios tell us whether we are in a slave society, perhaps, but do not tell us about the expansion and contraction of the space of choice in the lives of individual slaves. They may be good guides to the macrosociology of freedom, to whether there has been governmental care on a given island to make sure that slaveowners are not forbidden to drive their liberties with slaves to the extremity, but they are not a good guide to the informal part of the sociology of slavery and freedom.

We can define the degree to which an island was a "slave society" as the degree to which the island government devoted itself exclusively to making the liberties of the planters in their property unlimited, and had the powers necessary to do a good job of that. This, then, is the first determinant here of how oppressed a slave was: how fully and effectively the government of an island devoted itself to making the property right of the owner in his or her slave unlimited. We will argue that the main determinants of the degree to which an island was a slave society were the degree to which an island was a sugar island (because sugar planters were the largest and most demanding users of slave labor), the degree of internal social and political organization of planters (because the better organized they were, the better they could build the island society around oppressive sugar slavery), and the political place of the planters in island government and of the island government in the empire (because the more powers local planter government had, the less limited it was in building a slave society).

But the conception of planter institutional power as the institutionalization of planters' liberty over his property means in its turn that the higher slaveowner power was, the more the owners could treat their slaves any way they pleased.[2] We now are inclined to moral judgment of the slave system by what was the worst that could happen to the slaves, and rightly so. But that was not the way a slave had to look at it in order to try to live a decent life within it. In particular planter owners could supervise them closely in gang labor in the fields and make no promises, or they could negotiate contracts with their slaves or even set them free, and which one the owner chose to do mattered a lot to the slave.

The very thing that made slaveowners powerful, the existence of a slave society, made what they wanted to do the main determinant of what happened to the slave. If we study who it was that the planters set free, as the extreme manifestation of owner liberty, we find systematic and powerful patterns in how far the "deals" slaveowners made with their slaves were like those they made with free people, including "deals" that set the slaves free, that extinguished the relevant slaveowners' liberties.

The core bourgeois liberty is the freedom to alienate property, to truck, barter, and exchange. The distinctive thing about slaves as a type of property is that one can alienate them to themselves, can give them the liberties to decide what to do. Hence manumission, the individual granting of freedom, is a sensitive tracer of which slaves were most treated as free people.

Our argument will be that the central determinant of treatment "near freedom" by owners toward slaves was the slaveowner's wanting the slave to be a responsible agent in unsupervised services or work, work involving care, or enthusiasm, or risk to the worker, or requiring loyalty that could be easily betrayed. Thus it was when the slaveowner wanted trustworthy agency by slaves that he or she treated them as if they were free, as if they had rights, and in the extreme gave them rights.

Sugar Plantations, Planter Solidarity, and Imperial Local Government as Determinants of Slave Society

The core variables of my analysis of the degree to which an island was a slave society are applied to most of the Caribbean islands in Tables 4.1 and 5.1. In the previous chapter we analyzed the differences in economic history of the islands that determined the degree of dominance,

---

[2] The "his or her" in the previous sentence is crucial, since women treated their mostly domestic slaves much differently than men treated their slaves, mostly field hands.

and the timing of that dominance, of sugar planters. That analysis was made up of two conceptual variables, the degree of dominance of sugar in the island economy, and how long that dominance had lasted by the time we take our reading in the late 18th century. The length of time is a proxy for the degree that frontier planters had had time to organize a complete round of social life with families, and to organize political interest groups and legislative power among such resident planters.

Table 5.1 and Map 5.1 combine the results of Table 4.1 (from strong sugar dominance at the top to weak sugar dominance at the bottom of Table 5.1) with the type of local government granted to or imposed on the island by its empire (along the top).

The basic argument back of the "data"[3] reported in Table 4.1 is that sugar planters were the whites most interested in restricting the freedom of slaves, so sugar planter power was a deep determinant of a "slave society." Economic dominance in the last part of the 18th century was greater when sugar was more dominant in the island economy (decreasing from top to bottom in the table) and when that power had lasted longer, as represented by the estimated maximum growth period in the acreage and slave labor power devoted to sugar (decreasing from left to right in the table).

Thus near the upper left of Table 4.1 we find the islands whose whole economy was dominated by sugar cultivation and which had had that dominance grow in the earliest period so that sugar was well established by 1750. These islands should all appear in the top row of Table 5.1 ("Settler Planters," the highest planter-solidarity category, for reasons discussed below and in note b to the table). Near the lower right of Table 4.1 appear the islands in which sugar was much less important and had become established much later, and these should all appear in the bottom row of Table 5.1 ("Few Planters," the lowest planter-solidarity category). (I have mostly not put the islands that were never really sugar islands into Table 5.1—for reasons discussed above, I do not expect then to have a thoroughgoing slave society.) The Spanish islands generally appear in the lower right or below the table, because the Spanish government actively discouraged the development of sugar exports up to the last quarter of the 18th century in all Spanish colonies except the immediate environs of Havana and of Santiago de Cuba. Even there they did not amount to much. In 1750, for example, the entire sugar

---

[3] The reason for the quotation marks is not that I do not believe the facts I have inferred to some substantial degree, but that they have been derived from a wide variety of original data in such a way that they violate the standard meaning of "given" facts in sociology. See the more complete explanation for the generation of these data in the appendix to this chapter.

TABLE 5.1
Factors Leading to High Planter Power

	Planter Representation and Island Autonomy, 1780[a]		
Planter Solidarity[b]	Autonomous Assembly, Justice of Peace	Governor-Chosen Council	Urban Cabildos, Strong Bureaucracy
Settler Planters with Few other Crops	Barbados	Martinique Guadeloupe Br. Leewards	
Adventurer Bachelor Planters or Other Crops Prevalent	Jamaica Surinam	Br. Windwards Haiti (St. Dom.) Guyana (Br.) Trinidad (Br.) St. Croix (Da.)	Trinidad (Br.)[c] Cuba[c]
Few Planters, Many Ranchers, Peasants, and Merchants	Curaçao	Dominica Bahamas, Caymans St. Eustatius (Du.)	Puerto Rico Santo Domingo St. Johns (Da.) St. Thomas (Da.)

Note: Planter power highest in the upper left; see notes a and b below.

[a] In these three columns, autonomy and control over administration of the law leads to high planter power on the left; urban representation and strong bureaucracy leads to low planter power on the right. The classification is impressionistic, and I have taken account of factors not mentioned explicitly in the table showing high island power in empire policy as applied to the island.

[b] When there were fewer planters and when they were birds of passage developing a frontier who did not form local families to use power consistently (when they were "bachelor adventurer planters"), then planter power was lower. If settler planters dominated the economy on the islands where they had the greatest organizing capacity developed over historical time, they had greater power. Again the judgments are impressionistic, but the sex ratio among whites and a low reported amount of absentee ownership, where available, were decisive in distinguishing adventurer planters from settlers.

[c] Cuba taken as a whole was never dominated by sugar, and Trinidad was not so dominated in the 18th century. Both had politically powerful sections dominated by sugar in the early 19th century, and most of the literature on slavery on those islands deals with that period. I have moved them up to make their slave society politics of the early 19th century understandable. They should be in the lower right corner in the late 18th century.

production of Cuba was about equal to that of the small Danish island of St. Croix (MacNeill (1985), p. 126; for a general analysis of Spanish colonial administration, see Sarfatti [Larson] (1966)). Trinidad, which was until 1800 a Spanish island with a small infusion of French planters, also would appear in the lower right cell if it hadn't been for vigorous British development of sugar planting there after 1800.

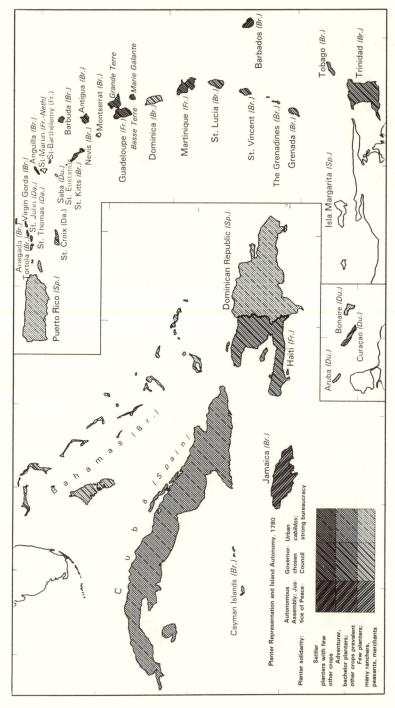

Map 5.1 Planter Social and Economic Dominance and Island Government. Darker colors indicate more slave society islands. Trinidad is treated here as after 1800 under the British; Isla Margarita is treated as not having its own government.

Anegada *(Br.)*
Virgin Gorda *(Br.)*
Tortola *(Br.)*
Anguilla *(Br.)*
St. John *(Da.)*
St-Martin *(Fr.-Neth)*
St. Thomas *(Da.)*
St-Barthélemy *(Fr.)*
Saba *(Du.)*
St. Croix *(Da.)*
St. Eustatius *(Du.)*
Barbuda *(Br.)*
Antigua *(Br.)*
St. Kitts *(Br.)*
Nevis *(Br.)*
Montserrat *(Br.)*
Grande Terre
Guadeloupe *(Fr.)*
Marie Galante
Basse Terre
Dominica *(Br.)*
Martinique *(Fr.)*
St. Lucia *(Br.)*
Barbados *(Br.)*
St. Vincent *(Br.)*
The Grenadines *(Br.)*
Grenada *(Br.)*
Tobago *(Br.)*
Isla Margarita *(Sp.)*
Trinidad *(Br.)*

Puerto Rico *(Sp.)*

Dominican Republic *(Sp.)*

Haiti *(Fr.)*

Aruba *(Du.)*
Bonaire *(Du.)*
Curaçao *(Du.)*

B a h a m a s *(Br.)*

C u b a *(Spain)*

Jamaica *(Br.)*

Cayman Islands *(Br.)*

Planter Representation and Island Autonomy, 1780

	Autonomous Assembly; Justice of Peace	Governor-chosen Council	Urban *cabildos*; strong bureaucracy

Planter solidarity:

Settler planters with few other crops

Adventurer, bachelor planters; other crops prevalent

Few planters; many ranchers, peasants, merchants

In the French empire the two Windward Islands[4] colonies (the ones France kept in the long run), Guadeloupe and Martinique, were developed earlier than Haiti. Haiti was at its maximum growth rate around 1750 or 1775, so that its planters in the late 18th century were much more often bachelors out by themselves trying to get rich, and its slaves were mostly born in Africa or first-generation creoles (i.e., born in the Americas; being slaves, they were of African parentage).

Much of the development of the British Windwards and Trinidad took place after England abolished slavery, and so much of the development of new sugar land was done by indentured East Indians rather than by slaves. But if we look at these islands in the late 18th century, planters were not yet in a position to develop a thoroughgoing slave society even if England had been in a mood to let them.

But planters could organize their economic power into class power if they had extensive ties with one another, had had much time to shape institutions to their liking, had established households, and were looking to the long-term health of their class and its wealth. So where there had been planters dominant for a long time in the economy, they came to be dominant in society and local politics. Thus even though Guadeloupe and Haiti were eventually as dominated by sugar as Martinique, they had not been so dominated long enough for slave society to dominate every nook and cranny of social life, or to have the extension of slaveowner power over slaves firmly institutionalized as the principal purpose of government.

The extensive apparatus of slave society that was imported into South Carolina from Barbados (Jordan (1969 [1968]), p. 84–85; Sirmans (1962)), or that is so beautifully documented in the legal studies of Goveia (1980 [1965]) on Antigua and the other British Leeward Islands, was not quite as developed in Jamaica, and was much weaker in Trinidad, Grenada, or Guyana.

Broadly speaking, then, the planters were more economically and socially dominant in the later 1700s on the islands listed near the upper left of Table 4.1, somewhat less dominant on the islands listed in the cells on the diagonal from lower left to upper right, still less dominant on the islands listed in the cells near the lower right, and least dominant on the islands that never became sugar islands listed at the bottom of the

---

[4] "Windward" islands are the small islands to the east and south, as mentioned in Chapter 2, conventionally starting with Guadeloupe in the northwest, but excluding Trinidad and often Barbados. The "Leeward" islands include different islands in the different languages, but always include the small islands between Puerto Rico and Guadeloupe, except when the term refers specifically to the government of the British Leewards and has a capital letter.

table. An approximation to this economic and historical base of planter class dominance and class organization appears as the vertical dimension of Table 5.1.

Planter Political Insertion into Empires

Table 5.1, then, combines into one dimension the two sources of planter domination of the economy and society of an island shown in Table 4.1 and adds a dimension that measures the powers granted to local legislatures by the empire. The biggest divide on local island government is between those empires that originally modeled colonial government on the government of commerce in the port cities of Europe, as outlined in Chapter 3, and those that modeled it on Spanish corporative administration. This divides the British, French, Dutch, and Danish islands from the Spanish ones, organized basically as a branch of the imperial bureaucracy. A further differentiation divides the islands of the commercial empires into those in which the powers of appointed European governors were higher, and where these consulted whomever on the island they chose, versus those in which there were locally elected councils.

Planters were more powerful when they had an assembly to which they were elected (column 2 of Table 5.1), rather than a cabinet of the governor (column 3) to which the governor appointed the local rich, so the same amount of planter dominance translated into more governmental power on the islands with effective legislatures than on those where a governor might consult with planters of his own choice. In general in the English legislative colonies the main agents in small localities were volunteer "gentry" justices of the peace, so implementation of all laws was in the hands of planters.

At the opposite extreme were the Spanish colonies, where the local councils were the *cabildos* of cities (last column of Table 5.1), where most legislation governing the colonies was not passed by such *cabildos* but instead by the Council of the Indies, and where the implementation of all laws was in the hands of civil servants who had been sent out from Spain (*peninsulares*). Planters had to apply to the *cabildo* for permission to turn their cattle ranches into sugar plantations (Riverend (1972), p. 111–12, 119–20; Marrero (1978), vol. 7, p. 15).

Thus to the upper left of Table 5.1, we have the islands where both demography and the structure of local government in the empire maximized planter power. Barbados was the high point of planter power, and had the fullest development of slave institutions, the greatest devotion to limiting slaves' liberties (and free colored liberties as well), and an inclination to defy the colonial office soberly and effectively, claiming imperial power for its own. But Jamaica, Surinam, the British Leewards, Martinique, and Guadeloupe were close competitors with Barbados.

The lower right of Table 5.1 is dominated by the Spanish islands that Klein used to illustrate the relative softness of Caribbean slavery,[5] but also has many of the non-sugar British small islands, the entrepôt islands of the Danes and Dutch, and many miscellaneous small non-sugar islands that did not have much autonomy.

Slave societies, then, were created when those people were dominant to whom slavery in its most extreme form was desirable, in the 18th century Caribbean, sugar planters. Three main factors made them dominant: sugar as a large proportion of the economy, a planter aristocracy with a solidary style of life and an interest in slave institutions, and empires' letting planters run island government. These served as multipliers of slave institutions, making them more elaborately oppressive. On the other hand, on the Spanish islands and Dutch islands, there were very few records of and regulations about manumissions, but very many free colored and black people. Most records of free blacks and colored people on Spanish islands are apparently based on censuses that asked them whether they were free or not. This was a very non–slave-society way of finding out who was free, indicating a low level of government interest in pushing slavery to its extremity.

The argument above has been that the power of planters was a product of how economically dominant they were on an island, of how long they had been dominant, and of how far the empire allowed them to run island government as they chose. We have then argued that the combination of those three conditions would produce, and did produce in the late 18th century, the extreme values of the variable "slave society." We have provided no direct evidence of that connection, for reasons described in more detail in the appendix to this chapter. I believe a

---

[5] Klein (1967). Klein compared Virginia, dominated by tobacco rather than cotton and so one of the softest slave regimes in North America (but with well-organized planters), with Cuba, where the region around Havana and Santiago de Cuba had some of the tough slavery of resident planters in the sugar islands, and the other regions had the very soft slavery of peasant farming with little rural access to the levers of power in the empire. Knight (1970) tried to refute him, but he looked only at the small sugar part of the only serious Spanish sugar island, and looked at the internal system within the plantations rather than at planter success in instituting governmental limitations of the options of blacks and free colored people. None of the places compared in this literature were near to Barbados, Antigua, or South Carolina in the degree to which they were slave societies. The political situation of Cuban planters was changing very rapidly in the late 18th century (Kuethe (1986). A very good overview of this whole debate is the background chapters of Scott, (1985).

summary of a good deal of qualitative evidence on the oppressiveness of slavery, much of it in the great debate about North American versus Caribbean slavery mentioned in note 5, would give approximately the same ranking of islands as is implied in Table 5.1, going on the diagonal from upper left to lower right.

Slaves as Agents: Ties and Claims of Slaves on Owners

But as we have argued in this chapter's introduction, the liberty of the planter to deal with slaves as he or she liked meant that slaveowners could make whatever deals they liked with the slaves. The main argument of the sections that follow is that quite often owners used such liberty to make what look very much like contracts as those were made with free men and women, except that one of the rewards was sometimes manumission. Manumission was in some sense often a "career" reward, the last promotion for a faithful and loyal slave. Like many such rewards in bureaucratic organizations, one does not know whether one gets the final reward until near the end of the career. We should, then, expect to find manumission in the same sorts of places in the economy we find bureaucratic promotions and generous pension schemes in modern society, where long-continued and skilled service showing loyalty, discretion, and good faith is required by the economic task.

Other features of the agency contract of modern civil law appear in the lives of some, but not all, slaves. Contracts with agents nowadays often have strategic principal monitoring of agent performance rather than close supervision, much agent discretion, agent reward proportional to results, and delayed agent reward until the overall results are in. These features are thought in modern agency theory to achieve the principal's purposes when the agent has more information and more control over effort and intelligence than the principal. Our argument is that treating slaves as almost free, and eventually as legally free, in the 18th century Caribbean was in general like an agency contract. Such contracts solve the problem of trust between slave and master better than coercion does.

Except in the case of sexual relations, such agency contracts reduce supervision costs whenever supervision is expensive compared with the incentives offered in the agency contract. In the extremes, when the slaveowner would have to be on the sea bottom watching the slave collect pearls off Isla Margarita, the cost of supervision exceeds the total value of the slave's labor, while supervising cane holing with a whip is cheap and effective.

Coercion, Norms, and Social Ties in the Formation of Race

Coercion was central to creating the slave population of the Caribbean and determining its racial composition. It was because coercion could be and was applied by white Europeans to black populations in West Africa, and could not be or was not applied as intensively in Europe, that the labor demand in the Caribbean was translated into an African slave population. Further, the slave system of labor relations in the Caribbean was dominated by coercion rather than any other kind of incentive system, and was most dominated by coercion in the core of the slave system, the sugar plantation.

The totality of the definition of the coercive relation was greatest on the islands listed near the upper left of Table 5.1, and least on those listed in the lower right. But people define the practical everyday meaning of such larger coercive and normative structures, even the most coercive ones, in the course of daily activity. What owners wanted out of slaves depended on the activities they were trying to carry out by means of the slaves. Insofar as one wanted love and intimacy, for example, coercion might possibly be a good way to get a relationship started (though the idea is deeply offensive to us now), but even in slave societies coercion was not a good way to elicit the free consent and spontaneous emotion that made love and intimacy valuable. The sexual tie was probably the most important one modifying the nature of slavery in the direction of freedom in the late 18th century (though obviously when one's prospect of freedom depended on a particular sexual tie, that freedom was substantially reduced as compared with free single women). A number of other relations between powerful whites and slaves modified the use of coercion and of class-conscious planter normative definitions in daily life.

Unfortunately the negotiations between slave and master tend to be absent from the historical record. The disappearance of negotiations in the daily life of the common people is frequent in historical work, but is more intense when the common people were slaves who did not have the right to appeal in court, had few or no property rights defended by the courts, could not sign legally enforceable contracts, did not pay taxes, were maintained in a state of illiteracy by social policy, and were not always regarded as actual or potential members of religious institutions that kept their own records.

There were five main conditions under which records bearing on daily life of slaves and slave-master relationships were generated. One was manumission, the establishment of a former slave as free by a governmental act initiated by the property owner. The documents about the conditions of such manumission often tell something about the relations of slaves and masters under various conditions, though as we have said slave societies generated more manumission documents per free black person than did societies whose central institution was not slavery.

A second source of documents was emancipation, the proposal by governments to treat slaves as at least eventually free people, whose rights therefore needed to be documented to be defended. Closely related was the abolition of the slave trade, which created the category of illegitimately imported (and therefore legally free) slaves, who had to be distinguished from legitimate slaves. The documents about which slaves fell into which categories of the emancipation law often tell something about the relations of slave to free.

A third was plantation accounting and the plantation books of exceptionally well-run (and exceptionally literately run) plantations or other enterprises dependent on slave labor, where the accounting value of the slave depended in part on the nature of his or her activity (Craton and Walvin (1970); Craton (1978)).

Fourth, governments had military or political reasons to treat some slaves (or former slaves) differently than others, especially if they had had military training and experience, had been to the metropole and hence had a claim to freedom, belonged to powerful maroon (runaway rebel) groups in the interior, or otherwise bore a distinctive relation to the coercive or normative system defining slavery. A troop of black soldiers obviously presents a different coercive problem than a gang of field hands.[6] Finally, some churches administered some religious activities that bore on the daily life of slaves, especially on their marriages, births, and deaths.

All of these sources are irregularly available. Religious records of marriages and baptisms are much more available in the Catholic empires (Spanish and French) than in the Protestant ones (English, Dutch, and Danish). Records generated by the enforcement of the abolition of the slave trade are essentially available only in the English islands, forming for example the basis of Higman's (1984) marvelous demographic analysis of slavery in the early 19th century, because only there was the imperial government really behind abolition of the trade.

We will therefore follow the "theoretical" method, widely and deservedly discredited in the discipline of history, in which "theory" means

---

[6] See Geggus (1982), pp. 315–25, for details on how the British thought about black and colored troops in Haiti during the British occupation.

guessing at the facts. We hope to follow it to the point at which it can be connected to the facts available, and to facts that others might generate. This theory then will form the basis for our interpretation of the nature and interrelations of the boundaries between slave and master, between slave and "free colored," between black and colored, and between colored and white. So first we go to the theory, which we will present primarily as a theory of manumission rates.

Ties of Slaves and Freedmen to White Power

Slaves had to form a relationship to owners or other powerful people in order to be freed. The simplest of these was, of course, to form a relationship with their own owner, and to persuade him or her (plantation slaves were very disproportionately owned by men; urban domestic slaves were very often owned by white and colored women) to give freedom either as a gift or by testament on his or her death. Sometimes ties to free people other than the master could become indirect ties to their owner, as when the other free person bought the slaves for the purpose of freeing them. Relationships to white employees of the owner, for example, fairly often resulted in freedom, when the employee bought the slave, or was given the slave by the owner in appreciation for the lover's or father's long service (Cauna (1987), pp. 134–35).

To understand here why planter liberties might depend on the sort of tie the owner had with the slave, we have to explain how ties varied between colored and black creole and African slaves; creoles were freer and more often manumitted. They also varied between small and large slaveholdings; more freed on small. They varied between city and plantation; urban freed more. They varied between colonies in which sugar planting was rapidly expanding and older colonies where sugar had filled its niche; older colonies had denser slave-master ties but more developed slave societies. They varied over time with the political situation; for example, the French Revolution and the abolition campaign in England substantially increased manumissions. They varied among empires, with the English planters being most heavyhanded with their liberties over slaves (though their liberties to do what they wanted were least constrained by their home governments), the French somewhat more likely to free slaves and to treat them in ways more similar to the way they treated free people, the Dutch and Danish more likely yet, though slaveowners' liberties were very little restricted, and the Spanish (to exaggerate) using slavery mainly as a coercive way to recruit immigrants to the islands, thenceforth often to be informally freed and managed by those means Spanish colonial government and powerful people used to manage "free" labor.[7]

These are the variables that shaped rates of manumission, so they must have been the variables that determined the sorts of ties slaveowners had with slaves. By extension, they must have shaped ties they had with people they had just given freedom to, and so determined the meaning in daily life of the boundary between slave and free.

Besides the powers of property, there were also powers of government on the islands, and ties of slaves to those powers also could result in freedom. When slaves rendered military service, during time of slave revolts especially, or against maroons or foreign invaders, the government often agreed to reimburse planters for government-promised freedom in return for loyal service.

Both France and England in the 17th century had explicit arrangements that slave ownership could not be enforced in the metropole, so slaves automatically became free if they got to Europe; they had no Dred Scott decision. But, at least in France, these arrangements were substantially modified in practice over time so that slaves could be brought into the metropole under various special dispensations that would preserve their slavery while in France (Peytraud (1897), pp. 373–400).

Sometimes treaties with rebels in the colonies (either white rebels with slave recruits, or slave or maroon rebellions) granted freedom. Quite often owners were not reimbursed; the presumption must have been that if it required great state expense and activity to enforce slave ownership, reimbursement was not an obligation of the state.

The general point is that legal freeing of slaves required slave access to power, either the power of property or the power of government. The power of property in slave society was particularly oppressive, but that very oppressiveness gave property owners great discretion to define what property relations meant for particular slaves. No contract or law guaranteed equality of treatment, so some could be freed and others kept slave without violation of property rights, or of human rights recognized at the time.

To understand what the boundary between slave and free meant socially, then, we have to interpret the data about manumission in terms of

---

[7] Americans are likely to think of freedom not guaranteed by law as a poor thing, as I explained in Chapter 1. I agree with the morality of that thought, but it is not of use to me in analyzing variations among slaves in their degree of freedom. It is clear that such variation within the slave population was very important to the slaves themselves, and while that criterion makes me uncomfortable I have to put up with it to do my job here. In particular, rights of the poor were less defended at home by powerful political institutions, especially churches, in the Spanish empire than in the Dutch or Danish empires, with England and France, I would say, somewhere in between.

what sorts of ties could produce freedom. Manumission is merely the extreme form of a stratification by planter will within the slave community that made some slaves able to make claims on (or against) white power holders, and left freed people who had "only barely" been freed unable to claim the full rights of citizenship (insofar as there were any rights so universally available that they could be called "citizenship").

Four Main Forms of the Slave-Master Agency Tie

Slaves had four main ways to form ties with white people that might result in freedom, which I will call sexual, domestic and managerial, commercial, and political.

Sex

Sexual ties between slave and free were mostly between white men and black or colored slave women, especially young, creole, colored, domestic servants. Of course, slaves might become domestic servants because of sexual selection, rather than be sexually selected because they were domestic servants. Peytraud quotes a letter from two island authorities about the ties between white male lovers and their black or colored mistresses:

> If we did not take care to stop the manumission of slaves, there would be four times as many as there are, for here there is such great familiarity and liberty between masters and negresses, who are well formed, which results in a great quantity of mulattos, and the most usual recompense for their obliging compliance to the wishes of the masters is the promise of liberty which is so gratifying that, together with their sensuousness, the negresses determine to do everything their masters wish. (Peytraud (1897), p. 409, quoting a letter of 1723)

Of course this causal analysis is a Just So Story, because it does not explain what a white male needed the consent of his slave for. It is clear that in such a coercive relation as that of master to slave, rape could as easily be part of the daily routine as seduction. The master had to promise something only when he wanted something more than a rape relation to his sexual partner. The sensuousness of women (aside from there being no evidence that sensuousness is related to race) is not now ordinarily elicited in rape, and so presumably was not then, even if the rape relation was no more coercive than the labor relation in the society. Like enthusiastic work, enthusiastic voluptuousness was not easily elicited by typical slave-master coercion. The statistical fact that the letter tried to explain with this Just So Story, that mistresses of owners were much more likely to gain manumission, was, however, there to be explained.

In self-reproducing free colored populations the sex ratio tended toward a normal one in which there were slightly more women than men (a sex ratio [men to women] about 0.8 to 0.9). However, in the slave societies in which most free colored had themselves been manumitted, the free colored sex ratio had a very high ratio of women to men. For instance Laurence ((1983), p. 40) gives the sex ratio in Tobago in 1790 among free colored with origin among the British slaves as a little over 2 women to 1 man, or 0.5 and the ratio among those with origin among the French slaves as a little over 3.5 women to 1 man, or 0.3. In Tobago at that time most of the free colored must have been created by manumission.

There are also more direct data on the manumissions themselves for most English colonies. Higman says:

> [Slaves manumitted] tended to be female, creole, young, and colored, and to work as domestics. In the sugar colonies females were roughly twice as likely to be manumitted as males in the period before 1820, but this difference narrowed significantly in many colonies as emancipation approached. . . . Females, however, more often obtained manumission through sexual relationships with whites or freedmen, and such relationships were by no means confined to the towns. (Higman (1984), p. 383)

The children of such unions may be considered to have an indirect sexual tie with white power. The patriarchal and "blood" ideology of European families in the 18th and 19th centuries reinforced these indirect sexual ties, though that ideology also downgraded blood ties for unmarried sexual relations, and even more for "miscegenation." Such manumissions of whites' own colored children were indirectly sexual, or "paternal."

Presumably sexual and paternal ties would have more effect when they lasted longer. Long-continued family-like relationships between more settled whites and their slave lovers and children would tend to develop more egalitarian relationships between members of the couple and in the paternal relationship, and thus to result in manumission. Sexual ties with domestic slaves and on smaller farms would then tend to result in more manumission.

Clients of slave prostitutes would probably rarely be involved in their manumission, but ties between owners and their prostitute slaves might result in commercial manumission, as discussed below. We should note in this connection that the manumission of mistresses because one wants honest love is not strictly transaction-cost agency, as was the incentive system under which prostitutes apparently worked. The reasons why one does not want to elicit affection with threats of whipping at each step, and why rape of slaves did not create manumissions the way concubinage did, are deeper than agency theory in economics explains. The effects of wanting slaves to make "free" affectional decisions and wanting commercial initiative from a prostitute in granting eventual freedom were apparently the same.

Perhaps another indication of the determinants of the strength of sexual and paternal bonds is that

> [i]n Bridgetown, where freedman slaveownership was concentrated, 2.6 percent of the slaves owned by freedmen were manumitted between 1817 and 1820, compared to only 1.0 percent of those belonging to whites. In rural St. Michael these percentages were 1.2 and 0.2 respectively. Thus, slaves of freedmen were two to three times more likely to be manumitted than those of whites, both in town and in the country. . . . [T]he highest manumission rates occurred where freedmen were already relatively numerous, for example in Trinidad, St. Lucia, the [British] Virgin Islands, and the Bahamas. (Higman (1984), p. 385; see Tables 4.1 and 5.1 for these islands)

Manumission of young women then can serve as a tracer of intimate relations between master and slave that tended toward love rather than rape or prostitution. Manumission of children of mistresses can serve as a tracer of those relations between master and slave children that tended toward paternity rather than breeding.

Agency in Cooperative Work in Maintaining an Establishment

By "domestic and managerial" ties I mean those that involve close continuing contact between a white owner (or owner's wife or agent) and a slave who has to be trusted to achieve objectives that cannot sensibly be monitored as "gang labor." Domestic servants who were not sexual partners were more likely to be manumitted than field hands, as were drivers, skilled workers, or stockmen. In general slaves were selected into these groups by skill and loyalty.

These groups were disproportionately creole and colored. For example, "[b]y 1834 at least 60 percent of slave domestics in Jamaica were colored, compared to 10 percent of the total slave population" (Higman (1983a), p. 126). Having been exposed to European culture, they could communicate effectively with the master and carry out the "agency" with an understanding of the owner's purpose. Such relations established an "unequal colleagueship" between master and slave, sentimentally and morally closer than in a field gang. Agency relationships were based on cultural similarities that produce trust, and produced fellow feeling on their own.

Agency often required the owner to set up an incentive system more like an employment contract than a slave-master relation. Such contracts often led the owner to conceive of the slave as having rights to the reward promised, as well as obligations. Among those rights could be the right to freedom.

Domestic slaves were generally much more likely to be manumitted than field slaves. For example, "[i]n St. Lucia in 1815–19 . . . only 11 percent of the slaves manumitted were field laborers, although they accounted for 44 percent of the slave population. On the other hand, 52 percent of those manumitted were domestics (17 percent of the population) and 15 percent were tradesmen (5 percent of the population)" (Higman (1984), p. 384). The ratio of the probabilities of manumission of domestics to field laborers was about twelve to one, and was about the same for tradesmen to field hands. Some of the higher probability of manumission for domestics was sexual, but a good deal of that advantage was preserved for domestic slaves of female owners.

Slaves on smaller rural holdings were more likely to be manumitted. Further, in the Spanish islands, in which slaves often worked in large ranching enterprises before the sugar boom of the late 18th and 19th centuries, the rate of "manumission" was much higher, though it left a large free colored population rather than manumission documents as testimony. This may be due to the impossibility of supervising cowhands in gangs and the damage that can be done to valuable animals by carelessness. These produced more "employment-like" relations between the rancher and his or her agents than was true on sugar islands (Boin and Serrule Ramúe (1985 [1979]), pp. 61, 63).

Commerce

By "commercial" ties I mean master-slave relations whose basic form was the exploitation of the slave by a formal contract with the slave, similar to the institution of *obrok*, or quit-rent serfdom, in tsarist Russia (ancient Spartan helots apparently had a similar contract, but with in-kind rents). The contract was generally one in which the slave exploited commercial opportunities on his or her own discretion: sometimes by women's carrying on a huckstering enterprise in the market; sometimes by men's hiring themselves out for episodic transportation work on the docks; sometimes by prostitution; sometimes by manufacturing or providing laundry services. The commercial opportunities that could be exploited by slaves were mostly urban, though traveling rural hucksters may have sometimes been slaves with such contracts.

These opportunities were not easily monitorable, so the owner

needed a contract with the slave to encourage the slave to seek out opportunities. The better the monitoring by the slaveowner, the higher
could be his or her share of the return. Slave prostitutes were often
owned by female entrepreneurs, often free colored women, and often
presumably exploited the commercial opportunities in houses maintained by their owners (see the painting reproduced in Hoyos (1978),
p. 170).

By the arguments usual in agency theory (an early exposition that
concentrates on this point is Heady (1952)), this required a contract in
which the slave collected most of the marginal product of his or her exploitation of those opportunities. Further, the contract had to give
rights to the agent (the slave), so that after effective exploitation the
owner could not change the terms and claim the whole product. On
18th and early 19th century plantations the owner claimed the whole
marginal product, which is why production had to be organized as
highly monitored "gang labor."

According to agency theory the optimum contract in such circumstances is that the agent pays a fixed rent for the use of the asset (the
farm in farm tenancy, the Russian serf in *obrok*, the slave in urban huckstering) and takes the whole product of the commercial activity. This
way the person who has the most information about opportunities and
who can determine by effort and attention the profitability of exploitation of those opportunities collects the full marginal product of the exploitation (Heady (1952)). Such a situation tends to create rights of the
slaves that the owner feels bound to respect, which give the slaves (with
luck) the means to accumulate money to buy themselves out of slavery.

This is why African slaves in cities had a high rate of manumission,
though otherwise Africans had the lowest rates of manumission. They
were disproportionately males on the docks, working in a system that
must have been a lot like the "shape-up" in longshoring on the American East Coast (Bell (1993 [1954])). Stevedoring entrepreneurs or merchants or ship captains—the loading was apparently normally actually
managed by the mate, or *maître*—needed strong men for casual labor
on an episodic basis, needed them to work very hard for a while, and
then wanted to get rid of them until they were needed again. Urban
male slaves were uniformly more likely to buy themselves out of slavery
than any other group (Higman (1984), p. 382). A similar mechanism of
wanting intense work for a while and then to get rid of the worker might
explain why houses of prostitution did not own many old women.

Everywhere before the 20th century commercial relations were much
more dominant in cities than in the countryside. Further, there was not
much gang labor in simple tasks requiring little skill and initiative in cities in the late 18th century. Much manual labor in pre-modern cities (at

least a quarter in cities like London) was carried on by independent arti-
sans, and much of the rest of it was casual wage labor or piecework labor
in temporary labor relations. Permanent relations between the people
who wanted the work done and those who did it were not the normal
way of organizing work in urban life in the 18th century. The same
forces that produced free labor contract incentive systems for free urban
manual laborers would have tended to produce the same conditions for
slave laborers in cities as well.

Politics

Finally, the slave political services leading to freedom were largely military and police services. The more monocultural in sugar an island was,
the fewer whites there were to defend it, yet the more valuable it was to
an empire. Islands largely devoted to sugar, such as Haiti [Saint Domin-
gue], Martinique, Guadeloupe, and Jamaica, were therefore militarily
vulnerable and commercially valuable in the frequent wars of the 17th
and 18th centuries. They were less vulnerable if their government could
recruit colored people and blacks to defend the island.

For example, Guadeloupe was less conquerable than Martinique in
the wars between England and France in the 1790s. Guadeloupe (specifically, Victor Hugues, a *petit blanc* (as low-status whites were called)
from Haiti, as agent of the Revolutionary French government) had
freed the slaves and recruited both black and colored troops into the
militia, and the British failed to hold it after a precarious conquest,
or to reconquer it. Martinique had not freed slaves or recruited colored troops extensively, and was fairly easily conquered.[8] Sometimes
treaties with organized rebel or runaway blacks were forced on colonial
governments. For example, after a war in Surinam between the Dutch
and maroons ("bush negros"), the French in Guiana agreed with the
organized blacks that they could settle as free negros ("de les établer
comme des nègres libres et les contenir sur ce pied," literally, "settle

---

[8] Napoleonic France did not actually reconquer Guadeloupe, but rather the colored general at the head of the troops "switched allegiance" to the empire government (Malgloire
Pélage—see Bangou (1989), *passim*). At about the same time the main revolutionary generals of Haiti were also "loyal" to the Napoleonic empire government, though Toussaint
occasionally put the civilian Napoleonic representatives under house arrest in order to do
what he thought he needed to do. In Haiti most "deserted" Napoleon when it became
absolutely clear that slavery was to be reestablished. Retrospectively, Pélage was a traitor to
the Revolution, and Toussaint, a revolutionary hero, because the consequences of the two
acts were different. For some explanation of why the consequences were different, see the
analysis of the combined effects of size and mountainousness on ease of conquest in
Chapter 2.

them as free blacks and restrain them on that footing" [Peytraud (1897), pp. 358–59]).

The empires had a great deal of trouble with military operations in the Caribbean, because troops from Europe quickly got too sick to fight. The planters tended to form militias (of "seasoned" men) that were not reliable servants of the empire, but instead would form alliances with whoever defended planter interests best. Planters also sponsored independence movements if it was proposed to tax them to support the defense of the empire (for Haiti, see generally Frostin (1975)). The empire's military officers had a great need for "seasoned" troops from the islands themselves, who would be more deployable than the local militias but who would not get sick. Free colored and slaves were often used for building fortifications and other non-fighting military work, and sometimes for international fighting. Sometimes they were used as "intelligence agents" to find out about rebellions or to hunt down runaways. In any of these cases they might be freed as a reward for political services.

The Theory of the Boundary between Slave and Free

In daily life, then, the high point of slavery was among the highly class-conscious and oppressive large sugar planters' field labor. Hardly anyone in field sugar plantation labor got manumitted; hardly anyone had intimate relations with whites, though they sometimes got pregnant in a nonintimate relation; hardly any managed work on a collegial basis with the owner or owner's agents; hardly any sought out commercial opportunities with autonomy and discretion; hardly any earned freedom as a reward from governments for loyalty and bravery; and all of them were subjected to the most class-conscious slaveowners, those most interested in the "health" of the slave system as a whole.

As this sugar plantation core of slave society sloped off into slave mistresses, slaves owned by freedmen, creole slaves in domestic service, skilled work, and first-line management, slaves in cities and especially in urban commerce, slaves in smaller enterprises, slaves of masters to whom the maintenance of the whole slave system was a secondary consideration, the slave relation became more like the relations among free unequals in 18th century urban society, or those between free peasants and landlords in western European countries. And that slope also led to the boundary between slave and free. And we have argued that the high freedom end of these slopes in fact became free colored or black freedmen, and if they were women, they maintained the free colored population thenceforth, because the children of free colored women were also

TABLE 5.2
Factors in Manumission Rates

Causal Process	Examples	Categories Most Favored
Intimacy	Sexual partners	Young, creole,[a] colored, women domestics
		Women held by small slaveowners
		Women owned by free colored
	Colored children	Creole, colored, domestics, young children in stable relationships
Trusted agents	Slave drivers	Male, creole, middle-aged
	Skilled	Male craftsmen, mechanics, artisans
	Domestics	Women, household domestics, nannies
Commercial opportunities	Dock workers	Male, African
	Prostitutes	Colored urban women owned by females (often colored)
	Hucksters	Creole women
Politics	Military and police	Young males
		Militia members
		Maroons

[a] "Creole" here means born in the Americas, as it is used in the British islands. In Spanish the comparable word implies white race, and in Louisiana it means of French origin.

free. With the exception of reconquered Guadeloupe there were no large movements of free colored back into slavery.

The pattern of higher manumission rates as suggested by this analysis is outlined in Table 5.2. The core of the argument here is that the "causal processes" on the left of the table are those that require discretion, loyalty, enthusiasm, skill, career training, or other aspects of agency relations.

Conclusions

The sociology of slavery and freedom has been crippled by not treating freedom as a variable. Part of the difficulty is that in the United States freedom is thought of as a legal concept defined in the Bill of Rights, or in France, as in the Declaration of the Rights of Man, so that it is either guaranteed or not. Part of the problem is that the size of the set of possibilities among which a group of people chooses, the core idea of freedom here, is clear enough conceptually, but hard to specify in practice because possibilities not chosen do not leave a historical record. The intellectual strategy chosen here is to specify freedom by its causes, the causes of more and less restriction of choice of the slaves of the late 18th century Caribbean.

These causes fall into two main groups: the causes of the societal power on an island exercised by social groups, specifically, sugar planters, that have a great interest in the restriction of the possibilities of slaves, and the causes of slaveowners' using their property rights in slaves as one of many considerations in making agency contracts with their slaves. Then the scattered evidence of what slaves and their owners in fact chose, such as manumission of the slave, or of what slaves could choose, such as how to spend their wages, or of what property rights slaves had, such as enough money to buy themselves out of slavery, suggests the shape and size of the possibility set under different causal conditions.

What was generally distinctive of the 18th century Caribbean colonies of all the empires (as of the American South at the same time) was the building of slave societies, societies whose principal governmental problem was holding slaves in bondage of varying degrees of restrictiveness. The characteristic attitude of such governments is captured by the epigraph to this chapter; the quotation is from Bryan Edwards, whose experience was mainly in Jamaica, a slave society of upper-middle intensiveness. But the intensity of governmental effort to restrict possibilities, the degree of totalitarianism of slavery, so to speak, was larger where planters were more economically dominant, had better class unity, and were well represented in the system of government of the islands in the relevant empire.

Within a given empire, the intensity of slave society varied. An Isla Margarita pearl diver who had to risk his life under the water, so that his owner could not monitor the work without risking his own, was a different sort of control problem than a gang worker digging holes to plant cane on the same island. So within the Spanish empire, the region near Havana in Cuba looked more like Jamaica, while Isla Margarita looked more like the Bahamas. This was because fishing off the Bahamas was more nearly like the agency problem of pearl diving than like the agency problem of getting more dirt moved by a gang of recent African slave immigrants in either Havana province or Jamaica.

As a practical matter, a thoroughgoing slave society was a utopian vision by planters, and in a lot of situations they could not get from that vision what they wanted out of real slaves. The more their society looked like Barbados, the more they could get hard work at low cost on their sugar plantations, but the harder it was to get the slaves to look after the livestock carefully, and the less fish they could get from the Caribbean and the more they had to buy salted fish from New England. The more their society looked like Curaçao, the more easily they could send their slaves off as their agents on business or household matters.

But in either kind of society those slaveowners who wanted commercial trustworthiness, initiative, courage, enthusiasm, or love, had to grant enough freedom to the slave so as to be able to make deals with elements of equality and choice in them. Absolute power may have corrupted absolutely, but it had the additional disadvantage that it would not get the pearls off the bottom.

Appendix

The Constitution of the Data

This appendix discusses the combined conceptualization and measurement process resulting in the evaluations of the variables for islands or for subgroups of slaves shown in Tables 4.1, 5.1, and 5.2. The data are "ecological," measurements of social structures, which tend to have higher reliability than measurements of individuals. But all of them are constituted by observations on several indicators, some of which are missing for each case, most of which are missing for some cases, and are sometimes derived from informal observation by historical actors or by historians. The data are closer to "diagnoses" than to "measurements." They are about named historical entities, so that experts in several of the islands can check for my errors, and future work can be better.

The first intervening variable in the text, explaining the practical daily deprivation of freedom in slaves' lives, is the degree to which an island had a "slave society" in the late 18th century. In Tables 4.1 and 5.1, this is measured by its presumed causes. The core meaning of this variable is the degree to which the island government has a disposition to react powerfully to suppress any source or symptom of slave free choice, regardless of costs of suppression in other values.

My first judgment of this disposition was derived from a combination of (1) defenses of slave society principles from defenders of slave domination as the principal end and purpose of island government, such as Poyer (1971 [1808]) for Barbados or Edwards (1801 [1793]; 2), pp. 39–46, 150–86) for Jamaica; (2) accounts by unfriendly observers at the time, such as the liberal slaveowner Lewis (1929) for Jamaica, or the first civilian English governor of Trinidad, quoted extensively in Naipaul

(1984 [1969]); and (3) general scholarly accounts trying to identify features of harder and softer slave systems, such as Tannenbaum (1946) or Klein (1967) contrasting Spanish and English colonies, Goveia (1980 [1965]) for Antigua, Tarrade (1972) for the French islands, with emphasis on Martinique, Bangou (1989) for Guadeloupe, Hoetink (1982 [1972], (1958), background chapters) for Curaçao and the Dominican Republic, Scott's (1985) background sections for Cuba, and miscellaneous sources for smaller islands.

The actual facts available on individual societies vary a great deal from case to case, since the different original authors were interested in different things, or had different theories about the same things. The facts range from passage of discriminatory laws against colored entrepreneurs in Barbados because entrepreneurial success might encourage insubordination among slaves, to slave right of ownership and sale of products from subsistence plots in Jamaica, to the colored mother of one of the post-slavery presidents of the Dominican Republic being bought as a slave, later treated as married to her owner and free, without apparent formal manumission, to a burst of laws imposing new restrictions, for example, against emigration or settling on mountain farms, passed immediately after emancipation in Jamaica (Holt (1992)). These facts provide evidence about which islands had the most intensive slave societies, at a level of "global coding" of whatever is said about the island by its historians and contemporary writers, and is not formally used in the data here.

With this tentative set of contrasts, I then looked at data on economic and political history to see what could explain the variation tentatively observed. Facts about economic and political history were in general much easier to obtain more systematically than comparable judgments of negative polity responses to marginal slave freedom. As it turned out, features of the economic and political histories of the islands were apparently the big causes. This availability of better data on the causes than on the symptoms led to the unusual strategy of measuring the effect by its causes. Estimates for the three main variables at the level of islands (in Tables 4.1 and 5.1) of the degree to which an island had a slave society were constructed from varying information as available.

The dates of the most rapid growth of sugar plantation frontier development were shaped by the general ideas obtained from the S-shape of most growth curves, often modeled by the logistic. I also used high slave imports; percent African and percent male of the slave population; high ratio of slaves to colored. New plantations' being opened only by substantial investments in roads to the interior indicated a late stage of frontier development.

As a last resort or a check on uncertain judgments, I have used a high ratio of the population reported in the 18th century to modern population as a measure of being near the end of sugar development, a low ratio as indicating low development. For example, in the late 18th century Haiti had a population about five to seven times as large as that of the Dominican Republic, while now they are about equal. This indicates that Haiti was near the end of its sugar development, while the Dominican Republic's sugar boom was mainly in the 19th and early 20th centuries. Since the time of sugar development is easily established in these two cases, the comparison on population growth since then validates the ratio measure to some degree. When we use it as a check on uncertain dating, for example, in Antigua (which has a high ratio of 18th to 20th century population), we can have some confidence that Antigua was an old sugar island by the late 18th century, sugar's having filled its niche before that time. These multiple sources, informally combined according to what was available, constitute the "timing of the frontier" variable in Table 4.1.

The proportion of the economy occupied by sugar when sugar had filled its niche is fairly well measured by the proportion slave when the frontier period was over, with three big exceptions. The first exception is that the peak of sugar production often came after emancipation including all of the Spanish islands except Cuba (the Dominican Republic, Puerto Rico, and Trinidad) plus Guyana. In that case one has to measure the ex-slave labor force and the free creole and coolie labor force after full development.

The second exception is that entrepôt ports, such as Curaçao, Charlotte Amalie (on St. Thomas), Havana, Kingston, St. Pierre (on Martinique), and St. Eustatius (a Dutch Leewards island) produced economic value out of proportion to their (mostly free and domestic slave) population. Sugar production as a proportion of the economy on an island with an entrepôt is overestimated by the proportion slave.

The third exception is that on islands with much foothill land, such as Jamaica, a varying but substantial part of the effort of slaves went into subsistence production. Some sugar slave labor produced part of its total economic production by producing provisions on such islands, and not all of their labor can therefore be counted as sugar labor.

For these reasons I have often used geographical correlates of a low proportion of sugar in the economy (e.g., mountains or insufficient rainfall predict low proportions). I have also used demographic indicators other than proportion slave: peasant or runaway slave populations in the interior; tobacco, coffee, or cattle exports; fishing or pearl-diving villages; mining villages or metal exports; entrepôt ports; shipyards, chandlery, and forestry for ship timbers; and peddlers to the interior from market towns.

Conversely, sugar booms after Spanish or French restrictions on sugar cultivation or trade were loosened, either temporarily (as with the British conquests of Havana and Guadeloupe in the mid-18th century) or permanently (as with the stabilization of independence of the Dominican Republic in the mid-nineteenth century, the British conquest of Trinidad confirmed in 1800, and the French conquest of Haiti and British conquest of Jamaica early in the colonial period), show that the above described demographic and economic indicators did not measure the size of the sugar niche, because the boom indicates previously unexploited opportunities. The failure of the same types of conquest to produce the same boom effects on the British Windwards or Curaçao shows they did not have such large sugar niches.

I did not construct a formal algorithm to adjust for such factors, because formal algorithms would run aground on missing-data problems. And sometimes a given indicator quite apparently gives the wrong result (e.g., Jamaica and Puerto Rico are about equally mountainous by the obvious indicators, but Jamaica had a fairly large sugar niche relative to the rest of its economy; Puerto Rico, a small one). This summarizes the construction of the data in Table 4.1 and its summary in the vertical dimension of Table 5.1.

The powers the empires granted to local island governments and the representation of planter interests in those governments, the combination of which gives the dimension of local autonomy in Table 5.1, are usually quite transparent in general historical treatments. For example, good treatments are found in Geggus (1982) and Frostin (1975) on Haiti, in Lémery (1936) on Martinique, in Pérotin-Dumon (1985) on Guadeloupe, in Halperin Donghi (1969) on Spanish America generally, and in Borde (1882), Naipaul (1984 [1969]), and Williams (1962) on Trinidad under the Spanish. There are thus usually multiple sources on the government of the important islands, especially the English ones. Sometimes, as with the Danish (now American) Virgin Islands and Swedish (now French) St. Barthélemy, I have relied on quite casual histories. Great Swedish or Danish historians have not been very interested in these small islands. Some of the best scholarly history is written in English, but is very sparse, and most of that in Danish seems to have been written for tourists in search of their tropical roots.

The dependent variable which the two causes in Table 5.1 are supposed to be measuring is the degree to which planters could create internal processes, through socially well organized classes with clubs and intermarriage and concern for heirs, and through legislative discussion, to decide on planter interests, and to mobilize on behalf of those interests. Here, too, I first used scattered incidents to create impressionistic paired comparisons among islands on planter solidarity. For example, early in the French Revolution the Martinique planters agreed to the participation of the free colored in the polity, as demanded by Revolutionary France. The Haitian planters (and apparently also urban *petit blanc* revolutionaries in both islands) split apart on this question (cf. Lémery (1936) versus Geggus (1982) and Frostin (1975) on this). Similar incidents would compare Barbados versus Jamaica in rejection of royal governor intervention in lawmaking, and Danish St. Thomas versus St. Croix reactions to impending emancipation and to slave demonstrations. Sometimes the incidents involved extraordinary care for the stability of the slave system as a whole, as in the Martinican help to suppress a quite successful slave rebellion on Danish St. Johns.

I then looked for an available structural correlate for these differences. The best I found was the time lapse between my estimate of the peak sugar-frontier growth period and the late 18th century (or whenever the incidents took place), controlled for the differences in the degree to which the island was a sugar island. That is, most of the more organized planter classes and coherent planter policies in the contrasting pairs were farther toward the upper left of Table 5.1; the less organized ones, toward the lower right.

I thought this was because building institutions of internal planter solidarity, especially unity in influencing the local government on the island, would take time and would work better when planters were living on the islands with families rather than planning to go back to the metropole with a fortune to marry. Resident planter families emerged late in the sugar cycle, except on the Spanish islands, where they were more resident than the government *peninsulares* from the beginning. But on the Spanish islands, they could not very well form their solidarities in island government councils, because they were mostly excluded from them.

For example, Barbados in the late 18th century had many more resident planters married to white women than did Jamaica, as well as more capacity to take power from royal governors, presumably joint results of the longer time since the sugar-frontier period and sugar dominance.

I then checked this indicator against similar incidents in previous periods. I also used incidents involving planter power after emancipation, used to introduce new limitations on now "free" ex-slave proletarians. The richest source for these last incidents was Holt's (1992) wonderful analysis of post-emancipation Jamaica. I looked for the presence or absence of similar legislation and government activity on other islands, to judge their distance on planter mobilizability from Jamaica.

Availability of the central indicator of variations within islands of the degree of freedom of subgroups of slaves, rates of manumission, is deeply confounded with the degree of slave society in the government of the island. When a government does not create a deep divide between slave and free, it does not take an act of government to destroy it. So documented manumission works as a measure where freedom of individual slaves mattered most, on islands where the main role of government was to preserve unfreedom of slaves against a varying array of forces, including individual planter generosity to slaves.

On a tobacco farm in the northern valley of the Dominican Republic or in a copper mine in the Sierra Madre of eastern Cuba, slaves worked alongside masters and poor peasants. When in some contingency it became no longer worthwhile for owners to enforce the line between slave and free (e.g., if the vein of copper was worked out), the slave could wander off, or continue cultivation of a subsistence plot, and the government did not care.

In such cases I have substituted (informally) the indicator of the ratio of the free colored population to the slave population as a measure of what was probably widespread manumission. As outlined in Chapter 4, it is also a measure of the average number of generations slave lineages have been in the colony. This cause of high ratios of free colored to slaves would, of course, occur in the same places as we predict high informal manumission, where the sugar frontier had not recently brought in new African cohorts on a large scale.

Occasionally documents betray the fact that informal manumission had gone on and the government, in an ambivalent fashion, was eventually willing to let it stand, as in the attempt by a local governor to reimpose slavery on descendants of copper-mining slaves in eastern Cuba in order to hire them out (probably to developing sugar plantations [Marrero (1978; 6), pp. 36–43]—there was a bit of formal manumission by slaves' buying themselves and their relatives from the king as well, indicating that the non-manumitted slaves owned property and had "their own" money). I have, then, inferred manumission rates indirectly, with another cause of a high proportion free unfortunately happening in the same places, exactly where we would most like to have the numbers to support our theory. (We must take what comfort we can in the freedom that they enjoyed, even if we cannot document where it came from.) We have predicted the distance between slave and free status to be lowest where contemporaries generated fewest numbers about manumission, and where a "normal" manumission rate would generate high ratios of free colored to slave populations.

For our purposes, we would prefer manumission rates cumulated over slave lifetimes, like total fertility rates. What we have instead, even in the British islands just before emancipation, are yearly rates, usually accurate to only one significant digit because numerators are small. They are usually for age-heterogeneous groupings of the slave population, which have, however, different age distributions, and usually age-standardized rates not readily calculable for the comparisons. These annual rates are based on more or less uncertain matches between the categories of censuses and the categories on manumission documents. We can guess that such rates are probably approximately a thirtieth or so of total lifetime rates, except for young, creole domestic female slaves, who often got manumission by way of sexual relations. Their lifetime annual rates were presumably lower than they were when they were young women, so their total manumission rates would be overestimated by simply multiplying their young-ages rates. Higman (1984) is very much more expert than I where these data are best, so I have almost always accepted his word both about the estimates and about their degree of uncertainty.

For the rest of the analysis about subgroups of slaves, I have made my analysis here in the form of predictions in case anyone manages to create good data. But I have informally checked these predictions against what population data on color of free and slave populations were available, or against travelers' impressions of population compositions. I have paid no attention to travelers' impressions of the rates themselves, because I believe people's impressions of all sorts of social mobility rates are useless as evidence.

6

Race as a Social Boundary: Free Colored
versus Slaves and Blacks

Introduction

The purpose of this chapter is first to explain the size of the free colored
population compared with the slave and free white populations, and second, to explain when the free colored formed a more or less separate
subsociety with endogamy and a distinct social and political status. To
put it another way, our problem is to explain how slave societies produce
racial stratification among the free population, as well as inequality in
social and legal standing between black slaves and white free people.
Racism and its social and legal institutionalization has been produced by
social structures other than plantations, but in the Caribbean the social
status of the free colored was clearly shaped by the slave status of some
of their ancestors.

Our basic arguments about both the growth of the free colored population and the social boundedness and distinctive status of that population uses our basic historical categorization into three time periods: before sugar, during the sugar-frontier period as slave society was being
built, and mature slave society. Before sugar (and this extends up to or
past emancipation for, e.g., the Dominican Republic, Dominica, the Bahamas, and Curaçao) the proportion free colored grew fairly rapidly,
and free colored were not very bounded in marriage or in occupation
from free whites, and had essentially the same legal, social, and political
status as poor free whites. During the sugar-frontier period, the free colored proportion of the total population decreased, were disproportionately themselves manumitted, and were developing strong social boundaries. In mature slave societies the proportion free colored tended to
grow at a medium speed, mainly by natural increase. The free colored
tended to be strongly bounded in marriage and occupation, and to occupy a distinct social, legal, and citizenship status.

The ratio of free colored to slaves increased with time before the
sugar-frontier rapid growth period. That ratio decreased (i.e., fewer free
colored per hundred slaves) with the rapid development of sugar plantations, and grew again slowly (a relative increase of the free colored pop-

ulation) after sugar plantations had filled their niche.[1] These differences largely explain the differences between empires and between islands in the ratio of free colored to slaves, with the English and French empires being lower (smaller free colored populations relative to slave populations) largely because they had sugar frontiers early in the overall development of their colonies, the Spanish, Dutch, and Danish having more free colored.

The Free Colored Population and the Sugar Frontier

Before the period of the sugar frontier the proportion of all people of African ancestry who were free was higher than that during rapid growth, and that proportion rose over time until sugar development started. This meant that in colonies whose rapid sugar development came late, the rapid growth took place in an environment with a large free colored population, as in the frontiers of The Dominican Republic, Puerto Rico, St. Lucia, and Trinidad. Trinidad also recruited free colored from other islands during the late Spanish period, further raising the proportion free at the beginning of rapid sugar development.

Islands that never had much sugar development generally had much higher ratios of free colored to slaves and colored to black: Dominica, Curaçao, St. Thomas, Anegada, the Bahamas, the Caymans, and Isla Margarita. The population details are not always clear in the sources, but presumably this high ratio reflects the combination of a much slower influx of new African slaves because the sugar frontier never happened and the lower barriers to manumission or informal non-enforcement of slave status.

During the rapid development of the sugar frontier the ratio of the free colored to the slave population tended to drop, as the slave population increased much more rapidly than the colored population. The more rapid sugar plantation growth and the more completely sugar dominated the island at the end of that growth, the farther the ratio of free colored to slaves dropped. Several factors were involved in this

[1] For data on free colored compared to other population groups that form the basis of these summary statements on population, see Frostin (1975), pp. 28–31, for Haiti (then Saint-Domingue), The Dominican Republic (then Santo Domingo), Guadeloupe, and Cuba; Cohen and Greene (1972b), pp. 3, 14, for Puerto Rico, Curaçao, Brazil, Martinique, Jamaica, Barbados, Cuba, and the upper South and lower South in the United States; Marrero (1978; 9), pp. 174–200, for details of the Cuban free and slave population with various color gradations given; for Puerto Rico at the end of slavery but before the major development of sugar cultivation in the 20th century, see "Documento número 206," in Centro de Investigaciones Históricas (1978), p. 167; for Martinique, see David (1974), p. 63; and in more detail for the British islands, Higman (1984), pp. 689–95.

lower rate of relative growth of free colored populations in times of sugar booms. The most important was no doubt simply that the rate of growth of the slave population was very rapidly increased by demand for more slaves due to the great labor-intensity of sugar cultivation

During periods of rapid growth of sugar plantations on a given island, because Africans were imported at a high rate, slaves were of higher economic value. They produced not only sugar but also capital value on new plantations, and the high rate of growth of demand for slaves generally outstripped the supply. Slave prices were higher in rapidly growing islands. So during rapid rates of frontier development slaves were more valuable and so less likely to be freed.

Further, the rate of manumission was low because the slaves were not of the sort who were often freed, being characterized by both high value and a low level of ties with the planter population. The correlation between percentage African-born and percentage colored among slaves in twenty British colonies is given by Higman ((1984), p. 316) as −.94. (The percentage colored among slaves is given for some of the British colonies, ibid., pp. 116, 152, 155.) Since the percentage African-born among slaves was a good measure of being a sugar-frontier colony, this meant that over time *after* the frontier was developed, the proportion of the *slave* population that was colored increased. Colored slaves were more often manumitted, so the fewer there were, the lower the manumission rate was likely to be.

Further during such growth periods, the ratio of slaves to whites was also generally increasing, because sugar plantations were larger than other types of plantations and larger than domestic establishments in cities, and sugar plantations employed only a few whites in managerial roles. Because the total number of whites employed on plantations was growing, either Europeans (typical in the English and French islands— some French islands partly substituted free colored for whites for this growth of plantation managers) or white island ranchers or peasants (typical in the Spanish islands) had to be recruited. During frontier periods in the French and English islands there were many white men for each white woman. In many places we have reports that it was usual for such bachelor adventurers to take a more or less permanent mate from among the slave population—since often their stay on a given plantation was short, less permanent was frequent. In such rapidly growing colonies most colored births would have a white father and a black slave mother. But colored births as a ratio to the slave population was probably decreased by the low ratio of whites to slaves.

The second factor accounting for the lowered relative rate of growth of the free colored population during sugar booms was that several forces besides the higher economic value of slaves on frontier islands lowered the rate at which slaves were manumitted while frontier development was going on.

Manumission rates were about five times as high for urban slaves as for rural slaves (Higman (1984), p. 382), though the sex ratios of manumissions were much more even in the cities. Since from 10 to 20 percent of all slaves were urban in the older sugar colonies, and very roughly 5 percent in the newly developing sugar colonies, this ratio means that the proportion of all manumissions that were urban might have been roughly half in the older sugar colonies, and very roughly a quarter in the newer ones. But the overall rate of manumission would be lower in newer colonies.

Creole slaves were much more likely to be freed than African slaves, though the rates of manumission by birthplace were more even in the cities (Higman (1984), p. 383). Colored slaves seem to have been freed about five times as often as creole black slaves in Barbados in the early 19th century.[2] Colored slaves were *relatively* much more likely to be freed in rural areas as compared to black slaves, and *relatively* less likely to be freed in urban areas. But since urban slaves were much more likely to be freed than rural ones, this still meant that colored urban slaves were much more likely to be freed than rural slaves. The overall effect of higher levels of urbanization after the sugar-frontier boom would therefore be to lower the rate of manumission during the frontier period, and to raise the rate of manumission after the boom was over.

From a third to a half of slaves manumitted in several British colonies were colored (Higman (1984), p. 383), while the percentages of colored slaves of all creole slaves for those colonies apparently ranged from around 12 to 16 percent (Higman (1984), p. 116). This gives a relative chance (ratio of rates) of being freed versus remaining slave for colored versus black creoles of about four to one. Since both the proportion of colored and the proportion creole was larger in the slave populations before and after the sugar boom than during it, this, too, would have lowered the rate of manumissions during the boom as compared to periods after the boom. The contrasts in rates of population growth by period are summarized in Table 6.1.

Colored slaves also had higher birth rates than those of African-born or black creole slaves. Since it appears that some of the low birth rates of slaves were due to difficulty forming permanent relationships or unwill-

---

[2] Computed from the proportion free versus slave of colored and proportion free versus slave of black, from data given in Higman (1984), pp. 116, 413, and 433, combined with the proportion of freedmen who were black given in Beckles (1990), p. 64. Almost all colored slaves were, of course, creole, born in the Americas—the point here is that even more of the free colored were colored *and* creole.

TABLE 6.1
Schematic Growth Rates of Population Groups

Population Group	Before Sugar Frontier	During Sugar Frontier	Sugar Niche Full
African slaves	Moderate	Very high	Very low
Creole black slaves	Moderate	Low	Moderate
Colored slaves	Moderate	High	Low
Bachelor planters	Moderate	High	Low
Creole planters and wives	Low	Low	Moderate
Manumitted free	Moderate	Moderate	Low
Colored born free	Moderate	High	High
Path of free colored population	Moderate increase of free colored to slave ratio; after about two centuries, free colored majority among those of african ancestry	Decrease of free colored to slave and white to slave ratios; colored slaves increase	Low increase of free colored to slave ratio; free colored growth mainly by natural increase

ingness to have children without some sort of a family, the choice of colored young women by white fathers may partly explain their higher birth rates:

> In the case of Tobago, the higher fertility of colored creoles was most apparent among females aged 15–24 years, whose fertility was more than double that of black creoles. At least half of the children born to colored creoles in Tobago 1819–21 were fathered by whites, another third by colored slaves or freedmen, and only 17 percent by blacks. On the other hand, 90 percent of the children born to black mothers were black. Thus, the fertility of colored creoles had more to do with the physical and psychosocial compulsions of miscegenation than with forces strictly internal to the slave community. In Tobago, as in Jamaica, at least one-third of all children born to slave mothers under 20 years of age were colored. In St. Lucia and Berbice, however, this concentration of colored fertility into the early childbearing years was absent. The existence of a free colored population in St. Lucia permitted relatively stable unions, and this may explain the higher fertility of colored slaves in the older age groups. But the permutations seem too numerous to permit reaching any final conclusions on colored fertility. The important conclusion that does clearly emerge from the data is that creole blacks were consistently more fertile than Africans [This is a per-woman rate comparison—the difference

was even higher than Higman's data here because of the high sex ratio of Africans.—A.L.S.], so that it is not necessary to explain the African-creole differential in terms of the creole population's colored component. (Higman (1984), p. 359)

Since creoles generally and colored children of whites particularly were both more likely to be manumitted, as we analyzed in Chapter 5, and since the proportion of the slave population that was creole and colored was reduced by rapid importation of more Africans during a sugar boom (see Chapter 4), the overall effect again was probably to decrease the growth of the free colored population by manumissions during the boom period. It may, however, have meant that a larger proportion of all newly freed people were fathered by whites.

White people without families probably had fewer domestics, and if they had domestics, they were probably on the plantation rather than in the city. So the bachelor adventurer planter composition of the white upper class during the sugar-frontier boom would probably depress the number of domestics and make the population of domestics more rural. Since domestics had a higher manumission rate and rural domestics a lower one than urban domestics, the smaller size and rural character of the domestic population during a boom period would tend to lower manumission rates. So the manumission rates would tend to be depressed during the boom period because domestic, urban, colored, and creole slaves, all of whom had higher manumission rates, were all less frequent.

The overall result, then, was a relatively low rate of "birth of a free matrilineage" from the slave population, running at a rate of about two to five such births per thousand slave women per year on the English islands. Note that the use of the word "matrilineage" here refers *only* to the way the statuses of slave and free were inherited, and has no implication for other forms of inheritance or other practices often associated with matrilineal societies.[3]

For the English islands, we have moderately good data[4] for the period after the end of the sugar-frontier period. After sugar filled its niche in an island's economy, the ratio of free colored to slaves started to rise again. The more dominant sugar was in the total economy, the slower the relative increase in the free colored population (barring revolution

---

[3] It seems that before the *code noir* of 1685, children on French islands were free if either of their parents was free; Bangou (1987a [1962]; 1), p. 102. In this case, then, the rate of birth of free African lineages was likely about doubled.

[4] It is to be remembered that informal methods of manumission that would not show up in the statistics would become more common as the fees for manumitting went up—as they did in Barbados and Antigua in the early 19th century—see Lazarus-Black (1994).

or general emancipation, of course). For example, Higman shows that manumission rates were higher for smaller slaveholders (Higman (1984), p. 385; this also partly explained higher urban manumission rates) and that sugar plantations were more likely to be larger units than other kinds of agriculture. All other important export crops (coffee, cocoa, tobacco, bananas, allspice, citrus fruits) had smaller slaveholdings than did sugar, and provisions were rarely grown with slave labor, so admixture of any other crops in an island economy would have tended to increase manumission rates.

So after the frontier period, the growth of the free colored population from manumission must have been slowest in the mature sugar-dominant islands, such as Barbados, Antigua, and Martinique, slightly faster when there was some admixture of other crops, as in Jamaica and Guadeloupe, quite rapid in half-sugar, half-peasant-and-ranching economies, such as 19th century Cuba, and hardly showing a hitch from pre-sugar rates (of course) in economies where sugar development took place mainly after emancipation, as in Puerto Rico, The Dominican Republic, and easternmost Cuba.

The difference between coffee and sugar in their implications for slavery gets almost experimental verification in Haiti, the most important sugar island in the late 18th century. When slavery was abolished during the Revolution and the abolition was confirmed by the wars of independence against Napoleonic France in the early 19th century, Haiti became the most important coffee island in the Caribbean; by 1859 Haiti was the fourth-largest coffee producer after Brazil, Java, and Ceylon, and an average of about 70 percent of Haiti's exports in the 19th century were coffee (Dupuy (1989), p. 95). Even in the 18th century many former slaves and other free colored grew coffee on "peasant" small plots in the hills away from former sugar areas, because the lowlands had become uncomfortably racist under the influence of sugar planters.

Between-Empire Variation

Clearly much of the difference between empires is due to differences in the timing and extent of sugar development. The Spanish islands (including Trinidad) had much later development than did the British and French ones, and the Danish ones (other than St. Croix), the Swedish one, and the Dutch ones never had much sugar development.

The Dutch case is a bit more complicated. The small Dutch islands of St. Eustatius and Sint Maartens (apparently mainly on the French part—the Dutch part being too dry) had a bit of plantation development, overshadowed in St. Eustatius by commercial development, but there is little information available on them. Dutch sugar development mainly took place in the Far East, especially Java, and on the Guiana coast of South America.[5] Once St. Lucia [Ste. Lucie], Grenada [Grenade], Dominica [Dominique], and St. Vincent became British in the latter half of the 18th century, the remaining three main French Caribbean islands (and Réunion in the Indian Ocean) were heavily dominated by sugar plantations.

Making allowances for this, and observing the behavior of French and British minorities on islands of other empires as compared with the dominant ethnicity, it seems to me that the free colored population as a proportion of all with African ancestry grew more rapidly on French than on English islands, and more rapidly on Spanish than on French ones.[6]

Some colonies had much higher manumission rates than others, though in many cases it seems not to have been legal and formal manumission, but an informal agreement between the owner and the slave that a person was free. Some differences seem to have been by the nationality of the empires, with owners on the British islands being most loath to free slaves, French owners somewhat more willing, and Spanish and Dutch Sephardic Jews much more willing. The islands in the British West Indies with a strong French or Spanish planter group and culture (St. Lucia, Dominica, Trinidad) had much higher ratios of freedmen to slaves and higher manumission rates (Higman (1984), p. 381).

This higher ratio of free colored to slave and white populations in Trinidad in particular was probably ultimately due to the policy of the Spanish governor of the late 18th century, who offered land grants (though of half the acreage offered to whites—land grants were, of course, a very big step toward citizenship in all early modern liberal societies) and full citizenship rights (such as they were in Spanish colonies) to free colored immigrants. These tended to leave the more oppressive

---

[5] Large, late-developing Dutch sugar colonies include Surinam (see Hoetink (1972), pp. 59–65) and Java (see Geertz (1963), pp. 52–82). Tentatively, Surinam seems to have been more liberal than, but otherwise similar to, say, Jamaica or Guyana, while Java was organized in a completely different fashion. Some of this liberalism may have been due to the relative ease with which maroons could get away to the jungle and organize themselves there, and it may have been an illusion due to the influence of the commercial offshore islands in moderating the law, but not the practice, of Surinam; Surinam slaves did not have much appeal to the courts. Java was so unlike the French oriental sugar islands of Réunion and Mauritius (île de France—it became Mauritius when it became English) that it does not provide supporting material for generalizations about how slavery was managed in the Dutch empire as compared with the French or British empire.

[6] The other empires had few enough sugar islands that one cannot "control" in one's head for sugar development. The Swedish island (St. Barthélemy [St. Barts]) never really had blacks. My vague impression is that the Dutch and Danish were about at the same level as the French in the policies that encouraged the growth of free colored populations.

English and French council-dominated islands for the liberal authoritarianism of the Bourbons (Millette (1985 [1970]), pp. 16–17).

The main purpose of our analysis of the different ratios of free colored to slave among empires is, then, to show how hard it is to attribute anything to differences in culture and law between empires, beyond the differences in culture and development policy that led to differences in the level of development of sugar plantations and the timing of that development. We must acknowledge, however, that there is probably such a cultural effect.

Increasing Endogamy of Free Colored Populations on Plantation Islands

When the sex ratio of the white population on sugar islands approached normal, which generally happened as the sugar-frontier growth period ended and a creole resident planter class came into being, fewer colored illegitimate children with white fathers were born. This seems to apply more to the English and French mature sugar islands of Barbados, Antigua (Lazarus-Black (1990)), Guadeloupe, and Martinique than to the Spanish islands. A creole mixed-race population was established in the Spanish islands before sugar development, with marriage and same-class cohabitation crossing the racial "line" between white and colored.

So the generalization seems to be that a thoroughly racist slave sugar society with a resident creole planter class produced many less colored illegitimate children than did that same society in its adventurer-planter phase. Less racist islands (which generally means islands with less development of sugar plantations) produced more legitimate and consensual-union colored children among a mixed-race proletarian and peasant population, but a relatively small population of colored children with rich white fathers. In settler-planter societies the free colored population grew more by natural increase than by the children and concubines of white fathers being freed, and so was more endogamous with respect to whites than it was in adventurer-planter societies during the sugar-frontier period.

For example, Higman ((1984), p. 156) says:

> In terms of the colored slave populations, however, only 35.3 percent had white fathers in Anguilla in 1827, compared to 92.3 percent in Tobago in 1819. [Anguilla was not really a sugar colony; Tobago was rapidly growing during this period.—A.L.S.] Without pressing the data too hard, it is at least clear that whites fathered a larger proportion of the colored slave population [which was itself smaller; see ibid., p. 147—A.L.S.] in the new [British] sugar colonies than in the old sugar colonies."

Another possible form of increased closure of the free colored was endogamy with respect to slaves. The data are very sparse, but this may have had roughly the same pattern and timing as the increasing endogamy of settler planters with respect to the free colored. Older and larger urban colored groups developed ideals of legal Christian marriage (or its near equivalent in monogamous consensual unions to be turned into marriage late in life), which tended to produce an endogamy boundary between colored and slave populations.

One way to look at both these closures by endogamy is that "Victorianism" and the sanitizing of upper-class sexual life that went with it had strong racial endogamy effects in sugar colonies, by confining more of the attentions of white men to their wives, both because more of them had wives and because having concubines as well as wives became less respectable. Roughly the same thing seemed to happen at about the same time with the increasing respectability (by "Victorian" standards) of the family behavior of the colored population. I think this Victorianism was stronger in the British islands, and so the endogamy boundary between free and slave ("coloured" and "black") populations may have been stronger there.

The Legal Status of the Free Colored

A separate legal status of colored people seems to have been a long-run product of plantation society.[7] The a priori legal assumption in the 15th, 16th, and early 17th centuries in the British, French, and Spanish empires was, roughly speaking, that people were legally either slave or free, and no legal (and few social) disabilities followed from slave ancestry. Colored generals were found in the French army, and black generals born slaves in the Spanish army, for example.

This assumption of legal equality of free people regardless of race lasted longer in the empire that had the latest sugar development, namely, the Spanish one. Although Spanish censuses on the islands sometimes distinguished *pardos*, or *de color libre*, the notion that whites were better than colored people seemed hard to establish even as an immigration policy (see Marrero (1978; 9), p. 88; also compare Spain's positive incentives for free colored immigration into Trinidad, mentioned above), let alone as a principle for organizing the island society. But even racist immigration policy efforts started after sugar plantations

[7] See the summary of enactments in Barbados in Handler (1974), pp. 66–109; for Martinique and Guadeloupe, see Elisabeth (1972), pp. 154–57, 159–65; for Haiti [St. Domingue], see Hall (1972), pp. 183–89 for the earlier tolerance and pp. 189–91 for legal closure against free colored in the plantation period.

started to develop rapidly under the stimulus of the Bourbon reforms of Cuba in the late 18th century (Kuethe (1986)).

Free colored people were everywhere legally distinct from slaves at least up to emancipation, and usually for some years after that. That is, mass emancipation did not immediately create legal equality between newly emancipated blacks and those free colored who had been free in slave society. Even in Haiti, those whom the revolutionary and then newly independent government tried to force to work on plantations were not the *anciens affranchis*. In the British islands ex-slaves were legally required to be apprentices, usually to their former masters, while the free colored were not.

The Free Colored as a Social Structure

In slave societies the freed (or free colored, or *affranchis*, or *de color libre*) were a population defined by race rather than by slavery, though obviously the ideology of slavery was central to it. The social meaning of being a slave was a good deal more variable than we are inclined to think, because we tend to define it by its dominant form, slavery of field slaves on sugar (or cotton) plantations. It was very different to be a slave on a livestock *hato* in The Dominican Republic [Santo Domingo] who got wages and could save them to buy himself out of slavery, who lived in a society where most people *de color* were free, and where political society was devoted to maintaining the power of *peninsulares* as against creoles rather than that of planters as against slaves. Being free was different when defined by opposition to that "near-free slavery" than when it was defined as against sugar plantation slavery. Being a *pardo* in the Spanish islands (especially in Puerto Rico and the Dominican Republic) was more nearly like being brunette in the United States than it was like being a free colored in Barbados or Antigua.

The last part of Chapter 5 tried to analyze the causes of differences among slaves in how near they were to being free. We urged that being creole and so culturally similar to the whites, being a concubine to whites, being a domestic or a skilled worker, being an urban slave working on the docks or as a huckster and paying rent on one's own value to a master, or being a slave on a small coffee, tobacco, cocoa, or provisions enterprise in the hills all were a good deal closer to being free than being a sugar slave was.

Most slaves in the Caribbean were sugar slaves, so it is proper to define slavery by its core. Sugar slavery dominated the main islands, the ones we read and care about, and so the sugar norms about what a slave should be were (oppressively) dominant. But we can see more clearly what the boundary between slave and free was like by looking at people closer to that boundary. The free colored were defined in large measure by being more similar to the freest slaves than anywhere near like a rich white planter. But they were also very far from being sugar plantation slaves.

The free colored population was of different size, different degrees of endogamy and growth by internal natural increase, and different legal status in different islands. It was during sugar booms, when new land was being brought into plantation cultivation, that the free colored were the smallest part of the population with African ancestry. Sugar booms did not happen at the same time or to the same degree in the different islands, and much of what we think of as the differences in race relations, among the empires and among islands within those empires, was apparently caused by differences in sugar booms rather than differences in cultural traditions. Sugar booms create slave traditions in a great hurry, and produce a colored population, some large part of it a free colored population, as bachelor adventurer planters meet black and colored female slaves.

Physically similar populations with somewhat the same formal status could be created in the peasantry and free proletariat of islands not having had their sugar booms. They quite often were described as colored to the Spanish colonial office in the censuses or reports for the first time when sugar started to be cultivated. That does not retroactively make them into "free colored" as it was understood in the English and French islands, because earlier they had not been not "free" as contrasted with the core meaning we now attribute to slavery, nor did color have the same significance it did on plantation islands. So they were free colored in a culture in which it did not matter much what color one was, in which free was not so very different from slave as it was on sugar islands, and in which being a slave was more often the first step in a career that led to being a free creole than it was on sugar islands.

The evolution of endogamous and legally distinct free colored populations, then, reaches its highest development in the old sugar colonies that had no other major kind of agriculture, such as Martinique, Barbados, and Antigua; it is still quite recognizable in the other major sugar islands, such as Jamaica, Guadeloupe, Trinidad, St. Vincent, Grenada, and even Cuba.

But when Luperón, Heureaux, and Báez became (in the late 19th century) presidents of the Dominican Republic, it was not really a revolution in Dominican race relations, but instead an independent Hispanic government with darker than average presidents. Luperón hurled epithets referring to Heureaux's Haitian ancestry. Luperón's mother was from the French Windward Islands, and, though black or colored, was not Haitian, as was Heureaux's. It was Haitians, not black and colored people, who elicited prejudice. Luperón's father did not "recognize" him (acknowledge paternity), while Heureaux's did, some time after birth. Báez's father was a mulatto goldsmith (*platero*), who bought, and then later married, Báez's "tobacco-colored" mother (Monclus (1983), pp. 21–22, 55, 85). The three presidents did not come from an ancient closed free colored community with clear boundaries. So both the race and freedom of the free colored meant something different in the culture of the Dominican Republic than on Barbados or Antigua.

Thus the much larger free colored populations of the Spanish islands indeed had fuzzier boundaries between them and whites, and probably fuzzier boundaries between them and slaves. But this seems to have a spurious relationship with the defense in Spanish slave law of various aspects of Spanish citizenship (such as the right to marry, the right to buy oneself out of slavery, the right to the services of priests). Spanish colonies did not have much sugar development before 1800, so they had milder laws, *and* they had larger and less racially defined free colored populations. The more one goes to the heart of Spanish sugar production in central Cuba, and the nearer in time one comes to the big sugar boom in the mid-nineteenth century, the more Spanish slavery looks like Jamaican slavery, and very likely, the more distinct the free colored population was. Thus Tannenbaum's (1946) use of the status of the free colored as evidence that Spanish slavery was different is fundamentally right, but the Spanish slave tradition had very little to do with it. The tradition was very similar to the tradition in the other empires, but was not broken because sugar development did not break it.

Part II

PATHS TO EMANCIPATION IN THE 19TH CENTURY

7

The Politics of Empires, European Democratization, Emancipation, and Freedom

Introduction

The overall purpose of Part II is to explain how slavery was abolished, and how the conditions of freedom for ex-slaves were determined. Since most of the pressures for emancipation ultimately came from the metro-poles, by way of the political links and channels that made the metro-poles and colonies into empires, that means we have to understand the politics of empires. All of the empires in the Caribbean[1] were radically federal structures, with different relations between the "empire govern-ment" and the colonies than between that government and regions and cities in the home country.

Different empires had different broad kinds of relations between co-lonial governments and metropolitan governments, which shaped both the local government structure the empire imposed on the colony, and the relations among metropolitan policies, political stuctures, ideas of government and government policy, citizenship, and what happened in the colonies. The Spanish empire was more different from all the others than the others were from one another. We have already discussed how the empire differences in conceptions of local government and of eco-nomic development policy created different structures of planter repre-sentation in the 18th century in Chapter 5, and how this interacted with the structure of the economy on a given island to determine the politics of slave societies.

But here we have to be interested in the structure of empire politics, because the thing we have to explain, emancipation, was not decided locally. Much of what freedom meant after emancipation was, however,

---

[1] The nearest to an exception was the United States's relation to its Deep South States—that is, the United States was the *most centralized* empire politically, which is presumably why it had a Civil War partly over slavery, rather than endless battles over amelioriation.

decided locally. In addition, different colonies in a given empire had different relations to the empire system, just as Alaska, Hawaii, and Puerto Rico did to the United States in, say, 1940. But in all of them the policies to be applied on a given island were determined by different mechanisms and structures than was the case for metropolitan regions and cities. In all of them the conditions of commercial life, tariffs and customs rates, were determined differently than the tariffs and taxes of metropolitan regions and cities. In all of them, and this is near the core of this book, labor law was determined in the colonies by a different interaction between local governments and empire governments than was true in the metropole. In all of them citizenship of island residents was determined differently than in metropolitan regions, gave them different rights to representation, and sent their representatives to different bodies with different lawmaking capacities.

For example, let us contrast the anti-slavery agitation and policies of the Wesleyans in the the 1790s and 1800–1810 in England with the anti-slavery Jacobins sent out to govern the colonies by the Revolutionary Directorate in the late 1790s in France. There was, of course, a different flavor to the anti-slavery position of the two "democratizing" bodies in the first place. But as a matter of the politics of empires, it was a different thing to petition the British Parliament to abolish the slave trade and then later to emancipate slaves than to send a Jacobin to the colonies to raise a black and colored revolutionary army and corsairs. The relation of the resulting anti-slavery legislation to the representative councils in the islands was different. The influence of anti-slavery ideas on the appointment process for new governors of the islands was different, as it was for new undersecretaries in the colonial office or in the "marine" department in France.

The military on the islands of the French and English empires in 1800 had different numbers of ex-slaves and colored people as officers and soldiers, and these were differently responsive to different revolutionary currents, so that the generals in Guadeloupe and Haiti were far more anti-slavery than the home government policy; those in Jamaica or Trinidad, or the admirals on British ships, were more aristocratic and royalist than Undersecretary Stephen in the Colonial Office.

In short, there is no aspect of the translation system that turned public opinion in the metropole into anti-slavery policy on the ground on the islands that was not radically different. The French and British empires in the 1790s were different kinds of political systems.

The radical federalism of empires with respect to colonies combined with the distinctive military situation of the islands, analyzed in Chapter 2, to make islands more dispensable parts of the empire, less easily defended against a powerful fleet. When wars came to an end, colonies very often were transferred between empires, conquered colonies were given back, and colonies were sold off. Islands that had French names were part of the Danish empire (St. Croix); islands with Spanish names, part of the British empire (Trinidad, Antigua); and I have had to invent a system for keeping straight the relation between the name of an island at the time of some events and its name at the time I wrote. Islands were systems enough so that as St. Lucie turned into St. Lucia, it carried French features into the British empire; but St. Lucie was different enough from French provinces that it easily ended up in another empire.

The key thing we want to learn in this chapter is how the politics of the metropole was transformed into the politics of the empire tie between the metropole and the colony, and thus ultimately into pressures on the island government. That transformation differs from case to case both because the empire governments and empire-island ties differ, and because the colonies were, to different degrees, intractable.

One of the reasons we have left the American Deep South out of our discussion of slavery and the Caribbean is exactly that the imperial tie of, say, Louisiana to the United States was so radically different from the tie of, say, Jamaica to England that anti-slavery movements and policies were transformed in radically different ways across that tie. The influences came from both sides in both sets of ties, so that slave societies were intractable and fought back against anti-slavery forces to establish unfree rural labor markets after emancipation in rather similar ways in the two "colonies." But Louisiana had votes and a Bill of Rights and seats in the electoral college, which made it very different in its relation to its empire than Jamaica.

We will first view briefly the material from the first half of the book in a rather different way, to analyze the difference in the "social constitution" of the empire-island tie. For example, the social composition of the political tie of the *peninsulares* to the Council of the Indies in the Spanish islands has come into the argument all through the first half of the book in explaining differences between that tie and the tie between planter legislatures and the Colonial Office in the older British islands. But that difference affected the translation of democratization movements in the metropole into island law and administration in a different way than it affected the timing of the growth of slave sugar plantations, the concern in the first six chapters.

Then we will outline principal sources of tension between planters and their governments and the empire as a political system in the old regime.

Finally we will turn to the general character of the transformation of metropolitan politics that usually goes under the name "democratization," and try to specify its relation to the empire political system. Since it was not, for example, "France" as we usually think of it that made policy in Martinique or Saint Domingue in 1775, but instead the empire political system, transformations in the politics of France in the 1790s had no transparent relation to transformations on the islands. The fact that the great Reform Bill extending "democracy" in Great Britain came near the time of emancipation of slaves in the colonies was certainly no accident. But on the other hand something very different was going on than simply extending the new rights of Englishmen to slaves.

The Tie between Empire and Plantation: A Review

The colonial political system in the late 18th century in British Caribbean colonies was organized around the tie between planters and the English government, as represented both in the Colonial Office and in the Parliament, with British mercantile forces and the military (especially the navy) around the periphery of this tie.

In the Spanish colonies the colonial political system was organized around the ties between the crown and an urban peninsular official upper class (including the higher clergy): people sent out from Spain, mostly as bachelors, to occupy posts in the colonial administration or in the merchant monopolies. Spain privileged *peninsulares* in the colonies because they did not trust the autonomist preferences of the *criollos*.

The Spanish crown operated through a collegial and patrimonial bureaucratic administration under the thumb of the crown (Sarfatti [Larson] (1966)), whose core institutions were in Spain itself.[2] Landowners, and particularly planters, were less important in politics because the Spanish government did not care much about agricultural colonial

---

[2] The *cabildo*, or municipal council, was more influenced by, and in some cases dominated by, creoles than was the rest of the governmental structure. The *audiencia*, or the high policy council and supreme court of the colonies, was dominated by *peninsulares* with a dominant loyalty to the Spanish crown. The *virrey*, or chief governor, represented the crown in the local government of the colonies, but his jurisdiction was much broader both substantively and in territory than that of the *cabildo*. The *virrey* had a different structure of conflict with the *audiencia* than with the *cabildos*, but tended to ignore all Caribbean *cabildos*. The governors of the particular islands were subject to the *audiencia* and to the *virrey*, and tended to deal with the *cabildo* of the capital city when dealing with local island matters. There was really no formal place for colonial agricultural interests to be represented; we analyzed some of the consequences of this in Chapter 5. A telling detail is that the cattle ranches near Havana, as a condition of holding their land, had to deliver a certain amount of meat to the capital. Proposals to intensify cultivation (e.g., to establish sugar plantations) required the legal *demolición* of the cattle ranch by the *cabildo* of Havana. See Riverend (1972), pp. 111–12—for other cities, see ibid., pp. 119–20. See the map of *demoliciones* near Havana by 1751 in Marrero (1978;7), p. 15.

products, and the landlords got what power they had by participating in urban politics and official society. In 1760 the sugar production of Cuba was roughly the same as that of the Danish [now American] Virgin Islands, where sugar was mainly produced on St. Croix (MacNeill (1985), p. 126). Planters became more important in Spanish colonies, especially in Cuba, early in the 19th century (Halperin Donghi (1969), p. 161).

Overall, then, the tie of island to metropole was built of different social materials on the British islands than on the Spanish ones. On the Spanish islands, agricultural interests and other creoles were peripheral, local councils were less powerful and less in control of administration, and cities were important because they served imperial military purposes rather than because they were centers of plantation commerce.

French colonial government seems to have been more or less between these two. The urban upper classes were more powerful on Martinique (and Guadeloupe was seen mainly as an appendage of Martinique), and there were more officials, especially more priests, appointed from off the island, making them more similar to Spanish colonies. The planters were more powerful (but less organized) on Haiti [Saint-Domingue], making it more similar to, say, Jamaica. But planter families were powerful in the councils of all three islands in the late 18th century, making the main French sugar islands more similar in social materials of the imperial tie to the main British islands. In the metropole colonial administration was treated as part of the ministry of the marine, and its relation to the sustenance of the French navy was central to the whole enterprise (Duffy (1987)).

On the Danish and the Dutch islands, there were no planters of significance (except in St. Croix), and a colonial urban-dominated government of merchants was legitimated by a merchant-dominated government in the metropole. Thus the central imperial tie was a merchant-merchant tie, and what looked like a navy was in many respects an aspect of the colonial activities of a league of cities. Surinam differed from the British colonies mainly in the fact that the home Dutch government was much more constituted as a federation of merchants from different home ports than the British government; in some sense there was no one to petition for the end of slavery, because the imperial tie was much more a private matter, or at most a matter of city government and civil law (for a related argument on the liberalism of southern U.S. planters, see Oakes (1991)). One would not petition General Motors on a labor relations matter the way one petitions the U.S. Congress—similarly for the Dutch empire (see especially Drescher (1994a); and for earlier Boxer (1988 [1965]); Tuchman (1988)).

The Issues Dividing Planters from the Metropole

To understand the distinctive politics of the slave system, we need to focus on the political issues that divided planters from metropolitan governments, since slaves were not participants in legitimate politics.[3] But planters were just about all there were in the politics of the main British and French islands (the Bahamas and a few other non-plantation islands were exceptions), while they were minor factors on Spanish islands, and were essentially absent on the Danish and Dutch islands (again, exceptions were St. Croix and Dutch plantations on the Guiana coast, especially Surinam). The distinctively urban character of Spanish colonial government, and its organization around the creole-peninsular conflict, decreased the planter role in Spanish colonial politics even more. But the urban character of the administration did not therefore make that administration more mercantile, as were the Dutch and Danish colonial political systems.

This implies that we have to start by outlining the nature of conflicts of interest, and of political representation of those conflicts, between planters and imperial governments. Then we will comment on how the radical differences in planter political placement among empires (and to a lesser extent among islands within empires) affected how these conflicts worked out.

There were four main areas in which there were active conflicts of empire-island interest, which were, to some degree or other, reflected in the empire political system. The first had to do with the imperial government's frequent policy of maintaining a system of mutual monopoly, tying all the benefits created by the colony to the metropole by way of granting trading monopolies in both directions.

A second major area of conflict was the provision of police and other public services in the colonies, and in particular a conflict over who was to control them and who was to pay for them. Roughly speaking, empires wanted to control the "police" system, but wanted the colonies to pay for it, and the planters wanted the reverse. Colonial legislatures were

[3] They were mainly participants in politics at all as recalcitrant instruments, whose possible flight, resistance, unwillingness to work, and the like became political problems. An indicative fact is that one of the main provisions of treaties negotiated with bands of runaways (maroons) was that they should discourage any further runaways. Such autonomous bands were of considerable political importance in Surinam, Brazil, and revolutionary Haiti. They were of peripheral importance in Jamaica and St. Vincent. Only in Haiti were they important determinants of military outcomes, usually, for example, being outnumbered by the black and colored members of imperial armies. More slaves were freed by fighting for the empires than by joining maroon bands, except in Haiti and perhaps the ten years' war in Cuba.

frequently rebellious about "voting supplies" (as the phrase was in the English colonies) to the colonial governors, especially, of course, when such governors were using those monies to enforce metropolitan monopolies against cheaper supplies from the Dutch or North Americans or to ameliorate the condition of slaves.

A third major area of conflict was over the general impulse of planters to think that the whole social system, and particularly economic development, should be shaped so as to maintain the maximum discretion and disciplinary power of the master over the slave. Because that maximum could be achieved only by suppressing all sorts of opportunities that might give slaves rights or economic alternatives, and because almost all progress in other areas of the economy or polity would tend to produce such opportunities, rights, and alternatives, slaveholders tended to support only economic development of sugar production by slave labor and political development only to enforce the slave system, and to supress all other economic and political development.

The intense conflicts over the end of the slave trade, over "amelioration" of the conditions of slaves, and finally over emancipation, got much of their fire from the "class interest" ideology of planters that the going wage (including privileges and subsistence) that slaves could get anywhere else ought to be systematically set to zero, including any going wage rate in alternative employments that the slave might possibly imagine, as well as the ones some slaves actually had.

A final recurrent source of conflict was the question of how the legislative representation of the colonies should be organized. The central question here was how far the island representatives that the island imperial government collected legislative information from were selected by the government itself, as opposed to being selected by some aristocratic or elective procedure that left representation at the discretion of the represented class. Just as one can represent proletarian interests in an authoritarian "corporatist" structure in which the government selects who runs trade unions, so one can represent aristocratic or planter interests through aristocrats and planters selected by the king. It is quite a different thing to point out that all the people the king selects for his cabinet are aristocrats than to say that the estate of nobles meets to approve or disapprove all new taxes, and perhaps to elect the king. The first is a patrimonial bureaucracy; the second, an aristocratic royalist oligarchy. Broadly speaking, the Spanish colonial regime was a patrimonial bureaucracy (see Larson (1966)), while the larger and older British islands (Barbados, Antigua, and Jamaica) were aristocratic oligarchies.

This meant that the upper classes in the Spanish colonies could be excluded from political discourse if they opposed the policies of the crown, or even if the bureaucracy thought they might oppose them later. In contrast, the planters in the British colonies could determine the law over the opposition of the home government, at least for a while, and they could lose in the long run only if the metropole was willing to pay a great cost. More detail on each of these conflicts follows.

Mercantilist Monopolies and Empire

The primary purpose of the government in supporting mercantilist policy seems generally to have been to make the trade easily taxable, to get advance payment for the monopoly privileges, and to make the colonies pay for the projection of empire power into the interimperial system. The exports of the colonies were, then, to some degree protected from foreign competition, and merchants from the metropole were given monopolies (of varying weight and importance) of the supply of both slaves and other goods to the colonies.

The empires differed in their policies of mercantilism, and the pattern of conflict was therefore different in the different colonies (a good short summary by a defender of the French *exclusif* is quoted by Tarrade (1972; I), p. 86). But one of the most frequent sources of rebellion of the colonial rich against the metropole was the imposition of mercantilist policies, or renewed enforcement of such monopolies already theoretically in place.

From the point of view of the colony, slaves, provisions, and often manufactured goods were almost always cheaper if bought in the local Caribbean trade, especially in the free Dutch ports of St. Eustatius and Curaçao, in the Danish free port of Charlotte Amalie on St. Thomas in the Virgin Islands,[4] or in the somewhat free port of Port Royal and then Kingston in Jamaica (especially important for Haiti and the Spanish islands).

The regulations varied somewhat among these places, but fundamentally being a free port meant that ships of any nation could ship into the port and those of any nation could ship out, without substantial interference by legal prohibitions, differential tariffs, and the like. Being a free port, then, enabled a harbor to become an entrepôt between metropoles that did not have rights to trade with particular islands and those who enjoyed a legal or practical right to trade with those islands, and between different islands that could not legally trade with each other. Havana and St. Pierre were entrepôt ports for intraempire trade for the Spanish and French empires respectively. This by and large made them beneficiaries rather than challengers of their empires' mercantilist systems.

[4] The Danes established free trade with the other empires' colonies from 1764 (Westergaard (1917), but St. Croix, the plantation island of the group, was not included in the free port area.

For example most islands had some sort of currency regulation that undermined free trade in coins, generally overvaluing those from the island's own empire. St. Thomas's [presumably specifically Charlotte Amalie's] prices for coins were therefore the main ones that could be trusted to be honest market-determined exchange rates. In turn that made bills on merchant houses in the Danish Virgin Islands into valid international currency, and facilitated the growth of the port's entrepôt merchandise trade.

Sometimes planters traded directly with North American ("Boston"), Dutch, and British ships "illegitimately" in their own harbors, or standing off just over the horizon, or on islands of another empire. English ships brought manufactured goods and provisions (e.g., salted beef from Ireland) to Kingston, which served then as an entrepôt in Caribbean trade with Haiti and Spanish colonies. Especially for the slave trade, but also for the *kleine vaart* (interisland trade, often smuggling, in smaller ships), Curaçao served as an entrepôt, with many of the ships engaged in interisland and interempire trade being Dutch.

The general point is that for the French and Spanish islands, manufactured goods, slaves, and provisions could more cheaply be obtained from English, Dutch, or North American sources. For the English islands at least, provisions could be more cheaply obtained in the Caribbean rather than from England, and slaves were often cheaper in Curaçao than from English ships, though slaves from English and North American ships were often cheaper than the French ones.

From the point of view of some merchants and all consumers in the metropole, the protection given to colonial products was an extra expense. Some merchants who specialized in colonial trade, especially if they had extended large credits to sugar plantation owners in the colonies, had an interest in the protection of colonial trade. It was, however, easier for them to adapt to free trade in sugar than it was for plantation owners (though there was a fair amount of movement of planters among empires as well), so their interest in protection of sugar was less intense.

By and large, then, it was only the imperial government that had a strong positive interest in both sides of this monopolistic tie. Colbert, the French prime minister who was the great innovator in mercantilist trade, seems to have thought that a system of such monopolistic mercantilistic ties would finance an overseas French empire. It would provide work in peacetime for the ships and sailors that would constitute the navy in interimperial warfare.[5] But Colbert had a great deal of trouble getting French merchant monopolies to supply provisions and slaves reliably to the colonies, and the merchants also had little interest in

---

[5] The English followed the same strategy with less singleness of purpose (Duffy (1987)); see Schumpeter (1954), pp. 346–47, for the dominance of the imperialist power interest, rather than short-run merchant profit, in mercantilist thinking.

giving their ships to the navy in wartime even if they might eventually get paid.

Where there was not much of an imperial government separate from the merchant class, as in the Netherlands, the monopoly was preserved only when it was to the advantage of metropolitan merchants, and even then not very strongly. When the protection of British colonial sugar came to be seen in Parliament as a way to make British consumers pay extra to have British slaves in the Caribbean, the imperial government lost interest in protecting British sugar because that was one thing British consumers would *not* willingly pay for. But failure to protect British colonies from competition undermined both halves of the mercantilist policy.

The Spanish government could not apparently get much interested in any commodities from the New World other than gold and silver, and these were not easily produced in the islands. The result was that the monopoly over trade between the colonies and the Spanish mainland, lodged in Sevilla and governed by the Council of the Indies, was never used to develop a vigorous trade in plantation-produced sugar. Sugar was moderately strongly developed in the Dominican Republic [Santo Domingo] in the 1500s. But in the latter part of the century there was a good deal of trading of coastal groups with Dutch ships standing offshore. In 1606 the Spanish decreed that all coastal areas except the capital should be depopulated, and the people moved to the interior, in order to preserve the monopoly (Boin and Serrule Ramúe (1985 [1979]), p. 33). This left the tobacco of the north (especially the interior valley of which Santiago is the main center), grown mainly on small farms, as the main commercial crop until the late 19th century. It is indicative of the Spanish difficulty in developing agriculture that in Trinidad Spain tried to use international difficulties between France and England to recruit French sugar planters from the Windward Islands (Borde (1882), pp. 136–69, 184–91; Millette (1985 [1970]), pp. 16–17.).

The general situation, then, is that without imperial governmental interests in preserving the mutual monopoly ties, for example, to finance France's otherwise too expensive navy in peacetime by giving it mercantile work, such monopolies tended to be the result of the play of interests of the merchants and planters in the colonies (*for* protection of colonial exports and *against* metropolitan monopoly of supplies) and of the metropolitan merchants (moderately *against* protection for colonial crops but *for* a monopoly over supplying the colonies).

As mercantilism waned as imperial government policy, both claims of monopoly became politically more precarious. Generally speaking the fight about the monopoly of metropolitan merchants over colonial supplies was a fight *between* the imperial government and the planters, and the fight over protection of colonial products was a fight *in the imperial country* between representatives of colonial interests (absentees and some merchants) against tax authorities, merchants and consumers (Tarrade (1972; I, II) is the most detailed study of such a conflict).

The legislatures or councils of the colonies in the 18th century Britain and France represented planter interests in the metropole mainly through their agents there and through communication with a "West India Interest" of absentee owners and some concerned merchants. In England, for example, in 1823 Dr. Lushington, an abolitionist M.P., counted fifty-six M.P.s in the House of Commons having a personal interest in slavery (Green (1976), p. 100). These petitioned Parliament and the Colonial Office (or the Navy Department in France) on behalf of their interests.

Planters also formally and informally represented their interests in favor of interloping trade through the governor of the colony, who often had some power to make emergency exceptions to the regulations establishing the monopoly over supplies. How much deprivation of goods from the metropole was a crisis was, of course, a matter of judgment. In general the planter members of councils and assemblies on the islands were inclined to take a liberal view of when there was a crisis, while often the colonial bureaucrats in Europe would take a hard line; the governor was never right no matter what he did. The merchants in the metropole who had not made it to the islands with provisions or slaves this year hoped to do better next, and so did not want the exceptions to be granted too readily.

The governors were, of course, immersed in the island upper class and sat in council to govern with planters and merchants. British and French governors, too, had to go without goods that were easily available offshore. Though their future careers depended in the long run on the metropole, they had to manage a successful term as governor in a system run, to a large extent, by the local planters and merchants. That system could not be managed very effectively by official letters from Paris or London.

Where the Spanish crown spoke to a powerful peninsular bureaucracy and clergy, letters and decrees were more effective communication. Sometimes interloping trade in Spanish colonies was legitimated by the legal fiction of conquest by the military power of (mainly English) traders, who then traded during the condition of conquest, and then fortunately left without doing too much damage. Where Dutch merchants serving in the metropolitan government or its chartered companies wrote letters to Dutch and Sephardic merchants in Curaçao, communication was good.

The planters on the British and French islands, and to some extent on the Spanish islands, were, then, "represented politically" in the international system by the Dutch, Danish, and North American governments that had approved free trade and free ports. That is, the indirect support of St. Eustatius (for example) for trade between the revolutionary colonies in North America and various Caribbean islands (including many English ones) was defended in the international political system by its being part of the Dutch empire, having a governor who could not be recalled by the British government (Tuchman (1988)). On the other hand, that support was only as strong as the Dutch navy, and when St. Eustatius was conquered by the English fleet, the interests of British planters in cheap provisions from New England were less protected.

The political and military protection of free ports was a "function" of the international (or in this case, better "interimperial") political system. But the late 18th century was perhaps the high point of interimperial war, so who was protected by whom against whom varied rapidly over time. When the Danes or the Dutch were at war with the English or French, the smuggling interest of planters in the English or French islands was not as well represented by the Danish or Dutch defense of their interloping interest. French smugglers, for example, were not immune from arrest or blockade when during a war they went to the wrong entrepôt ports, and in the extreme were not immune when the port itself was taken.

Both the Dutch and the Danes (as well, of course, as New Englanders) were heavily involved in the trade between New England and the Caribbean (provisioning the French, Spanish, and to some degree the English islands). During the American War of Independence, planter sympathy in the British islands for the Virginia wing of the American movement was supplemented by a Dutch and Danish sympathy for the "Boston" wing. Alexander Hamilton (see the photograph in Mentze (1966), p. 55) was serving an apprenticeship as a countinghouse clerk on St. Croix, the main Danish plantation island, in the early 1770s, and perhaps felt more comfortable with the Southern wing of the American Revolution for that reason. (Westergaard (1917), p. 249). George Washington had moderately close ties to planters in Barbados (Wessel and Leacock (1957). But the New England merchants had more contact and solidarity with the interlopers who wanted to buy their cheap goods.

The privateering interest was closely connected in spirit to the smuggling interest, and the Danes and Dutch (and the British in Port Royal–Kingston) were often accused of encouraging "piracy." British indignation against the Dutch at St. Eustatius trading with the Americans was closely followed by indignation over their trading in goods taken in privateering by Americans and French (Tuchman (1988); Pérotin-Dumon

(1989a)). Often the Dutch, and to a lesser extent the Danes, were politically close allies of planters wanting more independence, especially independence to trade locally for provisions and slaves (for an early [1605]
example in Barbados, see Poyer (1971 [1808]), pp. 52–59). In considerable measure the freebooters and smugglers working out of Port
Royal and Kingston were also defended by imperial British authority, so
imperial Britain was on both sides of the conflict at various times, and
sometimes simultaneously.

In general, then, mercantilism produced a conflict of interest between
planters and the metropolitan authorities in the colonial government,
though before the late 18th century one could say that Spanish mercantilism was so draconian that it nearly prevented the development of a
planter class, so there was less conflict. While the alliance between Colonial Offices and planters was the core of the system maintaining the slave
system politically, the planters wanted the slave system with freedom of
commerce for themselves, but a protected market for themselves in the
metropole. When they did not get either one or both, they were most
intransigent. And, of course, they were more intransigent where they
were more powerful.

Spain got some degree of military security out of its system of suppressing trade in staples, because it had very little creole opposition to its
policies. Havana served as an effective secure port for organizing trade
between various mainland colonies and Spain, and for repairing and provisioning ships. Havana was supported by a subsidy from México, rather
than by the rich returns that might have been possible from its hinterland. But that hinterland then did not challenge Havana and its Spanish
officials for control of the island until the 19th century, and by that time,
peasant and rancher development of the interior provided an anti-
imperial force that often opposed pro-slavery policies.

The Police of the Colonies

Public administration was generally expensive in the West Indies, because each of the islands needed a separate local administration nearly as
complete as a whole province would in the metropole. Economies of
scale in local government were difficult to achieve when all of the Leewards, for example, had a population less than many English counties,
or when Martinique was about the population size of the somewhat
mountainous French area of Franche Comté.

But perhaps more to the point, the planters wanted a different thing
out of the system for maintaining public order than did "the government." This was perhaps clearest in the case of marriage of slaves; the

Roman church was powerful in the French and Spanish colonies and interested in the sacrament of marriage. The *code noire* of the French colonies, or the corresponding *cedula* for the Spanish colonies, tried to protect slaves' right to marry and, more difficult for masters, to live with their spouses.[6]

In contrast, the Anglicans believed, along with the English planters, that the slaves were in general incapable of understanding marriage, and at any rate it would give them ideas above their station (see Higman (1984), pp. 351, 368–71). Marriage created rights, defended to some degree by the church; Anglican ministers were not about to defend any rights of slaves.[7]

The sort of slave code introduced into the English colonies reads more nearly like the following quotation from the South Carolina code, "first borrowed in 1696 from Barbados and reiterated as late as 1735":

> WHEREAS, the plantations and estates of this Province cannot be well and sufficiently managed and brought into use, without the labor and service of negroes and other slaves; and forasmuch as the said negroes and other slaves brought unto the people of the Province for that purpose, are of barbarous, wild, savage natures, and such as renders them wholly unqualified to be governed by the laws, customs, and practices of this Province, but that it is absolutely necessary, that such other constitutions, laws, and orders, should in this Province be made and enacted, for the good regulating and ordering of them, as may restrain the disorders, rapines, and inhumanity, to which they are naturally prone and inclined; and may also tend to the safety and security of the people of this Province and their estates. . . .[8]

The conflict here was between the empire and the local government over whether public administration ought to be about protecting the sacred status of slave marriage, preventing slave fornication, and similar

---

[6] See Peytraud (1897), pp. 158–66, *code noire* articles 8, 9, 10, 11—the date at Versailles was March 1685; Peytraud gives various dates at which it was adopted for the Lesser Antilles and for French Guiana (Cayenne), Haiti (Petit-Goave), and Réunion (Bourbon) in the Indian Ocean. For an English translation of the Spanish *cedula*, see Borde (1882), pp. 389–97, article 7. The Spanish *cedula* was more liberal in that it provided for the master of the man to buy the woman being married, or failing that, the reverse, so that the married slave couple could live together; such a policy might increase the slave birthrate.

[7] I do not really know why they were more reluctant to do so than Spanish or French Catholic priests; perhaps those who would have defended slaves' rights had gone to the Wesleyans. One should not exaggerate the effectiveness of Spanish or French priests in defending the Christian sacramental rights of slaves.

[8] Jordan (1969 [1968]), pp. 109–10, quoting Cooper and McCord, eds., *Statutes, S.C.,* VII, 352, 371, 385. For a similar French quotation, see Bangou (1987 9[1962;1]), p. 103, quoting the Minister of the Navy (which included the Colonial Office) in 1766; note the difference in who originated the different statements.

matters of slave welfare and godliness, or about preserving the unlimited power of the slavemaster. This made the fundamental line of conflict be over the question of local police autonomy. The question then became whether the coercive control of everyday behavior should be "deployable" by the imperial government, that is, bureaucratically subordinated to public purposes and to public legislation by being done by paid officers with training, careers, and a civil service occupational subculture, or "gentlemanly," that is done by amateurs "trusted" by their communities, who acted whenever they found it worthwhile to serve the local public interest.

To illustrate the distinction, jury duty in the United States nowadays is preeminently organized in a "gentlemanly" way, done by amateurs trusted with citizenship rights and serving out of the goodness of their hearts (as encouraged by mild penalties). When sheriffs were the main police force, this was true of the police as well. The "police" as we know the institution now have essentially a monopoly over legitimate coercion, are employed and not usually elected, and are subject to public legislation and an ethic of service that is supposed to govern all working hours, not just whenever it seems worth their while. Posses and other voluntary services, and neighborly social control, constituted the police in "gentlemanly" administration.

The question was, then, whether the colonies should organize the use of coercion the way we in the United States now organize our jury system or the way we organize our police.

The British "justice of the peace" system essentially took gentry or merchants from their lucrative roles on a volunteer basis, as they were recruited by communal pressure from other gentry and by their sentiments about the value of public order, and made them judges and executors of the law; judges were recruited in much the way suburban city councilors or school board members are recruited today. The militia was the collective-coercion branch of a voluntary police system (as well as occasionally useful in international wars).

Such a system got its legitimacy from being run by "notables," people from appropriate social classes who have shown themselves to be reputable, public-spirited, and even-tempered (or at least only bad-tempered in a good cause). Such volunteer justice is often called a rule of law rather than of men because it is the most reputable and disinterested of the local ruling class who volunteer for service, because such voluntary service is formally authorized by a ruling apparatus that appoints or elects justices of the peace or sheriffs, and because there is some special subculture of legal consciousness that is supposed to be adopted by volunteers. This special subculture is exemplified for example in the judge's "instructions to the jury" in modern U.S. courts—the juror is not supposed to be acting in his or her private capacity, but instead as an agent of the law, which he or she has to learn for the purpose.

Broadly speaking, then, Caribbean planters, like the North American revolutionists, favored a system modeled on juries, sheriffs, posses, and militias, while the empires favored a system of judges, uniformed police forces, and armies. The empire ideal tended toward an overarching system of authority and law administered by trained employed experts who were given a monopoly over the exercise of coercion in daily life (e.g., the right to arrest) and a monopoly over legitimated coercion subsequent to an expert "judicial" decision (e.g., the right to imprison, or to confiscate goods for a debt). But the empires then hoped the planters would pay for it.

In particular, volunteer public administration meant that all the prejudices of slaveowners, whenever they differed from that of the legal-bureaucratic system, would permeate the local administration of the law. This planter-as-gentry system of administration was most developed in the British islands, and is neatly described in a quotation from the permanent undersecretary in the Colonial Office, James Stephen. Stephen himself came from an anti-slavery family and religious tradition, so his attention was acutely called to the powerlessness of the administration in London:[9]

> It is a problem admitting of no intelligible solution, how wise and safe laws shall be made for the government of a Society in which confidence cannot be reposed in the judicial administrators of the Law. . . . Whether it is better that good Laws should be made to be executed by bad Judges, or that a country possessing bad Judges should remain destitute of such Laws, might seem to be the alternative in which the choice is to be made. . . . (April 1839, quoted in Green (1976), p. 92)

From the point of view of the British Treasury, a great advantage of the justice of the peace system was that the administration of such a voluntary system extracted only those services from the planters that they were willing to give, and consequently administrative costs did not have to be paid for by the treasury (in the extreme version of such a system, the public budget is also provided by voluntary gifts of notables—see Veyne (1976)). It is the ultimate in administration by consent of the administered, except for those who are not gentry. Until the abolitionist

---

[9] Green (1976), pp. 65–95, gives an excellent general summary of the structures of representation of planter interests on the British islands; Pérotin-Dumon (1985), pp. 74–77, has a good brief summary of local government for the French islands; and see Bangou (1987b [1962]), pp. 108–13. French colonies' island governments look much like the English ones for representation, but had salaried judges, more troops, and generally many more bureaucrats rather than volunteers.

movement made slaves' grievances politically real, it had the additional advantage for the English Parliament that law and administration voluntarily supplied by the local powerful produced a low flow of grievances to England. This was more true on islands, such as Barbados, that were "well administered" in the light of the standards of such a system.

The islands with the most voluntary government by local notables were probably the English colonies with representative institutions (the older sugar colonies including especially Barbados, Antigua, St. Kitts, and Jamaica) and the Dutch and Danish commercial colonies of Curaçao, St. Eustatius, and St. Thomas; next come the English crown colonies (the newer sugar colonies taken from the French in the Windwards, plus Trinidad, and Guyana [British Guiana, at that time Demerara, Essequibo, and Berbice] and the marginal crown colonies in the Bahamas, the Caymans and Belize—these had legislative councils, largely chosen by the governor), and probably also Surinam; next come the French colonies in order of age (Martinique was most informal; Haiti [Saint Domingue], most bureaucratic); then the peripheral Spanish colonies (especially Trinidad before it was taken over by the British [Naipaul (1984 [1969])], but perhaps The Dominican Republic [Santo Domingo] and Puerto Rico as well), which were informal mainly in the sense that the bureaucracy was so inefficient; and finally the Spanish island most involved in the trade in gold and silver, Cuba, which was quite heavily administered by metropolitan authorities.

As one moves down this list, one has more dominance of officials over notables in police and administration, more importance of regulations and less of local culture, more attentiveness to the state of the immortal souls (and to the marriages) of the slaves and more political control over the clergy that cared for them, more intervention by the metropole in the daily life of the colonies through crown-appointed judges, and more military garrisons.

A convenient indicator of all this for our purposes is whether there was a *code noir* or its equivalent issued by the royal government or whether slavery was regulated by a jumble of local laws, or later on, whether there was effective emancipation legislation administered by judges sent from the metropole.

Eventually all the empires imposed emancipation on unwilling planters in their remaining colonies, though the degree to which that deprived the upper classes of coercive power to extract labor varied a good deal. In general the English colonies, with representative institutions and justice of the peace administration, had their labor relations less undermined by imperial authority after emancipation than had the colonies of other empires (see the analysis in Chapter 10 of the attempts by the planters in the British islands to undermine the freedoms granted with emancipation—note the date, after emancipation, of Stephen's complaint, quoted above). The English colonies where sugar was still expanding more rapidly at emancipation (Trinidad, Guyana, some Windward Islands, and to some extent Jamaica) recruited more Asian labor under coercive coolie contracts. But former slaves were much freer after than before the emancipation that planters first opposed, then undermined, even if they were still not "free" in the modern sense.

In many other ways the "rule of law," in the modern sense of trained judges and bureaucratic police who can be appealed to by lower-class people on more or less equal terms with upper-class people, increased greatly over time in all the empires. Such a rule of law is what Adam Smith called "arbitrary" authority (see the quotation below), by which he meant that it was not under the control of even the local rich governed.

The Spanish, for example, so conducted their colonies before emancipation that they freed a lot more slaves (or let them live as free), and gave them more formal civil rights while still slaves, than the British colonies did. Still, Spain, when it finally got around to it, had to impose abolition of the slave trade, then emancipation, against the will of a considerably weaker planter class. And to do that, it had to concentrate more power in the deployable organs of coercion in the colonies than they had had in the late 18th century. For Spain to concentrate power anywhere in the 19th century, even in the peninsula itself, was quite a problem.

Because in the first period of colonization, in the 16th and 17th centuries, the metropolitan governments were so weak on the ground, and because there were much weaker status group cultures in the helter-skelter process of exploring and claiming the wilderness, it would perhaps be better to characterize the original form of government on most islands as "anarchic" rather than as a "justice of the peace system."[10] Even the relations between slave and master in the early days of the colonies were very variable and apparently sometimes bargained out, rather than being clearly organized by general colonial or empire legislation. Especially for the empires other than the Spanish one, the returns to early colonization on the islands were "adventure" returns in the strong sense of pirate movies, the direct outcome of episodic and opportunistic coercion and trade.

[10] The nicest account is that of Trinidad and Guayana-Cumaná in Venezuela by Naipaul (1984 [1969]), pp. 17–152. I have seen similar accounts for Columbus's time in the Dominican Republic, and for early colonial settlement in the Dutch Leewards, the Danish Virgins, Barbados, and for Tortue and the nearby coast of Haiti. They all sound a good deal like the communes studied by Benjamin Zablocki (1980), in the 1960s and 1970s in the United States, and they tended to break up nearly as quickly as those communes if there were enough boats.

Settlement, peaceful cultivation, and trade, as always, tended to produce more orderly government even when it was almost entirely locally organized. Or perhaps it would be better to say that there was either order or civil war after stable settlement. Order emerged more quickly when (1) congregational churches organized whole colonies (for instance, in the Providence colony on what is now the Colombian Isla de Providencia) or parts of colonies (e.g., villages organized by Baptist missionaries among the free colored or freedmen on Jamaica), (2) when the merchant company given a colonial monopoly had more people more continuously in the colonies (e.g., in Curaçao, in Martinique versus Guadeloupe), (3) when the gross returns from trade came to be larger than the returns from privateering (e.g., in Haiti [Saint Domingue] by about 1700), (4) when the planter elite was more a settler elite (e.g., in Barbados as compared to Jamaica and the Leewards, on Martinique and Guadeloupe as compared to Haiti), or (5) when the metropolitan government took a great interest (e.g., in Cuba as compared to Trinidad or the Dominican Republic [Santo Domingo] among the Spanish islands, or in the Leewards as compared with the Bahamas among the British islands).

By and large all these order-producing variables eventually moved over time in such a way as to increase the degree of local order in the modern sense of administration and justice guided by law and defending some rights of the lower classes, and also usually to increase relatively the power of officials as against planter aristocracies and their representative and volunteer administrative organs. But where they met planter resistance they could move awfully slowly in protecting the rights of blacks.

The Planter Interest in Political Defense of Slavery

Adam Smith argued in *The Wealth of Nations* that representative government (including voluntary justice of the peace administration, I would say) in the English Caribbean colonies probably meant that slaves were more oppressed there than in the more authoritarian French colonies. He said:

> In all the European colonies the culture of the sugar-cane is carried on by negro slaves. . . . But, as the profit and success of the cultivation which is carried on by means of cattle, depend very much upon the good management of those cattle; so the profit and success of that which is carried on by slaves, must depend equally upon the good management of those slaves; and in the good management of their slaves the French planters, I think it is generally allowed, are superior to the English. The law, so far as it gives some weak

protection to the slave against the violence of his master, is likely to be better executed in a colony where the government is in a great measure arbitrary, than in one where it is altogether free. In every country where the unfortunate law of slavery is established, the magistrate, when he protects the slave, intermeddles in some measure in the management of the private property of the master; and, in a free country, where the master is perhaps either a member of the colony assembly, or an elector of such a member, he dare not do this but with the greatest caution and circumspection. . . . But in a country where the government is in a great measure arbitrary, where it is usual for the magistrate to intermeddle even in the management of the private property of individuals, and to send them, perhaps, a lettre de cachet if they do not manage it according to his liking, it is much easier for him to give some protection to the slave; and common humanity naturally disposes him to do so. . . . Gentle usage renders the slave not only more faithful, but more intelligent, and therefore, upon a double account, more useful. . . . That the condition of a slave is better under an arbitrary than under a free government is, I believe, supported by the history of all ages and nations. (Smith (1976 [1776]), pp. 586–87 [original pages, 3d ed., 394–96], sec. IV, vii.b, pars. 53–55)

Smith is saying here that the planter ideology of slavery was so class-conscious that it overrode the planters' own interests in getting more initiative ("intelligence") from the slaves.

Tensions, Structures, and Movements in the Metropole

These tensions in the empire political system were the main ones around which empire structures, especially the structure of the empire-colony tie, were organized. Often above we have mixed together discussion of the social bases of tensions, the structures in which they were managed, and the resulting organization of the colony-metropole tie. This is not because we neglected to keep them straight, but because they were historically deeply confounded. It looks like a detail of level of bureaucratization when one asks whether the judge is a justice of the peace or a *peninsular*. But that structure relates to a general tension about who controls the execution of policy, "police," and therefore of how far the empire has to truck and barter with the local authorities to get its policy executed. And this was related to the deep question of whether that judge could be trusted to enforce strictly the mercantilist policy that planters should not buy provisions from the Boston merchants offshore, but should wait for the boat from St. Malo to bring fish from the same cod banks by way of France. And then it was related to the other deep question of whether the judge would use his power to enforce ameliorative legislation that said that the slaves should get enough of that fish.

Thus the structures, the tensions, and the social groups that made up the empire-colony tie were intimately intertwined, and cannot be discussed apart. Every question of "democratization," of who should influence economic policy, of whose side the police would be on, of who could appeal to the government on what ground, of how representation in court and in the making of laws was arranged, was a strain on one or more of those tension-filled links in the ties between empire and colony.

In the next chapter, for example, we will give a chronology of the French Revolution in the French colonies. But it will not make sense to confine ourselves very exactly to the years of the Revolution itself, because in the colonies the Revolution took place in a context in which one or the other of the colonies had previously rebelled, under planter leadership, against the empire government of the old regime. They had done such "democratic" rebellion under much the same sort of assumption of who it was whose democratic rights were to be improved that George Washington, Alexander Hamilton, or Thomas Jefferson had, and very little of the notion that Tom Paine had. They went into the French Revolution with much the same notion that it was going to be a planter democracy.

A Definition of Democratization

By "democratization" I mean an increase in the average *political incorporation* of the population of a country or other political unit. I mean by "political incorporation" the effective ability to have a group's or person's grievances discussed, and perhaps solved, and have those solutions backed by law and responsive state administration (cf. Stinchcombe (1987 [1968]), pp. 173–81; Stinchcombe (1975), pp. 569–84). In this sense democratization can increase when a ruling class is better incorporated into the discussion and controlling the execution of public policy, even if they use such access to increase their advantages against the ruled. Thus I would call Adam Smith's "free" governments above more "democratized" than his "arbitrary" governments, though I would agree with his generalization that islands had more totalitarian slave societies when they were more "free" or more "democratized" in this sense.

The elements of such a definition, then, are:

1. Organs of *public discussion*, such as legislatures and appeals courts. These are ordinarily collegial bodies, to which petitions, public opinion, legal briefs, and the like can be addressed, within which disagreement is legitimate, resolved after discussion, and resolved by some means in which all collegium members have weight, often by voting.

2. *Responsibility* of legislatures and appeals courts then has to be in part to the people or groups whose grievances are to be addressed, usually by *election* or *legal rights to sue or to appeal.*

3. *Control* by the laws, by decisions that are the result of legislation, which in turn requires oversight by the collegial bodies of state officials and courts that administer the powers of the state. Sometimes control is by joint election of the head of administration and the collegial bodies, sometimes by control of administration by "parliamentary" responsible governments, and always by legal limitations of administrative discretion by the purposes and decisions of collegial bodies and by courts in which both sides can be heard.

4. *Citizenship*, meaning legally and politically protected rights of access for the people or groups to the fora of public discussion, to have responsible legislatures, to have the power of public officials over one limited by law and by appeal to courts or legislatures, and to sue and be sued.

Obviously movements of political systems along these variables need not march lockstep over time, and the movement need not be uniformly toward more democratization. For example, public discussion of court cases developed in old regime France before responsible elected legislatures were the ultimate source of law during the Revolution (Maza (1993)), and were accompanied by a strong movement to make the administration of justice more public and more controlled by collegial (but unelected) appeals courts. Further, as British Caribbean slave societies so clearly indicate, movements toward democracy for white planters ordinarily led to *more* complete exclusion of slaves from political incorporation than did more authoritarian peninsular governments in the Spanish colonies.

So political incorporation (or "democracy") is a variable that can be different for different social groups at different times, rather than a dichotomy. One of its big determinants has been formalized political competition between well-organized parties in elections. Another has been voluntary organization of interest groups and social movements participating in elections and in public discussion. Another has been revolution, since uncertainty about who rules and on what basis has usually made it a good bet to organize new interest groups, social movements, and alternative governments that might have political influence both during the revolution and in the new government afterwards. Perceived inevitability of government action has discouraged public discussion of whether that action should be otherwise, and revolution has tended to destroy inevitability.

But the reverse causation also holds, that democratization causes party systems, social movements, petitions to the government and legal cases representing social and political groups, and increased participation in politics. Citizens speak mainly when they think someone is listening; this generalization applies to political groups as well as to individuals. Democratization generally produces a burst of organization, mobilization, and agitation. Rapid democratization therefore tends to produce uncertainty about who will rule in the future, and to turn democratization into revolution, into massive uncertainty about who is to rule.

Thus, for example, when I discuss the revolutions of the late 18th and 19th centuries in France as "democratization," I mean to assert that they increased the level of discussion of government matters in legislatures and appeals courts, that public opinion became more important in government, that collegial bodies had more control over the administration of laws and of administrative discretion, that elections included more people than before, and the like. When I speak of "restorations" restricting or turning back democratization, I mean such things as censorship, lower levels of control of laws and decrees by legislatures, less electoral competition, state administration less responsive to collegial bodies, restrictions of suffrage or decreases of offices with substantial powers subject to elections, and the like. And if I sometimes exaggerate the movements on these components, by asserting "democratization" during or after the various revolutions, I should rightly be called to account. I am not, by my lights, to be called to account for the fact that many of the people most influential in democratization in France in one or another of the components outlined above were not enthusiastic about slave emancipation.

Similarly if such lack of enthusiasm for emancipation characterized Washington, Jefferson, Jackson, and even Lincoln before 1863, that does not mean to me that there was no democratization in the American Revolution and the following eighty or so years of political development in the United States; or that there were no "restorations" in American politics during this period when some of these democratic achievements were turned back. I imagine it will be clear that generally speaking I am in favor of more democratization, and also of more equality in the resulting incorporation. Like most people with those preferences, I am troubled by democratization that reinforces political inequality, as it often did in the Caribbean colonies.

Democratization, Empire Politics, and Antislavery Agitation

In the first six chapters I have argued in part that various elements of democratization as defined above *on the islands* were part of the causes of the degree to which there was a slave society on the island. If local discussion in planter legislatures had great legal power and legislatures were responsible mainly to planters, if local administration was under the control of planters through those legislatures, if planters were citizens and almost no one else was, then the island tended to be more of a slave society. If peasants, ranchers, and maroons were effectively out of reach of the administration in a hilly and mountainous interior on a larger island, if planters were exlcuded from most island councils and those councils had small powers, if the administrators were shipped in from the outside and were concerned with the gold and silver trade, and if creoles in general had no substantial citizenship defended in law, then the island tended to be less of a slave society. But this is all about only the island half of the empire-island tie. The democratization of the metropole, I will argue in the following chapters, was the central cause of the emancipation of slaves, because it changed the empire end of the empire-island tie.

But because of all the complexities of the empire as a political system outlined above, the translation of democratization in the metropole into emancipation, or into local political incorporation and freedom for ex-slaves, was a very problematic business. One has to look at the empire as a translation system that transforms metropolitan democracy into pressures on the islands, and at the character of the democratization in the metropole itself, as well as a system whose island parts are differentially "democratic" for planters but nobody else.

The central questions about translation fall into two parts: the first is whether anti-slavery popular or elite forces in the metropole had a channel into the legislatures or courts of the metropole that in turn connected to the metropolitan end of the empire-island tie, and in particular whether they *believed* they had such a connection. Social movements only mobilized to control authorities when the authorities were both thought to listen, and thought to control the relevant administrations and policies.

When the English Parliament was thought to listen and to have authority over all executive, military, and colonial matters, it was sensible to direct petitions to end the slave trade and later to emancipate slaves to the Parliament. When Napoleon made foreign policy and controlled the military, when the French colonial administration was a branch of the navy department, when assemblies for discussion of policy had a precarious overall political status for Napoleon regardless of the issue because they had been too leftist, when the high courts had little jurisdiction over colonial laws and there had been a tradition that French laws did not obtain automatically in the colonies, there was really no place to address a petition.

The anti-slavery wing of the revolutionary movement of the late 18th and early 19th centuries in France was relatively weak and often had no effective arena to work in. When the Napoleonic military authorities of the metropole decided on a strategy of trying to coopt the black and colored troops of Guadeloupe and Haiti and put down any rebellion against reintroducing slavery of those who would not be permanently coopted, the question was not what the anti-slavery movement in France would do but what the black and colored generals on the island would do. They were more thoroughly and permanently coopted in Guadeloupe, and the rebels were more militarily effective in Haiti.

But to illustrate the importance of empire political structures, the Jacobin revolutionary authorities in the 1790s, sent out to Guadeloupe and Haiti to mobilize black and colored forces for the defense of the French empire, promised emancipation (at first only to soldiers, later to everyone). They represented the French left, which included (even if it was not dominated by) much of the anti-slavery and colored citizenship movement of the time. And the revolutionary armies and corsairs dominated by colored and black officers and men were creations of that Revolutionary govenment.

As we will argue, the experience of this contrast in empire ties as a result of revolution meant that there was a latent revolutionary empire structure that could be recalled by black and colored people on the French islands. It was during one Revolution (1848) that emancipation was imposed on the French Windward colonies, and during another (1870) that political citizenship of the black and colored poor was imposed there. And it was the failure of French revolutionary mobilization to defend their freedom about 1800 in that empire structure that moved the black and colored military in Haiti into rebellion and a war for independence.

The main point here is that the empire was not a homogeneous system of political access. The islands always had different political incorporation in their local governments and in the developing "national" governments of the metropole than did metropolitan social groups, so democratization in the metropole did not have uniform effects on the islands.

What this means is that the dismal state of the main theories of abolition of the slave trade and emancipation, outlined in Drescher (1990b) and especially clear in his wonderful analysis of what it means that the Dutch had almost no abolitionist or emancipationist movements (1994a), is due to looking only for motors of the movement and never for transmission belts. Theories of the main motors of abolition and emancipation movements include those that look for failing plantations, for lessened dependence of the metropole on colonial profits, for expansion of the doctrine of free labor that was the hegemonic ideology of industrial capitalists and of much labor agitation, for religious moblization by congregationalist or anti-clerical movements. No doubt there is something to all of these as theories of where the ultimate abolitionist pressure and the weakness of countermobilization came from.

But if one looks for uniform effects of a small and peripheral abolitionist movement among the French Revolutionists, a strong Wesleyan agitation in Britain, and nothing much happening in the Dutch empire, empire transmission differences overwhelm differences in the strength of the metropolitan movements. Changes in those transmission effects between the Jacobin and the Napoleonic period of the Revolution overwhelm the changes in the political status of that weak movement in France itself. And the character of the links goes far toward explaining the mobilization of the strongest emancipation movement of all, namely, that of the black and colored military on the French islands during the Revolution. The British fleets that took Martinique to maintain slavery and took Trinidad to expand it were transmitting policy from a government probably under stronger popular pressure against slavery than the French government that was abolishing slavery and incorporating black and colored people into the revolutionary army.

Because the empire structures themselves are helter-skelter, and relatively changeable over time, the last half of the book cannot be as theoretically integrated as the first half. But insofar as it has theoretical unity, it is unified around the proposition that the empire as a system transformed movements of democratization before they reached the islands, because of the sorts of complexity in those links analyzed above. Political incorporation in the metropole provides the motors, but what force is delivered to the islands depends on the larger forces that shape the empire structure that translates such political incorporation into pressures on island-empire ties, that themselves were made out of different social materials to start with.

We are much nearer in the second half to the kind of social history where one has to tell various stories of various empires rather than make theories. But I would argue we got there by formulating a theory of why it is that the theories that look for the main drivers in anti-slavery movements are generally following the wrong strategy, because political power runs through imperial channels differently than through political channels within the metropole.

8

French Revolutions and the Transformation of the French Empire

Introduction

France was the first empire to have a democratic imperial policy that included slaves and free colored, during the Revolution (the French Revolution of 1789–1799 will be denoted by the capital *R*). That policy did not last very long, being introduced late in the Revolution and being abolished by 1802 by Napoleon's empire. But that part of the Revolution lasted longer in the Caribbean, both before and after it was imperial policy. Democratic libertarianism as an ideology undermined the ideologies of both slavery and racism, though to different degrees, and the anarchy of the Revolution undermined the coercive mechanisms on which slavery and the slave plantation were based.

The French islands were divided during the Revolution from "left" to "right" between "patriots" and planters; as with the French nobility, planters were first revolutionaries favoring autonomy of local oligarchies, *parlements*, and Estates General, and later royalists and pro-English against the Republic; then the planters became French imperialists again under Napoleon.

The Revolution also divided the French ethnic groups on various British islands (on Saint Lucia [Saint Lucie] and Grenada, and to a lesser extent the other Windward Islands conquered in the late 19th century, and on Trinidad after British conquest in 1800–1802) and Spanish islands (Trinidad before 1802, Cuba, and Puerto Rico). That Revolution also divided the Spanish from the French and the French internally on Hispaniola. Diplomatically from 1795 the Spanish part of Hispaniola, now The Dominican Republic, was part of the French colony, now Haiti, but on the island itself, this was a lot more complicated. When the Dutch States General became pro-French and the Stadhouder took refuge in England, Curaçao divided between the pro-French council and the pro-English governor (Goslinga (1979), pp. 67–75).

The nationalistic power generated by the democratization of France during the Revolution, and then tamed and mobilized for a policy of authoritarian liberalization in the international system by Napoleon, also drastically changed the nature of the international equilibrium in the Caribbean. Probably the French empire's main effect was to mobilize England; since England was a naval power whose comparative advantage was greater in the Caribbean than in Europe, several of the French islands fell to the English.

In addition, the shift in the balance of power between democratic France and reforming Bourbon Spain in Europe increased the imbalance of the intensely developed area of Haiti [Saint Domingue] and the sparsely populated and economically insignificant Dominican Republic on Hispaniola. After the independence of Haiti, Haitians conquered the Spanish-speaking part of the island almost at will for nearly half a century, reflecting the basic power situation manifested in the Treaty of Basel in 1795.

The American Revolution had likewise changed the international situation of the Caribbean, for after independence the North Americans completed their near-replacement of both the Dutch and the English as the central "interlopers," or smugglers, of the Caribbean. In particular this meant that the price difference between smuggled supplies and manufactured goods and those supplied by merchants from the metropole increased. Lémery ((1936), p. 8) estimates that many provisions were 50 percent cheaper when *not* bought from France in the mid-18th century; even slaves were apparently about 30 percent cheaper from North American merchants (see also Pérotin-Dumon (1985), p. 66). The North Americans could get more goods to the Caribbean more cheaply than could either the British or the Dutch; Boston, New York, and New Orleans replaced Curaçao, St. Thomas, and Kingston as the centers of free trade.

Roughly speaking, the American Revolution provided a model of a planter revolution against a weakened metropole for the planters of the French islands and the merchants outside St. Pierre.[1] The planters on the French islands had been more restless than usual since the American Revolution (Frostin (1975); Pérotin-Dumon (1985)) in their political rebellions against the constraints of mercantilism.

The French Revolution, more than the American one, provided a model for changes for the free colored and eventually for the slaves in the other colonies—the island colored and blacks could "merely" introduce changes that had already happened in France but that were stopped by local planter governments. The Club Massiac of Haitian [Saint Dominguan] planters in Paris, for example, specifically avoided the question of free commerce because its conservative allies against equality of

---

[1] For example, merchants in Basse Terre and Point-á-Pitre in Guadeloupe were more rebellious. An administrator from Martinique complained in 1773, "It remains true as always that there is in [Guadeloupe] a well-known tendency to separate from the metropole" (Pérotin-Dumon (1985), p. 74). They wanted to separate in particular from Martinique's Saint Pierre merchants, who used the official position of their port against the interests of merchants outside it.

the colored in France's political system were the monopoly merchants in France (Debien (1953), pp. 280–81). But when in the course of the Revolution those allies were converted to support the rights of the free colored to try to get colored allies in the civil war in Haiti, the planters' anti-colored policy was doomed.

Chronology of French Revolution in the Colonies

1717	"La Gaoulé," Martinique Assembly arrests Governor and Intendent and ships them to France in a conflict over enforcement of *l'exclusif.*
1723	Revolt of planters and *petits blancs* in Haiti [Saint Domingue].
1759–1763	England holds Guadeloupe; free trade results in sugar boom; many slaves introduced.
1769	Revolt of whites in Haiti [Saint Domingue].
28 Mar. 1790	Constituent Convention adopts a law *not* extending the constitution of France to the colonies.
7 July 1790	New Martinique Assembly claims substantial "nullification" rights and, for emergencies, rights to legislate even where the metropole has laws.
15 May 1791	Decree, free people of color to be treated equally, to have all the rights given by the Decree of 8 March 1790 to all whites. Nothing for slaves.
24 Aug. 1791	Rebellion breaks out in the north of Haiti [Saint Domingue]; within two weeks perhaps 10 percent of the slaves in Haiti are participating in the revolt (estimate by Pérotin-Dumon (1985), p. 147).
24 Sept. 1791	Decree gives the colonies jurisdiction over their internal regime, including the status of free colored.
Early Nov. 1791	Colonial Assembly of Port au Prince rejects mulatto-white equality.
12 Dec. 1791	Assembly of Martinique (dominated by planters) calls a General Council of the French Lesser Antilles (Martinique, Guadeloupe, St. Lucia [Ste. Lucie], Tobago), giving eligibility for office to quadroons, the vote to mulattos, who satisfy the same respective qualifications as whites.

Apr. 1792	Pitt leads British House of Commons to abolish slave trade; stopped in House of Lords.
4 Apr. 1792	Approval by the French king of a law that free people of color are politically equal; colonial assemblies had to be reelected under the new suffrage rules.
10 July 1792	New Assembly meets in Guadeloupe.
16 Sept. 1792	Assembly in Martinique mock-arrests the governor (so that he cannot be convicted of aiding a rebellion), prevents the landing of Rochambeau as the new governor, insisting they do not need the commissioners charged with enforcing colored equality; Rochambeau and the fleet go to Haiti.
13 Jan. 1793	Rochambeau returns to Martinique from Haiti to find LaCrosse, the civilian commissioner, already in charge in Guadeloupe and Martinique.
1 Feb. 1793	France declares war on England and Holland.
7 Mar. 1793	France declares war on Spain.
27 Apr. 1793	Planters take the west of the island of Martinique, and await the British, after hearing from Du Buc.
21 June 1793	Sonthonax, Commissioner of the Directorate, promises freedom to Haitian slaves who join the army under the command of the Commissioner; taken as general emancipation.
June 1793	Rochambeau defeats a much larger British invading force in Martinique by fighting at night.
mid-1793	Spanish invade Haiti from Dominican Republic [Santo Domingo].
Sept.–Dec. 1793	English take several parishes in the south and west of Haiti, and the naval base at Môle St. Nicolas in the northwest across the windward passage from Guantánamo.
4 Feb. 1794	Abolition of slavery by the Convention; proclamation never gets to Martinique.
Mar. 1794	British invasion takes Martinique; Du Buc, planter leader and former president of the Martinique Assembly, becomes governor under the British; British take Guadeloupe.

6 May–Sept. 1794	Conquest by Victor Hugues of first Grande-Terre, Guadeloupe, then Basse Terre, from English.
22 July 1795	Dominican Republic [Santo Domingo] ceded to France by Spain in treaty of Bâle [Basel, Basilea]; controlled by the French military or local Spanish much of the time up to 1802.
16 June 1799	"War of Knives" in Haiti between colored under Rigaud and black under Toussaint starts with Rigaud's invasion from the south and colored uprisings in the cities of Toussaint's west and north; mass killings of colored in all three provinces by Dessalines and Toussaint.
26 Dec. 1799	Napoleon's constitution does not recognize the colonies as integral parts of France.
Jan. 1801	Haitian invasion of Dominican Republic [Santo Domingo] under Toussaint L'Ouverture and Santo Domingo declared part of Haiti; slavery abolished there; force withdrawn to deal with internal conflict in Haiti. Jefferson becomes President of the United States and withdraws U. S. support of Haitian Revolution.
July 1801	Haitian constitution, with advice from Alexander Hamilton, has a strong executive, President for Life.
1 May 1802	Toussaint surrenders to Leclerc; is allowed to retire. Arrested 7 June 1802; dies in prison in France, 7 April 1803.
6 May 1802	Army from France arrives to remove the black and colored troops from Guadeloupe
20 May 1802	Slavery reestablished by law of Napoleon. Delgrés blows up Fort Mantouba on Basse Terre in Guadeloupe rather than surrender to the French.
13 Oct. 1802	Pétion, Cristophe, and Dessalines revolt in Haiti with their troops; they had joined the French.
18 May 1803	England declares war on France.
1804–1805	Dominican Republic conquered again by Haiti.
1809; diplomatic 1814	Spanish restoration in Santo Domingo; slavery reintroduced.
1808–1814	Guadeloupe (1809), Martinique (1810), Réunion [Bonaparte, Bourbon], and Mauritius [île de France] taken by England—England kept Mauritius.

1815   Slave revolt on Réunion.

1821–1822   Haiti conquers Santo Domingo after its declaration of independence from Spain, abolishes slavery (again), rules until 1844.

The reins of local power in the old regime were generally in the hands of the colonial assemblies, made up almost entirely of planters (with the crucial exception of the governor and intendant, who were metropolitan higher civil or military servants). The planters had been running rebellions against mercantilism for a long while. So the first effect of the disorganization of imperial power by the Revolution was the drastic relaxation of *l'esclusif*, the restriction of island imports to those from France. The merchants of the colonial monopoly ports, especially of St. Pierre on Martinique, were somewhat torn between their bourgeois preference for the bourgeois government of France and their short-run interest in the preservation of the monopoly of the ports they were established in.

Of course most of the politics of the *exclusif* took place in France.[2] In the long run the monopoly merchants adapted to the new, more competitive, economic situation (and at any rate, had no mercantilist empire to appeal to), so lost their strong tie to the old regime. Further the Napoleonic empire and its more royal successor took most of the democracy out of the imperial tie, so the attraction of the commercial middle classes to the empire was reduced by the disappearance of the oligarchic council part of bourgeois democracy.

The alignment in the French islands, then, roughly speaking, eventually put the planters on the royalist, sometimes pro-English, right, and eventually the pro-Napoleonic right; the white merchants and the richer of the colored merchants in the Girondin, or "Patriot," middle; and some very few intellectuals, blacks when they were freed and mobilized in Haiti and in Guadaloupe, and some colored on the Jacobin left.[3] Some, especially blacks, were eventually even on the "Haitian" left. On emancipation questions and black participation in government, the Hai-

---

[2] See, e.g., Tarrade (1972; I), pp. 223–85, for an extended discussion of a prerevolutionary debate in France on exceptions to the monopoly.

[3] The first Jacobins in the islands were mainly *petits blancs*, poor whites, in the cities. Many of them were sailors, often only temporarily in the islands. At least those living in the islands tended to be quite racist, opposed to abolition of the slave trade, emancipation, and equality of the colored. It is sometimes not clear how far the racism of a given movement was due to such poor whites and how far it was due to the planters. The more a movement was urban, and the more it was a riot rather than an organized military or governmental enterprise, the more likely was it that the racism was poor white racism. Such racist poor white movements give great problems to the general Whiggish conception of "democratization" I put forward in Chapter 7, as they do in the United States. See Pérotin-Dumon (1988).

tian black and colored center were far left of the French center, and the Haitian left was very left indeed.

Over time during the 19th century the intellectual civil service (especially teachers) grew in the colonies as well as in the metropole; the colonies as well as the metropole became more urban; the metropole became more democratic, and even metropolitan conservatives eventually supported universal citizenship modified by populist authoritarianism; slaves were freed; and planters lost their nearly complete monopoly over island representative institutions.[4]

As in France, then, the center of gravity of the political system in the colonies moved leftward in the 19th century, with roughly the same relative positions of political traditions, producing majorities and policies further left, as the royalists weakened and the socialists grew. By the late 19th century the French islands were a good deal more democratic than the English islands, having essentially French metropolitan institutions but with public opinion and the "median voter" probably usually left of the metropole.

The alternation (if periodic revolutions and restorations can be called alternation) of the French metropolitan government between republican coalitions and "parties of order" produced an irregular path of two steps left, one back right in this general leftward drift. The crucial step leftward for the colonies was in 1848, when the slaves were freed for good and the electorate in the colonies substantially expanded, though most of the expansion was taken back in the 1851 restoration.

The Questions of Representation

In order to relate the class and party system described briefly above to the details of revolutionary politics in the 1790s in the islands, we must straighten out the way questions of representation were posed in the colonies. There were (and are) in general three main constitutional representation questions that determine which grievances of the population can get resolved (or at least incorporated into compromises) through the political process (this treatment is based on the section on "political incorporation" in my *Constructing Social Theories* (Stinchcombe (1968), pp. 173–81)). The first was the question of suffrage, of who gets to vote (and to a lesser extent who is eligible to stand for office); the question where there are no formal elections and the governing bodies

---

[4] Bangou (1987a [1962];1), pp. 190–92, "Les différents brèches dans le système esclavigiste," gives a concentrated chronology of the French enactments. See also ibid., pp. 201–7 and (1987b [1962]; 2), pp. 45–52, 75–77, 119–136—it's enough to persuade one of a view of "history as the story of progress."

are informally defined, of course, has to use different criteria for what constitutes "effective suffrage."

For example, when there was never a question of differential electoral rights of free colored, as on Réunion [Bourbon] in the Indian Ocean (Scherer (1965), p. 40), or in communes, such as St. Marc or Léogane in Haiti [Saint Domingue] (Geggus (1982), pp. 65, 71), or where the planter assembly granted colored suffrage early (as on Martinique), the conservatism of the colored population and the unity between white and colored during the Revolution was greater. This presumably is because planter power was not consistently used to create colored grievances, because colored people were politically incorporated.

Many of the colonial assemblies in the French empire had had councilors at least partly selected by the governor and serving at his pleasure, and were in some ways more similar to a modern cabinet than to a modern legislature; a dominant question of the late 18th century, and particularly of the Revolution, was whether and how the colonial assemblies should be elected, and who should determine the question of suffrage on what basis.

Once it was determined who was represented in a legislative body, the second question, whether they could make coalitions so that their central purposes could be achieved (or at least compromised) in the decisions of the body, was crucial. For example, when the St. Pierre merchants were granted very small representation in the first assembly on Martinique, they withdrew because their core interest in their monopoly over commerce of the island and of other Lesser Antilles was clearly opposed by the great majority of their colleagues—they had no chance to get into the governing coalition. The planter-dominated rump merely declared itself the assembly, which gave the merchants even less representation (Lémery (1936), pp. 40, 45–46). Of course the likelihood of getting into the governing coalition was substantially affected by whether the suffrage was equal (in the case of more or less universal suffrage) or if one's class elected many representatives (as did planters in Martinique).

The third big determinant of whether the grievances and interests of a group got dealt with politically was the powers of the representative body. For example, the question of whether metropolitan laws (whether of the king or of the National Assembly) were valid in the colonies before they were accepted or "registered" by the local assembly or governor was a question of how many of the grievances of the locally represented planters would be dealt with according to their preferences. After it became clear that the metropolitan Assembly was not friendly to slavery, the planters became very interested in local autonomy ("nullification"), independence, or government by the English rather than the

French metropole. In Haiti [Saint Domingue] the autonomists were called *léopardins*, presumably for their pro-English leanings. In Réunion [Bourbon], The Assembly declared on February 26, 1801: "The assembly declares that the will of the colony is not to break the ties that have inviolably attached it to France; but it declares at the same time that it will never adopt the decrees of 16 pluviôse an II [abolishing slavery] . . . and that it will reject it with all its means" (Scherer (1974 [1965]), p. 48).

The object here was, then, not to detach the island from the metropole, but to deny the national government the right to legislate for the colonies. The issue of local autonomy meant different things from a class and race point of view under the old regime (when the colonial office in the navy department was favorable to slavery, but against planters' trading with nonmonopoly merchants or foreigners), under the early revolution (when the metropolitan government ambivalently favored equal citizenship for poor whites and colored, but did not touch slavery, and tolerated freer trade in the colonies), and under the late revolution (when the metropolitan government "favored" emancipation of slaves, democracy, the exile of aristocrats and planters, and free trade).

In a revolution the question of suffrage, who and what interests will be represented, gets intimately tied up with what bodies and authorities will do the representation. Thus when the representatives of St. Pierre in Martinique withdrew from the new colonial assembly, they were not only questioning the allocation of power within the assembly as determined by the suffrage regulations, but also questioning whether that body was the governing body that should be registering laws and advising the governor.

When a revolution was under way then, what policy to follow on fundamental issues turned into a question of where the authority to decide such issues should reside.[5] When the metropolitan Assembly decided to abolish slavery, local planters did try to fight out the question in metropolitan politics. But they also tried to relocate such questions in the colonial assemblies, by turning the islands over to the British, by urging independence, or by claiming the right to nullify national laws as inappropriate to the colonies.

---

[5] Jurisdiction issues are always also substantive issues, and so all social classifications related to representation in various jurisdictions are political. But one criterion of a nonrevolutionary period is that jurisdictional issues are less uncertain, more permanently decided, than substantive issues. In federal structures, as the empires were, the equality of uncertainty about jurisdiction and substance in revolutions produces an uncertainty about citizenship as well, so that all social classifications tend to become political issues. Revolutions in which questions of jurisdiction are in dispute are always therefore about citizenship, and in federal structures always about territorial citizenship and the place of territorial government in the total constitutional scheme of things.

But further, the Revolution was going on in the metropole at the same time, which meant that who was being represented, what issues were to be treated by legislatures (versus courts and or the navy department), and what parties organized the governing coalition in one or another of these political arenas were all fluctuating there as well. Hence at any particular time it might seem wise for the planters, for example, to claim autonomy from the metropolitan legislature by refusing to register their legislation for implementation in the colonies, but to work closely with the colonial administration (especially the military) because it was controlled by aristocratic officers. But at some other time it might seem wise to register the law giving the colored equal representation in order not to have a military unit dominated by the revolutionaries land to enforce equal representation. A revolutionary army might enforce many other revolutionary policies.

The Revolution and the Evolution of Extremism

To understand the social and political implications of any particular representation conflict (or "the same" conflict at a different time) we have to have a comparison of the suffrage, party control, and powers of both (or of all of the set) of the bodies in contention. And in time of revolution the bodies in contention always include military units. When Toussaint L'Ouverture temporarily conquered the Dominican Republic [Santo Domingo] in 1801 (Ott (1973), pp. 116–19) it was taken as a serious danger to the control of the colony by Napoleon. Napoleon had confirmed Toussaint as Commander in Chief "for the purpose of fighting the English only." When Napoleon's military established Marie-Louise Ferrand as governor in Santo Domingo, it was clearly a last-ditch effort to deprive that same Haitian army of the control of the colony.

Part of the reason radical representatives of a group usually have a comparative advantage in time of revolution, moderates, in time of stability, is that what Trotsky called "dual power" is an alternative in times of revolution (Trotsky (1960 [1932]), pp. 206–15). Rather than competing within a designated governing body or authority for control of legislation to be implemented by an executive subject to that body or authority, one can compete in the establishment of a new body or authority with an executive devoted to implementing the resulting policy.

Of course one still may lose because the dual power established may be weaker than its competitor. But the radical policy may win without compromise. For example the "dictatorship of the proletariat" was a realistic winning policy in Russia in time of revolution; it was a minority policy in times of stability of governing bodies.

Thus in a revolution the range within a planter social movement from moderate to conservative tended to break apart on the question of whether to advance the group's grievances in a body in which they would have to be compromised, or to advance them by creating a body to administer an uncompromised policy. An analogous thing happened on the left. Just as "Soviet" versus "Constituent Assembly" or "Provisional Government" tended to divide Menshevik from Bolshevik, so assembly with colored and merchant republican representation versus planters-only councils tended to divide centrists from royalists.

When there are local representative bodies responding to a colonial society with different divisions than those of the metropole, as when ethnically homogeneous metropoles of free people (or at least free men) govern colonies with slave and free, colored and white free people, creole and metropolitan whites, there is a ready-made dual power situation between autonomous local legislatures and metropolitan powers. This is one of the reasons so many revolutions are nationalist or secessionist. Almost everyone in the colonial society could imagine a situation of "more autonomy" in which their group interests and grievances would be advantaged. Of course they could imagine also a situation of more autonomy in which they would be more severely disadvantaged than anything the metropole was likely to impose.

In particular the effect of the opportunity to create a representative body unique to or dominated by an interest group or an ethnicity is much like the effect of proportional representation on the structure of political parties (Duverger (1959 [1951]), pp. 206–54). It makes it possible for small parties to form on an ideologically pure basis, to represent a small interest, or to emphasize some institutional or ethnic connection, without perceiving that they are losing power by not being in a majority. Both revolution and proportional representation do so by decreasing the cost of "not winning" that the existence of an agreed-upon constitution imposes on minority parties, particularly in plurality systems, as I have outlined for proportional representation in my "Social Structure and Politics" (Stinchcombe (1975), pp. 560–69). That is, because in a revolution one does not know whether one's representative body could become the government, one does not know whether one would pay a heavy cost for sacrificing the marginal voters or the compromisers. This makes compromise less likely.

In French revolutions in the late 18th and 19th centuries the people in the middle tended to drop out of politics because the value of compromise was much reduced, and militants were not motivated to select compromisers as leaders in hope of gaining power. They might instead gain power by enthusiasm, dogmatism, and militant activity. People became more "revolutionary" in the ordinary sense during a revolution, much as they become more revolutionary when they can organize but are shut out of the legitimate channels for gaining political power (e.g., the German Social Democrats under Bismarck were shut out of power and less compromising than, say, the British Labour-Liberals); the reason is in both cases that they can gain no more political power by compromise than they can by purity of ideology, or defense of a minority, with no compromise.

The stability of an open constitution, especially one with plurality elections, then, produces a premium on political compromise. Revolution, isolation from political power, or proportional representation all reduce that premium on compromise, and so increase the tendency for extremists to be the best organized and most powerful.

But this in turn means that solidarity within groups has tended to grow during revolutions, and organizations devoted to the service of an ethnic group, an ideology, a class, or a race have tended to develop during revolutionary times, when the structure of representation is uncertain and potential governments in a dual power situation are competing to become the government.

Armies as Representative Bodies in the Revolution

Of course, in time of the Revolution, the rate of change of the representational structure and policies of the metropole and the colonies both changed rapidly. The bodies in competition under a regime of dual power, of uncertainty of jurisdiction, changed rapidly as well. In particular, armies with policies distinct from that of the authority that had created them tended to become more prominent as policymaking bodies, and all the geographical and epidemiological contingencies that determined the military situation of a given locality therefore changed the power environment of a particular interest or grievance.

In general in the West Indies the relative power of creole troops versus metropolitan troops changed with the seasons (rainy seasons increased the sickness rates among metropolitan troops much more than among creole troops). It also varied with time: the longer metropolitan troops were in the colony, the more of their troops were sick or dead from disease (up to about three years, when the troops that were left had become "seasoned").

In the early part of the Revolution, the metropolitan troops tended to have policies made exclusively by officers, and were often more conservative and pro-planter than the democratic metropolitan governing bodies. From about 1793 to 1801 the metropolitan troops tended to have policies made by political commissioners of the French legislative assemblies, often reinforced by more or less democratic bodies created within the military. In particular the corsairs (privateers), who were often the bulk of the French navy in the Caribbean, were considerably more left (and more creole) during this period than the navy was (or especially than the navy had been earlier). Corsairs were quite democratic on the ship, and the navy had had a particularly reactionary officer corps. In the Napoleonic period after 1801, the metropolitan military was considerably more conservative than the republican creole colored and black military that controlled Guadeloupe and Haiti.

When coalitions were made between creole planter military forces and regular troops (as in the English occupations of Martinique and southern Haiti), over time the relative influence of the creole officers tended to increase, in some cases leading to creole planters' switching sides or creating regions with autonomous creole policies.

When the coalition was between conservative metropolitan militaries and black troops, as between the Spanish and various blacks, including Toussaint L'Ouverture, in what is now The Dominican Republic [Santo Domingo], or later between the Bonapartist military and various black generals, including Pétion, Christophe, and Dessalines, a growing autonomy of the black forces tended to produce a switch to a more antislavery policy in regions controlled by the blacks, and eventually to a formal break with Napoleon.

When the coalition was between Republican metropolitan military forces and mulatto forces or black troops freed for the purpose, as on Guadeloupe with Victor Hugues or Haiti with Sonthonax, the greater "seasoning" of the creole black troops reduced the relative power and the discretion on questions of color and slavery politics of the white republican leaders, and increased black and colored influence on who got to make the decisions. For example, it was the readiness to compromise of the colored general Malgloire Pélage on reconquest Guadeloupe that enabled the Bonapartist troops to land at Pointe-à-Pitre, although the local civilian democratic bodies opposed it. It was the eventual willingness to revolt against Napoleonic rule by the black and colored generals of Haiti that prevented such a compromise holding up there.

The orderliness of this growth of the relative power of the policies defended by creole troops, and the new switches in policy often introduced by sending new troops from the metropole (especially sending republican troops around 1793–1794, and sending Napoleonic troops around 1801–1802), show that the dual power that has to be taken into account in the French colonies very often involved the competition between a representative body and a military body. The military bodies in the colonies as well as the representative bodies had an evolution over the course of the Revolution. In particular that evolution tended to make the military bodies more creole over time (except for new injections of metropolitan troops), and tended to make them more autonomous as policymaking or "legislative" bodies over the course of the Revolution.

To some degree all this theoretical observation does not help make sense of the details at particular historical times, because the people on the ground were nearly as confused and mystified about the political meaning of a particular move as we are. For example, the Haitian planters took a much harder line toward the free colored population early in the Revolution than did the Martinique planters, and this was one of the many factors that led it to be easier and more effective for planters to surrender Martinique than to surrender Haiti to the English occupations of 1794 and late 1793, respectively.[6]

But the point here is that the situation was sufficiently unclear to the participants that the same interest group in one colony went one way, in the other colony, the other way, on the same question of representation, and paid the respective differential costs at a later time. So part of what makes the theory no substitute for the historical detail is that revolution is a time of uncertainty about what any particular issue of representation or loyalty means, and consequently a theory of what people might rationally choose to do is not as much help in predicting what they will actually do, until one knows what *they* thought the situation was, not what we think it turned out to be with hindsight.

French Washingtons and Jeffersons

It is less of a mystery why the French Enlightenment reached Martinique than why it reached Virginia, but in both cases it reached planters with extensive experience of local representative institutions and of local armies and militias, and with an interest in cheap provisions by free trade with northern colonies. A gifted planter statesman, Louis-François Du Buc, led the assembly of Martinique to adopt (over several frustrating steps) the political equality of the free colored early in the Revolution. That is, colored people became formally equal to the whites; whites' representation became more democratic during the Revolution in France and in the colonies still controlled by France; before democracy in the sense of emancipation was clearly transmitted to the colonies, Du Buc was Governor on the English island of Martinique.

The American revolutionary coalition between Virginia planters who wanted cheaper provisions and New England bourgeois who wanted to

---

[6] It helped that the English invading force in Martinique was much larger, the defending force much smaller, and the island easier to control militarily. See Geggus (1982), and Chapter 2.

sell them started to be reproduced in Martinique, or rather in the ports of Martinique, between "Boston" ship captains and planters. In the United States that coalition was easier because there was an enlightenment wing of the planters and a secular wing of the Boston bourgeoisie; there was a similar relation in Martinique. Du Buc then played more or less the role of Washington for Martinique (except he welcomed the English in, rather than kicking them out, while Washington welcomed the French in, rather than kicking them out). At times the members of the enlightened oligarchy dominated by planters were called federalists in the Antilles, too, though these favored decentralization to the colonies rather than the strengthening of the colonial central government, as in the United States.

The planter-dominated assembly of Martinique tried to organize a combined conference of the Lesser (French) Antilles (then St. Lucia [Ste. Lucie], Tobago, Guadeloupe, and Martinique) to incorporate the colored on a uniform basis in 1791–1792 (Lémery (1936), p. 138). The committee report gave eligibility for officeholding to quadroons with three white grandparents, and gave the vote to mulattos (at that time this probably meant all people with color somewhere in the middle) born free. In contrast, the whites of Haiti [Saint Domingue] were completely uncooperative with the enfranchisement of the colored, maintaining that it would undermine slavery. There was not even a temporary coalition between planter assemblies and colored leaders in Haiti, and there was much less compromising tendency later among the colored of Haiti because they had not learned that whites could compromise.

But much more consistent than this very tentative attempt to incorporate wealthy colored people into the planter-dominated oligarchy was an enthusiastic assumption by the planters of the right to declare all the ports of an island to be open to foreign trade, and all nationalities of ships to be eligible to participate in that trade. There were no differences between Haiti and the Lesser Antilles on that question; nor was it necessary to construct complicated interisland committees to compromise on the question, as had been necessary on the suffrage of colored people.

Only on Martinique, where the most powerful merchants were in the Lesser Antilles monopoly port of St. Pierre, was there a serious conflict between the merchants interested in preserving their monopoly and the planters interested in freer trade. The argument of the St. Pierre merchants was that the opening of other ports meant that planters who owed them money could ship through other ports and escape immediate payment of debts secured by liens on the crops. Eventually St. Pierre merchants lined up with the merchants in other ports on Martinique and with the merchants of other islands to support the middle tendencies of the Revolution. But the first burst of activity was violent St. Pierre opposition to the enfranchisement of colored people and an attack on a colored militia company.

As France itself moved "leftward," and as the democratic principles started to be applied to the colonies, the representative institutions of the old regime were used by Martinique planters to mount a rebellion against the Revolution. In principle what happened on Martinique was that their analogy to the American Civil War broke out in the middle of their analogy to the American Revolution. Planters used their control over local representative institutions to mount a rebellion against a central government increasingly inclined to defend slaves, colored people, and poor whites. If one can imagine John C. Calhoun and Jefferson Davis being powers alongside Washington and Jefferson, and inviting the English back in rather than compromising on the Constitution in 1783, it might be a model for Martinique.

Anne Pérotin-Dumon gives evidence from Marie Galante, an island of Guadeloupe, in 1791, where thirty-nine out of fifty-nine members of a Jacobin club were planters ("*habitants*" meant planters, not inhabitants, on the islands at that time):

> But in contrast to the counterrevolutionary sugar planters, they are planters of coffee or of provisions. The patriots are not only merchants and lawyers. At Marie Galante the [59] Jacobins had [only] six lawyers and notaries, five shopkeepers, five merchants, the priest, and *l'instituteur de la jeunesse*. (Pérotin-Dumon (1985), p. 144)

And Moreau de Saint-Méry had already noted about Haiti that tobacco was compatible with a freer labor regime: "It was only and exactly at the time when tobacco was the principal and even the unique object of colonial commerce that [French] indentured workers were found appropriate for the same tasks as negroes" (quoted in Pérotin-Dumon (1985), p. 44). Thus the revolutionary reliability of Virginia planters may be due to the similarity of tobacco planting to the crops of Marie Galante planters, who were also more reliable revolutionaries.

While the analogy is a bit stretched, the central point is that the Revolution as it appeared in its later phases in the Antilles was partly analogous to the American Civil War. Earlier, the issue of the powers of representative institutions relative to the king had been at the center of the Revolution. The planters could be leaders of such a revolution even more than the nobility in the Estates General could be, for the representative institutions in the colonies were made up entirely of planters, rather than them being only one of the represented estates. As abolition of state-enforced monopolies became central to the revolution, the planters and merchants outside St. Pierre could combine against *l'exclusif*, the monopoly of French merchants and ships over trade with the Antilles. The merchants of St. Pierre were core beneficiaries of *l'exclusif*.

Only as the questions of emancipation and extension of the franchise, of liberty, equality, and fraternity, came to be central did the sugar planters take the same position as planters did in the United States when (much later) liberty, equality, and fraternity in the South came to be central in the American polity. By then, of course, cotton, which is much more similar in its organization of cultivation to sugar, had replaced tobacco in much of the American South. This replacement partly explains why John Calhoun was different from Thomas Jefferson. The processes by which the question of freedom of slaves, equality of the franchise, and fraternity with southern blacks came to be salient in the United States, were, of course, quite different from those in the French Revolution.

The planters in the different French colonies organized their rebellion against the Republic, their appeals to the British for military support, and their demands to the king for freedom of commerce in case of a restoration at slightly different times. The accidents of the military situation, the white Haitian indignation over the proposals for a colored franchise, the degree of mobilization of the colored and black population by the left all varied between the islands. The British arrived with enough troops to take Martinique shortly after the open rebellion of the planters was defeated by the republican general Rochambeau, and Rochambeau was not the sort to free and mobilize the slaves to fend off the second British invasion without metropolitan approval. Martinique was in the hands of the British by the time the French abolition of slavery could have got there, so there was never really a chance to mobilize Martinique blacks for the Republic. Martinique was well garrisoned by the British and the garrison well led, so that it could not be taken back by a democratic mobilizing invasion, as Guadeloupe was.

The result of this was that slavery was never abolished during the French Revolution in Martinique, that the colored population had memories of deals with the local oligarchy that contrasted favorably with their experience of the British rulers, and that planter power was reestablished without civil war on the island, to be confirmed by Napoleon.

Tobago and St. Lucia were conquered by the English without substantial difficulty, and remained English colonies. In Tobago a very small French population was essentially deported by the British. In St. Lucia French planters maintained some power in a government dominated by the British, but British planters also moved in. Census returns of slaves were, however, dominantly in a French dialect when the British started to conduct systematic counts so as to enforce the end of the slave trade. Sharecropping was still called *metayage* there toward the mid-19th century. These two islands, so to speak, dropped out of the system in which their history during the French Revolution had any meaning. People do not write many books on the revolutionary politics of these islands.

Revolutionary French Guadeloupe

In Guadeloupe the political position of the planters was weaker before the British conquest, and the support for the Revolution in both the city of Basse Terre (the official seat of government on the west side of Basse Terre island; the island is sometimes called *Guadeloupe proprement dit*) and Point-à-Pitre (the commercial center and main port, on Grande Terre across the Rivière Salée from Basse Terre) was more uniform than on Martinique. Marie-Galante throughout was more to the left than the other two islands, and this was partly a populist leftism of a commercial peasantry rather than sugar planters.

For example, when Captain Lacrosse, representing the Republic, with the task of imposing equal citizenship of the colored on the islands, conducted a propaganda campaign from St. Lucia [Ste. Lucie] asking for support, he was invited to become the governor of Guadeloupe in late 1792, before the Martinique Assembly invited him to become governor there.

But the crucial fact was that Guadeloupe (having been conquered in 1794, about the same time as Martinique, by the large British expedition) was taken back from the British by the Republicans, under the leadership of Victor Hugues. In the process, Hugues enforced the freeing of the slaves, the political equality of colored men, the mobilization of both blacks and colored people into the military, and the political dominance of commercial Point-à-Pitre over official Basse-Terre. Hugues built an economy to support the patriot government in part by organizing privateering, on which he collected a 10 or 15 percent tax (sources differ; see Bangou (1989), p. 98, for Hugues's budget revenue estimates, and also for the 15 percent rate). He also rented out the expropriated plantations and was not as dependent on planter-owners, or as exclusively dependent on maintaining sugar production. Hugues tried to organize revolutionary government-backed coercion for former slaves to continue to work on the plantations, at least to raise provisions, just as Toussaint L'Ouverture did in Haiti, and he seems to have had slightly better luck.

Thus the end result was the local enactment of French revolutionary principles under the formal authority of the French government, maintained throughout the period in which revolutionary Haiti claimed independence from France and organized to defend it, and a period when the British dominated the surrounding seas and the surrounding islands. Guadeloupe had to be reconquered by Napoleon to reimpose slavery. But Napoleon (and the British and Spanish) failed to conquer Haiti, so slavery was never reintroduced there.

The French Revolution in Non-French Islands

The French Revolution from the first challenged the legitimacy of royal governments, which included most of the governments that gave legitimacy to the authority of slave systems at the end of the 18th century (the Dutch government was only nominally royalist, being really a merchant oligarchy; the U.S. government was republican). By 1794 the Revolution specifically denied the legitimacy of slavery (and by 1802 it specifically did not). The shape of the challenge was specifically political, and aimed to abolish slavery by taking power in colonial societies. Further, where the later (post-1794) Revolution did take power (Guadeloupe and Haiti), it organized military and propaganda campaigns in nearby islands to undermine the slave system and the power of the empires that supported slavery (in Haiti far more consistently than in Guadeloupe—see Pérotin-Dumon (1988, 1989a, 1989b)).

Further the diaspora created by the Revolution in the Caribbean moved both pro-slavery and anti-slavery people to other islands; the anti-slavery immigrants were, of course, more disturbing to the planter governments elsewhere.

The challenge to the legitimacy of empires and slavery was most intense where there were large concentrations of French-speaking people, as in the formerly French islands of St. Lucia [Ste. Lucie], St. Vincent, Dominica, and perhaps Grenada, Tobago, and St. Croix (these had very small French settlements), in Trinidad because the Spanish had invited French planters, their slaves, and free colored in both before and during the Revolution, in Cuba, Jamaica, Puerto Rico, and the United States because Haitian refugees, mostly planters, came there in large numbers, and in Santo Domingo and Sint Maarten because they shared islands with a French colony.[7]

The challenge was also strong because the Revolution in France was mounted on top of commitments to institutions and ideas that the *ancien régime* had shared with other European empires, including especially the Enlightenment; the descendants of feudal representative in-

[7] The sources for the comments in the preceding paragraphs and the following comments are mainly the passages dealing with the period of the French Revolution in the general histories of various islands: Amelunxen (n.d.); Boin and Serrule Ramúe (1985 [1979]); Borde (1882); Breen (1844); Brereton (1981); Dietz (1986); Duffy (1987); Geggus (1982) for comments on Jamaica; Goslinga and van Yperen (1985); Hall (1983); Halperin Donghi (1969); Higman (1984) for French speaking by slaves and masters in English islands; Hoetink (1958); Marrero (1978; 9), pp. 140–53; Mentze (1966); Naipaul (1984 [1969]); M. G. Smith (1965a); Trouillot (1988); Welles (1928); Williams (1962). With rare exceptions, these are not specifically concerned with the variables into which I have organized the explanation of the penetration of the French Revolution here.

stitutions (*parlements*, estates general, cabinets and councils of the kings, multi-member courts or juries); property, contract, and equality before the civil law; a relatively free press and other institutions of public discussion; and the basic prohibition of slave and servile labor in the metropoles.

Many of the principles of the French Revolution had resonance with many of the principles of Protestantism and anti-clericalism. The sorts of principles that led Quakers eventually to exclude slaveowners from their congregations, the sorts that led to congregational church government, adult baptism, and other norms related to "freedom of conscience" and freedom of association, were close to some of the norms of the Revolution. There were powerful "Arminian" wings within many of the Protestant churches, rather like the humanism of the National Council of Churches nowadays, that had a large overlap of ideas with the Enlightenment.

The fear in the English islands of Quakers and Wesleyans had much of the same tone as their fear of propagandists from Guadeloupe or their fear of Dessalines applying coercion to rebellious whites. Although Calvinist Dutch and Nonconformist Liverpool merchants engaged in the slave trade, they did not organize themselves as a slave society should, and many of their friends and relatives were in anti-slavery organizations.

How deep the structural similarity of orientation between the Revolution and other empires was is perhaps measured by the fact that Pitt led the House of Commons to vote to abolish the slave trade in 1792 (it was stopped in the House of Lords), and the Danish king forbade participation of Danes in the trade in 1803. None of the 1790s ideological and political tendencies other than the French Revolution freed very many slaves, but the same conflicts over slavery that got great political force in the middle of the French Revolution had "milder" forms in the other empires. Anti-slavery was no doubt stronger in the metropole in England, but because the empire government was constructed differently than the revolutionary French one, it was weaker in the colonies.

Those milder analogous forms were stronger in colonies where there were French minorities (or in St. Lucia and Dominica, majorities) or French republican armies or navies, where the Enlightenment had more followers, where the Nonconformist wing of the Protestant Reformation was better organized and more numerous, where the populist version of representative institutions had more legitimacy, and, perhaps, where there were fewer slaves. They were perhaps strongest where there were free colored majorities, especially in Isla Margarita and Cumaná in Venezuela.

Those same places created more trouble by the importation of French ideas and institutional proposals on other islands during the latter part of the French Revolution, and more fear and loathing among the planters and their military and political organizations and among the conservative military and bureaucratic representatives of the empires. The conservatives could hardly wait for wars against republican France to start before accusing democratic movements on their own islands of treason.

The French Revolution as the Beginning of the 19th Century

As the American and French revolutions marked the beginning of the 19th century in European politics, so the French revolution in the Caribbean, especially in its Haitian and Guadeloupe versions, opened the 19th century in the Caribbean. After 1794 the questions of slave emancipation, universal (male) suffrage, and democratic local autonomy were explicitly there, if often in the background. Planters had their *bête noir* in Toussaint L'Ouverture; and a white *bête* in Victor Hugues; the white one was a beast because he had black and colored allies, emancipated slaves, and black armies and corsairs. The radical left from that time forward had a vaguely French tone on many islands (the main exceptions are the English ones other than Trinidad and the Windwards). After World War II until the Cuban Revolution, most of the Caribbean communists probably spoke French.

Simón Bolívar took refuge and sought support in Haiti rather than in any of the Spanish Caribbean colonies, and his favoring of emancipation of slaves in Venezuela is sometimes interpreted as recruiting of powerful colored leaders in Margarita and Cumaná (Halperin Donghi (1969), pp. 100, 120), sometimes as part of a bargain in return for Haitian support. In any case his policy on slavery looked very different from any autonomist movement before 1789. The nightmares of planters, other than the British ones, had a French tone in the 19th century.

We see in the French Revolution that the question of how far the empire was to be the same system in the colonies as in the democratic metropole was to be a matter for decision, for political movements, in the 19th century. The central racial, citizenship, and class issues that came up in the other islands came up first in the French colonies, and one knew what two different left versions of the democratic solution, Guadeloupe and Haiti, had looked like.

The central novelty of the French Revolution for the Caribbean, then, was that the *empire* government imposed democracy, including emancipation, on two islands against the will of the planters (and would have imposed it on Martinique if the British had not got there and stayed there). The *empire* mobilized slaves and colored people into armies to defend liberty, equality, and fraternity, and got them into representative bodies to decide on the political aspects of that defense. We see for the first time on the French islands the alignment of the issues of emancipation, suffrage, class, freedom to hold peasant farms, and race equality into a single right-left division on the islands.

On the English and Spanish islands in the 19th century, those who wanted to stay in the empire were pretty uniformly on the right on a quite similar dimension. In British and Spanish colonies being for the empire was being against democracy in the colonies. The French Revolution established a different possibility in the French islands, that the empire could be democratic, could liberate black and colored people, defend the class interests of workers, and receive the communist deputies from Guadeloupe and Martinique. Of course it established the Napoleonic empire as an alternative as well, which implied that the only way to defend the interests of slaves, blacks, workers was a leftist revolution against the empire. The only sugar islands that are still with their 18th century empire are Martinique and Guadeloupe. We make the argument here that this is an outcome of the French Revolution.

But the possibility that Haitian ex-slaves, and so perhaps others, could mount a revolution, beat off English, Spanish, and French invasions as well as the planter government, bring emancipation of slaves to a Spanish colony by force of arms more than once, and substitute peasant cultivation for sugar plantations also was established by the French Revolution. The organization of the empires into a world system to isolate this revolution was a central feature of the early 19th century. The slave states of the United States, from Jefferson's presidency on, supported in this project of isolation. Cuba is not the first Caribbean revolution the United States has isolated from the world, and there was no Soviet Union to help the revolutionary colony (as there is no longer for Cuba, in 1995). So from the Napoleonic restoration on, the history of Haiti and its relation to empire can no longer be treated together with the histories of Guadeloupe and Martinique. We continue inside the empire here, and leave Haiti's distinctive revolutionary experience and its independence and isolation for Chapter 9.

1830, 1848, and 1870 as Gradual Approaches to 1794

The July Monarchy of 1830–1848 introduced something that would have been called "amelioration" in the British islands: political equality for the free colored, easier manumission (temporarily delayed by an attempt at nullification by the island legislatures, who said that the monarchy did not have jurisdiction over emancipation), census of slaves so that those not counted were presumed free, the doctrine that French soil frees slaves, and open discussion of general emancipation with a general tone of "inevitability." In general the pro-black commissions were peopled by "republicans."[8]

In 1848 the slaves were freed and politically enfranchised, and in 1851 the restoration took away political rights, leaving the ex-slaves with much the same situation, "free but not politically enfranchised," as obtained in the older British islands after their emancipation in the early 1830s. Until the next revolution, the autonomous local political system was determined to return them to as near to slave labor relations as could be managed without ownership of the person.

In the early 1870s universal male suffrage was introduced again, putting the legal situation back to where it had been in 1794, but the planter counterattacks from 1870 to 1900 were much more moderate than those of a century earlier.

The older colonies (this phrase usually refers to Martinique, Guadeloupe, and Réunion, but sometimes includes French Guyanne [or Cayenne] and sometimes Corsica, i.e., excluding Algeria, Indochina, and black African colonies) from 1870 to 1900 had a legal situation such that they were equal parts of France "constitutionally"; they participated equally in making laws for France as a whole. But the laws passed in the French parliament did not apply automatically to the colonies, because "local conditions" were different. The main local condition was the financial health of the sugar industry, especially as determined by labor relations and the security of capital in all three islands.

Victor Schoelcher, one of the two deputies elected from Martinique in 1871 (he was elected in three different electoral districts, and chose to be Martinique's representative rather than one of the others), was born in France and active in French politics and had been the chief actor in a commission that had recommended general emancipation just before 1848. It is characteristic that a main hero of the free colored (blacks had the franchise but in general did not vote at the time) on Martinique should be a white French republican political activist of a relatively sober and moderate sort, who had made his lifework the amelioration and abolition of slavery by parliamentary and administrative action in the metropole.

The general problem of popular leaders on the islands was that they could not win in the island political system with popular support alone: the planters were too powerful. By 1851 suffrage had been taken away twice and emancipation once in Guadeloupe, and suffrage once in Martinique (suffrage and emancipation had not been granted during the

---

[8] Martineau and May (1935) have convenient chronologies: for the metropole, pp. 97–106 and 108–15; for Martinique, pp. 169–73; for Guadeloupe, pp. 214–28.

Revolution on Martinique); blacks lacked political organization and education; trade unions were not organized and legitimate; and the governor, who administered elections, was a friend of the planters. Experience
had shown that one could not win island political power without "republican" support in the metropole.[9]

Of course experience had shown the same thing on the English islands without showing that island black and colored forces could mobilize metropolitan support, except perhaps for the brief period of
dominance of "the town party" mobilizing the Colonial Office liberals
in Jamaica (Holt (1992), pp. 214–61). In England the Whigs tended to
be radical with respect to slaves but conservative with respect to the proletariat; in France a wing of the revolutionary tradition was radical with
respect to the proletariat and could be persuaded to be radical with respect to slaves.

It was, then, a unique feature of French island politics that a deputy
of one of the islands to the French parliament could be a symbol of black
and colored emancipation and political enfranchisement. No blacks or
colored people in the British islands mobilized to get William Wilberforce, the anti-slavery British Member of Parliament, elected. But it was
also a feature of the period of 1790–1900 that the only time such a symbol could be created was when the republicans, the heirs of the French
Revolution, were in power in France. Always otherwise the fact that the
laws of France did not apply automatically in the colonies meant that in
practice that planters ruled the local system, since they produced the
"special" laws. Popularity among the free colored (and at least indiffer-
ence among the now free blacks) therefore did not translate into the
capacity to govern as long as the laws of the islands were "special," and
the applications of French laws to the colonies were made in a special
council that whites (though not entirely local whites) dominated.

Thus the construction of a channel between local black and free colored populations and the metropole depended first on the capacity to
create local power in an environment heavily (but not monopolistically)
controlled by local creole whites, with planters generally dominant but
not as dominant as on the British islands. But, and this is the crucial point here, it also depended on connecting that local mobilization
to republican centers of power in the metropole that were willing to defend the most elementary bases of mobilizing local power and translat-
ing it into power in the imperial political system. Only the metropole
could, given sufficient left power, defend some island freedom of speech
and organization, universal suffrage, trade union recognition, eligibility

[9] See generally for Guadeloupe, Bangou (1987a [1962];1), pp. 187–205, and (1987b
[1962];2), pp. 2–119 in the 1962 edition; for Martinique, Constant (1988), pp. 15–66.
The legal history is in Alcindor (1899), pp. 92–109.

for office, limitation of force and fraud in elections, and power in the governing coalition for the deputies when they got to the French parliament.

Such channels could then carry, as well as "constitutional" defense of republican power in the colonies, grievances from the workers and peasants of the islands to the metropole and remedies back to the islands. Except in Haiti and (oddly) in St. Croix in the Danish Virgin Islands (Hall (1984)), Caribbean black and colored organs of power had never won in the face of failure of political support in the metropole, and even the Haitian and St. Croix movements were at some times near failure.

The metropolitan restorations of 1802 and 1851 that restored, respectively, slavery and black exclusion from suffrage on the islands (thus destroying the effectiveness of the island end of the channel) and repressed activities of island republican and socialist allies in France made it clear that the interests of the colonial lower classes were aligned with the left in French politics. But they also created a combined symbolic and real channel within the imperial system for processing the grievances of the colonial lower classes. We need to explore the nature of that link, for it eventually resulted in the colonial communist parties' leading a nearly unanimous political coalition in 1946 to apply for incorporation into France as departments with the same legal status as other departments. In particular the movement wanted to produce an incorporation such that the laws of France, including those of political representation, rights of organization, and forms of local government, would apply without special approvals to the islands.

Becoming a Part of the Metropole as an Anti-Colonial Position

In 1881 the colored deputy from Martinique, Ernest Deproge, gave an address at Lamentin (the one in Martinique), saying that after the Revolution of 1848,

> the empire . . . wiped out our political liberty and all possibility of intervening directly in the regulation of our affairs. (Constant (1988), pp. 32–33)

The generation of 1870 had formulated its hopes as follows:

> We want to transform the fictions into realities; we want to be equal to all other Frenchmen. Thus our first care and attention was to ask to move into all the duties of citizens of the metropole. We did not want to be exempted from the duties of justice; we asked obstinately for jury duty. We did not want to benefit from any privilege, any exemption. But we wanted also all the rights,

all the privileges, of other citizens. We resemble them in every particular. . . .
In the French *patrie*, we do not want to be inferior to anyone. (Ibid.)

Here the republican colored left is claiming democracy on Martinique
by way of asking to be equal to other French citizens of the Republic.
We note that the dates 1848 and 1870 are the dates of republican revolutions that extended both liberty and the vote to colored and black men
on Martinique.

These republican movements of France also extended secular state
schooling to the masses, and the same claim was extended by the colored left to the islands on the instance of the colored left deputies,
Hurard and Deproge. But a governor of the day, Bruot, was of a more
traditional opinion:

> The schools should not take on an extensiveness prejudicial to the develop-
> ment of agriculture. It is to be feared that having received only an imperfect
> instruction that will not even qualify them to become white collar workers in
> the administration or in commerce, children who have attended schools will
> develop a distaste for work on the land. . . . I have tried hard to make the
> masses understand that it is to their best-defended interest to abstain com-
> pletely from political conflicts in order to occupy themselves more completely
> with their work and their welfare. (Constant (1988), pp. 44–45n)

Whenever republicanism was precarious in the metropole, it was difficult for local black and colored leaders to imagine the metropole sustaining leftward movements in the government of the islands in any systematic way. The established wisdom was that the islands had different
laws. Such special laws for the colonies might be passed in the French
parliament, but they were passed as a different issue than the laws governing France, with different relations to local government and to metropolitan French naval and colonial administration. This meant that left
local political success translated directly into influence in national
French politics, but only indirectly and with difficulty into influence in
island politics.

As the Third Republic consolidated republican institutions in France
during the last quarter of the 19th century, the problem of the republicans and socialists in the islands turned from one of representing the
values of the Republic in the political system of the island to representing the islands' interests in the continuation of the Republic in the metropole. Their problem was much like that of civil rights leaders in the
United States in the 1960s to 1980s: supporting the left in Congress
and the presidency to try to pass civil rights laws, and also trying to turn
the civil rights laws into an implemented reality by financing and giving
legal powers to civil rights commissions, equal opportunity commissions, special federal voting rights marshals, and the like. The first prob-

lem was to get emancipatory legislation of various kinds passed in France; the second, and more difficult, was to get it implemented on the islands.

Socialists for the Imperial Tie

By 1910 two candidates for the office of parliamentary deputy from Martinique, one of the "radical socialists" (Victor Sévère) and one of the "socialists" (Joseph Lagrosillière) signed an electoral pact called *L'Entente Républicaine*. The joint platform included the following statement:

> The *entente* ought henceforth to work toward the amelioration of the fate of all categories of workers of our colony, toward the consolidation and perfecting of our democratic institutions, and to the assimilation of the old colonies to the metropolitan *départements*, toward the realization of all that can elevate us and make us better. (Constant (1988), pp. 50–51)

Both were elected, and then fell out. But what is striking is the close conjunction of the proposals to forward workers' grievances and interests, and to work for making the colonies into departments of France, like the departments on the mainland. This is something like statehood for Hawaii (a plantation colony that never had slavery), except that the French legal and political system is much more centralized than the American one. Legrosillière was one of two authors (with Boisneuf) of a proposed law in 1915 asking for the extension of departmental organization to the old colonies (Bangou (1987b [1962]), vol. 2, p. 242 of the 1962 edition).

The socialist party of Lagrosillière split in 1919, when he proposed to create "an alliance between capital and labor," and the "Friends of Juarès" who left became the embryo of the Communist party (Constant (1988), p. 54). But to some degree they carried with them the conception that socialism against capital (rather than allied with it) was still to be defended by defending it in France (ibid., p. 65).

The workers' movement was also interpreted by its opponents as an imitation of France. For example, the journal *Les Antilles* wrote of the strikes between 1882 and 1900,

> [S]trikes in such a small country! Is it not ridiculous at the same time as it is disturbing? . . . Why, then? To do like the others, beyond the waves of the Atlantic, to walk in the wandering footsteps of other strikers in France . . . to associate themselves with their disastrous progress, to affirm like they do and just as ridiculously as they do the rights of man, of the citizen, of the worker, of the proletarian.

Legitimus, the first socialist elected to the French parliament from Guadeloupe, was elected to the General Council of the island in 1894, and then to the national parliament in 1898. Bangou calls his party the party of blacks, as opposed to the (Republican and Radical) colored parties (Bangou (1987b [1962]), vol. 2, p. 183 of the 1962 edition). In 1894 collective bargaining with arbitration or mediation by the governor took place between sugar workers and the sugar factory heads, and between the small sugar growers and those same factory heads (ibid., pp. 179–80 of the 1962 edition). After 1910 the discretion of local governors to register or promulgate French labor law in the colonies led to local movements to get them to do so, which gave an *assimilationiste* character to many of the local agitations of the socialists and communists and to the trade unions (Blerald (1986), pp. 126–27; also see Elisabeth (1972), p. 170).

After 1917 the social-democratic wing of the socialist movement was favorable to a partial assimilation to the status of a department (leaving financial control of the colony's local expenditures to the local legislature), while the communist wing favored full assimilation, with the fear that otherwise the local planters would have too much power. The radicalization of the 1930s and especially of World War II legitimated the communist movement, and de Gaulle's incorporation of the communists (temporarily) into his government and his support for full assimilation legitimated the essentially full equality of the *departements d'outre mer* to the *departements* of continental France.

To Be a Patriot in the Tropics

Anne Pérotin-Dumon's wonderful book on the Revolution in Guadeloupe has a title, *Être patriote sous les tropiques* (1985), that would not make sense in the British or Spanish islands or in the United States. What "patriot" means in the title is to be a French revolutionary supporting a revolutionary government or movement in France. Thus the title says as much about the public it was addressed to in Guadeloupe or Martinique in the 1980s as it does about the Revolution of 1789. In the United States or Britain to be patriotic usually means to have an authoritarian view of colonial policy. The word calls up the vision of a retired colonel in a pub complaining about how we let India go, and now all the wogs are pushing us around. Patriotism in the other large metropoles of Caribbean colonies means a more or less unreflecting loyalty, praise of things as they are (except that taxes are too high), and rejection of the right of protest of the oppressed because it undermines the national community. In France there is a version of patriotism that is emancipatory abroad as well as at home.

It is not that the normative systems by which the other empires define their national essence do not have generous emancipatory implications for colonies. North American radicals such as Mark Twain could write wonderful anti-imperialist diatribes that were distinctively part of an American tradition, but no one would think of calling them patriotic pamphlets. Wilberforce was after all an important British politician as well as an anti-slavery agitator, though the colonel in the pub would hardly recognize him as a patriotic hero. The same "Enlightenment" aspects of the normative tradition that led to expansion of citizenship and welfare rights within the country could also lead to defense of expansion of the rights of colonial populations.

"Reconstruction" for the American South was not so different from the periodic French revolutionary outbursts of concern for the position of blacks and colored people in the islands. The 20th century location of black people's hope for reform in the federal government and their solid support for whatever they thought was the left on the national scene had some similarities to the identification of the island left with the French left in Martinique and Guadeloupe, and was similarly partly a consequence of Reconstruction and similar movements in the "progressive" North.

But like the British islands, the American South had a tradition of local laws' being made by local legislatures. In the 19th century, American constitutional interpretation and congressional tradition left suffrage, union organization, schooling (or rather lack of schooling), and welfare in the hands of local legislatures. In the South that very often meant in the hands of planters, especially where the decentralized tradition left much of the state's jurisdiction in the hands of county and municipal governments. So the difficulty of emancipatory national movements' penetrating into black belt county governments in the American South was generally similar to the difficulty of the British anti-colonial left's penetrating Jamaica or Trinidad.

The tradition that local governments could routinely follow policies that were contrary to national policy, in contrast, was not characteristic of the Third Republic in the last three decades of the 19th century. The autonomy of the colonies from the national government was an anomaly in French government. The autonomy of the South was much more the way things always were, *except* for Reconstruction, in the U.S. government.

But a crucial aspect of French centralization was applied to the colonies in the constitution of 1870: suffrage for national politics was universal male suffrage. Further, the nationalization of representation in parliament, and the reliably republican character of the colonies, gave colonial working-class grievances access to the metropolitan press. French black grievances went somewhere else besides the Rockefeller Foundation, where they went in the United States.

And another aspect, mass elementary education and secondary education open on the basis of talent and earlier school success, was vigorously pursued in the colonies as well as the metropole by the relevant ministry. The education ministry was quite used to having to fight local right-wing and populist forces in order to administer national republican educational policy, because it had to fight Catholic claims to control education in many areas of France. Being welcomed by the population, if not by the upper class, made the colonies already a more propitious environment for a republican education ministry than much of France.

On the British islands, then, both independence and effective representation in the British political system seemed impossible, especially after local autonomy was given up for crown colony status just as the black and colored electorate became likely to win. There was then no particular reason not to go for broke, and for left movements to favor independence.

In the French islands defense of worker and black rights in the French political system did not seem impossible, though there, too, there was a wing of the island left that thought that autonomy would make *real* socialism possible on the islands. But it was not simply foolish on the French islands, the way in was on the British ones, to be a left patriot in the tropics.

9

The French Revolution in Haiti and Haitian Isolation in the 19th Century World System

> In the Haitian revolution, the men of color won
> and were able to enjoy their independence; in our
> [United States] Civil War, they were freed but
> they had to go on living with their ruined masters.
> (Edmund Wilson)

Revolutionary Autonomy, then Revolutionary Independence, in Haiti

Haiti [Saint Domingue to 1802] had three major regions that were partly politically and militarily autonomous during the Revolution, and that had different histories. The north, near Cap Haïtien [Cap de France], was the earliest densely settled and earliest devoted to sugar, largely because its agricultural plain could support rain-fed sugar cultivation. The earlier settlement and the history of being the core of French government and French monopoly commerce produced a better-organized sugar industry (e.g., more of its sugar was white sugar), more of a creole planter culture and more resident planter families, and more governmental experience in the north. It was somewhat militarily vulnerable to the relatively large internal valley of the northern Dominican Republic around Santiago, which in turn meant that Santiago was vulnerable to it. It was also militarily fairly easily accessible from the Artibonite valley in the northern part of the western region, which became quite densely settled. The northern region produced roughly two-fifths of the sugar of Haiti by the beginning of the Revolution, a bit less tonnage than but equal in value to that of the western region.

The western province had been more recently settled by sugar planters at the time of the Revolution, probably largely because it was semi-arid and required irrigation for successful sugar cultivation. It had two main producing regions, a northern one dominated by the valley of the Artibonite and Ester (the mouth of the Ester is at Gonaïves, where

Toussaint L'Ouverture[1] had his main base for much of the Revolution; that of the Artibonite is between Gonaïves and St. Marc), and a southern one in the Cul de Sac region near Port au Prince. Both these subregions were fairly militarily accessible from the southern part of the Dominican Republic, and of course vice versa.

The western region had more of a frontier spirit, fewer women, a more African slave population, and a lower level of governmental organization. It also produced about two-fifths of the sugar exported by the beginning of the Revolution, with its slightly larger tonnage being compensated for by a lower level of refinement (more brown, less white).

The southern province produced roughly a fifth of the sugar exported, in pockets around the coast. The whole region was more mountainous and more lightly governed, and had a larger concentration of smaller coffee plantations in the mountains, largely run by white proprietors in the western tip and colored proprietors elsewhere (Geggus (1982), pp. 235–36, and *passim* to p. 240). Its bays, coves, and harbors were more accessible to contraband trade from Jamaica, and were more vulnerable to any military force that controlled the mountains, as the colored troops of Rigaud did during the early part of the Revolution. Both during the Revolution and in the immediate post-revolutionary period the southern region often had an independent army, usually dominated by free colored.

The southern small town and productive areas were also relatively easily conquered by the English during their invasion, because each had a small hinterland to mobilize, even compared to the small forces the English brought to bear. In general the mountainous terrain and the low amount of resources one got when one dominated any particular valley made the area relatively invulnerable to conquest as a whole from the western region around Port au Prince. There was a relatively long southern tradition of successful rebellion (e.g., against *l'exclusif*), and in quite a few of the small concentrations of population the relations between white and free colored had been relatively egalitarian for a long time.

[1] The last name L'Ouverture was adopted when Toussaint was adult, already a general in the revolutionary army, and bears no relation to the name of his father, of his owner, or of the plantation. Toussaint is the name of November 1 in the French ecclesiastical calendar, and may have been his birthday, as he and apparently his family were serious Catholics. The name of one's father had no legal consequences for slaves in St. Domingue (now Haiti), so slaves known by French names, such as Toussaint, presumably had no need of surnames denoting their fathers, and his father himself had no surname. Some of the Haitian black revolutionary generals were apparently commonly known by a "given name" and a "surname" (e.g., Christophe and Pétion), and some were not (e.g., Dessalines and Toussaint); this may be related to whether they were free before the Revolution. Given names or surnames in the index are therefore sometimes not ones the people would have recognized as children.

Probably there was a higher ratio of peasant to plantation production in this region than in other regions, and more mountain and foothill crops rather than sugar among the plantations, which might partly explain the more peaceful race relations in parts of it.

Geggus's map titled "Approximate distribution of forces in Saint Domingue, 28 April 1794" (Geggus (1982), p. 115), in which areas controlled by the republicans, the Spanish, the British, and "indeterminate" are outlined, shows the complexity created for the Revolution by this regional differentiation. The fact that Geggus has to specify a single date rather than a month or a year indicates how indeterminate it was which government controlled a given area, so whose representative institutions one ought to have been oriented to in that area. Each of these governments with shifting territories in their turn had shifting political structures and shifting balances of power among the elements of those structures; for example, in the south at that time, "republican" meant a colored army under Rigaud, while in the west and north it meant a largely black army under Toussaint L'Ouverture.

The main events in the chronology of the Revolution in Haiti and its immediate aftermath are included in the chronology in the previous chapter. In the long run the army commanded by Toussaint, then by Dessalines, and civilian representative bodies created by it, won control over all of Haiti. Toussaint represented slaves, if necessary in opposition to free colored, represented Jacobins rather than anyone further right when they came into conflict, represented the Haitian balance of power among the factions and armies rather than the one in the metropole, represented the republican army whenever it was in conflict with civilian authority, represented racial compromise between black and colored and (with black dominance) between black and white, and represented the maintenance of sugar production and export in a modified plantation system (roughly what we might call producer's cooperatives, or perhaps better, "War Communism") rather than the creation of a small-holding peasantry. Or more briefly, he represented the compromising branch of the Jacobin and pro-black Haitian left.

However, by the time Toussaint made peace with the Napoleonic army and then was betrayed into prison by it, he and his (various) allies had already defeated the planters and the first revolutionary local government (which rejected freedom for the slaves), the British, the Spanish, and the colored southern army. Much of the time after independence his government (or army) and its successors controlled Santo Domingo as well (Haiti was apparently the Indian name for the island as a whole, and at any rate the Haitian government for a long time claimed to be a successor to France's claim based on the 1795 Treaty of Basel, in which Spain ceded its part to France).

By the time Haiti was independent, Dessalines had succeeded Toussaint. By then almost all of the factions had killed large numbers of prisoners of the other factions, the three racial groups (white, colored, and black) had killed masses of innocent people of the other racial groups, and each of the four invading metropoles (Britain, Spain, republican and Bonapartist France) had killed a great many residents of Haiti who would otherwise (if Haiti had been recognized as a nation) have been recognized as prisoners of war. War is a nasty business and corrupts morals always, and civil wars are nastier than wars between nations, but the wars of the Haitian revolution were among the nastiest of the 18th century.

Mass killings of rebels have always been characteristic of slave societies, and the self-righteousness of planters who talk about the gentle government of England and the horrors of French revolutionaries, or about wild slaves burning cane, a few pages away from describing a heroic genocide by British troops of whole communities of rebels, including women and children (a particularly obnoxious example is Shepard (1831)), are enough to make a decent person sick to the stomach.

But the way political culture was organized into fighting groups, each trying to impose its institutions in a system of dual (or multiple) power, in the Haitian revolution exaggerated such tendencies, generalized the morality of planters to the contending races and elicited the planter morality rather than the rules of war in the contending conservative invaders. And the longer the revolution went on (this one lasted from about 1790 to 1802), the more each faction learned and justified the tactics of terror by the behavior of its opponents. It was the same Trotsky who wrote about the structure of dual power in revolutions who wrote *Their Morals and Ours* (1973 [1939]), justifying the use of terror by the Bolsheviks because the Russian right wing used terror on a massive scale. Haitian revolutionaries less often wrote books.

In such circumstances it is difficult to keep one's own morals straight when writing about it. I probably should say at this point that, on net balance, I think the Haitian revolution contributed more to human happiness, by destroying slavery and eliminating racist planter power from building oppressive institutions of post-emancipation society, than it destroyed by provoking massive terror of each against all and isolating Haitian society from the good parts of the international system (there was not all that much civilization in western civilization's international system in the 18th and 19th centuries) for fifty-odd years. But I often despise the actions, sometimes even the people, who made that contribution to human welfare.

Besides its effects on Haiti itself, the success of the Haitian Revolution threw into relief the relationship between the international system and slavery. The same international system that eventually abolished the slave trade, then even slavery itself on each empire's own islands, also isolated Haiti from the diplomatic system. The United States, after being quite encouraging to the Haitian revolution in its first years,[2] refused to recognize the new Haitian government until after the Emancipation Proclamation in 1862, for example. The translation of the class, race, and democratic revolution in Haiti into an issue for the politics of the world system, for diplomatic reactionary activity, was clearly partly an outgrowth of the revolution itself, for the blacks had to defeat English, Spanish, and French invading armies in order to establish a society without slavery. They never had to defeat the United States, yet the United States took up the fight of imperial Europe to isolate the Haitian revolution.

The Political Sociology of Diplomacy

My purpose in this chapter, then, is to develop the theory of the sociology of diplomacy so that it can be useful for explaining the diplomatic isolation of Haiti for the first two-thirds of the 19th century. Independence won by warfare is after all a distinctive relation to one's empire, and, as it turned out, to other empires as well. The independence of the United States did not produce isolation because of a remarkably generous set of treaty provisions, including early recognition, by England (apparently largely to destroy the American alliance with the French).

But Haiti was unrecognized by the United States, and by the South American countries, although Haiti had aided their revolutions. The United States campaigned against invitation of Haiti to a Pan-American conference of newly independent Spanish colonies with the United States, and those states went along with their new friend. Haiti was unrecognized by the European powers until the 1830s.

The French Revolution, more or less against the will of the Revolution in the metropole, established a black revolution in Haiti that eventually led to Haitian independence. That black revolution was never defeated on the island in the 19th century by anything except Haitian rebellions. It had a strong form of factual independence, being able to defeat all contenders for power on the island. Haitian rebellions and civil wars did, at various times, establish regional governments in separate parts of Haiti, and eventually (1844) a separate independent govern-

---

[2] It was clear that a revolutionary government would not maintain the *exclusif* that gave a monopoly over trade with Haiti to French merchants, which I suppose was the core consideration for U.S. non-slave states.

ment was stably established in the Dominican Republic, replacing the
previous Haitian government of that part of the island.

What unified the foreign policy of the various governments of Haiti
and its parts from Toussaint through the U.S. Emancipation Proclamation was a class issue, the abolition of (and the opposition to reintroduction of) slavery. That class issue was at the same time a race issue
(though colored and black Haitian governments and factions were unified on it) and an international issue; the Haitians saw the international
scene as through a class darkly. The lines of class, race, slavery, and black
suffrage (though by and large black political participation in the Haitian
government should be called "suffrage" by analogy only) were drawn in
the world system, between Haiti and the rest of the Caribbean and its
imperial governors, by the Haitian Revolution.

The central question of this chapter, then, is why diverse empires,
many of them with a substantial democratic tradition and some with a
solid revolutionary tradition, were swept up into a reactionary diplomatic alliance against a black revolutionary republic. In the Realpolitik
of an unconquerable black class–revolutionary government, the outcome of the political process in Europe was non-recognition until the
1830s, and in the United States and South America, non-recognition
until the 1860s. The European imperial governments made their peace
earlier than the north and South American revolutionary ones, and that
needs to be explained.'

To understand this, we need a sociology of the politics of foreign policy in the 19th century, to see how the political definition of the place of
Haiti in the world system could be so far from the military and governmental reality. The democratic and emancipatory elements in the traditions of both the American and the European powers might have given
them sympathy for the same elements in Haiti. One might think that the
problems of Realpolitik of empires who could not defeat Haiti in the
Caribbean would lead to recognition. Our problem is to explain why
this did not happen, why reactionary forces dominated the Caribbean
diplomacy of the core members of the world system.

The sociology of diplomacy here has to be about the question of what
determined what sort of object Haiti's government and policies were in
the political universe of the imperial countries. Our central argument
will be that this is not a single question, but two different questions. The
first question is the relation of the Haiti and its policies *as a symbol in the
domestic politics* of the imperial countries, which governed what happened to it among people who did not care about that country as a reality. The second question has to do with the experience of various groups
to whom the reality of Haiti was very salient, for example, the experience

of Josephine, Napoleon's wife, who was born into a family with plantation interests in and contacts with Haiti and Martinique.

Thus, for example, the place of Haiti in the American political cosmos was dominated by those who could not care less about Haiti as a reality, and who located it as a symbol in the light of their relation to it *as a symbol of slave revolt* (rather than, e.g., as a symbol of anti-imperial revolution, as the South American revolutions of the 1810s and 1820s and the Irish revolution of the 1920s became). That it should be Jefferson as a hero of anti-imperial revolution but a slaveowner who first excluded Haiti diplomatically, and Lincoln, right after the Emancipation Proclamation, who first recognized it, is indicative of this core symbolic role of Haiti. Neither Jefferson nor Lincoln was benefited or endangered by Haiti, nor did they belong to groups with extensive experience with Haiti. In fact, most Americans with experience with Haiti were New England shipowners, not slaveowners.

In contrast in England, France, and Spain there were small but powerful groups who had experienced Haiti as a threat to slavery in Jamaica or Martinique, or as a particularly difficult part of the military problem of French-English imperial rivalry, or as a source of irritating if unimportant problems in the government of the Spanish part of the island and the possibility that those problems might bring the South American anti-imperial revolution to the Caribbean (the Spanish were actually worried about Cuba, not the Spanish part of Hispaniola, the island that Haiti and The Dominican Republic now occupy).

The possibility of reimposing slavery in Haiti had disappeared by the 1830s, the English were (sort of) abolishing slavery in Jamaica and the English islands, and British-French imperial rivalry had moved to the Indian Ocean. Non-recognition in the 1830s, then, failed to serve the concrete interests and salient colonial and military worldviews in English, French, and Spanish internal politics that it had served in the early part of the century. There was no appreciable pro-slavery voice in European domestic politics, so Haiti was not incorporated into the symbolic system of domestic conflicts by slaveowners, as happened in the United States. The British Wesleyans at the core of the anti-slavery movement in England, for example, would hardly take the deeply Catholic Toussaint or the anti-white and anti-colored terrorist Dessalines as their anti-slavery hero, and no British landlord in England (in Ireland the revolutionists were free white peasants) was threatened by a revolution like that in Haiti. Haiti then became a "merely diplomatic" problem in Europe in the 1830s, and Realpolitik could then determine the outcome.

There are, then, two dimensions of political sociology we have to analyze. The first is the place of a country (here, Haiti) and its policies in the symbol system of domestic politics among those who do not care about the foreign reality. The second is the place in the empire or metropolitan national political system of those who have had extensive and salient contacts with, and often interests in, the foreign political reality. It is such a combination, different in different countries, that determined, for example, the differences in the starting and ending dates of Haiti's diplomatic isolation.

Part of the outcome of this reasoning is that it is only in the most abstract sense that "the world capitalist system" acted. The diplomatic isolation of the Haitian revolution was partly the product of domestic politics in the United States and U.S. dominance over its South American "client states" (even over the independent governments whose revolutionary struggles Pétion in the south of Haiti had supported substantially (Leon (1974), pp. 440–51; Verna (1980 [1969])).

But North American objections to Haiti as a symbol of anti-slavery and black equality combined with the world system interests of very small parts of the capitalist and governmental class of the empires of Europe. The result was that the isolation of revolutionary slave rebellion came to an end earlier in the part of the world system most occupied with maintaining exploitation of colonies, and later in the part that was heading toward a civil war over the domestic place of slaves. The world system, then, acted differently in the different states of the core depending on their different politics of diplomacy toward Haiti.

Diplomacy and Revolution

We usually think we know what diplomacy is and how it works, because in modern societies in peacetime it is fairly isolated from everyday politics, much of it is secret, or "preliminary," and it is mainly the work of bureaucratic specialists rather than political representatives. During wartime, diplomacy becomes quite different, because the costs of war are paid by the society as a whole and wars lead to a reorganization of civil society onto a wartime footing.

In times of revolution the revolutionary society such as Haiti and its factions tend to become symbols in the domestic politics of societies not having a revolution. Because of the meaning of their revolution in other countries, actors in the revolutionary society have to take account of the fact that diplomatic and warlike means are likely to be used by other societies for or against the revolution.

Because European states in the late 18th century were built mainly for warfare, and because even their domestic parts were often secret and bureaucratic rather than public and representative, the divide between domestic and international politics was not so sharp in the 18th century as it has been in the 20th—18th century domestic politics was more like the modern politics of diplomacy. Further, the most powerful western European states in the late 18th century were largely financed by taxes on wholesale trade, especially international trade (see Tilly (1990)). The diplomatic milieu was therefore filled with people who had commercial interests in other countries, and that commerce was crucial to the finance of the government. Those parts of the state that dealt with the colonies were even more dominated by people with commercial interests in the trade and production of the colonies.

The Haitian Revolution was therefore a major political event in the international political system, as the American Revolution before it had been. However Haiti's place in the politics of the other powers, including now colonial politics and colonial commercial policy, was unique because it symbolized class and racial equality and revolutionary state-building by black ex-slaves. That revolutionary state-building was a deep challenge to European state finance as well as, of course, a symbolic challenge to the welfare of slaveowning sugar and cotton planters, especially in the Caribbean and North America.

Haiti was the first of a number of third world revolutionary societies to become important objects in the politics of the hegemonic or core powers, especially those of the United States, and suffer the consequences of diplomatic isolation and systematic attempts at subversion by those core powers. Revolutionary and Napoleonic France was a somewhat similar example to Haiti among the European core powers in the late 18th and early 19th centuries.

The Place of One Polity in the Politics of Another

When a country, ethnic group, or political movement with which people in a given society have not had much daily experience is an object in their politics, it is placed in the cognitive space of what they *do* experience. Thus Haiti was not something that the slaves on the other Caribbean islands experienced in their daily lives, with a very few exceptions of slave emigrés. But planters thought that if it did become a symbolic object for them it would help slaves interpret their own slavery and would introduce new possibilities of a way out. For example, when Senator Thomas Hart Benton of Missouri said that the United States should not have diplomatic relations with Haiti because having black or mulatto consuls and ambassadors "puts on exhibition the fruits of a Negro insurrection that has succeeded" (Price-Mars (1953), vol. 1, 149), he was complaining not so much about what Haiti symbolized to Haitians (which he would no doubt have been equally horrified about), but what it might symbolize to American black and mulatto slaves.

People in general have a very simplified notion of the foreign group, shaped by their own politics and society. Such use of another group as a symbol in interpreting one's own life tends to be labile and unstable. I will call such people "the public," and their interpretation of the country (Haiti in this case) "public opinion." A smaller number of people have a more complex experience and set of ideas, usually about a small part of the foreign group. Their experience and ideas are shaped by economic contacts, political and diplomatic occupations, emigré status, journalistic specialization, missionary interest, and the like. I will call such smaller groups the "diplomatic milieu" of one country's relations to another or to a linked set of others. A diplomatic milieu is, then, a social circle within which diplomatic milieu will generally divide into subgroups according to the kind of contacts or interests its members have.

During the Haitian revolution the British conquered much of the south and the Port-au-Prince area, and had strong outposts along the west coast up to the Môle St. Nicolas, and many British officers and Jamaican merchants were involved in the administration of the occupied territories. These people had had considerable experience with parts of Haiti, contacts with merchants and officials of the occupied parts, military alliances with emigré white troops and perhaps some colored and black troops, and battles against or diplomatic relations with the Haitian military and political authorities. These contacts were by and large through translators, restricted to the matter at hand, and restricted mainly to the south and Port-au-Prince (an excellent account is Geggus (1982)). These officers and merchants would then form one subgroup of the diplomatic milieu with respect to Haiti in the Jamaican and British polities.

Coffee planters from the south of Haiti fled the revolution and settled in the far east of Cuba in the hills to cultivate coffee. When Napoleonic France later went to war with Spain, they were eventually mostly driven out. They had brought to Cuba the experiences of white planters isolated on small coffee plantations, where they worked with their slaves, far from the commercial and governmental centers, a sort of "kulak" experience of old regime Haiti. They also brought the experience of warfare against the colored troops that had created a republican government in the south.

They developed a populist-racist worldview akin to that of royalist Cossacks in imperial Russia, Boers in South Africa, *pieds noirs* from Algeria in southern France, and perhaps even the tobacco and horse-raising planters in the foothills of the Appalachians (such as Andrew Jackson, who knew how to deal with the national bank and knew how to remove Indians to the west better than the fancy people on the Supreme Court).

The experience of these planters with Cuba was even more segmental than their experience of Haiti had been and more unrepresentative of Cuban society, since by and large they did not speak Spanish and the Spanish officials of Oriente Province usually did not speak French.[3]

In Jamaica and in Britain, a population of officers and merchants was created for whom the occupied slice of Haiti was real. They could categorize its inhabitants into different groups; they knew their enemies in Haiti by segregation from them and fighting with and against them within the same society. In sum, they had an ambivalent and experienced view of their allies and enemies in Haiti. In particular they had an ambivalent and experienced view of the coffee planters; for example, the British had been much less intensely committed to defeating the colored troops that took over southern Haiti after the British withdrew than the French-speaking white coffee planters.

In Cuba, and to a much lesser extent in Spain, the group of populist, white, slaveowning small coffee growers 125 or so miles from their old home (only 75 from Môle St. Nicolas, the nearest part of Haiti) were a group immediately affected by Spain's going to war with Napoleonic France. While Bonaparte and Spain had been allies against Haiti, they had been thought to be reliable allies of the Spanish. But after Bonaparte and Spain fell out they were thought by their Cuban neighbors (especially the important ones, the *peninsulares*, who ruled and would go back home to Spain) to be Bonapartist allies, who could easily conceal conspiracies by speaking French.

The British officers and Jamaican merchants were, then, part of the diplomatic milieu, at least of Jamaica, and the French coffee planters, part of that of Cuba; to some extent they were both part of the diplomatic milieu of the empires as well.

Other important parts of the diplomatic milieux in the empires relevant to Haiti included white sugar planters or colonial government officials who became emigrés from Haiti, especially in France, the United States, and other Caribbean islands; military officials whose job had been to conquer Haiti or to protect the other islands from rebellions; planters in the other empires and the other islands of the French empire, whose own property and prosperity were at stake if their slaves followed Haiti; governors of slave islands charged with keeping peace and collecting the taxes on sugar and other export products; merchants with monopoly advantages in the colonial trade or a portfolio of bankrupt plantations that they had taken over for bad debts; and the Dutch, Danish,

---

[3] See Marrero (1978;9), pp. 140–151, for their impact on Cuba; Geggus (1982), pp. 236–37 for the area they came from; Debien (1953–1954) for an account of their adaptation to and ejection from Cuba.

and North American New England and Mid-Atlantic shippers, merchants whose success depended on productivity combined with poor customs enforcement in the slave islands.

These diplomatic milieux differ from the cosmopolitan educated elites of the metropolises and the capitals of empires, who form the part of the general public with the highest saliency of diplomacy. To put it another way, high saliency of foreign policy can be a matter of a highly sophisticated appreciation of one's country's position in the world, or a matter of life experience with part of that world. The two causal origins of saliency of foreign policy have different consequences for the politics of diplomacy. Such cosmopolitan elites are distinguished from the ordinary domestic public by a much deeper and more complex view of all other countries or ethnic groups, but it is still a view that interprets other countries as objects in a cognitive system to make sense of the cosmopolitans' own country's politics.

The experienced diplomatic milieux differ from the cosmopolitan part of the general public in their slant and in their orientation to a very small part of the world. The place of a particular foreign country or ethnicity in the diplomatic milieu depends on people's particular places in the flow of people, commerce, and ideas between societies.

No doubt the British officers were, on the average, more politically right-wing on such questions as the citizenship of small farmers than the French coffee planters in the east of Cuba, and probably as racist and pro-slavery as those planters. But for British officers an alliance with the colored armies in the south of Haiti was an alternative to defeating them; it was not for most of the coffee planters. For this and other reasons, the Haitian revolutionary government occupied a different place in the political cosmologies of the British officers than of the French coffee planters; they knew different things about the Haitian revolutionary government and evaluated it along different dimensions. So even when, in a few cases, they were part of the diplomatic milieu of the same country in its relations to Haiti, they would be part of different subgroups in that milieu.

In particular different parts of the diplomatic milieu would have their futures shaped very differently, and more or less intensely, by different diplomatic events. When the French and the Spanish fell out, the French subgroup in Cuba who had been recently welcomed as allies against the French Revolution in general, and the Haitian subpart of it in particular, become potential enemies. The British officers in contrast had some slight increase in their freedom of maneuver when the French and Spanish fell out, and had to be cautious about slightly different things. They did not have to go into exile again because of the declaration of war, as the French coffee planters in Cuba had to do.

The way this segmental experience of diplomatic milieux affects diplomacy differs from the normal political effects of such segmentation within a country by race, class, region, industry. Of course, the Haitian population was itself divided by differences in experience with their own government and society. Haitians would have a much livelier appreciation of the impact of foreign policy on Haitian society if their "ecological range" was the whole society, or if they were deeply involved in exports of the main goods produced by planters, or if their political power would become precarious (or, for others, greatly increase) if the French were to reinforce their small garrisons in Santo Domingo City or at Samaná in the Spanish part of the island, or if their children were being educated in France. But they would have *different* views and interests than those of other people within Haiti, and in particular combine those foreign policy experiences with different positions in domestic politics and economics. The political system on which they would ordinarily act would be the Haitian government rather than the government of an imperial power. A given subgroup of the diplomatic milieu concerned with Haiti was ordinarily a larger part of all the people concerned with Haiti in France than a given segment of Haitian society was of all the people concerned about the Haitian government in Haiti.

To many of the Haitian population in the late 18th and early 19th centuries, no doubt, Haiti was not really an entity whose fate was a central part of their psychology. Almost all were black, and they might well think vaguely that Haiti was a black rather than a white government, and that that government was favorable toward the liberty of ex-slaves from the French, but perhaps unfavorable toward their liberty to stop working on the old plantation now that a black colonel in the Haitian army was running it. But a complicated picture of Haiti as an actor in the world system was likely not part of "public opinion," not even to the degree to which there is such a conception of the United States acting on the world scene among modern North Americans.

The Dynamics of Public Opinion Relevant to Diplomacy: A Definition of "Nationalism" as the Response of a Structure

But the picture above is a static one. Events are not interpreted only in cognitive structures determined by social location, by experiences of a part of the diplomatic milieu, or by cognitive pictures of domestic politics that include a few foreign political objects. Events also shape opinion. People are, for example, recruited to the diplomatic milieux by events—the defeat of the British and the whites in the south of Haiti recruited the French coffee planters to Cuba as a part of the diplomatic milieu of Cuba and Spain, especially concerned with Spain's relation to Haiti (and hence indirectly Spain's relation to France). For British officers the evacuation of Haiti made their knowledge of Haitian occupied territories mostly irrelevant. Such officers likely became passive bystanders in British diplomacy toward Haiti after that time, complaining in the bar at the inn perhaps about the decline of empire through softness.

General public opinion changes too. The more rapidly public opinion changes with events in such a way as to support the diplomatic stance of the country (as Page and Shapiro show for the United States (1992), pp. 172–284), the more "nationalistic" the country would be said to be. Particularly if the public is easy to mobilize to a much more active level, so that it is easy to recruit armies and to divert expenditures to war purposes at the beginning of a war, then the country is effectively nationalistic. By the end of the Revolution in 1802, at least with respect to mobilization against the French, the Haitian public was very nationalistic in this sense compared with most poor people in third world countries. It is the deposit of this nationalistic consciousness in the identities of modern Haitians that Edmund Wilson describes in the epigraph to this chapter.

Diplomatic milieux in general track the course of events much more closely than does the public. When different parts of the actively concerned diplomatic milieux, that is, those whose members are most concerned in their lives with foreign policy, move more together in the same direction as the general public and the diplomatic apparatus, then the country is still more nationalistic. "National interest" then dominates "particular interests" in foreign policy. When diplomatic missions from France came to both Pétion, the head of the Republic of Haiti in Port-au-Prince, and Christophe, the head of the Kingdom of Haiti in Cap Haïtien, and when, though they were only in a truce in their civil war, they both reacted with exactly the same anti-colonial, anti-French policy, then Haiti was more nationalistic than most dual governments in the midst of a civil war (Price-Mars (1953), vol. 1, p. 135; Léger (1930), pp. 27–47, esp. the text of the proposed terms on pp. 38–39). Since they had both been generals in the Napoleonic army, they should unequivocally be considered a part of the diplomatic milieu in Haiti, aside from being heads of state.

Christophe in the north had one of the diplomats shot as a spy and published his instructions, much to the dismay of both the French and the British diplomatic apparatus. France and Britain had agreed that if the French conquered Haiti (the diplomacy was to prepare local alliances for the French taking over the island, which would have to be by conquest), the British ban on the slave trade would be lifted to "repopulate" the island—genocide did not have the bad name then that it has now, but this was pretty strong medicine for public opinion, particularly in Britain (Léger (1930), pp. 35–36). One might imagine this would increase the level of nationalism of Haitians of all levels of sophistication, at least increasing their mobilizability against the British and French.

As nationalism in this sense developed, of course, the Haitian nation itself became a bigger part of the cognitive apparatus with which people within Haiti interpreted the meaning of other countries. In particular the nation came to be seen as an entity operating on a world stage, with interests, powers, rights, and dignity. When the French diploma*ts then proposed good terms to Pétion as president of the south of Haiti and Christophe as king of the north as people (they were apparently proposing to take *both* sides in the civil war), but humiliating terms for the Haitian nation (e.g., keep the people working on the plantations until their legal masters could take them over again), then a nationalistic public and these national leaders felt the humiliation.

The French also pointed out that *their* king felt humiliated at being asked to recognize a government whose constitution excluded whites (and most clearly French whites) from the island. Reintroduction of owners onto plantations was incompatible with the Haitians' conceptions of their nation's dignity as an international actor; the exclusion of French people from property on the island was incompatible with the conception of the French about what they were owed in the way of respect (and, of course, in the way of property). Since the Haitians had seen a good deal of French massacres before winning the local part of the French Revolution and, later, in repulsing the French after declaring Haitian independence from Napoleonic France, they probably suspected (even before King Christophe opened the pouch) that the outcome would be worse than humiliation.

This event then moved France even more clearly into the position of eternal enemy in the cognitive map of Haitian public opinion. When a few years later (1821–1822) a movement in the Spanish part of the island [The Dominican Republic] proclaimed independence, Haiti's President Boyer (by then there was a unified government of what is now Haiti) interpreted this as an opportunity for the French to move into the island, and decided to occupy it. At that time the Haitian constitution said that Haiti governed the whole island, that Haiti was a black nation, that colored people were to be counted as black, and also that "white people no matter what their nation could not set foot on Haiti as masters or proprietors and could never in the future acquire any property" (Article 12 of the declaration of 20 May 1805, as quoted in Price-Mars (1953), vol. 1, p. 39).

This was clearly a perception of the eastern part of the island in terms of the politics of the Haitian revolution, not in terms of a constitution for an island with Haitian and Dominican-Spanish subsocieties. This contradiction between Haiti's claim to the whole island and its constitution as a black society created substantial difficulty in making alliances and constructing a government for the Spanish subsociety out of the population, about a third white (the other two-thirds were dominantly free colored, with some free blacks; these fractions are my very speculative estimate). Most of those whites were peasants and small proprietors who had never had slaves.

From a geopolitical point of view the Haitian nation was conceived *in Haitian politics* as the whole island. But from a revolutionary point of view the relevant universe was the French part of the island, and when the constitution said "all whites" they had been thinking of French planters and French, English and Spanish invaders, not Santo Domingo peasants. The events of their conquest clearly then posed the difficulty of the contradictions in the constitution (and probably in the mind of Boyer as well; see Léger (1930), pp. 73–87). Or perhaps better there were contradictions between the view of the constitution as a conception of the Haitian nation in the French part, and the constitution as a guide to what was wise "semi-foreign relations" of that nation with the conquered Spanish part. So Santo Domingo's being an object in the political cosmology of Haiti did not resolve the contradictions in the image of the Haitian nation: Haiti had to have defensible boundaries and so to control the whole island, and Haiti was a black society created by a black revolution.

Haiti as a Symbol in the Empires, and Empires as Symbols in Haiti

With slight variations Haiti occupied the same place in the political cosmology of the different empires. First, Haiti symbolized a social revolution: freeing slaves, breaking up and expropriating plantations, establishing a new government, applying terror to reputable whites as well as to rebellious blacks (in fact, the empires hardly noticed that the Haitians also applied it to rebellious blacks), all using the symbolism of the left of the French Revolution. These several characteristics seemed to be all one symbol on the right wing of all the empires, and by and large right wing people were all that cared. In particular Haiti was seen as exporting revolution, although actual help to other revolutions seems not to have been very common. Pétion's help to Simón Bolívar (Verna (1980 [1969]), pp. 150–90) has to be balanced by Toussaint L'Ouverture's betrayal of French agitators sent to Jamaica to raise a slave rebellion (Geggus (1982), pp. 381, 385, 465 n. 23 to chap. 14, 19 to chap. 15). Whatever Haitian governments did in fact, Haiti was a symbol that meant export of revolution.

Second, it was a racial symbol of powerful and rich blacks, black rulers, black generals winning wars. The delicate shadings of color in which colonial specialists in racism occasionally took such aesthetic pleasure disappeared, so all the rulers of Haiti seemed black. The constitutions of Haiti supported this interpretation, for when they specified black rulers and no white landownership they specifically included colored as black. Sumner Welles (1928), who spent much time in the Dominican Republic, is a good American example of the way this racial line got defined, as is the quotation above from Thomas Hart Benton. For Welles people of all different colors with detectable African features were all called "Negro," and their perceived blackness (Welles knew Spanish, so "Negro" meant black to him) was the cause of all their bad characteristics. Non-American versions of the symbolism are to be found in Tolentine Rojas (1944), Shepard (1831), and Breen (1844).

The language was very slightly more guarded when the Colombian foreign minister wrote memos of instruction to deputies to the Hispanic-American Congress in Panama:

> The government of Colombia feels much repugnance to maintaining with Haiti those considerations of etiquette generally accepted among the civilized nations, but at the same time wants to avoid all cause for disputes by means of a temporizing conduct. [The government] would not, nevertheless, make any objection to continuing to admit the Haitian flag in Colombian ports for purely mercantile purposes. (José Rafael Revenga, letter of September 24, 1825, quoted in Verna (1980 [1969]), p. 443).

"Repugnance" over the requirements of diplomatic etiquette was misrepresented in Colombia's normal diplomatic correspondence as caution about offending France during a war with Spain,[4] or in writing to the United States delicately by recognizing the different statuses of blacks in the United States, in Haiti, and in "the rest of the American countries." Realpolitik was already more legitimate than open racism in diplomacy in South America (partly because Bolívar was strongly pushing for recognition of Haiti), but racism backstage was very thinly veiled indeed. And Haiti was a symbol of the trouble of treating blacks as equals among the rich and powerful, like other diplomats.

---

[4] Verna (1980 [1969]), pp. 379–81. The general diplomatic problem of Haiti's exclusion from the Congress of Panama being organized by Colombia is outlined *ibid.*, pp. 439–55.

Haiti and the Dominican Republic

Haiti's diplomatic situation was complicated by the fact that the diplomatic status of the Spanish part of the island (what was then Santo Domingo and is now The Dominican Republic) was uncertain. It had been ceded to the French in summer 1795 but never actually turned over to them locally. Toussaint L'Ouverture led an army to take Santo Domingo "for France," against the wishes of Napoleon. The governor of Santo Domingo surrendered to him on January 21, 1800. Toussaint wrote to Napoleon, saying: "Having decided to take possession by force of arms I found myself obliged before setting out to invite Citizen Roume [the formal head of the French government in Haiti—A.L.S.] to desist from the performance of his duties and retire to Dondon until further orders. . . . He awaits your commands. When you want him, I will send him to you" (James (1963 [1938]), p. 239).

But as James points out, Toussaint "took no trouble to explain. It was dangerous to explain [because it would be flaunting his determination to repel an anticipated French invasion reinstituting slavery—A.L.S.] but still more dangerous not to explain" (ibid., p. 240). Toussaint was the first of a long line of Haitian heads of state who lost or almost lost power in part because they wanted to conquer the Spanish part of the island and while they were gone rebellion grew up behind them in Haiti.[5]

Haiti, having about five or six times the population of Santo Domingo and no special trouble with tropical diseases' decimating its troops, had no particular difficulty conquering the Dominican Republic. But Haitian leaders, even Toussaint, had trouble explaining to their public why it was worth the cost to conquer and reconquer the troublesome and unprofitable Spanish part of the island.

The general reason was that first the French and then the Spanish (and sometimes both together) were suspected of wanting it to serve as a base for the reconquest of Haiti and the reimposition of slavery. After 1844 the Dominican Republic negotiated with the British, the Ameri-

---

[5] Dessalines, who carried out the first reconquest after Toussaint's, seems to have lost power for other causes. Boyer, who carried out the reconquest in 1822 and held the territory until his resignation in 1843, had no particular difficulty, partly because the Haitians were apparently welcomed in, but left a substantial difficulty for his successors. See Leger (1907), pp. 195–99 for losses or near-losses of power by Presidents Hérard, Guerrier, and Riché, either because they were fighting in the east or because they gave up, and pp. 201–3 for Soulouque, or Emperor Faustin, who lost power during an attempted invasion.

cans, and the Spanish about establishing a relation of "protection" in return for a base or commercial privileges.[6]

Since Spain still supported slavery in its colonies at the time, since the United States encouraged it at home and southern interests were generally central in North American military diplomacy in the Caribbean, and since France was still proposing to take Haiti back as a colony for much of the time, all these suspicions about the diplomacy of The Dominican Republic with imperial powers were well grounded. The reimposition of slavery in Haiti was nevertheless a remote contingency, not an immediate threat, and so not a very real threat in Haitian public opinion.

But what the distance of the threat meant in turn was that Haitian war objectives were not very clear, and it was not very clear what had been won when the Spanish part of the island was subjected, or what had been lost when it became independent again. When a Haitian president or emperor was absent conquering the east, local rebellions against the government that demanded taxes and men did not have to answer insistent foreign policy questions. This distinction between the level at which diplomatic policy was decided and the level at which local rebellions were organized was general in 18th and early 19th century societies. The old regime in France itself had got into trouble not for losing wars, but for exacting very large contributions for wars (such as the American Revolution) that did not bring much apparent benefit to France.[7]

England and the Netherlands were the main 18th and early 19th century European societies in which leaders of local politics helped choose war objectives and voted on war policies, so they were the main societies that did not confront many local rebellions (or in the extreme, revolutions), when they went to war (Tilly (1993), pp. 52–78, 104–41). Napoleon succeeded in organizing the French state from about 1795 to 1815 so that it could wage war without provoking revolution (ibid., pp. 179–82). But otherwise the absolutist states of Europe had to increase troop levels at home so that they could send troops abroad. The Haitian state was just a particularly weak state having the same problems that most European states were all having at the time. War was getting more expensive, but the people in general and local political leaders in particular were not being asked whether it was wise before being subjected to its costs.

---

[6] The Spanish did take over the protection of The Dominican Republic in the 1860s and established a government along Spanish colonial lines, which turned out not to be very popular even among those who had invited them in. They called Spain *España boba*, stupid Spain, during and after the occupation, and they were right.

[7] Cf. Skocpol (1979), pp. 54, 60–64, who attributes the weakness of the French state that led to the Revolution in large measure to expensive wars with ambiguous outcomes.

Thus Haitian leaders got into trouble even when they easily won their wars, in Santo Domingo or later the Dominican Republic. To fight such a war they had to try to extract resources from local or regional power centers in Haiti that could fairly easily become autonomous, to organize those resources above the level of those local centers (for instance, by having soldiers stationed in the east rather than at home), and then to devote the resources and troops in distant lands to purposes that did not immediately feed back to give local benefits. The costs were clear and present, but the benefits fuzzy and long term.

So when the objectives were "purely diplomatic," countering suspicious moves by one or several empires in another country, Haiti was not effectively "nationalistic." The personal authority of the leaders was not a strong enough basis of legitimacy that trust could be transferred from them to the diplomatic objectives of the state. When Leger, from a Haitian diplomatic family, writes that Great Britain, France, and the United States "prevent[ed] Haiti from availing herself of the opportunity of subduing her former citizens" (1907, p. 202), it is clear that such objectives seem to him clearly in the national interest. It evidently was not clear to early 19th century Haitian public opinion that these white Spanish people were fellow citizens, that subduing fellow citizens was anyway worth a very high cost, or that the malevolent intentions of these empires were close enough to fruition to be worth fighting Santo Domingo to frustrate them.

Of course, when Haiti did govern the Spanish part of the island, it created for itself a diplomatic milieu within its political system with extensive experience with both French and Spanish rule, and after 1822 with a bit of experience of independence. That experience was particularly distinct from their experience under Haitian rule for the white part of the Dominican population. The experience of Haitian rule, then, created a high sensitivity that lasted into the 20th century among The Dominican Republic's population, and that created severe military conflicts as The Dominican Republic's population, military power, and diplomatic status approached that of Haiti.

The Difficulty of Diplomacy as Class Warfare

Even in the most literate of publics during times of greatest mobilization for foreign affairs, such as world wars, it is difficult to build the connection in public opinion between foreign affairs and daily life. The costs of warfare have to be extracted from the society, and the translation from public purposes to the payment of taxes obviously has to be based on some system of distributing the costs.[8]

Obviously the costs imposed on enemies of different degrees of war guilt, or the bargains made with allies, are even less matters where the details of policies are thoroughly debated in the public forum. Military elites and diplomatic elites are in general much more secretive even in a popular war than other political elites. In peacetime one could almost say that they do not have to be secretive because so very few even of the leaders of domestic politics have any substantial opinion.

This is why it is so important to distinguish those small parts of the population who have more extensive, and often internally segmented, experience with and interest in foreign countries. We have called those parts the diplomatic milieu in a country. Our problem here is exactly that social classes are not parts of the diplomatic milieu, except in very exceptional circumstances.

A Haitian government of class warfare based on an ex-slave population that was largely illiterate, and beyond that politically illiterate in a deep and fundamental sense, with experience only of the diplomacy of defending a revolution on their own island, was even less prepared for popular participation in the niceties of diplomacy. Diplomacy for Haiti consisted primarily in making deals with sworn enemies, slave empires. Haiti as a government preferred one kind of hostility to another, made bargains with enemies because bargains with enemies were often the best diplomacy could do. The enemies made the bargains because they had what they hoped were short-run difficulties carrying out the conquest of Haiti. It was therefore even more difficult to mobilize on the basis of the class significance of maneuvers in a proslave world system. *Raison d'etat* was even farther from the reasons that made class sense to Haitians than it was for, say, the English working class.

---

[8] Even Great Britain's home population, probably the most literate of the undefeated participants in World War II, used "borrowing" to be repaid in inflated currency, a melange of rationing systems, including rationing of labor, restriction of the right to strike, complex conscription systems, special war taxation schemes that were as much rhetorical as fiscal, and other methods of dissimulating the relative burden of the war on different sorts of people. They hired George Orwell, a left socialist of the most transparent integrity, among others, to explain to the colonies why they, too, should pay their part of the burden as determined by the imperial government. Orwell did not believe in colonialism, but did believe in the war against the Nazis; for the British government to be forced to such expedients shows what a difficult problem they thought they faced in extracting resources from their colonies. Even governments of relatively solid legitimacy tend to move sharply leftward after serious and protracted wars—patriotism produces Tory workers only at the beginning of wars (see Gallie (1983), pp. 224–51, entitled "War and the Crisis of Legitimacy," for an excellent attempt to explain the greater interwar militancy of the French left than the British left in terms of the way costs were allocated in World War I.)

In addition, the Haitian political system that translated complex diplomatic matters into class terms was not itself very legitimate. The ties that linked local populations to cosmopolitan political systems were by and large through local heroes who had become significant personal leaders of a local coterie or military band. These personal leaders were then part of a coterie of a "general" who moved on the national scene, as a part of the coterie of a *caudillo* or potential challenger to the *caudillo*.[9]

The system of legitimacy, for all its preeminently class character, was implemented in a sort of pyramid of personal loyalties, tied together in the entourage of the political leader. There were no "mass organizations" that could be "transmission belts" between the political elite and the mass public. The crucial thing about mass organizations is that their leaders are to some degree subject to a governing system made up of the masses and the lowest-level activists that can keep them in line. They are responsible downward. Their deals, to some degree, have to be approved by the masses. That is what made Lenin call them transmission belts, because the long-run trust of the masses in their leaders had a more or less solid organizational base.

In a pyramid of personal loyalties, the basis of trust is the notion that the local leader is loyal to the local follower, the broker with whom he or she has contact within the coterie of the national dictator or *caudillo* is loyal to the local leader, and the dictator or *caudillo* is loyal to his or her coterie. But the qualities of the personal ties above the local level are not readily monitorable. And when the broker in the *caudillo*'s coterie has the contract for supply of the troops venturing into The Dominican Republic and is obviously getting rich off it, the whole system looks untrustworthy from the bottom (or, of course, from the outside). The long-run diplomatic aims for the class of ex-slaves of bargains with slave power tended to get lost to public view in a welter of personal relations and personal advantages. This is presumably because people are wise about what diplomatic objectives are likely to be lost in a welter of personal advantages in such a system of pyramidal personal loyalties.

When the threat of the reimposition of slavery by France was immediate, as, for example, when the same Napoleon whose local governors were bargaining for support of ex-slave troops had reimposed slavery in a bloody repression on Guadeloupe, the Haitian people and their leaders could easily relate the class issues of their revolution to the costs of the war of independence. Their experience of white terror against rebellious

---

[9] I use the Spanish word because the phenomenon of personalistic politics of regional and military chiefs, who sometimes take precarious control as *caudillos* of "national" governments, is quite similar in Haiti and the South American countries after the latter's independence. I do not know of an equivalent word in French or English.

blacks made a racial definition of who among the enemy should pay the costs easy for Dessalines, and made his race-based terror approach make sense. If Toussaint had still been in power rather than being deliberately starved in a prison in France, Toussaint's anti-genocidal policy, his personal mercy, and his sensitivity to the long-run diplomatic costs of terror against whites, with whom all the Caribbean empires identified whatever their sins, might have been defended effectively in public opinion. But racially based terror, "genocide," was at least understandable diplomacy to Haitians, given what they had seen from the other side.

The general point, then, is that running diplomatic policy as an aspect of class conflict is difficult under the most ideal of political conditions. It became more difficult when the diplomatic problems were inherently "matters of technical judgment" in an unfavorable environment, as Haiti's were. It was even more difficult when the transmission belts between the diplomatic elite and local powers were not governed by class-conscious organizations controlled from below, but were instead a pyramid of patron-client relations that were inherently untrustworthy. They were very likely seen as even less trustworthy than they actually were by those who did not make a business of politics. Thus diplomatic policies appeared in the political public as "machinations."

Even when we can reconstruct a sensible class meaning to policies, it is hard for us to imagine a way to implement those policies by using as the main resource the class loyalty of Haitian ex-slaves. The best James (1963 [1938]) could suggest was that Toussaint should make a speech. There is no doubt that the level of class-consciousness of black ex-slaves in Haiti in the early 19th century was as high as it has ever been in an illiterate and politically inexperienced public. And there is no doubt that when Haitian national policies were clearly class policies defending the population against slavery, Haiti was one of the most successfully nationalist poor third world societies in world history. But even that was not enough to make diplomacy in a hostile environment of slave societies an effective tool in that class conflict, except in cases of invasion.

Conclusion

The central explanation for the diplomatic isolation of Haiti for two-thirds of a century, then, is that it was a sort of political object that did not elicit loyalty from those with class-based grievances in the core imperial societies, except for slaves. Jefferson and Jackson could go their populist pro–small farmer way without appealing to solidarity with black slave Haitian rebellions, though these created large small-farmer populations, or with the aspirations of rich and powerful blacks in Haiti or elsewhere. Where the appeal was strong, namely, among slaves, they were systematically denied the capacity to organize and to respond to Haiti as a political object. The influence of slaves themselves on diplomacy was primarily as a problem of governance: what do we have to do to keep them from rebelling, or keep them working hard at things that make us a profit if we free them. Thus Haiti did not symbolize class conflicts in democratic societies (or the democratic part of the United States), and among slave societies, the slaves who would side with Haiti's had no power to influence diplomacy.

But a second reason was that the diplomatic milieux of the empires' relations to Haiti were disproportionately made up of white emigrés from Haiti, military officials whose job had been to conquer Haiti or to protect the other islands from rebellions, planters whose own property and prosperity was at stake if other slaves followed Haiti, governors of slave islands charged with keeping peace and collecting the taxes on sugar and other export products, or merchants with monopoly advantages in the colonial trade or portfolios of bankrupt plantations that they had taken over for bad debts.

The Dutch, Danish, and New England and Mid-Atlantic merchants were the main exceptions. And we do repeatedly find exceptions to nonrecognition of the form quoted for Colombia above: the Haitian flag on a merchant ship was recognized as a legitimate flag, immune from confiscation or piracy like other ships. Haitian ships loaded with coffee (Haiti went out of the sugar business and into the coffee business, for coffee can be cultivated and dried on peasant holdings) were welcome, while Haitian ambassadors from a revolutionary government were not.

The third reason for the continued isolation was Haiti's peculiar class struggle–based nationalism. The only people Haitians would allow to dismember their country were Haitians. Although there were many rebellions, it was rare that one of the empires could take advantage of them to break off a piece of Haiti that they could then recognize. The last substantial one was the colored rebellion led by Rigaud in the south during the early years of the attempted Bonapartist restoration, which seems to have had foreign support of a substantial kind. It seems likely that the suspicion that the foreign support meant the return of slavery sapped the morale of Rigaud's rebels, since Pétion (also colored) established autonomy with much the same geographical base soon after Rigaud's. But Pétion had no substantial support from imperial powers and a very class-oriented program of breaking up plantations (and other lands) into peasant properties. So in Haiti, "divide" worked fine, but "conquer" did not follow. Even in civil war the Haitians could unite against the French. When the possible reintroduction of slavery was in question, there was no disunity that could be recognized by an empire interested in slavery.

The upshot of these three types of causes is that the world system did not move as a unified body. France, especially the France that returned to power with the Napoleonic restoration, had a diplomatic milieu filled with colonial governors, military men, and planters. England had slave islands, especially Barbados, Antigua, and Jamaica, that played an important role in the English upper class, while the Wesleyan and other abolitionists made domestic English politics symbolically anti-slave, but by no means enthusiastic about symbols of anti-white rebellion (much as in the U.S. North). Spain had a large governing class in the Caribbean, but a small slaveowning class without much power except in Cuba, and a vague feeling that by rights Santo Domingo (and Trinidad, lost to the British) ought to belong to them. Spain's domestic politics, insofar as those politics had to do with foreign policy, mainly revolved around complex and shifting relationships to France, rather than having to do with Haiti.

It was in the United States that Haiti had an almost entirely symbolic role, as a symbol of slave rebellion. The anti-slavery northerners (like the English Wesleyans) were not very enthusiastic about black violence and black power, being quite ambivalent even about black voting, let alone black armies and presidents. Up to the 1860s, and specifically up to the Emancipation Proclamation, the south was much more concerned with symbols of slave rebellion, and so it easily kept the U.S. government from formal recognition. The main part of the U.S. diplomatic milieu that had an interest in Haiti, northern shippers and merchants, could get by with the half-recognition implied by recognizing the Haitian flag on ships as legitimate and by gaining access to Haitian harbors.

Except for Simón Bolívar most South American and Central American political groups had had no experience with Haiti; slaves were freed by the 1830s in the former Spanish colonies with no substantial rebellion by blacks. They easily followed the American symbolic interest in non-recognition (under pressure) up to the 1860s.

Thus diplomacy toward Haiti was shaped by its revolutionary class nature as a symbol and by the concrete interests of imperial diplomatic milieux. North American shipping capitalists in the U.S. milieu wanted to trade with Haiti rather than own slaves, so except for ship flags, diplomatic isolation was a symbolic and nearly costless acknowledgement of the symbolic sensitivities of the south. The French diplomatic milieu was mostly cleaned of its Haitian emigré subparts by the 1830s, so it could recognize Haitian independence, in a grudging bourgeois fashion. The

English were abolishing slavery by the 1830s in their own way, not at all similar to that in Haiti, and so had no objection to recognition, even if Haiti was not their kind of symbol. Spain went along because only its Cuban planters really cared, and they were peripheral, mostly not residents of Spain itself, and were less than half of creole Cuba.

But until the Civil War resolved the question of symbolization of the slavery-abolition debate in domestic politics, the United States and its South American followers were not ready to confront the reality of black class-conscious states. From the point of view of materialism, it was non-recognition in the U.S. ideological superstructure that lasted longest, while that grounded in French and British material interests could be sooner bargained away.

10

Establishing Monopolies in Free Labor Markets: Semi-Servile Labor in the British Islands

Empire Government Structure and the Definition of Freedom

In Great Britain the empire government found it easier to abolish the slave trade, in all the other empires as well as their own, than to abolish slavery within the empire. Either England or the United States had the strongest popular movement against the slave trade, and given moderately democratic structures in both countries, these put great pressures on the respective governments. The empire government in Britain and the national government in the United States were quite radically federal, in the sense that it was not automatic that laws passed in the national government were valid in the plantation colonies or states. In both, the federal subgovernments in plantation areas were moderately "democratic," in the sense that whites had elections not under the control of the empire or national governments and those elections produced bodies and officials that had great local powers. In both, the sea and international commerce were the province of the empire or national government.

It was the fact that the sea was under the direct control of empire governments in all the major empires (the nearest to an exception to empire control of the navy was the Netherlands) that made treaties among the sovereign states effective in ending the slave trade. It was the fact that all the empires had "federal" relations to their colonies (this was least true of the Spanish empire) that made simple abolition an ineffective way to end slavery in the colonies. Thus in some sense a popular movement in Great Britain was more effective in the French or Dutch fleet than in Jamaica, Barbados, or Antigua. The core of the world system was a less federal structure than the British empire, at least on matters that were clearly world system matters, such as the structure of the market for slaves from Africa.

In both the United States and the British empire, the attempt to govern slavery in the subgovernments' jurisdictions produced constitutional crises, the American Civil War and the fall of an English government over the government's proposal to reduce the powers of the Jamaican legislature. Jamaican powers were being challenged by the anti-slavery movement, but that movement could not successfully pass the constitutional revision that would have been required to allow Parliament to administer the citizenship of slaves and ex-slaves directly. It was this failure to weather the constitutional crisis that left the power to say what emancipation and freedom meant for ex-slaves in the hands of British West Indies planters, the main topic of this chapter.

The constitutional story of the American Civil War is a good deal more complicated than that, but by about 1876 the American Deep South was in more or less the same situation constitutionally as the British West Indies after emancipation, with more or less the same effect, the effect outlined in the epigraph to Chapter 9 by Edmund Wilson about ex-slaves living "with their ruined masters." We leave those complications aside here by leaving the United States out of our analysis.

As outlined in Chapter 8, the question of whether laws of the metropole obtained directly in the colonies in France depended on the fate of the revolutions. The more conservative metropolitan governments of the 19th century administered Martinique and Guadeloupe in a federal way, that is, so that national political bodies could not abolish slavery and so that island blacks were not represented in French national governments, more or less along the lines of the British empire. The French empire under conservative governments had somewhat more intervention and more empire military and police power on the ground in the West Indies than the British had.

The revolutionary French governments were "nationalist" on colonial citizenship questions, more or less like the Reconstruction Republicans in the United States (see Brandwein (1994), chap. 1, for an analysis of the Civil War as a crisis in federalism). Thus the empire constitution was one (a not very important one) of the several constitutional questions that lay at the heart of the Great Revolution and the revolutions of the 19th century in France.

The primary purpose of this chapter is to develop an analysis of the definition of what freedom meant in the British islands after emancipation. Because of the federal structure of empire government, this turned out to depend strongly on the strength of planter power on the islands, combined with the island labor market situation. The argument about planter power can be briefly summarized in the light of the analysis of Chapter 5 as follows: The more a British island was a slave society before emancipation, the more it was a slave society afterwards. The argument about the labor market situation can be summarized as follows: The less the sugar frontier period was already over at the time of emancipation, the more the labor market monopolies that made free labor more like slave labor were applied to East Indians in coolie labor contracts, rather than in limitations on the freedoms of ex-slaves. The more an island was a slave society with its frontier expired, the more oppression was organized as deprivation of freedom of ex-slaves rather than of East Indian coolies.

Planter Monopolies in the Labor Market as Local Colonial Policy

To apply the analysis of federalism to the British empire, our first problem is to develop a theory of what a class-conscious attempt by planters in the British islands to develop monopolies in the labor market after emancipation could do. Then we will analyze the two main variants of these monopolies, represented by semi-servile imported labor under what we will call coolie labor contracts, and restricting the alternative opportunities of the island colored, ex-slave, and resident Asian free labor force.

The coolie alternative involved a monopoly by the owner of the contract to the labor services of the immigrant for a term of years, provided the planter lived up to the contract in the eyes of the island officers of the law. Those eyes were often very tolerant of planters' misbehavior and very stringent with coolies' misbehavior, because they were often planters' eyes. The monopoly was, however, limited to a term of years, provided the laborer lived up to his (or more rarely her) side of the contract. It is indicative of the nearness of such contracts to slavery that Bridget Brereton in her general history of Trinidad describes East Indians who had finished their indenture as "'free' Indians" (Brereton (1981), *passim*, e.g., p. 94); her use of quotation marks presumably indicates that they were not quite fully unfree when indentured. They were, of course, free in the sense that they were not slaves.

The second alternative involved various devices to restrict the resident labor force to work on plantations, by denying them alternative opportunities. For example, at the end of slavery most of the houses and garden plots to which emancipated slaves could have access were on the plantations. If part of the terms for renting a house to live in was to furnish labor at below the competitive market rate, and if the plantation owners who owned most of the houses were unified in not renting houses for cash to those who worked elsewhere, then a tenantry system for residences could provide the plantation with island labor coerced to work by the prospect of being deprived of housing. Similarly, restricting access to crown lands to planters developing plantations, or keeping bankrupt plantations from being broken up into peasant plots, both deprived the labor force of the alternative of being a peasant. Eric Williams quotes a Committee of the House of Commons on the West Indies Colonies of 1842 on the problems of the colonies with extensive fertile land, namely, Jamaica, Trinidad, and Guyana:

> (9) That the cheapness of land has thus been the main cause of the difficulties that have been experienced; and that this cheapness is the natural result of the excess of fertile land beyond the wants of the existing population. (Williams (1962), p. 95)

Clearly something would have to be done about that, so a systematic policy of only selling off crown lands in large lots and suppressing squatting tried to keep free laborers from cultivating their own subsistence, or export crops like cocoa and coffee. Since the interior and east of Trinidad and most of Guyana were quite inaccessible by road, suppressing squatting only suppressed peasant export crop cultivation, not peasant subsistence cultivation.

Creating a monopoly by political means is, of course, creating a boundary between people and alternatives they would otherwise take advantage of, a boundary, then, between the jobs on plantations and those on peasant plots, for example, or between those eligible to occupy plantation houses because they work at below-market wages and those not eligible. Monopoly also creates social and especially political and class boundaries between people advantaged by maintaining the boundaries and people restricted by them.

The boundaries created by coolie labor contracts were most obvious, since they fell at the boundary between foreign and domestic labor, between those free and those temporarily unfree, those whose contracts were made in an Asian (or Portuguese, etc.) labor market and those who would make a labor contract in the local market. In 1906 in Trinidad indentured unskilled labor on plantations earned 25 cents a day, while unskilled "creole" and "West Indian" free labor on the roads earned between 60 and 80 cents a day, or even $1 (Ramesar (1976), pp. 12–13). Those boundaries lived on in their ethnic and cultural form after they lost their servile form, after East Indians, for example, competed in the local labor market.

The coolie labor contract method of establishing planter monopoly raised the saliency of the creole trade union alternative, a monopoly by local labor over jobs on the island by restriction of immigration. While the poor of Asia needed some sort of credit to make the trip to higher-wage Caribbean economies, that credit might theoretically have been provided by banks so that the contract involved no ties to particular labor contracts. A bank might bet that a worker in India could make more by emigrating to Trinidad because there was a higher wage in Trin-

idad, might arrange security for debt payment without regard to particular employers, and therefore might detach the credit for migration
expenses from semi-servile conditions in the labor contract.

It would of course be difficult to make money in that sort of banking
business because there would be poor security that the worker would
work and would repay the debt. But the point here is that such "guest
worker" competition would reduce the wages of Trinidadian black and
colored plantation workers in much the same way that semi-servile labor
contracts did. So the alternative policy for workers is a boundary against
East Indian competition, forbidding immigration.[1] It is because the island boundary is so salient, and the ethnic boundary between highly Eu-
ropeanized black and colored creoles and East Indians or other immigrants so clear, that the split in sources of labor can result in an ethnic
split in the labor movement and the citizenship movement, and a conflict over the right to live on the island.

But boundaries were also created in the political system by planters
occupying most positions in the legislature and forbidding black and
colored free people from "squatting" on crown land, or preventing
bankrupt plantations from being broken up. No representative of the
workers or peasants would vote for such restriction if they knew what
they were doing.

Such a planter monopoly over legislation created a boundary involving a conflict of interest between enfranchised, white, wealthy planters
and disenfranchised, black and colored, poor workers. When that same
line was repeatedly drawn by limitations on emigration, by enforcement
of labor contracts connected to rent of houses by eviction rights, by un-
dersupply of elementary schooling, by vagrancy laws, it was deeply
marked in the future politics of the island. "Everyone knew" that the
question of extension of the franchise was a question of the wage of
workers, because the wage was systematically held down by political
means.

This identification of citizenship, the franchise, class interests, and
race interests along a single left-right continuum was established rapidly
in the French islands by the processes of the French Revolution. In some
sense that alignment never disappeared afterward because Haiti was a
continual reminder, and because the memory of earlier freedom of the
slaves of Guadeloupe, taken away by the Napoleonic empire, reminded
Guadeloupe blacks and colored people who was on their side, who on
the other side, in metropolitan politics. When the French islands estab-

---

[1] Boswell (1986); Boswell and Jorjani (1988); Bonacich (1972, 1981); Thomas (1985),
pp. 35–77, 103–34, 202–25.

lished many of the same policies to establish monopolies in the labor market after emancipation, it took place in a context in which French metropolitan politics defined a leftist assimilationist alternative, an abolition of the federalism that kept island labor relations under different laws than metropolitan labor relations.[2]

That same identification grew slowly in the English islands because emancipation was carried out by a capitalist imperial power without open civil war. But it grew in the same direction because British planters could not resist using their political power to reduce the price of labor farther than capitalism itself would reduce it.

And while the importation of Asian and other foreign labor under coolie contracts created a split in the working class along ethnic lines, stronger in those colonies that had been sugar frontiers at the time of emancipation, it, too, was part of a process that aligned questions of citizenship with questions of class and race interest; it just made the citizenship question more complicated.

This complex of establishing labor market monopolies decayed in part from democratic processes transmitted from Europe and induced by the class interest of the poor in democracy. As mass slaughter came to be less legitimate as a response to black and colored rebellion, and citizenship of the (male) poor became politically legitimate even in England, the imperial link transmitted a less and less reactionary political culture, and provided less and less support for political repression. Black and colored people traveled to Europe and the American North, read books from Europe, heard (distorted) news from Haiti, and watched the American Civil War go against slavery. And perhaps more important, they traveled among islands, carrying news of ways to respond to political oppression, learning what race leaders said elsewhere, learning what trade unions looked like, meeting black socialists who did not breathe fire after all.

But in addition the decay of plantation economic health put a further burden on the monopolistic system. Where that system was in firm control, as in Barbados, when sugar prices went down, planters simply cut wages in half, because they had eliminated practically all the alternatives to plantation work. Elsewhere[3] the plantations went bankrupt rather than the workers, and planter political power was sapped because bankrupt planters went back to England to live out their lives of quiet desperation.

---

[2] Blerald (1986), pp. 87–27; esp. 126–27; and Elisabeth (1972), p.170; for a few moves in a similar direction in Cuba, see Scott (1985), pp. 28–35, 110, 218–26, but these had little significance for left-right differences in attachment to the Spanish empire.

[3] As in Jamaica (Green (1976), p. 252) and the British Virgin Islands (Harrigan and Varlack (1991)).

The Organization of Planter Monopoly Advantage

The purpose of this section is to give a typology of monopoly advantage of employers in labor markets after emancipation. The types are distinguished by the difficulties and benefits of enforcement of the advantage. For example, some types of advantage depended on the geography of islands combined with the fact that planters tended to control inter-island migration. Thus, for example, Antigua, St. Kitts, and Barbados had almost no provision grounds, and all the arable lands were under the control of planters. This meant that it was easy to deny workers the chance to get a peasant "provisions" plot without permission of a planter on those islands. Since workers could not easily move among islands without planter permission, having a job on one and a plot on another, this situation provided a chance to keep the alternative of becoming peasants from the work force; the same monopoly was more difficult to establish and monitor on Jamaica, Trinidad, and the Windward Islands other than Barbados, and on the plantation colonies on the coasts of the Guianas.

Thus the chance of establishing a monopoly advantage over labor by limiting the peasant alternatives was much more possible on Barbados, Antigua, and St. Kitts than on others. On those islands it was easy to monitor and enforce anti-squatter laws as long as planters stuck together. There were no French or Spanish islands with no easily available mountainous peasant plots like these. There were hardly any plantations on Curaçao and the neighboring Dutch islands, but there were no real opportunities to become peasants in the deserts either, and something of the same sort was true of the Bahamas.

Thus we want to distinguish Barbados, Antigua, and St. Kitts by the ease with which the denial of peasant opportunities could be organized by planters. This means that we need a typology of monopolies that will immediately distinguish the type that was easy on the all-plantation colonies, hard in the mountainous and desert colonies. The reason we want to do this is that we can then form a theory of what sort of social structure is likely to develop to be enforced by planter-dominated governments on islands without mountains or deserts. We will then not be surprised when we find that Antigua did not take advantage of the British government's alternative to establish "apprenticeship" of former slaves after emancipation. Apprenticeship established a two-way bond between former slaves and masters, in which masters exchanged support for apprentices when they did not need them for labor in return for guaranteed labor when they did. Antiguan planters figured that they could be assured of the availability of labor when they needed it without supporting it when they did not, because peasant alternatives were not available to their workers. The monopoly of apprenticeship for a term of years was inferior, in their mind, to the monopoly established by island isolation combined with lack of unclaimed land (Thome and Kimball (1969 [1838]) pp. 7–52).

It turned out that apprenticeship, a close simulation of slavery for a term of years, did not work well anywhere, and was soon abolished. But in many colonies other than Antigua, planters were tempted by it. We have to explain why the planters of Antigua, no more noble or anti-racist than any others, should have insisted on complete emancipation. And for that purpose we need to have a typology of monopoly advantages in the labor market that will distinguish Antigua from most of the rest of the Caribbean (except for Barbados and St. Kitts).

It is therefore convenient to divide the types of monopoly according to the main object to which the monopoly rights were attached, so as to distinguish the types of difficulties of organizing enforcement of the monopoly. I will argue that it is convenient to discuss monopolies that attach (1) to the person whose labor is monopolized (e.g., slavery); (2) to alternative productive activity (e.g., peasant tenures); (3) to worker consumption (e.g., tenancy of houses or debt for consumption supplies); and (4) to restricting the opportunities of alternative employers who might compete for worker labor. The argument will be, then, that the enforcement of the monopoly over labor of slavery (or of apprenticeship for a term of years after slavery) attached to the person of the slave (or ex-slave) presents different problems of enforcement than does denying access to peasant tenures, which in turn is different from the enforcement problems created by the chance to attach labor dues to residential housing and so have monopolies created in the consumption market. Preventing other planters from selling their bankrupt plantations off as peasant plots is a different sort of problem than preventing prosperous planters from offering other people's laborers a higher wage.

Monopolies of the Person

Our intuition is that slavery, ownership of the person, is different from all other forms of coercion of labor. This intuition reflects the fact that the slaveowner can interfere with all freedoms, can limit all alternatives, can force a particular choice. Slavery is boundless coercion in the sense that if one form of limitation of alternatives does not work, an owner can try another. The reason limitations of planter power built into slave codes usually have little effect is that there are many substitutes for the form of coercion forbidden. The general point is that any alternative open to the person can be forbidden by the slaveowner. Slavery, then, is different from the monopoly created by denying potential peasants plots because if a free person cannot find a plot, then there may be other things he or she can do to avoid plantation labor. Other modified forms of owner rights in the person, then, are similar to slavery to the degree that they create rights to interfere with all the alternatives available to the worker.

We have analyzed in Chapter 5 the variations within the slave status created by variations in the problems of control of the slave by the owner in various types of enterprises. What we want to analyze here are types of coercive relations that approximate slavery by giving free rein to the employer to intervene in many aspects of the worker's life, with the object of limiting the alternatives of the worker so that he or she is forced to work as the employer wants. And in particular we are distinguishing here such arbitrary rights of intervention by particular "owners," rather than the right of the planters as a class to create legislation about all the alternatives. Where planter legislatures were powerful they tried to create all sorts of limitations of opportunity for the emancipated working class. But the right, for example, to remove a squatter off a piece of "crown land" pertained to the body politic, and not particularly to the owner of the slave.

The nearest approximation to slavery after emancipation was the "apprenticeship" system created by the English Parliament for emancipated slaves. The apprenticeship was supposedly to train slaves to be free men and women. The former owner was supposed to get coerced labor for a term of years, longer for agricultural workers than for domestic slaves or craftsmen (and craftswomen when women were so classified, which was almost never). In return for this the owner was supposed to provide essentially all the requirements of life for the apprentice.

In the narrowest interpretation (that of Barbados) this meant in particular that since children were born free after emancipation, the planter did not have to provide food for the children (Green (1976)). The worker lived on the plantation, and had no rights (not granted by the master) to any usufruct of that plantation. The master governed the amount of provisions provided (subject to legal minima enforced, occasionally, by stipendiary magistrates) and selected the work. About the only freedom guaranteed fairly definitely was the right not to be whipped, a considerable and valuable right but not a very extended definition of freedom. The amount of coerced labor was specified, and former slaves could do more than this for wages; they could sometimes use those wages to buy themselves out of apprenticeship early.

This system limited dramatically all the alternatives for the freed person in a way not characteristic of the limitations of other free people, and put the control over those limitations in the hands of their former owners. The limitations were attached to the person of ex-slaves, and control was attached to the person of their ex-owners. Apparently the freedmen and freedwomen thought this was a lot like slavery, and we have to agree.

Broadly speaking, this system failed, and in the colonies with sugar frontiers, immigration created a similar temporary slave-like bondedness. The immigration of East Indians and some other ethnicities was at first carried on in such a way that it merely supplemented the labor force available in the plantation colony. The colony's government signed up the laborers in Asia (or elsewhere) and left the signing of labor contracts to pay back the passage until after the immigrants were landed. This would create a pressure to lower the labor market wage rate, but would otherwise leave the labor market a free market with competitive wages, much like the American urban labor market in the late 19th and early 20th centuries.

The system was soon modified so that the immigrant had an obligation to work for whoever bought his contract on arrival, with many traditional planter rights owed by "apprentices" or "engaged" European labor in the early days of the colonies. This was semi-servile labor for a term of years, with the terms of the servile tenure specified in a labor contract signed in a very low-wage Asian environment but interpreted so as to reduce wages in a high-wage environment in the Caribbean. People with such coolie wage contracts often thought that when, for example, the planter did not pay the wages the contract said, the contract was abrogated; local magistrates often did not see it the same way, partly because they did not speak Bengali, but partly because their salaries were ultimately allocated by a legislature of planters.[4]

So immigrant status eventually not only carried the general obligation to pay off the debt contracted to get to the high-wage labor market, but the specific obligation to live on a specific plantation, to work there, to accept the provisions provided there, and so on. The general set of limitations and dependencies were attached to the person who had agreed to the contract, and enforced by the person to whom the contract was sold. Of course the creation by the British colonial authorities of a general obligation to pay off the debt for passage created an obligation to

---

[4] "Fell into arrears in wage payments" is Green's phrase ((1976), pp. 278–79). They were sometimes held to be criminally vagrant if they left only because they were not paid. Perhaps worse, East Indians even went wandering about and died of tropical diseases without supervision. They died of African and European diseases quite a lot anyway, but it is particularly offensive to the colonial administrator's mind if they die without supervision. Green is a good example of the colonial administrative mind, perhaps shaped too much by reading only administrators' views in the archives.

work, enforced in various ways. But it was turned into a system much more like slavery for a term of years after the local legislatures got control of it.

Many of the devices for monopolization in the labor market that we will discuss below also had an aspect, for some of the workers who suffered from them, of monopolies attached to the person. For example tenancies in houses and yards on a plantation that had labor dues as part of the rent, in contracts in which the standing crops in the yard passed to the planter in case of non-performance of the labor dues at a value assessed by other "objective" planters, obviously created a special monopoly by the planter over the labor of the particular person who occupied the house (or in some cases, of all the family members who lived there). Similarly a debt to the plantation company store tended, in the system of justice of the colonies, to involve debt peonage of the debtor to the particular planter on whose estate the store sat.

Wages in arrears often created ties as well, for the likelihood of ever collecting was greater if one stayed on the same plantation. Whether it was the planter or the worker who was in debt, it created peonage for the worker, a source of coercion for the planter.

Slave provision plots traditionally used by a particular slave family in the foothills quite often were owned by the planter (though the frontier work of developing them into arable land had been, of course, the after-hours accomplishment of the slaves). The right to continue as a peasant farmer on a plot developed by oneself and one's family thus often carried the obligation to work on the plantation to which it "belonged." That fact enabled the planter to demand more than a labor contract would have given (e.g., it often required the labor of family members as well as the lessee). In a well-developed planter political system shaped by a history of slavery abolished, all sorts of coercive power in the labor or commodity market tended to get turned into an attempt to control all the alternatives of particular people, as had happened in slavery. Planters were not satisfied simply to have workers compete with one another and so drive down wages; they wanted to drive down particular people's wages by particular powers over them.

Consumption Monopolies

Cheap goods for consumption were not, from the beginning, a value for those who founded colonies. The basic idea of mercantilistic colonies was very close to that defining private property in any modern corporation. The king or other sovereign was the owner of property rights in the colony, which therefore should be so organized as to make money for the king. Like any other stockholder, the king might then organize a corporation, sometimes with other stockholders, to administer that property. The king or the corporation might give or sell parts of the enterprise, for instance, pieces of land for producing consumption goods, but that was part of an incentive system for making the colony profitable, not in order to produce things valuable in themselves.

The basic notion that the returns from colonies were to be counted in the metropole, not in the colony itself, and that they did not include fat peasants or long life for the workers or any other consumption value, continued to dominate the metropolitan part of colonial administration. Likewise, the welfare of workers is not normally a direct purpose of corporate law, and people do not ordinarily create corporations to be able to pay wages. But in modern society at least macroeconomic policy is supposed to create jobs and wages.

Such a system, then, created a basic empire-colony organization that automatically thought of increases in value from the point of view of the stockholders, rather than from the point of view of the workers or middle management. Since many of the basic ideas of how kings should run their business involved the notions of legal property in land or other estates, because the king could not supervise everything in detail, and since colonies in particular were very hard to administer in detail when the mail took three to six months, the colonial incentive system tended to create "property rights." These rights were held in general by planters and other capitalists, and by merchants who managed the translation of production in the colonies into returns in the metropole, especially returns to the government. The legitimacy of the system, however, depended on returns in the metropole rather than on returns to the workers or the planters.

This in turn meant that no one in a mercantilist system could see the use of modifying the flow of consumption goods unless someone, preferably the king or the upper political classes, made a profit. Island boundaries across which flowed things to eat were opportunities to make a profit (or to collect taxes), rather than an obstacle to be overcome. The fact that people could eat much better (because more cheaply) if they bought food from the nearby North Americans rather than from the European metropole was not therefore a value in the original imperial system. The flow of food was to make a profit from or to collect taxes on, not to feed people.

In particular, as we have noted frequently, the value produced by a peasant family on land it cultivated that went into their stomachs was of no interest to the imperium. One collected taxes and profits on sugar, not on plantains or manioc or fresh fish. It was perfectly in order for a colonial officer or planter to complain that provisions were too cheap in

Jamaica (Green (1976), p. 307), so people were not forced to work; the modern argument that this shows the efficiency of capitalism for the workers had hardly been invented.

After emancipation this still meant that island productivity was measured in the flow of goods salable in Europe, or flows for consumption that could be taxed. If a monopoly created by a planter government was used to produce goods for export that could be taxed or on which profits could be made, it was clearly a good thing, prima facie legitimate.

Further, the apparatus was in large measure already there to create and administer such monopolies. All housing and yard gardens for the slaves had been built so as to be monopolized by planters on plantations. Roads and coastal shipping docks were built to supply plantations, not peasant farmers. Subsistence plots were arranged so they could be cultivated on weekends by people who worked on plantations, and the allocation mechanism was in the hands of planters. Permission for hucksters to pass onto the plantation to sell their goods was routinely administered by overseers. Urban elites had claimed the right to administer provisions markets populated by peasants and higglers because such trade was not a right valuable in itself, but valuable because it facilitated exploitation of the colony as a whole.

Since these traditional ways of fitting control of the flow of consumption goods into the incentive system of the sugar export productive system were created by imperial island governments with the help of local legislatures or councils, and since this governmental system was not destroyed by emancipation in the English islands, it was available for use in disciplining labor after emancipation.

Houses and yards on all the islands, and provision grounds on the islands with extensive uncultivated land (i.e., all except Barbados, Antigua, and St. Kitts), were defined as the property of the planters after emancipation, though of course the buildings had been built and the provision grounds cleared by slaves, mostly on their days off. The standing crops on provision grounds and yards were generally defined as the property of the slaves, but upon expulsion of the tenant, the crops were usually assessed by a group of planters and paid for before becoming property of the planter—there was no option not to sell, of course (see the summary of legislative provisions in Gibbs (1987), pp. 26–27).

It was a frequent practice, as mentioned above, for the rent of these properties to be explicitly included in a labor contract, rather than in a separate tenancy contract, creating coerced labor of particular residents (and often their families) with the punishment being expulsion from house, yard, and provision ground, with forced sale of the crops. For example, such a contract including housing and a yard in Antigua had a special name in the law on the labor contract after emancipation, namely, "general hire" (Lazarus-Black (1994), pp. 130, 142, 283n.8). For this reason, many of the freed families preferred to find housing else-where, or campaigned for rental contracts separate from labor contracts. In the long run many planters agreed to create a separate village ground at the edge of the estate and to sell plots in it. This, of course, still cre-ated a monopoly to the degree that working off the plantation would create additional transportation costs for the worker, but that is not as coercive as a tied tenancy contract.

The workers did not in general like this system, and many of them moved out of plantation housing when they could. For example, Wil-liam Sewell, a reporter for the New York *Herald Tribune*, estimated that there were 11,000 field workers living on plantations in 1834 in Tri-nidad, when plantation labor was still coerced. By 1859 only 4,000 still lived on estates, while 7,000 had left (Brereton (1981), p. 80).[5]

It was easy for a planter to turn his old provisions supply system into a company store with the same basic staples, creating a great accessibility advantage both to the workers' houses on the plantation and to their work. Further since he could use his control over the wages to collect on any credit advanced, he was better placed to extend credit, often having a monopoly over credit purchases. His monopoly was stronger if he de-layed paying the wages. Debt created by such credit purchases could then be used to create debt peonage, which may have had a precarious legal existence in the British empire but had an effective practical exis-tence in the colonies, where planters controlled enforcement. While the planter could not keep plantation workers from trading with higglers who traveled between plantations, he could make it more difficult for the higglers to reach workers who lived on the plantation. And higglers could not usually give credit.

The late 18th and early 19th centuries decreased the scope and influ-

---

[5] Starting in 1882 in Trinidad, and more or less dominant by the turn of the century, the sugar production system went over to a pattern of a large central sugar-processing factory with several commercial tenant farmers producing cane, a thoroughly capitalist relationship rather similar to that obtaining between landlords and tenant farmers in rural England. The same sort of arrangement was common on St. Lucia (Green (1976), p. 255). Such a system of central processing plants with commercial contracts with smaller sugar cane growers had started developing earlier in the French islands, especially Guadeloupe after an earthquake (Schnakenbourg (1980,1)), and developed rapidly in Cuba at about the same time as in Trinidad, after a much later emancipation. Besides depending on technical advances in sugar production, this transformation usually also required local rail connections between the fields and the central processing plants, restricted production to large open land areas (e.g., the ones on Marie Galante in Guadeloupe) and excluded small valleys (e.g., the ones around Basse Terre in Guadeloupe), and the like. But this restructuring of plantation capi-tal came, in most places, after slave society features of the rural labor market were already much weakened, and probably was not in itself a big factor in that weakening.

ence of mercantilistic policies, and this in turn meant that the great advantage of the United States and Canada in supplying food was reflected in much cheaper prices. Already in the late 18th century Americans could sell provisions at about half the price that European monopoly suppliers charged. When the rapid growth of peasant agriculture on many of the islands was added, the living standard that could be bought for a given expense must have been much higher after emancipation than in the heyday of slavery. If free people's wages were as high as slave provision expenses, then, the living standards of freed families must have been much higher, even not taking into account those goods (such as practical ability to marry) that were the direct result of freedom. Farmers complained of a glut of provisions pushing prices down and could not see anything but tragedy in a generous supply of provisions causing low prices, which must mean that people ate better at the same wages.

Overall, then, the planter governments and individual planters used the traditional mercantilist and plantation apparatus of control over the flow of consumption goods to create monopolies to give them advantages in the labor market. There was, broadly speaking, a drift away from attempts to use these to recreate coercive freedman-to-master relations similar to slavery by transforming them into monopolies over the whole of a person's life, and toward relationships more similar to wage labor with a managed price. Resistance (by voting with their feet) of freed workers generally transformed personal coercive systems gradually into general politically organized pressures on workers to earn money somehow, under as severe competition as could be arranged. These general pressures, combined with reduction in productive alternatives, were supposed to create worker demand for jobs as plantation workers at wages plantation owners thought they could pay.

Monopolies by Reduction of Alternative Productive Opportunities

In some of the British islands planter governments could drastically limit the alternatives of the labor force by limiting emigration. The same islands appear on this list as have repeatedly appeared in discussions of which islands were old colonies, versus which were sugar frontiers, which had imported provisions versus slave provision grounds, which had nowhere for slaves to run away to versus islands with maroon settlements, which were entirely dominated by sugar versus those with coffee or cocoa plantations. The old colonies with imported provisions, no refuge, and sugar domination were Barbados, Antigua, and St. Kitts.

From the point of view of the Caribbean labor market, these colonies were overpopulated; the men in them, and perhaps the women and children, would be more productive elsewhere, in the newer sugar colonies. Their relative overpopulation is reflected in the fact that they are now only about twice to three times as densely populated as they were in the late 18th century, while the other colonies have added population steadily in the 19th and 20th centuries. Thus if one could deny emancipated people the right of emigration, one could turn them into a reserve army of the unemployed (Green (1976), pp. 257–89). That army would be smaller in the harvest season than in the off-seasons, but it would enable the labor-intensive, low-wage exploitation of exhausted land even in a market where more fertile colonies (or colonies with slave labor) were competitors. Barbados plantations competed successfully with more fertile Cuban plantations with slave labor in the 19th century.

The main danger of absorption of that reserve army in these colonies was the possible division of bankrupt plantations into plots for peasant cultivation. We mentioned earlier (Chapter 4; Barrow (1983), p. 94) that in Barbados those few plantations that were divided sold for up to twice as much per acre when sold as peasant plots than they were worth as sugar plantations. If some large part of the sugar plantations had been broken up, the increase in the going wage rate would have made more of them unprofitable, and would have turned them, too, into peasant plots, a slippery slope toward capitalism with a competitive wage.

Since, as it happened, many of the mortgages and other debts on these plantations were in the same hands, and these were Barbados bankers' and planters' hands, and since the Barbados legislature had kept control over bankruptcy within the courts of the island, planters collectively could keep plantations from becoming peasant plots. In Jamaica and many other islands, sugar lands became peasant plots both by being broken up and sold and by rentals. This was partly because it was already a lost cause on islands with mountains to keep peasant tenures inaccessible to freed families, but also partly because bankrupt plantations were handled in England and turned over to English merchants to dispose of. These merchants had no concentrated interest in maintaining the prices of plantation properties, no capacity to run the plantations themselves, and no real objection if peasants could work for themselves rather than for low wages in the islands.

This combined strategy of preserving plantations and limiting emigration worked best in Barbados, partly because Barbados had a more effective government and a more solidary planter class. But it worked quite well in Antigua, which went directly from slavery to free labor rather than passing through apprenticeship of former slaves (Bermuda, a non-plantation colony, also skipped apprenticeship). The Antigua government passed an anti-emigration ordinance within a few years after emancipation (1836) that "they [workers] should not be allowed to leave the colony unless they could show that they had no relations dependent on them or for whom they had not made satisfactory provision" (Mathieson (1967), p. 44); of course, whites could leave even if they left dependents behind.

Immigration was another alternative to effect the island-wide scarcity of labor. In several colonies (for instance, Trinidad and British Guiana; see Green (1976), pp. 276, 290) the expense of obtaining Asian immigrants was shouldered largely by the public treasury. It was natural for planters to imagine that decreasing the wages of labor was a public good to be paid for out of the public purse. Further it was often just as natural that taxes should be shifted from sugar to imports of provisions, so that the workers paid for their own competition. Much of the time what happened is that the wages for ordinary year-round labor were decreased by the competition of East Indian immigrants. Black and colored laborers were in better physical shape, so harder seasonal labor, such as holing for planting and cane cutting, was paid at a higher rate, and creole peasants were hired for it, usually on a piecework basis (called a "task system"). Immigration characterized those colonies that were still frontiers, especially Trinidad and Guyana, partly because their public purses were prosperous enough to finance immigration and their wages were highest (so most needed lowering).

Planter governments in British colonies that had hills and mountains, provision grounds, maroon settlements, and cocoa or coffee cultivation generally tried, and generally failed, to declare all cultivable non-sugar land crown land. They sold crown land only in large lots for sugar cultivation, tried to suppress squatting, and otherwise tried to limit peasant cultivation. Where there was relatively little sugar cultivation and where there was already a substantial small-plot peasant cultivation of coffee, cocoa, or provisions, this policy might not be tried. Both were true in British Dominica and Montserrat, and Puerto Rico in the Spanish empire was similar. There was little attempt to restrict peasant cultivation on these islands (but see the discussion of Dominica's tax policy below). Where there was substantial sugar cultivation and already substantial small-plot cultivation, as in Trinidad and Jamaica, policies were enthusiastically enacted, and then very large police expenses made it difficult to enforce them. This simply put a brake on commercial peasant production while not stopping peasant provisions cultivation. Naturally the planter interpretation of this was that black and colored small-plot cultivators were too lazy to produce commercial crops. Shortly after the crown lands were legally opened up to small-plot buyers in Trinidad (by Governor A. H. Gordon [1866–1870]), cocoa exports, mostly cultivated on peasant plots, were of higher value in Trinidad than sugar (Brereton (1981), pp. 89–91).

On Dominica, where there was a great deal of land that could be cultivated in small plots, heavy taxation on peasant activities, land, and export crops pushed many small farmers to the point of bankruptcy, where they could not pay the taxes. Sometimes peasant land was taxed at a rate as much as ten times as high as plantation land, and comparable discriminatory export tax rates were put on cocoa, arrowroot, coffee, and root crops that peasants could and did cultivate, so as to restrict the prosperity of smallholders. And as if this were not enough, the tax laws were unfairly administered so that the actual tax rates were even more discriminatory against peasant enterprise than the planters had managed to legislate (Trouillot (1988), pp. 106–13).

Limitations on Labor Market Competition of Other Planters

In addition there were some attempts to restrict competition in the labor market itself between planters. There were early attempts to use legislation to forbid planters from "enticing" laborers away from their "contracts," usually contracts whose only existence was testified by the worker's working for the planter (Gibbs (1987), pp. 26–27) ("enticing" by emigration agents was also forbidden in many places). If the presumption was that a free laborer had a contract if he or she was at work, then anyone enticing a worker was encouraging that worker to violate his or her legal obligations.

But more important were attempts to impose labor market–wide wage rates for plantation labor, especially in times of strikes or other agitation. For example, the workers in Jamaica found out that their labor had been evaluated at one shilling sixpence in computing planter compensation for the abolition of planters' rights to coerced labor of apprentices, and they thought if their labor was worth that much, their wages should be that much, and organized themselves (with the help of Baptist ministers) to refuse to work for less. Attempts to organize planter solidarity to maintain a lower wage rate were used in opposition to this movement. More straightforward evidence of the principle of surplus value would be hard to find.

Similar conflicts in British Guiana produced similar attempts to organize planter solidarity around a published wage rate. Obviously the lower the wage rate, the more the higher returns from peasant cultivation than from plantation labor would wean creole labor away. Collective bargaining and petty bourgeois peasant cultivation are alternative worker strategies to the same end. Property in peasant plots was also, in the British democratic system of the time, a big step toward citizenship.

The Class Meaning of Citizenship

All these arrangements to use many aspects of legislation and administrative regulation to establish planter monopoly advantages in the labor market made the class nature of representative institutions in the British colonies transparent. Because the imperial government then supported these institutions, with some variations in enthusiasm, and because whenever citizenship and representation of the colored population became strong, the planter legislatures wanted to abolish their own autonomy in favor of the more reliable Colonial Office, the British imperial tie became transparently a class tie. Citizenship in the ordinary sense of being able to elect members of legislatures that could enact laws thus became primarily a class matter.

Because citizenship had been a matter of race before emancipation, and because class was also a matter of race in Caribbean slave societies, citizenship's being a class matter also meant that it was a race matter. Class was most related to race for the emancipated slaves, since their class position had been explicitly connected to their race. This meant in turn that class was most related to race among blacks generally, and citizenship had clearer class implications for blacks than for many colored people. The most egregious uses of monopolies established by legislation after emancipation to establish slavemaster-like relations between employer and employed were applied especially to former slaves. It was former slaves who had had customary rights to a house, garden, and subsistence plot that were now declared sole property of the planter. It was the class-conscious large sugar planters who had been most interested in slavery as a class matter, and it was those same planters who were most interested in creating and maintaining monopolies in the free labor market for the planter class as opposed to the new proletarian class. And in most colonies it was planters who in fact were in the legislature and who were in fact petitioning the Colonial Office to allow exceptions to that office's general free labor market conception of what emancipation meant. Just as individual negotiations of the slave labor contract were more common in non-sugar enterprises and in domestic life, so the new legislation creating coercion in the free labor market was most ignored in urban, peasant, and hill crop enterprises.

Thus the exquisitely anxious negotiations about the representation of the free colored were, from the planters' point of view, negotiations over whether the coercive "requirements" for plantation labor stability and cheapness would be the dominant purpose of government, or one consideration among many. In particular, such negotiations brought up the question of what considerations would be dominant in deciding the citizenship of the blacks who worked on plantations. That was central to the whole project of using government to establish semi-coercive plantation labor regimes by regulating immigration, tenantry contracts, vagrancy, squatting, and the like.

In its turn the question of island autonomy came to be tied in with the class conflict aspect of citizenship. By and large in the British islands post-emancipation movements for autonomy, and eventually for independence, had the opposite class implications from those they had had before emancipation. In the slave societies autonomy was primarily a matter of planter government, and partly as a consequence of this, it was a matter of whether the islands could trade freely for provisions and manufactured goods rather than having to buy from the imperial metropole.

This sometimes pitted the merchants holding the monopoly against a free trader planter group, as clearly happened in Martinique in the French Revolution (discussed in Chapter 8). Such autonomy movements in slave societies rarely went so far as to claim independence, because the preferential tariffs for colonial sugar advantaged planters. Thus the imperial tie would be broken by planter autonomy only by accident, and usually then replaced by some other imperial tie. Further, until the French Revolution in Haiti, no one had proposed to use the autonomy to introduce slaves into political citizenship or to equalize the political power of largely urban colored people with that of planters. Some moderate push in that direction came from the British Colonial Office in the years immediately after emancipation.

After emancipation the general tendency, especially in the Colonial Office, to apply the same criteria for the franchise for colonial legislatures to all free people meant that planters became more likely to lose control over the colonial legislatures than over administrative influence. Where the planters had firm control over the legislature and the legislature had a great deal of autonomy, as in Barbados, autonomy was little mixed up with political citizenship for plantation laborers, and planters continued to favor autonomy (see Hamilton (1956)).

At the other extreme where colored people rapidly came to have power in colonial legislatures, as in Montserrat and Dominica, planters tended to push for crown colony government in which the governor picked much of the legislature and held agenda-making power for it. In Jamaica and most of the Leewards the planters wavered to and fro as political contingencies dictated, but by and large they drifted toward giving up legislative power and emphasizing the colony-empire tie as the guarantor of prosperity and security.[6]

This arrangement of the battle over citizenship in the islands, then, reproduced in more repressive and racist form the nature of the same battle in the 19th century in Britain. Insofar as there was colored political activity, it then tended to be of the Whig variety, searching for allies and resources among the movements of the more reputable and moderate of the disenfranchised. The chance of getting any power in the government at all varied between the islands, being very small in Barbados, relatively good in the long run in some of the smaller islands and in Jamaica, and confused by the large immigrant communities in Trinidad and Guyana. Their chances also varied over historical time, with the changes of ministries in England (with Whigs being more open to widening the franchise for the colonies as well as in Britain), with disorganization and desperation of the planters (especially in Jamaica after the abolition of preferential tariffs for colonial sugar), and with the normal shifts in political fortunes and alliances.

However the colonial part of the empire differed from England in the close identification of disenfranchisement, working-class membership, and blackness. After the liberal period of about a decade after emancipation, when the Colonial Office pushed for freer labor markets and a more equal franchise, the colonial system also differed from the British one in the much greater intensity of the identification of colonial Tories than English Tories with imperialism. For Caribbean planters imperialism was the core value of English Tories; in contrast, Protestantism was the core value for Tories in Ireland, and anti–working class ideologies were the core value for Tories in Wales and Scotland.

Thus by the turn of the 19th century the intertwining of the issues of citizenship, repressive class-consciousness, and racism had produced an alignment of races from white to colored to black on the extension of the franchise, on class issues, such as squatter tenures, immigration, and labor union organization, on independence and island legislative autonomy, and, insofar as it was relevant, on political preference among English parties. Whites had the most conservative position on all issues and blacks the most left position. Usually not all of these issues were salient at the same times, and they were differently salient in different islands. The division was probably most intense in Jamaica, least intense in Barbados (where the powerlessness of the left made all issues only rarely salient) and in the non-plantation islands.

---

[6] For the development of opposition between a planter "country" party and a colored and liberal "town" party in Jamaica, and the decision by the country party to abolish its own power because the Assembly was dominated by a "destructive minority," of colored representatives, see Campbell (1976), pp. 202, 356–65.

Thus the pattern of alignments of issues in the British islands by the late 19th century looked much like that in the French islands other than Haiti (there was no white right wing in Haiti). The principal difference is that the *girondin*-like movements of the colored and urban liberals in the French islands were much more strongly identified with the principle of universal citizenship than the Whig-like movements of the colored in the English islands. A related difference was that there was more of a liberal civil service and professional class in the French islands than in the British ones, and there was a stronger democratic movement among the petty bourgeoisie there. And a final difference is that the center-left in France used the imperial tie more vigorously to promote equality of citizenship during democratic regimes, so the identification with France penetrated much more deeply into the colored population, with the reservation that it was the France of the Revolution they identified with rather than the France of order. Nevertheless in both empires the class and citizenship questions were intertwined, and in both, that intertwining was strongly related to race in the same way.

The Political Incorporation of Multiple Institutions

The slave societies of the late 18th century British empire often incorporated subparts with substantial "institutional completeness" (Breton (1964)). For example, Spanish law with a British executive and judiciary was valid in Trinidad from around 1800, when the island became British, until the 1830s, and legally recognized communities of free Negroes and colored people managed institutions quite separate from those of plantation society in the highlands; many French institutions continued to rule the daily life of many planters and slaves in Trinidad (where the Spanish had invited French planters in) as well as in Tobago, Grenada, St. Lucia (see Breen (1844) for a British reactionary view), St. Vincent, and Dominica—all of these except Tobago still have relatively large Roman Catholic communities, as does Montserrat; a large community of former Irish indentured servants led a more or less separate life on the mountain Montserrat, reproducing the separateness created by the Irish Sea by altitude; many Dutch institutions continued to organize daily life in Guyana [Berbice, Demerara, Essequibo]; during short English occupations of French (e.g., Martinique and Guadeloupe) and Dutch islands (e.g., St. Eustatius) during wars of the late 18th century even more of the institutions governing daily life were not English.[7]

---

[7] Though sometimes the freedom of trade introduced by the English produced major transformations in a short time. For example, during an English conquest the slave population of Guadeloupe roughly doubled between 1759 and 1763—see Pérotin-Dumon,

This was a common pattern in the late 18th century Caribbean: from 1795 on, France theoretically governed the Spanish part of the island of Hispaniola [now The Dominican Republic] as well as what would become Haiti, but except for the army and the law the institutions in Santo Domingo were clearly Spanish, and remained so under the Haitian occupation up to 1844. The dominance of French law, however, lasted into the late 19th century (see Hoetink (1982 [1972]), p. 107), but there were no social boundaries created by loyalty to French institutions in daily life. Sint Maartens-St. Martin had French and Dutch separate governments with informal treaties separate from those of their respective empires as their common government. At some times the Jamaican government had treaties with quite autonomous maroon "states" in the mountainsplanter state in. The normal number of governments on all but the largest islands was usually one, but the number of systems of institutions with social validity was often more than one. This was a pluralism of empire cultures. It perhaps reached its linguistic extreme in Curaçao, where a quite ordinary lower-middle-class white had to learn Papamiento (a sort of Portuguese dialect), Dutch, Spanish, and English, and many times it would be useful to know French.

These plural societies were quite often unified by one of two sorts of coalitions between planter elites of the imperial power and the rest of the society. First there was the alliance based on the common planterhood, as when the French planters in Trinidad relied on the same coercive apparatus (Spanish with English implementation) as did English planters. Whatever the social tensions and paranoia in times of war between the empires, the French could trust the British to supply reliable coercion to maintain slavery, and the British.[8] could rely on the French to show solidarity, at least when the enemies were slaves.

Second, there was an alliance based on mutual isolation, between slave-dominated lowlands versus peasant highlands (Jamaican maroons; Irish servants in Montserrat—see Fergus (1978)), separate islands (ethnically diverse planters on St. Croix, a plantation island, versus the commercial St. Thomas in the Danish Virgins), or separate geographical sections (on St. Maartens versus St. Martin; Saint Domingue versus Santo Domingo; St. Vincent between the Caribs and the English)[9] with more

---

(1985), two different figures on pp. 51 and 72. A comparable sugar and slave boom for the Havana region of Cuba happened about the same time—see Kuethe (1986), pp. 3–23.

[8] Though British planters in Trinidad might complain of the inadequate racism and excessive humanitarianism of Spanish law—see Smith (1965 [1953]), p. 98; Naipaul (1984 [1969]), pp. 384–85. One central trouble seemed to be that Spanish law allowed the court sometimes to listen to slave evidence, at least after torture (ibid., pp. 153–368, 381–82)

[9] See Shepard (1831) for an extremely contentious account of the alliance between the Caribs and French revolutionaries.

or less contested borders and a complicated scenario of imperial and local international relations.

M. G. Smith (1965 [1960]) argues that this sort of division of society into groups living by different institutions is different to some considerable degree from a society with different styles of life determined in large measure by the same institutions, such as the difference between planters and slaves. The daily lives of the people brought into contact by slavery are intertwined by the institutions—political, productive, and the plantation as a "community"—that constitute the slave system. Slave and planter are divided by the legal boundary, but slaves are not permitted freely to build institutions with autonomous legitimacy on their side of the boundary. The subcultures produced by stratification on each side of the employment relationship thus do not qualify, he says, for being "plural" because they do not generate partially isolated institutional systems. They are more likely to produce class conflict than to produce secession, though the fantasy of secession may play a role in the moral philosophy of class relations (Roemer (1982)).

Smith's point is in particular that plural societies produce different problems of social integration during nation-building and the growth of political citizenship, because they pose the problem of building separate institutionalized ways of life, not already integrated in daily life, into a common political community, rather than settling the issues of class conflict (perhaps by collective bargaining in an ongoing productive enterprise) and moving toward enfranchisement of the poor (e.g., in party competition over franchise issues). Many of Smith's examples come from the place of East Indians in democratizing Trinidad and Guyana.[10]

The degree of institutional completeness of the East Indian community varies a good deal across islands. For example, compare the religious distinctiveness of Trinidadian East Indians (documented in Jha (1976)) with the Christianization reported for East Indians in Grenada (in Steele (1976)). Compare this with the variation across immigrant groups in Montreal by Raymond Breton (1964), who argues that the social and cultural closure of the groups depends on the degree of development of distinctive institutions, in turn determined partly by size and degree of segregation The same argument is implicit in M. G. Smith.[11]

Planter citizenship for the French planters in Trinidad and the British Windwards early in the 19th century, rather than their suspicious exclu-

---

[10] See also Braithwaite (1975 [1953]) for a more geometrical version of the problem, similar to that of the W. Lloyd Warner and "caste and class" school on U.S. race relations.

[11] A similar variation in the Indian Ocean is the nearly complete Catholic assimilation (see Scherer (1974 [1965]), p. 80) of the East Indians, who amounted to about 20 percent of the total population, in Réunion. But in Mauritius, with a population about 70 percent East Indian, Indian culture is highly preserved (Paturau (n.d. but after 1986), pp. 112–13).

sion from government, would probably have strengthened the political position of the British planters, both with respect to their home government and in local crises with the non-planter colored and the slaves. But as Naipaul (1984 [1969]) teaches us, such governmental institutional pluralism makes everything in government complicated, and provides nooks and crannies to be exploited by conflicting personalities, conflicting foreign (e.g., Venezuelan) and domestic revolutionary and reform currents, and conflicting career and property interests.

Planter power can have other bases than planter citizenship when they are not citizens. For example, the French elite in Trinidad showed a great capacity to assimilate Roman Catholic immigrants, so many of the leading "French" elite members have Irish names, and some with French names gained their revolutionary experience in Irish revolutionary movements.

The general point of these examples is that a given ethnic subcommunity of plantation immigrants on different islands have had different degrees of institutional completeness, which depended heavily on the gross size of that group. But when planters were ethnically plural as well, as in Trinidad, the stability and totalitarianism of planter rule has been precarious.

Similarly, if the mutual distrust, conflict over cultural matters, and conflict of interest in political civil service jobs, government contracts, and trade union power between the black and East Indian proletariats and peasantries of Guyana and Trinidad had not been so severe, there might have been more rapid movement toward full political and economic citizenship. By the time proletarian and peasant unity became relevant, the planters were unified across ethnic lines, if somewhat disorganized by the breakup of the empire and the policies of the Labour governments in England.

The ethnic pluralism that enters the political system, then, is in large measure a projection of communal institutional diversity on the canvas of state definitions of political interests. For the century or so after emancipation, the planters were dominant definers of the channels by which political interests could be expressed, who was enfranchised to express them, what sorts of interests would be filtered out and not heard in the political system. The conjunction of interests that gave meaning to enfranchisement, then, was some combination of the ideological lenses of those behind enfranchisement movements in the metropole, as refracted in part through the Colonial Office, and those defined by race, immigration, labor market monopoly, and restricted economic development by planter local governments.

But the conjunction of institutional interests and channels of possible representation of communal groups was *also* defined by the ways these groups got married, organized family and communal claims on property, trained their children for the labor market and for politics, conceived the relation between their own religion and the dominant Anglican religion, and the like. Even identical channels for claiming civil, political, and welfare rights would mean different things to the East Indians, the colored, and the blacks, because those institutional patterns were different.

And, of course, the planters saw to it that immigrants had different channels than did colored and black (for otherwise the communal group of East Indians would not have given planters monopoly advantage in the labor market), that colored and black often had different channels, that those still working on plantations had different channels than did those who had moved into cities or got peasant plots.

So the definition of political interests was different for different communal groups; differences in the internal organization (e.g., size, segregation, institutional completeness) or political status of a given communal group between islands had reflections in their definitions of their political interests. All these definitions varied over time, as the empire and the imperial culture defined the problems of citizenship, of civil freedoms and rights, of political representation, and of welfare rights differently, and drew political lines differently in the islands and in the metropole.

The central metropolitan cultural influences on these developments in the British colonies were the enfranchisement campaigns of the Whigs and the British labor movement, especially the Labour Party. For those with French connections, the French Revolution and its variations and the competition between parties of order and parties of the Revolution during the 19th century had echoes in the internal politics of the Caribbean islands even if they were not French islands, and after our period the anti-colonial movements of India and Africa had distant echoes.

Roughly speaking the end result of these factors was two distinct "left" movements in the colonies with large East Indian immigration, a black colored and an East Indian one, each separately ranged from radical-labor to liberal-Whig or reformist labor. The liberal-reformist wing of the black colored movement tended, first of all, to be more colored and less black. Second, it tended to be associated with the more conservative of the Protestant sects, but rarely Anglican, in cultural tone; more oriented toward marriage and the virginity of unmarried women; more in favor of partial independence rather than complete independence; and sometimes more French (French reactionary planters were much like English ones, but French middle-class movements were more radical, and more powerful in the French colonies, because there were larger bureaucratic classes there than in the English ones). By and large, the more conservative or reformist wing of the East Indian movement has been both more dominant and "more communal" than it has been in the colored and black movement.

Thus the extreme of two large labor movements, dominantly oriented toward populist politics rather than toward collective bargaining and trade unions, one East Indian and one creole black and colored, have dominated those colonies with the largest Indian immigration and the most complete development of separate institutions, Trinidad and Guyana. The creole colored and black movement has been more divided between radical (more black) wings and more moderate (more colored) wings than the Indian one, which has been in some sense "more communal."

At the opposite extreme, where there was essentially no or a small East Indian immigration on mature plantation islands, as in Barbados, Antigua, St. Kitts, there has been no real institutional development of the immigration population and no racial division of the left. The clean correlation between degree of whiteness and degree of moderation, with very white people being positively pro-imperial, is not interrupted by communal politics about such questions as how well churches of non-Christians are supported, or Indian marriages recognized.

In between are three main kinds of mixed islands: (1) islands with essentially ethnically homogeneous upper classes, mainly facing colored moderates and black radicals, but with enough ethnic diversity in the working class to make for some special considerations, such as Jamaica (see Ehrlich (1976)) and perhaps Grenada; (2) islands with ethnically heterogeneous white populations (e.g., French or colored populations so large and powerful that they make the institutional unity of the upper class problematic, such as Montserrat, Dominica, St. Lucia, and perhaps Trinidad); (3) islands where the whites have fled, or where racial boundaries and slavery were never central issues, where queer, Whiggish governments of mixed color pursue tourists and other economic development, as in the British Virgins, the Bahamas, the Caymans, and many small islands, such as the Grenadines.

Conclusion

The interaction of island class powers, democratization movements, and the constitutional structure of the island-empire tie acted together to determine what emancipation meant in the British empire. Rather similar conjunctions of local planter dominance, democratization in the ruling society, and radically federal "empire" structures resulted in rather similar niggardly definitions of the freedom of freedmen in the U.S.

South after about 1876 and in the French islands during the reigns of "parties of order" between the revolutions in France.

What anti-slavery movements in non-slave metropoles meant, then, was shaped and limited by these constitutional features of empire governments. The British empire was extreme in the degree to which island governments were in a position such that they had to approve and administer anti-slavery legislation. The United States came close to this extreme before 1860 and again between 1876 and World War II. The French government in conservative periods had an empire government that regarded all the colonies as having to be separately legislated for and administered, with consent of legitimate local authorities, though with increasing deposits of revolutionary centralism in the definition of citizenship as the century went on. Thus the British islands administering emancipation are perhaps the best place to study the construction of limitations on ex-slave liberties after slavery was abolished.

Broadly speaking, the first burst of legislation and planter activity in the free labor market for ex-slaves was to invent devices to recreate the personal coercive relationship between a master and a slave, out of the legal materials of freedom of contract and the social materials of a slave society. The basic devices were variants on the peonage contract. East Indian immigrants were in servitude to particular owners who had bought their contracts; ex-slaves who wanted to continue to live in the houses they had built or to cultivate the subsistence plots they had cleared for cultivation were bound to work on a particular plantation; consumption credit was only available when backed by a plantation owner, and so on. These attempts to create a comparable level of individual-to-individual dependence as had obtained under slavery usually failed in the long run, basically because the ex-slaves "voted with their feet."

Other devices involved systematic attempts to cut off alternative opportunities. The most important of these were attempts to keep ex-slaves from effective ownership of plots of land that could be subsistence farms, local truck farms, or small plantations of cocoa, coffee, ginger, or other export crops. The basic fact was that, all told, if there was a viable peasant alternative, hardly anyone chose to work on a field gang on a sugar plantation. Presumably this was because peasant cultivation brought higher total welfare to the worker than did work at the going wage on plantations. The factors in the availability of the peasant alternative are outlined in Chapter 4. Our purpose here has been to explain variations in the intensity to which islands developed devices to destroy opportunities offered by the various natural and social factors discussed there. Our basic answer is that opportunities were destroyed more where the complex of empire federalism and planter-dominated island politics shaped the empire-island tie, so that anti-slavery movements could not go so far as to provide peasant plots on the ground in the Caribbean.

Many of the devices first used to recreate person-to-person labor relations without exit continued to be used after that effort had failed, especially when they involved plantation owners' monopolies in consumption goods: houses, provisions plots, credit for provisions, and the like. One can increase the degree of dependence of workers so that they more often choose to stay where they are, without trying to turn that into a re-creation of lifelong authority relations.

Finally, planters organized themselves into conspiracies in restraint of competition among themselves in the labor market, and they did so better where they controlled the local government and the empire government did not intervene in local matters, such as labor market contracts. The speed with which the practice of letting East Indians look for a job when they got to the islands disappeared and was replaced by an auction for the contract in which the worker had no voice shows this unwillingness to compete, by offering workers more, in clear form. Capitalism ideally means that workers compete for jobs and that employers compete for workers. The employer competition for labor half of this has always been less popular with employers. We diagnose exceptional employer political and social power when employers manage to dispense with that half. Though employers' cartels, like other cartels, tend to break up over the long run, they lasted longer on sugar islands that had been slave societies.

Our final argument in this chapter has been that a transparency of the connection between citizenship of blacks and immigrants and class interest was created by this set of strategies. When the empire tie was deeply implicated in the failure of democratization in England to reach the islands, so that citizenship for blacks and East Indians was unequal because of the empire, then independence was linked to citizenship and working-class interest. Suffrage, independence, race, and socialism were closely aligned by the end of the century in the British islands. That alignment was created in large measure by the systematic exploitation of island power and empire federalism by planters to reduce the wages and freedom of workers in the labor market by political means.

11

Spanish Colonies: *Caudillismo*, a Split Cuba, and U.S. Intervention

Introduction

Our purpose in this chapter is to analyze the big exceptions to the picture we have spent the book drawing: Haiti after independence, The Dominican Republic after its independence from Haiti, Cuba, and Puerto Rico. While the exceptions do not make up a very large proportion of the islands, they make up most of the land area and much of the population of the 19th century Caribbean. The fundamental argument of this chapter is that although these societies all had had slavery, and all abolished it in the 19th century, their political and social dynamics cannot be explained by those facts. The past existence of slavery had different historical consequences when, as in the Spanish islands, sugar planters had not used the slave legal tradition to construct a thoroughly slave society. And it also had different consequences when the slave and plantation system was thoroughly destroyed in a revolution and in an independence movement governed by ex-slaves, as in Haiti.

But to show effectively that the governments of these four political systems (on three islands) were not the governments of slave societies, I need to explain how they *did* work: how politics was connected to the mode of production in a different way than in slave societies, how race meant a different thing after emancipation, and how the sugar slave enclaves in Puerto Rico and especially Cuba did not undermine the essentially "South American" style of government and society of these islands.

Because the book's purpose is not to build a theory of how societies with minor slave aspects to their colonial histories modernized politically, the bits and pieces of theory of the dynamics of the Spanish islands and Haiti outlined here are not integrated into the theory of the book. This will give this chapter something of the character of "a brief outline of whatever happened in the Spanish islands and Haiti," rather than a theory of why one slave society was different from another. There is nothing to be done about this. These societies are too important to be left out of an account of the 19th century in the Caribbean, but *not* having been very extreme slave societies, the role they have played so far in this book, of being low-intensity slave societies in the lower right of the tables, is not much of an account. If it turns out that, at the peak, only about half of the sugar workers in one of the most intensive sugar plantation areas of Puerto Rico (near Ponce) were slaves, and most people in Puerto Rico did not work on sugar plantations anyway, the main theories of this book apply only peripherally even to that valley, and leave the rest of Puerto Rico out. It is a misfortune about social life that it makes social theory messy, perhaps, but it is a misfortune that we have to live with.

Obviously if I am going to convince the reader that the dynamics of Haiti were essentially South American, I will have to explain how South American governments worked in the 19th century,[1] and how they were caused in a way that did not require a Spanish cultural tradition, so that I can include Haiti among them.

My fundamental argument in this chapter is that the history of colonialism had produced the conviction that "a real government" could exist on these islands, and left behind cultural and social materials out of which such governments could be constructed. Because the whole Caribbean was a colonial enterprise, many of the materials of which governments had been constructed were world-system materials: customs tolls, international alliances, immigration and slave trade policies, appeals to public opinion in core European societies, and the like.

But because Spanish island societies and Haiti were more creole than all but the oldest slave societies (because they had not had the recent massive immigrations of the sugar frontier), many of the social materials that had to be incorporated into viable island governments were local, not world-system, forces. Most people who were to be governed on these islands did not have careers in the larger cosmopolitan world system; they were not going back home to Spain or France to marry and build country houses. Political leaders had to have a local power base, either to raise a civil war or to govern.

After independence Haitian local power bases could not be built out of the principles of legitimacy of the French old regime, because that was a slave system. And in the Spanish islands local sources of power had to be connected to powers generated in the world system in a new way. The Spanish had done it with a patrimonial bureaucracy that did not work very well even for Spain in the 19th century. It left most promising sources of local political power on which independent governments had to be built outside the imperial system of legitimacy. It was impossible for independent governments in Haiti and the Dominican Repub-

---

[1] I will not actually study such governments other than the Caribbean ones; for an analysis of variations among South American governments in the mid-19th century, see Safford (1985).

lic or the United States in Cuba and Puerto Rico to build an island government based on special privileges of peninsular Spanish bureaucratic
immigrants.

The first (and longest) part of this chapter is, then, devoted to the
processes by which local forces in three of the four countries (excluding
Puerto Rico) built state power. The most convenient way to do this is to
analyze the reasons why that process produced a system that is commonly called *caudillismo* in the literature on South America (an excellent summary is Safford (1985), pp. 348–49, 375–83). From the point
of view of the argument of this book, what this is supposed to show is
that such a system is nothing like the slave societies we have been discussing, because it is like something else. I need not argue that nothing
about Spanish culture encouraged a personalistic style in politics on the
Spanish islands, but only that the same structural situation could produce personalism in politics in Haiti as well. The Bonapartist or absolutist tradition in French culture could perhaps substitute for Spanish heroic culture.

The second part of the chapter is devoted to the analysis of the complex criss-crossing causes in the political system of Cuba in the late 19th
century, in which the instabilities of a society half slave and half free
(which were giving trouble to the most stable democracy of the time)
were added to the other instabilities that grew out of the Spanish colonial tradition and the extraordinary instability of the government of
Spain itself (Tilly (1993), pp. 79–89, esp. 82–83) and its empire (Halperin Donghi (1969)).

Caudillismo, Coteries, and Charisma

Political systems characterized by what Hispanic American countries call
caudillismo (or, in its more peaceful forms, *personalismo*) have dominated post-independence Haiti, the Dominican Republic, and Cuba.
Military bands in the mountains and deserts, hero worship,[2] leaders in
fancy uniforms whose main point is that they are not in fact not like
anyone else's uniform, irregular finances ("banditry" and "corruption"), ties of personal or patron-client loyalty, exchanges of "loans"
and "gifts" between persons embedded in relations of political loyalty,
political responsibility to persons rather than offices, elections as plebi-

[2] Including extraordinary praise of themselves by *caudillos*, it sounds paranoid to modern ears, but one has to recall that the first person who believed he was Napoleon was
Napoleon Bonaparte, and he turned out to be right. See Hoetink (1982 [1972]), pp. 123–
27, for examples of self-praise

scites confirming leadership selected by military means or by deals between *caudillos*, tests of manhood by violence with a justification of honor insulted (and a corresponding exclusion of women from politics and rejection of "courtier" civilization and culture) all occur together at the same times and places in Latin American politics. I will show they take place in Haitian politics as well, so they cannot be attributed to Hispanic culture alone, by showing that the same forces that produce *caudillismo* in the Dominican Republic and Cuba also produce it in Haiti.

These features give the islands a tone of Arthurian legend: the gathering of the host, trial by combat, heroic virtue except for some "manly" troubles with women, and personal riches with no mention of a mode of production.

It is clear that this complex formed a system: *caudillismo* did not mean that "history is the lengthened shadow of a man," as Emerson put it. That system arose in particular social environments. I will give an explanation of that system in three parts. First, I will try to show that the social structural conditions that brought the symptoms of the complex together occurred when political action (or other collective action) had to be taken on a larger scale than the local scale on which loyalty and responsibility were generated.

For example, a *caudillo* acted on a "national" scale with resources generated through "friends and neighbors" loyalties of local villages or regions, or generated within a military band. But no taxation system with autonomous legitimacy, for example, made local resources available for public purposes at the national level. Personal capacity to act at the level of a state without the normal sorts of legitimacy that related stable cosmopolitan states to their local subsystems is, then, the essence of the social structure of *caudillismo* in our argument.

The second part of the explanation specifies how the hero-and-personal-loyalty culture functioned in such a situation to make local loyalties into resources at a higher level. The basic point is that only successes in the macroscopic system generated resources for the *caudillo* to maintain the status of hero and of object of personal loyalty in the local system. The exceptional qualities of the leader were mysterious because evidence for them was available only in successes in, and resources from, a system beyond the ken of local daily life. But the fact that the national system had few autonomous resources or sources of legitimacy that reached local levels where resources were generated meant that leaders could not reliably generate successes on a national scale; and in particular no routines were organized on the local level that reliably guaranteed successes in public civil and military policy on the national level.

While the supralocal national system soon after independence had few resources, many that were available had sources and ties in the international system. These came in the form of tariffs on international trade and treaties with, or incorporation into, empires (empires in the Caribbean generally spent more on military and administrative expenses than they obtained in taxes, so there was a "flow of resources" from the empires to the local governments).

Roughly speaking, in the Dominican Republic in the last half of the century the main "parties" (called "red" [led by Santana and Báez] and "blue" [led by Luperón and Heureaux]) differed primarily in whether the resources of the system (especially the ones for defending it from the Haitians) could come from within the island or whether they should instead depend on the international system.

The Santana-Báez party, which held power in the third quarter of the 19th century, consistently attempted to create resources to defend the Republic's independence by making treaties with, or becoming incorporated into, empires that could defend them from the Haitians.[3] They negotiated for incorporation into the French and Spanish empires, and into the United States, for protection in return for granting rights to military bases (especially in Samaná Bay), and they asked for the empires' sponsorship of diplomatic negotiations to get the Haitian Emperor to recognize Dominican independence and end the border warfare (Rodríguez Demorizi (1981), pp. 76–96).

The Luperón-Heureaux party, which, roughly speaking, held power in the last quarter of the century, after the Haitian threat receded somewhat, favored independence and monopoly over the "national" territory, and based its powers mainly on control of tariffs on commerce, especially that through Puerto Plata.

The argument of the Santana-Báez party was that a small country next to a large, belligerent neighbor (Haiti had something like five times as large a population), that claimed all their territory and had conquered it several times, needed large strong friends. Since in the long run the nationalist ideology of Luperón and his party dominated the Dominican Republic, the Santana-Báez argument is portrayed in the modern literature as cowardice or treason (*vendepatria*). Our point is only that in poor, small Caribbean countries, cosmopolitan resources useful for constructing a national government were largely generated by the relations of that country with the world system, not by taxation of local productive activities, land, or local flows of commerce. Taxing international trade to support a government is not markedly more nationalistic than making international treaties for military protection.

[3] Monclus (1983), p. 27, describes the feedback system in which Dominican fear of Haitians led to international negotiations with slave powers, which then made the Haitians fearful of reintroduction of slavery.

The more forms of legitimacy such as law or electoral representation a *caudillo* could build into the cultural system whose core was his own virtues and successes, the more regular could be his extraction of resources and his capacity to produce successes. Plebiscites, for example, might not create democracy in the usual sense, but they tended to regularize authority for taxation. Particularly crucial was the extraction of resources sufficient to maintain the loyalty of the army and police force. The more regular the extraction of resources, the more we now know a *caudillo* as a dictator or tyrant or king. The diminutive *-illo* no longer seems appropriate to modern writers when a personal entourage became an institution; we do not attach a diminutive to the pope's title.

The construction of "personalism" as an ideological system, and the entailed question of what sort of things such a system can legitimate, is therefore the second part of the explanation of *caudillismo*. Our argument is that such an ideology of personalism was one of the few ways of connecting local sources of loyalty and power ignored by the Spanish colonial system and the loyalty of slaves repressed by the French system to the cosmopolitan world in which independent states were built.

The third part of the explanation is to outline the social structural situation that gave rise to this complex of scattered local resources and a cosmopolitan system in which the resources for building a state were available above local levels. By defining the *caudillo* complex by what it could do and how it could do it, we more easily understand where it solved problems people had. When did people's problems have their solution on a more macroscopic level than their resources and ties of loyalty normally reached? When did taxation or military recruitment have to be legitimated by personal successes of a *caudillo* rather than successes of the government as a social organization?

This third part of the theory, then, needs to explain why independence from Spain and France by way of revolution gave rise to *caudillismo*, while *caudillismo* was generally of minor importance in Saint Domingue or the Spanish islands (and the Spanish mainland) before independence. Why was it not such a severe problem in the United States after the American Revolution? Why was the Napoleonic form of *caudillismo* in France so much more stable, and particularly so much more of an institution-building movement, than the Haitian and Hispanic American forms? Why was King Arthur perhaps in a similar situation to a president of The Dominican Republic?

It also might be expected to explain why the Jamaican colony or the French Antilles colonies had relatively little *caudillismo* on land but the pirates and privateers operating out of these places had their heroes and bands and irregular budgets; why *caudillismo* reminds historians of South America of the social system of the *conquistadores*; why loose ("liberal") government in Curaçao or Charlotte Amalie on St. Thomas did not look like loose government in the Dominican Republic or Haiti.

In each case we have to ask how personal ties to a *caudillo* substituted episodically and precariously, in the Spanish islands and Haiti, for other ways for local loyalties to generate successes in a large-scale political system and then to explain why there were more stable ways to translate local loyalties into resources for cosmopolitan government and government outputs into generalized local loyalty to the system on the other islands, the United States, or Napoleonic France.

We may sometimes point out analogies as we go along to other systems in which charismatic legitimacy and the shifting coteries of heroes or geniuses are endemic, such as science, the performing arts, or entrepreneurship. In all these cases people bigger than life tie locals to cosmopolitan events when there are few legitimate and effective channels for locals to act directly on the cosmopolitan scene. In these systems, too, there are rewards from the cosmopolitan scene that flow to heroes and geniuses, rather than to the locals, and these ultimately make genius or heroism possible.

The Detached Shells of the State and *Caudillismo*

Lévi-Strauss (1966a [1962]) argues that cultural forms and elements are like scattered pieces of machines or bits of material scavenged from previous artifacts, and that these cultural forms can be woven into myths whose elements show associations from their origins, just as the shell casing become a lamp base for a *bricoleur* gives the lamp a warlike cast. Now let us imagine an environment in which the bits and pieces of a cosmopolitan cultural and social structure, bits of a possible state but without assembly into an effective state, were lying around unused, but ready to be assembled into a new structure with resources, skill, and energy.[4]

For example, the traditional flow of tobacco from the large northern interior valley around Santiago in the Dominican Republic after 1844 had been going through Puerto Plata on the northern shore to St. Thomas, 400 miles away, or Hamburg, 8,000 miles away. A customs

---

[4] In Lévi-Strauss the pieces of culture do not have operating action routines built into them, because he is discussing the constructions of myths. Many of the pieces of the state in, say, The Dominican Republic in 1844 were perhaps underutilized organizational and political routines more than "patterns of culture" as we usually think of them. But like an underutilized shell casing, that is not a shell because it has no powder, in the hands of a *bricoloeur*, such routines were not really a "state" until they were assembled into an organization to monopolize violence, tax collection, and legislation.

house there had traditional, somewhat corrupt relations to local warehouses and shippers, which could generate a flow of tax revenue if a reliable supply of coercion could be provided from the island government. In times of state disorganization, local corruption or urban needs took the lion's share of these tolls, but the structure was ready for a *caudillo* to make use of.

The island government was in a sleepy town of around eight thousand in the underdeveloped south of the country, where Spaniards, then Frenchmen, then Haitians, and after 1844 *criollos* tried to organize coercion. The cultural remnants of armies, tax collection systems, and perhaps even budgets were in the cultural repertoire of that town, but without the Haitian (or French or Spanish) army, those cultural remnants were not in its administrative structure. One could imagine a Santo Domingo island government in the city of Santo Domingo with the cultural materials at hand, but it was hard to construct one.

General Pedro Santana in the south could build an army more or less on the model of the peninsular army of the Spanish, and perhaps generate a flow of funds by granting sugar concessions. Puerto Plata could generate a flow of funds from taxes on the tobacco trade, roughly twice as large as the sugar trade in the mid-19th century (Hoetink (1982 [1972]), p. 65), and perhaps General Gregorio Luperón could combine that with a peasant army more or less on the Haitian model, because tobacco was a peasant crop. But neither could succeed only on the basis of the principles of legitimacy of the three empires (Spanish, French, and Haitian) that had made the cultural shell of a state a reality in colonial times.

The same sort of story, *mutatis mutandis,* could be told of General André Rigaud in the south of Haiti and General Toussaint L'Ouverture in the north and west just before the Napoleonic invasion, or President (formerly General) Alexandre Pétion in the south and the southern part of the west and King (formerly General) Henri Christophe in the north and the northern part of the west after Napoleon's army was defeated. During the 19th century "the government" was usually in Port-au-Prince, which dominated the Cul-de-Sac hinterland, and the "revolutions" usually had their origins in Cap Haïtien in the north, in more than one town on the southern coast, or in the Artibonite valley (the northern part of the western province). The recurrent problem of such revolutions was to create a national government out of regional military forces and loyalties; the recurrent problem of Port-au-Prince was to generate loyalties and flows of military and economic resources from those regional political enclaves.

The regularity with which a state structure competitive to that in Havana was created in the peasant-dominated hills and mountains of the far east after the mid-19th century, with various generals or *caudillos* in various relations to one another (and after independence, varying relations to *caudillos* in Havana), indicates the same sort of system in 19th century Cuba in the hills, especially in the east. Havana had a strong monopoly over legitimate violence in the 19th century, but the geographical range of legitimate violence was quite restricted. In Cuba, unlike the two countries on Hispaniola, the *caudillo* system did not dominate the state in Havana until after 1900, though it dominated various state-like revolutionary structures in the east.

The general situation, then, is that there was a historically real cosmopolitan colonial organization that *had been* able to generate an organization of commercial flows and flows of tax funds, rewards and privileges, land tenures of moderate to high security, and infrastructure investments, and had had the reliable capacity to defeat rebellions should any arise. One major set of elements of that historical supralocal structure was a state with a territory-wide monopoly (or near-monopoly) of violence, a system of courts, a hierarchy of office with regular salaries and other perquisites, records, and legitimacy through councils and through appointment powers of the king and church.

In the Spanish colonies (Cuba, Puerto Rico, Santo Domingo, and Trinidad, though because of the English conquest it never mattered in Trinidad) that structure had been manned—especially at the top—by *penisulares*, mostly bachelors hoping (if they did not die of yellow fever) to go back to Spain to marry and be rich or, for soldiers , to inherit their father's small farm. Creole civil servants and soldiers were, of course, much cheaper than *peninsulares*, and there was always a tendency to substitute locals for immigrants. But the Spanish government was always more worried about the imperial loyalties of creoles, and followed a wavering and uncertain policy on the composition of the bureaucracy. So the recruitment of creoles to some bureaucratic positions did not create structures of local loyalty and legitimacy as much as it did in the British and French colonies. Wavering and uncertain policies tended to create creole revolutions rather than creole loyalty.

In Haiti the colonial structure had been manned by Frenchmen, also mostly bachelors and hoping to become plantation owners before they went back to France. In the 19th century *peninsulares* no longer manned the Dominican Republic, and whites did not run much of anything in Haiti. The ties to the metropole that had legitimated the system and in particular had provided reserves of soldiers and money, to be sent in time of need, had gone.

Although the forms were remembered, they had always been hollow in the sense that they were not filled with local loyalties. The Spanish had never really tried to set up flows of imperial loyalty from the creole population in exchange for creole claims on the imperial system (though they did so more in Havana Province than anywhere else in the Caribbean; Kuethe (1986)). Even less had the French set up ways to elicit the loyalty of Haitian slaves or the free colored, who were the only ones left in Haiti after independence. So the shell of sovereignty was not naturally filled by local representative institutions the way it was in Martinique during the early part of the French Revolution, or in Jamaica or Barbados when, much later, they got their independence from the British.

In this field of remnants of shattered states, then, *caudillos* had some chance of bringing something valuable back from adventures into the larger system, because the construction of a state with those materials was known to be possible and the social technology of state functioning was culturally available.

Caudillismo and the Size of Political Forces

When Hoetink talks of the system of *caudillismo* as like a market (Hoetink (1982 [1972]), p. 137), he mainly emphasizes the competition between coteries. But what is most characteristic of an ideal-typical market as compared with a state is that the rate of growth of firms in competition is determined by success in their local niche (then in the next-larger niche, and so on). When Scherer and his sources ((1980), pp. 145–50; see also Simon and Bonini (1958)) build models of the size distribution of firms in an industry, they assume that all firms have a minimum size to get into the market at all, and that above that size they all have the same expected rate of growth. The actual rate of growth of a given firm involves a random component around that expected rate of growth. Such a process gives rise over time to a skewed distribution of the size of firms, in which the most successful more or less "dominate" the market.

In the political system the crucial process in a growth that involves the transition from local to cosmopolitan is the transformation of resources from locally "bound" to "liquid" in the cosmopolitan environment. This is beautifully exemplified by the problem of the transformation of local military power (and the economic power that supports the military power) into power that could be used in the Cuban revolution of 1868–1878, the War of Ten Years. The political and military leader of Camagüey [then Puerto Príncipe] province, the large-scale landowner Ignacio Agramonte, got into a series of conflicts with authorities of the revolutionary army and government: Carlos Manuel de Céspedes (the president), Manuel de Quesada (the commander in chief, removed from his post by the legislature dominated in large measure by the Agramonte faction from Camagüey), and Thomas Jordan (an American general who was co-commander in Camagüey with Agramonte, an appointee of Céspedes). All of these conflicts had to do, one way and another, with the division between locally bound resources and those available to the cosmopolitan revolutionary movement as a whole.[5]

Much of the conflict revolved around the question of whether the revolutionary troops would live in military camps or live at home, to be called from home when fighting had to be done. Jordan resigned his post and went back to the United States because "two millennia of military experience" showed that troops had to be "concentrated," so that they would be deployable so as to do the most damage to the enemy and to the enemy's strategic position, rather than just being willing to fight to defend their homes. Jordan thought, for example, that after causing very serious losses to a larger Spanish force, the revolutionaries should pursue that advantage rather than leaving the Spaniards to recover.

Here, the central problem is whether the troops were to be used for cosmopolitan purposes of defeating the enemy, or for local purposes of defending what the recruits most wanted to defend. But a subsidiary problem was that the psychological and real costs of serving as a soldier were larger if one could not go home to tend the crops and livestock, or to make love to one's wife, or to supervise the socialization of one's children. A very similar conflict over whether troops were to live in camp or at home occurred when the Dominican general Máximo Gómez was appointed by the Cuban revolutionary president as commander, replacing Julio Grave de Peralta, in Holguín (Guerra y Sánchez (1972), vol. 2, pp. 36–37). Grave de Peralta was "the natural political and military chief of the jurisdiction," and favored the troops' "grouping themselves only when they had to fight."

The supply of military provisions had the same two aspects. For example, Agramonte complained when cartridges were sent from the supplies delivered by ship to his province to the rebels to the west in Santa Clara; he complained also when the revolutionary president, visiting a shoe factory making clothing for Agramonte's local troops, insisted on taking some of these shoes for the civilian members of his cabinet.

But he complained especially strongly about the revolutionary troops' burning the houses and sugar mills that would be useful to the Spanish troops when the rebels had to abandon them, and about an order to take work and meat animals wherever they were found for the supply of the troops. From the point of view of a local leader, such exactions were an

[5] This account is based on Guerra y Sánchez (1972), pp. 7–27; for the revolutionaries' position on emancipation of slaves and the position of the free colored, an issue on which the local military interests in the revolutionary east and the national-strategy cosmopolitan interest in possible planter allies in the west conflicted, see Scott (1985), pp. 45–62.

excessively heavy taxation on those whose houses, mills, and work animals were taken, without proper representation of their interests or due process of law in asserting "eminent domain." Part of the difficulty was, then, that the destruction was an unfair burden with no system of compensation. But another part was that the purpose of the destruction and requisition was winning the national fight even when it meant destroying the local benefits of that win, a clear local-cosmopolitan issue.

From one point of view the transition here was from military forces as voluntary associations to military forces as bureaucratic structures. But what that "bureaucracy" made possible was the transfer of the resources from the local to the cosmopolitan level. Such liquidity of resources was central to using local power on the cosmopolitan scene.

The crucial question of the stability of cosmopolitan systems ("states") themselves had to do with whether those systems could shape the constituents of growth of cosmopolitan power. That is, could the larger system reach in to shape the growth of the smaller one at the point when and where the locally collected resources were to be turned into resources valuable at the cosmopolitan level? The control of that transition from local to cosmopolitan power *by the cosmopolitan system* was crucial to the stability and the capacity to take action of the cosmopolitan system. In this case the cosmopolitan system was a government in civil war with the Spanish government. But the structure of its problem was the same as that of the Dominican or Haitian governments discussed above.

The control over the creation of more liquid resources in the local system was the core of cosmopolitan dominance. The control of troops *that could be moved around on the orders of cosmopolitan authorities* was thus the core of that "monopoly of violence in a given territory" that Weber took to be the core characteristic of a state. The state monopoly of the legitimation of force was what made local legitimations irrelevant for all political problems that reached above the locality. Taxation by cosmopolitan authorities could then yield resources to be used at the discretion of those authorities if it was money taxation; but if taxes were shoes made in a factory in Camagüey, it was not clear that the revolutionary government could control who got to wear them. Of course both money and troops had to be earned and taxed or recruited and trained in some particular locality, as they always do. But it was a crucial transition when the Agramontes and Grave de Peraltas of this world could no longer specify how they were to be collected and how they were to be used.

In politics, for example, elections provide a regular way to translate local support into cosmopolitan political authority. Maurice Duverger and V. O. Key (Duverger (1959 [1951]); and Key and Heard (1949)) have argued that plurality elections tend to produce parties with near half the vote that might possibly win the election, but also produce high rates of decline of small factions (see also my reformulation in Stinchcombe (1975), pp. 560–69). That is, what mystifies us about *caudillismo* is not that the coteries compete, as Hoetink seems to imply in comparing the system to a market: Democrats and Republicans compete, and candidates compete for their nominations. What mystifies us is that local chieftains with small coteries could sometimes grow to be large *caudillos* with control of governments, whereas small parties tended to decline in majoritarian electoral systems. It is as if, in the market, every auto repair shop were well on the way to becoming Toyota.

After reading a bit one is not terribly surprised in a system of *caudillismo* to see a group of twenty or thirty people proclaiming a revolution, and then bringing it off.[6] There did seem to be some discontinuity in growth rates of political groups, an increased rate of growth of the *caudillo*'s coterie at the point at which the *caudillo* took over the state and instituted an effective dictatorship. A great many dictators in both Haiti and the Dominican Republic failed, however. They were usually beaten by revolutions that started with a few dozen people. The discontinuity in rates of growth, so that only large parties grow or remain stable, was clearly not as great in *caudillo* systems as it has been in North American states. For example, the coterie of a defeated dictator was not as regularly the dominant opposition in Haitian or Dominican history as the party of a defeated president or governor has been in American history.

To put this another way, the North American party structure has traditionally been determined from the top (from the "state") down, by the electoral rules and the past history of the state's party system, rather than by rapid growth of winning surge movements following a new candidate. Haitian and Dominican Republic 19th century politics (and Cuban politics within the independence movement and immediately after independence), in contrast, were more determined by conditions in the *local* environment that determined the rate of increase of a *caudillo*'s power. But as usual, winning state power gave a *caudillo* a substantial advantage in winning the next round, though perhaps not as much advantage as it gave an incumbent in American politics at the same time. We imagine dictators to be more immune from challenge than

---

[6] For example Guerra y Sánchez (1972), pp. 3–10 (War of Ten Years in Cuba, 1860s); Luperón (1939 [1895–1896];1), p. 110 (insurrection against Spanish authorities in The Dominican Republic, mid 19th century); Mejía Ricart (1980), p. 11 (insurrection against urban criollo government, The Dominican Republic, 1840s)—these were brought off, of course, after many vicissitudes, and the first ended in a treaty rather than in taking over the state.

they were in these three islands in the 19th and early 20th centuries, because they were immune from "legitimate" challenge.

Thus after the Spanish and Haitians left the Dominican Republic, after the French left Haiti, and after the Spanish during rebellions lost control of eastern Cuba, the cosmopolitan system no longer assembled the pieces of culture on whose patterns states could be built. And this in turn meant that the liquidity of local resources on the level of the state as a whole had to be created within the *caudillo's* own movement, or in a coalition. One of the things specifically political leaders who built parties and states rather than coteries (such as Céspedes in the Cuban War of Ten Years and José Martí in the Cuban war of independence) could do was to build institutions within the movement to make resources liquid. These very often took the conventional forms of state-building: councils of representatives, general staffs of armies, taxation systems, encouraging commerce so that it could be taxed in money, borrowing from world bankers at exorbitant rates, selling or mortgaging lucrative taxation rights. Political leaders created cosmopolitan political resources by creating citizens; *caudillos*, by creating networks of patron-client relationships with local leaders.

The core thing that the *caudillo* did in the 19th century Caribbean was to translate local loyalties into political resources (military power and money, especially) that could be used on a national scale. This translation could not be done from within the cosmopolitan system itself, as it had been done in colonial times, because the Spanish empire had not built routines to represent these local interests into the colonial system of government. With independence, then, the government to be constructed would look much like the Spanish government, except that it had to generate its resources from loyalties within the island. Spain had not taught people born in the islands how to do that very well, because it had kept them politically nonparticipant. France had only taught how to get resources for governing out of planters, not out of ex-slaves. *Caudillos* taught creoles to make cosmopolitan power resources out of local loyalties, and then assembled the unused pieces of island government by using the powers they had generated from their local bases. Once constructed, those national structures could reinforce the solidity of the local loyalties that had generated the capacity to create them in the first place, creating a moderately stable system of "*clientelismo*."

A first step for understanding how *caudillos* could legitimate their construction of state power is to outline their own and their contemporaries' conception of what a *caudillo* was. Even if the culture of *caudillismo* was not exclusively a Spanish creation, it was the backbone of the dominance of national government over local powers that *caudillos* constructed. So we turn to the culture of *caudillismo*.

The Legitimacy of Heroes: Big Men and Charismatic Culture

All of us in bourgeois culture learn the culture of heroism in Western movies, detective stories, war stories, romances, children's biographies of famous scientists, tales of the saints, Robin Hood or King Arthur legends, and the like. But if these are not all known as fiction, at least they clearly apply to different times and places than where we live. We all know people who are bigger than we are (even for the things we are especially vain about) but we are inclined to think that they put their pants or slacks on one leg at a time.

But what we have to explain here is a cultural system in which *caudillos* were so *much* larger than life that both they and their followers thought they were qualitatively different, had access to special sources of power and wealth, were, in Max Weber's phrase defining charisma, "specifically exceptional." The culture of *caudillismo*, then, had to have an equivalent to the concept of the "gift of grace" that made saints and gods sacred, because *caudillos* as persons were endowed with mysterious powers, not like the powers you and I have. And for this culture to have political effects, people had to believe they could collect evidence in this world about which people had such powers.

We can roughly outline the culture of *caudillismo* under the following six heads: (1) the belief that the leader could manage the uncertainties of politics, and so would be able to reward followers—this legitimates power more where politics is more uncertain; (2) the belief that good luck (especially in politics and military ventures) was a virtue, a result of "political genius" of a mysterious sort, occasionally with supernatural sources; (3) the belief that ruthlessness and corruption were practical or responsible, and that a politics of principle or of lawfulness was utopian or idealistic; (4) the belief that loyalty was the main responsibility of followers (and perhaps of leaders as well) and that there was always a substantial risk of disloyalty for which the proper response was revenge; (5) the belief that sumptuous consumption (mistresses and mansions, for example) and generosity to followers were obligations of (and so virtues of) political leaders; and (6) the belief that conflicts, disintegration of social relations, and political troubles generally should be solved by concentration of power and discretion on the leader, because unity, loyalty, and the application of genius all require absolute power.

1. *The quality of leader.* The Spanish phrase *calidad de líder* means the combination of qualities that go to make up qualification for being a leader, or roughly "leadership" in the phrase "he shows leadership" in English. But the word *calidad* has the sense of high quality or nobility,

as in the phrase "quality linen" or "people of quality." ("Quality" in the sense of "characteristic" or "attribute" is a different word in Spanish from the same Latin root.) The phrase also has a connotation that being leader was an office and that one might act in office differently than one did in everyday life.

But generally the *calidad de líder* was an inner attribute of a person, rather than situational, or derived from official appointment, or acting on behalf of higher powers. It was more like "genius" in artistic or intellectual circles than like "charisma" in religious circles; *caudillismo* as a cultural system was more like the bohemianism of artistic circles than like revivalist movements.

It is hard to tell how far the reconstructions by hagiographers who write about *caudillos* reflect the same culture that influenced the military and political bands. Presumably they are transformations of cultural materials of *caudillismo* for the purpose of mythmaking, but whether the transformations still represent the original is hard to tell.

An example of characteristics attributed to leaders in such literature is Rufino Martínez's characterization of Gregorio Luperón, a 19th century *caudillo* from the northern region of the Dominican Republic: Luperón

> seemed to act under the influence of a mysterious force that induced him to accomplish a mission to which he was predestined . . . suggestive power, intuitive prevision of action . . . , brutal impulsiveness, when he erred he mended his error, authoritarian—enemy of any brake and therefore undisciplined, proud, not accepting being outdone . . . love of country above all other loves . . . ambition for glory . . . when courage was the first of virtues he had it . . . as if by enchantment [when he took over leadership], confidence in the success of the enterprise was reborn . . . an oratorical vocation. (Martínez, Preface to Luperón (1939 [1895–96];1), pp. 13–14 16, 19)

It is noticeable, for example, that nationalism is here turned into a personal virtue, love of country; the structural definition as close tracking by public opinion of the diplomatic and war-making policies of the society, that we used in Chapter 9, on Haiti, would not resonate in the *caudillist* cultural environment.

Similarly the mythic origin of the surname L'Ouverture (often written now without the apostrophe), which Toussaint, Haiti's liberator, adopted, was that a French governor said something to the effect that when there was no opening, Toussaint made one.[7] Toussaint was also supposed to have asserted that black soldiers were more willing to fight

[7] In a contentious field, such myths have answering debunking myths. For example, an alternative myth about the name is that Toussaint had an opening between his two front teeth.

in the face of great odds and to die when he was there, and favorable biographers certainly believe that.

Toussaint reported on the effect of this in action in the following passage:

> [I explained to them t]he position of the enemy and the absolute necessity of driving him off. The brave republicans, Moïse, J. B. Paparet, Dessalines, and Noel answered in the name of all the chiefs that they would brave any sort of danger, that they would go anywhere and that they would follow me to the end. (quoted in James (1963), p. 147)

The fact that he thought of this as a characteristic of himself rather than of the role he was playing was shown in the following sentence: "Remember that there is only one Toussaint L'Ouverture in San Domingo and that at his name everybody must tremble" (quoted in James (1963), p. 220).

In both cases, then, the mythical picture, often also affirmed by the charismatic people themselves, was that *caudillos* had inexplicable powers in the political and military system.

2. *Belief in luck*. When Luperón defended a town with thirty-five men against hundreds of "Spanish" troops (many of the troops defending the Spanish government were Dominican troops of Santana, the president and general who had asked for Spanish protection in the early 1860s), several of the other officers were killed but he got away; that he took the risk showed what a great leader he was, and that he got away showed what he was predestined for (Luperón (1939 [1895–1896];1), p. 110).

When Toussaint L'Ouverture got away from enemy troops met by surprise when he and another officer were moving between their detachments in the mountains between the Cap in the North and the Artibonite valley, it showed that he was always attentive to the details, and constantly going around at great risk to himself to encourage the troops.

In general in very high-risk enterprises like combat or fishing, or in athletic competition, people believe in luck. In uncertain systems of *caudillismo*, politics was assimilated culturally to combat, and the belief in luck was part of that. The stories of bravery in battle were often intensified by painting the hopelessness of the military situation as worse than it really was. But surely tackling an apparently stable government with what starts as a group of a few dozen men was not for the timid. The point here is not whether the *caudillos* were really as irrationally brave in military matters as the myths made them, but rather that having run the risk and come out of it whole was counted as a badge of honor, qualifying one as a leader.

Erving Goffman has emphasized ((1967a); see also Carol A. Heimer (1986, 1988)) that the level of risk determines "where the action is" in violent sports generally. "Manliness" or "courage" was, then, a central virtue; confronting risk and being lucky was a quality of character. In "manly" sports those who have survived and become powerful did so by confronting risk cooly and coming out all right. Goffman quotes Hemingway a lot to show what this is all about, and no doubt Hemingway's having lived in Cuba and Spain made him see virtues in bullfighting and other tests of courage that peaceable folk find harder to see. It is, however, the complex of increasing the narrated risk, and so the bravery required, and then attributing the luck of coming out all right in spite of the risk to a quality of character, that ties bullfighting and *caudillismo* together culturally.

3. *Belief in practical politics. Caudillismo*, like other charismatic principles of legitimacy, tends to downplay other principles of legitimacy besides personal qualities. "It is written . . . but I say unto you . . ." In politics what I say unto you has very generally been that I have an offer you cannot refuse. The legitimizing of the holding of power because the *caudillo* was a powerful person and by nature destined to rule took the form in the Caribbean of justifying violence and corruption as the means to personal power. Violence and corruption were legitimate, it seemed, because they worked, as well as because they showed courage.

Ulises Heureaux, formerly a member of Luperón's coterie in Puerto Plata, became president of The Dominican Republic. He had a serious conflict with Luperón, partly apparently motivated by Luperón reproving him for unprincipled behavior. He was a fount of defense of "practicality" in politics. Hoetink (1982 [1972]) quotes a number of wonderful aperçus: "I have paid my homage to the democratic republican principle; I respect it, although I do not use it in certain selected cases" (p. 129). Because Luperón traveled in the "civilized, powerful world" he could not see that principles were useless: "If you were here in the saddle, you would see at each step the inertias, the obstinacy, the hostility, the resistance of friends and non-friends . . . , in such a heap of obstacles that to remove them it would be necessary to dispense with all law and in its place establish an army and a guillotine" (ibid., p. 130). "The General [Luperón] does not want to understand that our situations are not identical, given that I assume the moral and material responsibilities of Government, being the target of the shots from the intransigents from all the circles of my personal adversaries . . . while they only search out him [Luperón] who today finds himself more distant from public matters . . . when they want him to sponsor them" (ibid.). "[P]olitical ability comprises many different things, but among them . . . attraction, dissembling, prudence, persistence, without ceasing to be opportunistic under any circumstances." (ibid., p. 131).

Luperón in rejecting the candidacy for president of the Dominican

Republic used the "practical politics" argument, that one can only rule by ruthlessness and corruption, as a reason for abstaining: "And as it would be necessary either to use the machete [on a pact he felt bound to] or to manage the intrigue [to annihilate his enemies], and in either of these ways, I would cease to be worthy of the presidency; rather than attaining it without dignity, I will remain content at home with my honor." And in describing the faults of one of his friends as president, he diagnosed the problem as, "Espaillat was not a good President because he was loyal, honorable, and moral, and he was not a squanderer or traitor. This is a harsh, severe truth, but it is true." (Hoetink (1982 [1972]), p. 113, quoting Luperón (1939 [1895–1896];2), pp. 281, 328; I have modified Ault's translation.)

4. *Belief in loyalty and risk of disloyalty.* Heureaux said of a general: "Liriano [a nickname] suits us, because his very defects oblige him not only to be loyal, but to live constantly alert" (Hoetink (1982 [1972]), p. 131). Loyalty in *caudillismo* was a particular form of political responsibility, of the willingness to run risks, take blame, provide what resources were necessary rather than what was owed (Heimer (1986)). But it was a responsibility to the interests of a particular other person who was of higher status, more powerful, and who controlled rewards, and in these respects it was different from the loyalty that, for example, a parent might feel toward a child.

One of the problems with responsibilities or loyalties of all kinds is that when they are advantageous, one cannot easily tell whether people are loyal or fair-weather friends. In particular when a kingmaker such as Luperón puts a henchman such as Heureaux in the presidency, he runs the risk that Henry II ran when he appointed Thomas à Becket as archbishop. The rewards and responsibilities of the presidency (or the archbishopric) may then outweigh the rewards and responsibilities of loyalty to the *caudillo* or king. Any *caudillo* with a normal run of successes and failures (and Báez in The Dominican Republic, for example, had a great many) had seen many friends of good times desert in bad times, to come back again with a turn in luck. The system was built on personal loyalties, and it therefore had a weak foundation.

In The Dominican Republic, politics, especially in frequent periods of civil warfare, had wide fluctuations in the costs of being responsible to the interests of a leader one was supposed to be loyal to. When the central way to get political purposes achieved was to make henchmen responsible for them, loyalty to the leader was the core definition of responsibility; it was the principle of legitimacy that was supposed to govern officeholders. They were often too busy pursuing their own interests to be loyal, and when the *caudillo* was down on his luck he tended to have very few friends.

5. *Belief in mansions, mistresses, and munificence.* I don't understand why a show of luxury was legitimating, but it seems to have been in these systems. It is clear that *caudillos* quite often flaunted their wealth, the number of their women, and the opulence of their largesse. The capitalist assumption that legitimacy comes with having a positive balance sheet did not reign here; instead a show of lavish consumption showed power and legitimacy, regardless of whether it could be paid for. I can't empathize with this part of the culture, so I can't tell why flaunting recklessness and huge appetites and the wasting of resources legitimates the caudillo. It seems to be a common theme in "big man" cultures.

6. *Belief in absolute power as cause of unity.* The ideology of *caudillismo* outlined above seems especially adapted to legitimating power gained with irregular troops recruited by the promise of gain. It does not seem an especially promising way to run a government made up of many interests, many regional groupings with power, many representative bodies with conflicting special values to defend. It was a relatively unpolitical political ideology; it had only power and personal virtues in it, not any proposals to confront the central dilemmas of values and their relation to legitimate force (Weber (1946 [1919])). In fact many of the governments created by *caudillos* got into serious difficulty in short order when confronted with complex problems of balancing interests.

The response to such difficulties was characteristic: to urge the concentration of even further power on the *caudillo*, rather than making deals or proclaiming principles that would render the *caudillo* government legitimate by other means. We have seen the denial of principle in some of the quotations above. But civil law is and was legitimate in large measure because people agreed to their obligations under it; "when he is bought he stays bought" is a comparable principle of legitimacy in politics. When an American president gets into political trouble, the most common response is to truck and barter to get his or her way. *Caudillos* instead concentrated power.

One after another of the precarious presidents of Haiti had themselves proclaimed president for life, or emperor, or king, sometimes after they had offered to leave power shortly before (see Leger (1907), pp. 202, 213). It is not quite true to say that being president for life was the last refuge of a scoundrel, but it was remarkably often a *caudillo*'s move in a desperate situation, not the culmination of a long series of political successes. One of the indicators of this orientation was that one of the main things that was changed in the Haitian constitution whenever it was modified was the length of the term of the president. In such a system a long term appears to be the way out of destructive conflict for a longer time. Salnave, who was shot after losing power in 1870, was, however, the last president for life. One of the problems with being president for life was that it made it too obvious how to get rid of the president.

The purpose of this section has been to outline the main elements of the caudillist ideology of government. It was a cultural system that gave a precarious legitimacy as long as the *caudillo* lived up to all the necessary principles, and delivered the goods to his followers promised in that ideology. It was especially necessary that the principles and the goods delivered should convince the military and the people with autonomous local bases of power.

The principal trouble it had as a way of organizing government was that it did not transform local powers routinely into powers for a national government, but transformed only those powers within the personal reach of the *caudillo*. That, for example, made it different from Napoleonic government in France, or from the elected governments of the United States at the same time. The Southern states in the American Civil War were not built on an ideology of the special qualities of Jefferson Davis or Robert E. Lee, but on voting and representative institutions that included at least the main people with local power, the planters. The South was much more a government in the sense we understand the word nowadays than was the Cuban caudillist revolutionary political system in the east in 1868–1878 or in the 1890s, or than Toussaint's following in the Artibonite was in the 1790s.

The system was, however, recognizable on both sides of the Haiti–Dominican Republic boundary, and in the hills of Cuba in the 1890s as well as in the Dominican Republic. Puerto Rico did not have much chance to show the features of this system, partly because independence from Spain was more or less immediately succeeded by a moderately effective representative government backed by American troops. But this system of legitimacy was nothing like the system represented by the Barbados slave code, or its post-emancipation approximation (described in Chapter 10), with representative government populated almost exclusively by planters.

Caudillismo and Latifundio

The general purpose of this section is to use a moderately frequent example of the social basis of the start of a *caudillo* movement, namely, a large cattle ranch, to illustrate the difference between slave plantations and *caudillist* sources of political power. In both the Dominican Republic and Cuba, some of the important *caudillos* were large cattle ranchers; the same pattern has also been observed in Argentina, Venezuela, and Uruguay. The national army was probably a more frequent source of *caudillos*, but the fact that both plantation owners and large ranchers were important landowners makes it illuminating for us to explain their different political behavior.

By *latifundio* in Latin America we usually mean large pieces of land of poor or middling quality, exploited by a combination of cattle herding, the *hatos* of the Spanish islands or the pens in Jamaica (Higman (1989)), and subsistence or provisions farming. Very large extensions of land-ownership, often including several villages or hamlets, were almost invariably created by political means, though money was often part of the mix of coercive and economic incentives by which large extensions were consolidated.

In European feudalism there was a formal identification of ownership of large expanses and political roles: for instance, positions in the House of Lords or in the Estates of Brittany depended on large landholdings. The feudal ideological presumption was that the ownership of a *latifundio* was determined by descent and kinship, and that political position derived from (or was identical with) ownership of a noble estate. But instability of political positions in feudalism often had immediate consequences for tenure in latifundio; *caudillo* systems did not have the stabilizing force of feudal ideology, and instability of latifundist tenure with changes in political fortunes was even more obvious. One understands Napoleon's and various Haitian *caudillos'* wish to call themselves kings and emperors, to recall that stabilizing feudal ideology. But that recall did not stabilize new leadership of independent Latin American and Haitian governments very well. *Caudillo* property in land tenure secured by coercion was politically precarious as well.

The key feature for the following argument is that this distinctively intense dependence of land tenure on political power was combined in large ranches with the capacity to mobilize the small beginnings of a *caudillo* movement. It is hard to get thirty to fifty people to come to a meeting even in intensely organized modern societies. To get thirty to fifty people to come to a meeting to organize a revolution in much less literate and organized societies, to risk their lives in a political enterprise, was even more difficult. But cattle workers were routinely armed, their arms were routinely not controlled by the state but by the worker or the landowner, they were mobile horse riders, and they knew their way around the mountains. In all those ways they were a radically different seed stock than slaves for growing an army. So the dependence of ranching tenures on politics was combined with ranchers' easy access to private military resources, making ranching a frequent source of *caudillos*, even though the private appropriation of state military resources was a more common source.

The systematic policy of underdevelopment in the Spanish colonies encouraged the intermixture of land tenure with political power. Settlement or increased intensity of exploitation of new lands was always a political act, because in general the Spanish crown thought of settlers as a potential alternative government. Tenure systems have practically always changed with increased intensity of exploitation; one cannot run an agricultural society with the tenure system of hunters and gatherers. The right to create the appropriate subtenures (e.g., the *agregados* granted pieces of land around a big ranch, who got protection of their tenure from the big rancher in return for watching out for thievery, strays, and so on) always involved an appeal to the state, if there was a state; it created state-like features of the agricultural community if the state was too distant to matter.

Access to the state therefore became more crucial when the intensity of exploitation of land was being increased, which happened whenever the Spanish islands were conquered by other empires, when trade restrictions relaxed with the Bourbon reforms in the last quarter of the 18th century, and again when they became independent. Such increases in intensity involving state intervention also took place on previously cultivated holdings that had fallen out of cultivation when royalists and *peninsulares* were exiled during wars of independence, or when areas had been devastated by civil war, as in the east of Cuba after 1878 and again after 1898.

The resources for such increased intensity in general had to be moved from elsewhere, and their control in the new location had to be secured by creation of political structures in that new location. The political controls for the labor recruited for sugar plantations, as we have seen, involved not only the international military, legal, and political system that moved African people into the status of slaves, but also planter governments in the plantation islands to keep them slaves. Such political systems had to be created, and had been created in large measure by calling on the legitimacy and military power of empires.

But the increased intensity of plantations differed from increased intensity of cattle ranches and provisions farming in their political requirements and impact. First, financial resources to buy slaves and build sugar refineries were much more important than political resources to establish land tenure for plantations. For a cattle ranch the political defense of land was the core of the resource: the herd (though the most valuable capital resource) would build itself (if it could be protected from rustlers—a core political task of holding the land effectively), fences could come later, watering holes needed only a few days' work, and God might or might not provide the rain (the best portrait I know of the work of starting and keeping up a ranch is Conway (1990), an account of an Australian sheep ranch).

Second, the intensity of sugar planting and harvesting made the property boundaries (excluding the provisions plots and pastures) almost self-policing, and at any rate made watchmen a relatively small item in a plantation account book. Patrolling, branding, fence-mending, and defense of the routes of transhumance were the essence of ranching, so policing was a higher proportion of landlord expense.

Third the square miles needed to generate enough resources of people and money to be a power on the national scene was much smaller in plantations than in provisions landlordism, and the size of subsistence "feudal" landlordism needed to become a political power was much less than that needed to become a political power as a rancher. Thus political competence to maintain a *latifundio* was more dependent on very large size in less intensive agriculture; it took a lot of mountain land to maintain a lord, but much less valley bottomland, and even less alluvial land in a sugar plantation. A ranch employing a hundred workers in the 19th century Caribbean would occupy tens or hundreds of square miles; a sugar plantation with a hundred slaves with some land not in sugar cultivation might run to 200 to 400 acres, or about half a square mile.

The workers on a ranch were much more effective militarily: they knew the mountains where a cow or a person could hide, they carried arms and learned to use them, they were used to carrying out work in a loyal fashion without supervision, their loyalty was private rather than being controlled by the state. So one hundred ranch workers generated much more military power than one hundred slaves.

Fourth and finally, the precariousness of slave labor relations and the technical and commercial complexity of a plantation meant that the upper planter class was less "dispensable" for politics than were latifundists. Or perhaps better, the cost of turning a plantation over to an attorney or a *régisseur* to manage was much higher because the absentee's attorney could make more, and more important, technical and commercial mistakes. In the colonies with reasonably stable government, a planter would only sacrifice his own presence on the plantation to be in Europe; he did not depend enough on local politics to maintain his tenure to make it worthwhile to devote full time to island politics. When plantation tenures became more precarious in the Haitian revolution, some absentees came back to Haiti to try to save their properties by political action. Ranch tenures were always precarious.

If a planter had to be on the island anyway he would attend to the plantation before politics. The complaint of, for example, the Jamaican governors about the unwillingness of the planters to attend the legislature when plantation work was intense was hardly heard on the Spanish islands before sugar became dominant. Ordinarily therefore a latifundist was more available for local politics than was a planter.

In sum, the variation in intensity of cultivation of large properties had its high end in the plantation, its middle in the hacienda, in the English manor, in a property devoted to cultivated pasture, or in a coffee or banana or cocoa plantation, and its low end in the latifundio cattle, work animal, or sheep ranch. That variable had a deep relation to the variation in the form of island government from planter aristocracy to *caudillismo*. Landownership was much more of a political career at the low-intensity end, much more of a capitalist enterprise at the high end. At the low end, a rancher like Santana from the east of the Dominican Republic might spend years as a *caudillo*. Planters at the high end were hard to recruit as *caudillos*, but easily unified into representative bodies to build a slave society. Ranchers (or *hacendados* in mountainous former Spanish colonies, such as Mexico, Central America, Colombia, or Peru) were not easily unified into a representative body, but easily formed bands that might grow into *caudillo* governments.

This does not mean, of course, that ownership of a plantation and control over slaves were not fundamentally political phenomena, as we have shown in considerable detail in Part I of this book. Instead it means that individual fortunes of planters did not vary as rapidly in response to personal political activity in plantations as they did in less intensive agriculture and ranching. Especially increases in intensity, turning a frontier into a personal fortune, were preeminently a political achievement in the mountains, a capitalist achievement in sugar plantation areas.

The great *caudillos*, especially those that became presidents, often got investments in sugar plantations and even merchant houses by what elsewhere would be called corruption. This was because the political requirements of even sugar plantations or merchant houses were not achieved without effort, and sometimes the effort took the form of corruption. Dependence on government was greater in frontier sugar developments and new commercial links than in running an established plantation system. But any particular capitalist enterprise could often use a friend in power, even when production had stabilized, and might offer an investment at derisory prices to make sure of one.

So the point is not that politics did not matter to the plantation; the point instead is that *caudillo* fortunes tended to be made by political development of *latifundio* of the traditional type rather than of plantations. Further, being a *latifundio* owner was a better place to start a political career than was being a plantation owner in systems of *caudillismo*, since *latifundio* ownership was fundamentally a political office. Plantation islands were unlikely to produce *caudillo* governments unless the plantation system was destroyed, as in Haiti.

Of course, *caudillismo* itself was a system of political instability, and so itself rendered all political conditions, including land tenure, more precarious. This was even more true when, as in Haiti, the revolution that created *caudillismo* was a rural social revolution against a particular form of land tenure, a revolution that exterminated or drove into exile the class of holders of plantation tenures. *Caudillismo* created more uncertainty of tenures also when the exile or death of important *caudillos* threw large *latifundios* on the political "market." Estates of former *caudillos* were rarely bought and sold in a capitalist market as ordinary land tenures. Such tenures were usually not very legitimate even by the loose principles of frontier extensive agriculture, besides having the illegitimacy of a political loser. Thus the economic base of *caudillismo* in underdeveloped tenure systems in underexploited colonies was sustained by the undermining of security of tenure by *caudillismo* itself.

The very large fortunes of dictators who lasted a long while in countries with *caudillismo* were thus only partly made up of flows of cash from corruption, or investment of corrupt gains in economic development. They were usually also made up of coercive creation of latifundist tenures by use of the powers of the state, and these tenures and agricultural fortunes tended not to last much longer than the dictator's control of those powers.

Thus while the lack of sugar plantations and the prevalence of ranching in Spanish colonies could not be counted as the big causes of *caudllismo*, they did their bit. The instability central to *caudillismo* was in part due to the widespread ability of various sorts of people to build a military band of thirty to fifty people with a "revolutionary" purpose. Large ranchers were such people, in a way that plantation owners were not. Plantations were generally sinks that used up coercive power generated elsewhere to sustain slavery, and planters were very careful to use their political influence to generate that power somewhere else than among their slaves; ranches were springs that generated coercive power under the ranchers' own control, and so ranchers moderately often ended up as contenders for national power as heads of coalitions of military bands.

Cuban Development on a Dual Path

Ortiz Fernández (1947 [1940]) gives a literary treatment of the dual development of Cuban economy, politics, and culture by taking plantation sugar growing and peasant tobacco growing as the central symbols. Negro slaves cultivated sugar; free whites gave careful manual care of the leaves of cultivated tobacco (pp. 57–61, 71). Rich capitalists had to invest a lot in sugar factories, while tobacco required few tools, so simple countrymen could become a free bourgeoisie. "All the colonial governments favored the sugar planters" (ibid., pp. 65, 68), while tobacco was more heavily taxed and state monopolies taking heavy cuts of tobacco profits were more persistent.

The plains of central Cuba (Havana province and Matanzas province especially) were the main centers of sugar production in the early 19th century, with the region near Havana growing first (starting in the late 18th century—the region near Havana had sugar exports about equal to those of the Danish [now American] Virgin Islands), the north coast of the Havana-Matanzas plain easily accessible to barge shipping to Havana next, the plain South of Havana next, and the eastern provinces mainly after independence. During the spread over the central plain, the pockets of suitable land in smaller alluvial plains elsewhere were developed. For example, the immediate areas of Santiago de Cuba (Cuba is and was the name of the municipality of which Santiago was the seat, as well as the name of the whole country) and Guantánamo were dominated by sugar and the nearby hills by coffee plantations, while the mountains and hills inland from them were dominated by peasant cultivation (e.g., the Spanish officials' name for the rebels of inner Oriente province in the 1870s was *labradores*, roughly, "peasants").

However not all the peasant cultivation was tobacco. Tobacco was the main peasant crop that the Spanish government took an interest in, because it was easily exportable and so easily taxable and easily monopolized. Even for tobacco, the Spanish government forbade the production of any more than could be handled by the royal monopoly factories in Spain, because extra tobacco would produce trade, and therefore smuggling. The Spanish government cared even less about local markets in subsistence provisions than the plantation island colonial governments did. From a political and cultural point of view, however, tobacco's commercial and industrial importance made it a good symbol of the peasant aspect of Cuban development for Ortiz Fernández.[8]

The core social base in Cuba of the defense of the Spanish imperial tie was always the *peninsulares,* people who came out as bachelors from Spain to make a military, civil service, or mercantile career. Spanish immigrants mainly worked in the cities, especially Havana, for the imperial government or for commercial houses with monopoly advantages.

But starting with the Bourbon kings in late 18th century Spain, the

---

[8] The same contrast could be drawn between the northern valley around Santiago in the Dominican Republic, which exported tobacco, and the southern plain where the city of Santo Domingo was located, which started to grow sugar. The summary description above may seem to be reversed to people familiar with developments after Cuban independence and U.S. intervention. U. S. investment created very large sugar-sharecropping enterprises with large mills and private railroads in Oriente and Camagüey provinces, and by 1939 these two eastern provinces produced over half of Cuba's sugar. See Guerra y Sánchez (1940), pp. 46–69.

Spanish empire formed a close alliance with Cuban sugar planters; in the first instance, those of Havana municipality and province (Kuethe (1986)). The alliance had a mixture of inducements and threats. The central threat was that if there were a serious independence movement supported by the planters, the Spanish would free the slaves without compensation; for the empire, slavery was less important than imperial control. The inducements were varied: commercial privileges for sugar, first in the Spanish market and then the right to trade with the United States; considerable local autonomy, by Spanish standards (e.g., the university in Havana was started as a secular state institution with hardly any trouble); titles given to leading planters, and military commands with honors attached made more available to Cuban creoles than in most Spanish colonies; trade made easier by allowing shipment from several ports.

The Geography of Revolution in 19th Century Cuba

The peasantry were therefore the core of the revolutionary tradition in Cuba. There was relatively little of the anti-mercantilist revolutionary movement led by the upper classes that was prevalent on the French islands, because the Spanish old regime threatened the Creole rich with social revolution, and relieved some of their grievances in Cuba that it had let fester in the other colonies. And this in turn meant that the geography of 19th century Cuban revolutions reflected the distribution of peasant cultivation in two ways: first, the revolutionary movement tended to be concentrated in the hills and mountains; and second, there was a big variation from Havana toward the east, with revolutionary fervor in both major 19th century revolutions increasing steadily as one went east.

The pockets of plantation export trade on the seacoasts formed conservative social political environments for landing counterrevolutionary forces. The garrisons of the forts in those sugar pockets provided peninsular troops for the defense of the sugar towns. The eastern mountains and foothills were dominantly white and free colored, dominantly peasant, and dominantly revolutionary. As a symptom and symbol of revolutionary consciousness, the formal upper-class Spanish custom of using two surnames (the patronymic followed by the matronymic, in the extreme with one or both hyphenated as well) was rarely found among the revolutionaries in the east. There was some moderate revolutionary sentiment even in the hills and mountains nearer Havana, but only peripheral revolutionary or bandit movements in the fewer and lower hills of Havana province itself.

The riches and population density of sugar production made railroads profitable. The Havana-Güines line was opened up in 1837, tying Havana to the southern plains of Havana province; by 1868 most of the railroad lines still connected Havana to its south and to Matanzas and other nearby sugar areas a bit to the east (Oostindie (1988), pp. 25–26).

The density of reliable transportation within the sugar region made it possible to create a much denser state apparatus in that region. Troops could get from one part of that central region to another; the telegraph lines that ran beside the tracks could convey governmental messages; the commercial flows that railroads facilitated also facilitated government taxation. Resistance could be quickly crushed in the semi-urbanized sugar areas tied by rail to Havana; it was much harder to crush in the mountains of Oriente province.

No part of the area west of Havana (which mainly consists of Pinar del Río province) was as inaccessible as the mountains south of Santa Clara or the various mountain groups of the far eastern end of the island. But the general 19th century tendency for the degree of urbanization and the degree of dominance of sugar cultivation to slope downwards as one moved away from Havana and towards the mountainous spine of Cuba obtained in the far west as well.

This meant that the peasant agriculture (tobacco, coffee, provisions) complex and the sugar complex on Cuba were geographically separate, as they were on most of the islands with substantial mountains. But what was distinctive of Cuban development was that the peasant and sugar parts of the economy had about the same population size throughout the late 18th and 19th centuries. In Puerto Rico, Dominica, and the Dominican Republic peasants were more numerous—in most of the rest of the Caribbean sugar cultivators were more numerous. The two populations in Cuba grew at approximately the same (very high) rate, and the white immigration and colored internal migration to the peasant part of the economy was of the same order of magnitude as the slave "immigration" that populated the sugar complex.

Cuban Urbanization

The city of Havana was more dominant throughout the population evolution of Cuba than on any other sugar island (with the possible exception of St. Pierre at some periods in Martinique), probably because it played such a central role in the larger commerce and defense of the Spanish empire.[9] Havana itself was somewhat similar to Curaçao, Char-

[9] MacNeill (1985), pp. 36–38, gives a careful estimate for the mid-eighteenth century of about forty thousand, or about a quarter of the population of Cuba.

lotte Amalie on St. Thomas, St. Eustatius, or to some extent Kingston in being an entrepôt port, with ship maintenance and supply a central industry.

If we abstract for a moment from the higher level of urbanization of Cuba, mainly due to Havana, Cuba was more of a sugar island than the islands in which mountain crops and peasant agriculture dominated (Dominica, The Dominican Republic, and Puerto Rico). It was less of a sugar island than islands where sugar was very dominant.[10]

The Mix of Social Tensions in Cuban Revolutions

The result of this growth of a dual agricultural society created an overlay of three main kinds of tensions over citizenship. The first was the classic Latin American conflict within urban life between creole and peninsular political influence, in a system in which urban government was dominant in colonial times; the creole urban elite typically had an ambivalent reaction during the wars of independence, wanting to preserve urban power but with creoles in place of *peninsulares.*

A second tension was the claim for rural representation of peasants and ranchers, partly represented by *caudillismo*, as we have analyzed above, which continued the revolutions of independence from Spain into the 19th century: a conflict between rural and urban forces that tore independent South American governments apart. Where this Hispanic system of urban-rural political conflict was dominant and the rural forces were strong, as in most of South America, slavery (which had taken precarious root on the coastal plains) was abolished by the mid-19th century and *caudillismo* was common. Where the urban forces were strong, as in Mexico, Buenos Aires Province when it was autonomous, and perhaps Venezuela, alliances between urban oligarchs and shifting groupings of other forces gave varying results.

The third tension was the claim of planters to run the political system to create and maintain a slave system, common to the Caribbean. As we have analyzed, on the other islands this early in the 19th century the process of emancipation produced the deep left-right split between ex-slaves and ex-planters (so between races). It was this split that turned the

---

[10] As outlined in the first part of the book, Barbados, Antigua, Guyana, Martinique, and Guadeloupe were much more dominated by sugar. Jamaica, Haiti, most important Leewards other than Antigua, and perhaps St. Vincent were somewhat more dominated by sugar. Cuba was perhaps somewhat less of a sugar island than Trinidad, which had a boom in both sugar and non-sugar sectors slightly trailing Cuba's. Trinidad's peasant sector was more populated than Cuba's by recruitment from the plantation sector, and in particular by East Indians after their indentures were up. The rest of the islands were either the same or less dominated by sugar than Cuba in the 19th century.

French Revolution into the Haitian one. Then in the 20th century the same division produced left-right splits as the backbone of independence movements (and their pro-colonial opposition) in the British islands. In a different context it produced left-wing colored and black deputies from the Caribbean to the French parliament. This left-right anti-slavery split was in general a very subordinate part of the ideology of the Cuban revolutions of the 19th century (see especially Scott (1985)).

What makes Cuban history so fascinating, yet so confusing, is that such a system of overlapping contradictions created an enormous variety of possible political combinations, all of them potentially powerful (or perhaps better, all of them roughly equally incapable of governing). Ordinarily societies that produced classic *caudillos* did not produce communist revolutions as the next stage. Ordinarily the tight tie between powerful planters and the right wing of the empire political system, created by the fear of the consequences of enfranchisement, did not have an extensive rural opposition organized after the fashion of *caudillismo*. Far left proletarian movements in islands other than Cuba did not ordinarily have, as a source of potential allies early in the revolution, a long tradition of poorly organized rural populism with ambiguous "idealistic" liberalism mixed in.[11] Everything that can happen anywhere can happen in Cuba as well.

The American Empire

The economic and naval power of the United States in the Caribbean grew continuously during the 19th century. It was more or less immobilized for the purpose of empire-building before the Civil War by the split between North and South. Most of the commerce with the Caribbean was carried on by northern merchants. Most of the American political allies of Caribbean planter governments were in the South. An alliance between the Haitian Revolution after 1802 and the representatives of the northern intellectual and political currents of the American Revolution would likely have started the Civil War before 1860. The proposed incorporation of the Dominican Republic in the United States posed the same problem of exacerbating racial tensions in milder form. The potential incorporation of Cuba as a slave state (sometimes other slave islands flirted with this option) would have exploded the precarious union from the other direction. Illegal filibusters (the analogy with French *flibustiers* was quite distant, because the American ones did not have the crucial ingredient of authorization from some empire) were the main operative American political intervenors in the Caribbean. They could not mobi-

---

[11] The Russian Revolution of 1917 was very similar in that respect.

lize the American split political system on any side of any important Caribbean question.

After the Civil War the United States had a more unified interest, which can be roughly described as wanting either Spain or the United States to rule the remaining Spanish islands. Spain was not dangerous to the United States, as indicated by the fact that the Haitians and the peasants of the Cuban interior were near-matches for them on their respective islands. France was not very dangerous, having been fairly easy to displace from Mexico, but was a more substantial threat than Spain. England, on the other hand, was a fairly serious matter.

Most of the active military-political interventions of the United States on land in the Caribbean came in 1898 and after, and involved Puerto Rico, Cuba, the Dominican Republic, and Haiti. Puerto Rico became an American colony, and a more or less democratic government with many North American features was established. For example, colleges were started on a large scale in Puerto Rico immediately after the intervention of 1898. American capitalist interest in Puerto Rico was heavily concentrated in the sugar industry, which was modernized but remained relatively small and had a labor relations system more or less like that of the central valley in California.[12]

Cuba was set up as a "self-governing U.S. colony." The colonial reservations of the treaty and the Platt Amendment essentially amounted to a military base at Guantánamo covering the Windward Passage, protection of North American sugar and other investments, and a sort of quasi-protectorate in which the United States had a relatively close monitoring of Cuba's foreign policy.

The U.S. interventions in The Dominican Republic and Haiti in the early 20th century were episodic, to change governments the United States did not like. In the Dominican Republic the policies that grew out of such interventions protected U.S. investments in sugar plantations and a few other branches of the economy. In Haiti the interventions seem to have been mainly directed at trying to get a government there that the United States could morally approve of, together with opportunistic neo-colonialism that never amounted to much.

Conclusion

In some ways the point of this chapter has been to show that the main argument of this book is not much use for explaining political and social life in the Spanish Greater Antilles and Haiti after 1800. None of them

---

[12] But in contrast to Hawaii, the main U.S. sugar colony, Puerto Rico, had few Asian immigrants.

were really slave societies, though Cuba came close. But even that close approach came after slave societies had lost much of their world-system support, when the other empires were disassembling their slave societies by fits and starts, and for much of the 19th century up to half the island was governed by (ambivalently) anti-slavery democratic independence movements.

The contrast shows how strong the governments of the slave societies were. If we compare the massive terror, civil war, and revolutionary reorganization of the economy that it took to overturn the Haitian old regime with any of the changes of *caudillos* in the Dominican Republic or independent Haiti, we cannot but be impressed with how comparatively weak the latter governments were. Slavery was a strong system of legitimacy that produced governments that were really hard to overturn, or even to turn toward ameliorative policies.

The Spanish left behind weak governments. And when they had not left (yet), the system of legitimacy of the colony did not effectively incorporate the major political and economic forces of the colony. The policy of the Spanish government in the Cuban independence war of the 1890s was much like that of the United States in South Vietnam in the 1960s: moving the local population into strategic hamlets because they could not be trusted to support the government being defended, sending soldiers who did not understand why they were there, collecting taxes to support the war from a recalcitrant Spanish population. And the reason was the same: hardly anyone really believed in the colonial government. The phrase *España boba*, stupid Spain, was from The Dominican Republic, but surely the Cubans understood well what it meant. Planters would have built a nasty government that could have held its own, if the Spanish had been willing to encourage them.

So this chapter has gone off in a direction more or less orthogonal to the main thrust of the book. But it is important to the argument of the book that failing to introduce a sugar slave system of production early and on a large enough scale made the Spanish colonies into variants of Latin American societies and politics, rather than variants of slave societies. And it also supports that argument that after destroying the slave society and its plantation mode of production, black Haiti looked more like a former Spanish colony (except for having a much denser population, so being militarily much more powerful, and speaking French) than like the other slave societies after emancipation.

12

Conclusion: The Sociology of Freedom

Definitions of Freedom, Liberties, Citizenship, Exposures

When Adam Smith ((1976 [1776]), pp. 586–87) argued that free governments of the colonies produced more oppressive conditions for slaves, and that "arbitrary" governments restricted planter autocracy over their slaves more, he was recognizing that freedom is a social relation. The freedom of planter governments in the colonies means by definition that arbitrary imperial governments do not have the right to interfere with their decisions. The freedom of the planters to do what they want with their property means that slaves do not have freedom, the right to do what they want.

John R. Commons (1924) describes the origin of protection of central capitalist principles as the establishment of a series of *liberties* to which there are corresponding *exposures*. Property in a piece of urban land, for example, is a group of liberties to use that land in a variety of legitimate ways: to sell it, to rent it, to build a drugstore on it. All other people have, then, an *exposure* to the owner's use of any of those liberties, in that they have to suffer any consequences to them of the owner's use of the liberties. If another person has a drugstore across the street, the competitive effects of the owner's use of his or her liberty also to open a drugstore are an exposure to the drugstore opposite.

Thus under an "arbitrary" imperial government the king had a liberty to intervene through his agents in the colony, and the planters there were therefore exposed to that intervention. If the king did not intervene under a "free" government, the planters had a wider set of liberties, to which the slaves were exposed.

The exposure of others to owners' or governments' liberties (government liberties are often called immunities, because others do not have the right to sue, or to bring criminal proceedings against, government officials for doing their duties and using the powers of office), of course, lets owners or governments set up incentive systems with their liberties, to motivate others to do their bidding. Liberties create deployable power to set up systems to get others to do what one wants them to do. Commons distinguishes them from *rights*, and the corresponding *duties*, that allow the right-holder to demand only what the other person is duty-bound to deliver. Looked at from another point of view, then, a system of liberties creates a flexible system of power. Power created by a system of liberties can be transferred to entrepreneurs; political power to take slaves in Africa can, for example, be turned into planter power over those slaves for a price. This is why Commons wrote about the development of legal concepts of liberties and exposures under the title *Legal Foundations of Capitalism*.

A particular type of system of liberties is embedded in our common notions of *citizenship*. Political entities of various kinds, "parties" in the broad sense of that word, can be created by systems of liberties in politics, just as capitalist entities, firms, can be created by systems of liberties in markets. The freedom to make speeches, to vote, to organize to petition the government can be used as incentives for political authorities, and can constitute party organizations, which then shape the incentives of others (by logrolling, for example) who also want to influence the government.

Parties constituted out of the liberties of people who are citizens look much more unstable to an authoritarian eye, but they in fact create stronger governments because they create more flexible political systems that can elicit loyalties under more various conditions. Part of the greater capacity of the Barbados government to maintain a slave society, both before and after emancipation, was due to the more solid liberties of Barbadian planters and the better organization of flexible governments constituted of those liberties.

The main defense of liberties is the interested defense by property holders or citizens of *their own* flexible powers derived from their freedom—derived, then, from the consequently large set of ways they can collectively use the powers generated by their liberties. The general ideological defense of liberties by social thinkers is that it creates more flexible social structures, markets rather than rule-bound hierarchies (which is to say that the hierarchies created in markets are easier to dismantle), or democratic political systems that can respond to changing needs and interests.

For example, as Holt (1992) has argued, there was little interest in letting Jamaican blacks do what they wanted, for instance, to start peasant plots and grow provisions, in the social theory behind emancipation. Instead, for many or most, freedom for blacks was conceived of as a different labor relations system with superior disciplining power, greater flexibility, and less production of violent rebellion than slavery. Freedom was a route to greater social discipline.

Schumpeter's (1950 [1942]) argument that only socialism could, in the long run, generate sufficient labor discipline to sustain industrial society is a similar example in the political realm. Schumpeter thought that capitalism was eroding the capacity to govern, to elicit the consent of the working classes, that capitalist societies had inherited from feudalism. Only by letting workers organize and take over the government, so that their organizations would have to take responsibility for wealth and welfare, could the political requirements of industrial discipline get consent in a democratic society. He thought that would slow economic growth (a similar argument is Olson (1982)).

We commonly make the same argument about science, that the system of liberty to publish everything a scientist believes is at the same time an exposure of everyone to having his or her ideas refuted (or at least loyalty to them undermined) by alternative publication (Hull (1988), pp. 303–19). This both means that science as an institutionalized system is more believable than other systems, because we almost all believe each of its elements could be overturned if any competent person thought them wrong, and that science is more flexible than many belief systems in adapting to varying needs for knowledge, new opportunities to establish knowledge, and the like.

The first point here is, then, that a definition of freedom has to describe the component liberties that make it up not only by what a given class of people (e.g., owners, citizens) are allowed to do, but also by what consequences of action all other people are therefore exposed to. The folk saying defining freedom, "Your liberty ends where my nose begins," is therefore exactly wrong for purposes of describing social systems. A liberty is socially meaningless unless one can carry out the relevant decision that uses that liberty in spite of the damages it does to others.

Freedom as the Expansion of Possibilities

But a second aspect of freedom or liberty is that it enlarges the set of possibilities among which one can choose. This naturally has both a social aspect, that more possibilities for more people are generated in a freer society, and a personal aspect, that each person's possibilities are increased if he or she is "freed," no matter what sort of servitude he or she had before. Otherwise we would not use the verb "to free" for manumission or emancipation. The best place to start the analysis of this aspect of the definition of freedom is with wealth or income.

It is clear that the richer a society is, the more things can be produced by the society. That means in turn that at least some people or groups in that society can do things they could not do in a poorer society; if wealth and income were distributed identically in two societies, one of which was richer, then all people in the society would have more possibilities. Realities are usually somewhere in between those alternatives: as a society gets richer, most people have more possibilities than they had before, but, for example, carriage makers may be able to choose from a *smaller* set of possibilities, be less free after automobiles make most people freer.

Likewise the wealthier individuals were in the 17th and 18th centuries, the more different properties they could buy, the more incentive systems they could set up to get others to do what they wanted, and so the more liberties (and corresponding powers derived from them) they could exercise. They had more choices than poorer people. The social welfare aspect of citizenship (Marshall (1992 [1950])) is, roughly speaking, a system for assuring that some minimum of economic liberties are enjoyed by all citizens and citizen families (and usually some selected classes of non-citizens and their families; cf. Hein (1992) for modern United States and France and the social welfare rights of "allied aliens"; Borde (1882) for French planters under the Spanish government of Trinidad).

Similarly the social creation of competitive parties is of the essence of democracy (Schumpeter (1950 [1942]); Lipset, Trow, and Coleman (1956), pp. 3–16, 268–69), because it expands most people's choices of how to have influence on the government. And between the 16th and 18th centuries the capacities of small countries, such as the Netherlands and England, to conquer and maintain empires was clearly partly due to the fact that all imperial adventures had to be approved by serious and somewhat competitive representative institutions, so resources could be devoted to imperial maintenance and conquest without leading to civil war at home.

The capacity during the 19th century of regions of Haiti to raise rebellions, and perhaps replace *caudillos*, whenever the dictator was off conquering the Spanish part of the island, also clearly limited the exactions of the Haitian government on the population. There is more total liberty to choose government policies in a society with competitive politics, just as there is more liberty to choose consumption goods in a wealthy society. And that usually means more satisfaction with and loyalty to the reigning institutions in societies with more total liberties, in what we commonly call "free" societies.

The increases of liberties of specific groups of the population, especially on such a large scale as emancipation of slaves, the granting of political citizenship in the islands to free colored[1] and to emancipated slaves, or the granting of autonomous island government when citizenship was restricted to planters and merchants dependent on them gener-

---

[1] In this chapter I will distinguish "free colored" as people who were free before emancipation, whatever their actual color—most were of mixed race, for reasons discussed in Chapters 5 and 6. I will call people who were free as a result of general emancipation "ex-slaves" or "emancipated blacks," again, whatever their color. The degree of racial mixture of ex-slaves varied a good deal among islands. Of course children born after emancipation had never been slaves, but I will call them ex-slaves for simplicity.

ally made the groups granted new liberties *less exposed* to the liberties of others. And conversely an increase in others' liberties increased one's own exposures to their uses of their liberties, so that slaves were exposed to being worse off when slaveowners ruled. There is a zero-sum aspect to increases in personal freedom that do not lead to greater total opportunities.

The debate over emancipation and its aftermath was a debate organized around conflicts within the idea of freedom. The imperial notion of freedom was expansion of productivity and government capacity by means of freedom. Slaveowners generally regarded freedom as a zero-sum matter, in which they lost their power over slaves. Slaves usually regarded emancipation as an expansion of their personal possibility set, especially opening up the possibility to set up as peasant farmers, outside the system of world trade in staple commodities if they chose.

Clearly the total definition of the freedom of planters with respect to slaves, slave lack of immunities against anything the owner might choose to do, found in the self-governing older British colonies such as Barbados or Antigua in the late 18th century, was an extreme of unfreedom of the slave. To be sure, planters could set up incentive systems for slaves with their system of liberties, and some of those incentive systems led to manumission of slaves. Total liberty included the liberty to give slaves rights, including the rights of free colored people. But the fact that slaves sometimes benefited from the use of the total liberty of the slaveowner never meant that slaves on a large scale preferred slavery.

In the slave societies free colored people much preferred to live out of the territory claimed by sugar plantations, in the cities and in the foothills and mountains. They formed definitions of freedom very closely connected with that of Commons (1924), that the central liberties constituting their own freedom were those connected to property, especially rural peasant property (Holt (1992), pp. 172–82, 436–37). After emancipation ex-slaves tried hard to defend their property rights to peasant-like tenancies they had held as slaves, in houses, yards, and provision grounds (Mintz (1974b)). And both free colored and slaves quickly bought up partitioned failed plantations when they could, and bought crown lands where, as in Trinidad, they were thrown open to sale of peasant-sized plots. Baptist congregations sometimes bought up whole plantations to divide among emancipated blacks and free colored people. Planters and colonial officers often saw these ex-slave claims to the freedoms of property as an invasion of the planters' right to hire them for low wages, and we analyzed many of the ways they tried to restrict the possibilities of ex-slaves in Chapter 10.

The image of the set of possibilities of a person that we learn from economics is closely connected with the "budget line," the amount of money the person might spend. Economics textbooks used to imagine that a person was choosing various combinations of peas and carrots. We put the quantity of peas along a vertical axis, the quantity of carrots, along the horizontal axis. Then we locate from the price of peas the quantity on the vertical axis the person could buy if he or she bought only peas, and on the horizontal axis from the price of carrots the largest quantity of carrots he or she could buy. Then the straight line connecting the two points is called "the budget line," and all the combinations of peas and carrots between the axes and the budget line are possibilities for a person with that amount to spend. The space between the axes and the budget line then is called the *possibility space*.

We analyzed in Chapter 10 how planters on the English islands (and in Guadeloupe and Martinique, under slightly different conditions) established various particular monopoly arrangements in the labor market after emancipation. They wanted the newly freed blacks to use their freedoms by taking low wages to work whenever the planters wanted them, and to go away and support themselves whenever the planters did not (Holt (1992), pp. 200–201). The strategy planters followed, then, would result in freedmen and -women having a jagged budget line. For example, peasant holdings from crown land around or below 10 acres were much more expensive than the same land in larger lots for sugar plantations or livestock ranches; rents of their traditional houses, yards, and provisions grounds could only be paid in plantation labor at a wage below market; leaving the island for higher wages was legally prohibited.

Such jagged possibility spaces are in general more common where the law or regulation enters deeply into the uses of liberties permitted, as in zoning regulations, in production or acreage quotas in agricultural subsidies, in the market for required courses (in contrast to elective ones) in undergraduate colleges, and the like. The discussion of how terrible it would be if students got to take the courses *they* thought they needed and wanted and what it would do to our language departments if they did, or what would become of undergraduate sociology if we did away with the statistics requirement (cheaper sociology degrees without statistics, like bad money, would drive out good degrees or money), are much like the discussions after emancipation of how to get free black people to choose the work planters wanted them to do for the wages planters wanted to pay. Similarly the zoning discussions of why letting a large estate near Lake Michigan be cut up into four lots for upper-middle-class housing would ruin the property values of nearby estates resembles the discussions a century and a half ago of cutting up sugar estates on Barbados into peasant plots. Such plots would have undermined the supply of plantation labor, and hence would have undermined the ability to repay debts of nearby sugar estates.

In all these cases someone is trying to cut off some of the possibilities of others by regulations, so that they will have as their new best alternative something more pleasing to the regulators. People who want more regulation talk of an "externality," which is what Commons called the "exposure" due to the exercise of a "liberty": an effect on the neighborhood or on professors with standards if liberties are not restricted. The whole idea of competitive capitalism is, of course, an organization of the negative "externalities" that firms faced with competition have to put up with, what Schumpeter called "creative destruction" of the value of out-of-date firms.

The general point here is that one can construct an incentive system both by the use of one's own liberties and by the restrictions of other people's liberties by creating jagged possibility spaces for them. The politics of carving out parts of other people's economic liberties to forbid them, so that they will do what whites want them to do rather than what they would choose for themselves, is a deep part of the definition of what emancipation meant in the Caribbean.

Much the same sort of tinkering with liberties was characteristic of citizenship conflicts. In general the autonomy of island governments was a structure to give a different distribution of political liberties to workers versus planters and capitalists in the colonies than in the metropole, with the colonial poor and the working class in general getting fewer of the "rights" of citizenship. This was why the left and the blacks on Guadeloupe and Martinique favored full integration of the government of the old colonies into the government of France. Where, as in the British empire after about 1860 (Holt (1992), pp. 312–42), there was not much hope for Caribbean workers' becoming full citizens of the metropole (the planters had given up being full citizens themselves, in large measure to prevent blacks from being full citizens; cf. Campbell (1976)), the workers and blacks instead turned against the empire because it did not lead to incorporation into the metropole and the liberties that incorporation brought. The exposure of the poor and black to the right to govern held by the whites was extreme in the British islands in the last third of the 19th century, considerably less in the French islands at the same time, fairly near nugatory in the Spanish islands and the Danish Virgin Islands, and nonexistent in Haiti.

Freedom and Slavery

The main brunt of the first half of this book is that a society and polity devoted to the maintenance of extreme unfreedom, of the absolute rightlessness of slaves, reached its hysterical extreme in the islands most dominated by sugar where old planter legislatures had the most unfettered power and local autonomy, Barbados and Antigua. Less sugar dominance or less historical depth to planter solidarity or less island government autonomy each produced somewhat less planter power, as on Jamaica, 18th century Haiti, the British Leewards, Martinique, and Guadeloupe. While sometimes on these islands the degree of hysteria of the politics of no-compromise oppression was equal to that of Barbados or Antigua, it did not have the same cool, stonewalling effectiveness of that of Barbados or Antigua. For instance, the local rejection of equal rights for the free colored in Haiti [Saint Domingue] early in the French Revolution was extraordinarily stupid racism, and the stubborn but somewhat ineffectual resistance of the Jamaican legislature to amelioration and emancipation had as its main effect infuriating the powers in the Colonial Office and Parliament on which its own power ultimately depended.

When slave plantations existed on a large scale, dominating the local economy, this produced strong causal forces toward creating a complete slave society, dedicated to maintaining unfreedom even to the extent of interfering with the liberties of masters (e.g., to manumit their slaves). The longer such a causal force operated (e.g., that causal force was oldest as well as strongest in Barbados and Antigua, and older and stronger in Martinique and Guadeloupe than in Haiti), the more thoroughly the society was devoted to unfreedom. Compared to such societies, the least bit of slave liberty defended in law or practice looked very much better than their present condition to almost all slaves. Freedom defined in contrast to sugar plantation slavery in old sugar societies could be pretty narrow and still look a great deal better than slavery.

Freedom was the major stratification principle of slave sugar societies. The distinction between slave and free defined both classes and races (with, of course, some fuzziness around the edges). All different ethnicities and genotypes of Africans were defined as one race because they were shipped from Africa as slaves and became slaves in slave societies. People of intermediate color were often defined as "of African descent" or "colored" because African descent was statistically the central feature of the distinction between slave and free; they could with equal justice have been classified as "of European descent," or "of free descent." In Haiti the colored were often called *affranchis*, illustrating the connection between slavery and race from the other side.

If we were to classify all societies in the history of the world that have had slavery versus freedom as a stratification principle by the degree of centrality of that principle in the overall stratification system, the English and French Caribbean sugar islands would be at the extreme high end, Cuba in the early 19th century and the American South taken as a whole quite high, and most other slave societies quite low. (Of course societies that have never had slaves would be very low, with prisons and asylums being the main forms of unfreedom).

When British people (other than black Caribbean ones) sing, "Britons never, never shall be slaves" (Jamaica Kincaid writes of one of her young female characters' refusing to sing it), they are using stratification systems of other societies (some of them, to be sure, British colonies) as a metaphor to describe their values, not to distinguish themselves within the stratification system of Britain. In the cultural system slavery is often used in this metaphorical way, to get out of the hard work of defining what one means by freedom. It is (and has always been) clear in everyone's definition that slavery is the core of what freedom is not, while not much else about the concept of freedom is clear (Patterson (1991; 1) pp. 1–5).

What was distinctive of slavery in its extreme form as compared with all other ways of regulating the liberties of workers was that the regulation was entirely at the discretion of the planter. Planters did grant rights to slaves, but with the exception of manumission, those were all explicitly precarious (informal manumission was also precarious). Slave rights to inherit provisions grounds, houses, and yards were generally recognized within the plantations of at least the British islands, for example. This was one of the best ways to get slaves to build the houses on weekends and evenings and cultivate provisions on holidays, so that the planter would not have to buy provisions. But when emancipation came it was clear to the planters and their governments (though not, of course, to the slaves) that their tenure in these lands and houses was precarious, and could be made conditional on whatever slave plantation work the planter decided to impose.

After some dispute, blacks generally left the houses and lands rather than submit to those limitations of their liberty, but the point here is that the rights of the slaves were not rights in the larger legal system, but only in the custom of the manor. And unlike the history of the law in late British feudalism, the custom of the manor was not considered legally as the terms of a contract between the free worker and his or her lord that could be enforced in the king's courts. Originally the British jury of one's peers was to testify to the terms of that contract, to the custom of the manor and tenures recognized by that custom. So whatever else freedom was, it was centrally *not* having planters determine all the possibilities in one's life. If under slavery one earned informal rights to make decisions about a provisions ground by mixing one's sweat and free time with the soil, but the planters could take those away before or after emancipation by free and unfettered decision, then one was less free than a peasant; but one was more free than on an island where slaves did not have informal tenures in provisions grounds. The slaveowners were at liberty to do with all rights of slaves as they would, and insofar as they managed to preserve those capacities after emancipation, the freedom of ex-slaves was reduced.

As we have tried to show in Chapter 5, there were some conditions even on the sugar islands under which it was to the advantage of the slaveowner to set up the tie to the slave in a fashion that gave the slave effective rights. The African dock workers who paid rent to their owners for their services, and then sold those services to captains or ship's mates or merchants, would seek out work a lot better and work harder at it, even if they were out of sight down in the hold, if they thought they would have rights to the extra money they earned. It was then to the advantage of slaveowners to create effective rights as part of their incentive systems, in much the same way as it had been to the advantage of the king and metropolitan merchant companies to give planters ownership rights in the frontier lands the planters developed into sugar plantations. Solid liberties of workers or other agents were often effective parts of incentive systems, whenever agency in distant or hidden areas on behalf of a principal was required.

But liberties also permitted planters to construct private systems, without recognition as "contracts," for example, with slave mistresses or skilled plantation workers or, especially for women slaveowners, with household servants. Some of the most valuable things we all get in life are things we are free to build into our households behind barriers of privacy. When these private constructions come into the divorce court to be enforced, they either cannot exist in the law or are not the same thing when they are enforced. In modern marriages, of course, husbands and wives create the benefits they create for each other because they are free to do so, but children who also get benefits are not free to set up private worlds according to their own tastes and agreements.

Likewise, when planters created households with their slave mistresses, behind barriers of privacy, relationships often brought the benefit of manumission to the mistresses and their children, and no doubt also brought other benefits that did not create legal and documentary traces. These informal rights and liberties were created because the planter was legally free to do so, but not because the slave was. The benefits took public and legal form only when the planter agreed to make them so, and slave mistresses had no claim against the fathers of their children in the courts of thoroughgoing Caribbean slave societies (such mistresses and their children often did have such public legal claims in other societies with slavery). This inequality of publicly defensible liberties no doubt created inequalities of power between men and slave women in their private relations, different from those between the same men and their wives.

After emancipation, the inequalities between rich and poor fell, for a long time, in practically the same place as the inequalities between slave and free had fallen. The greater set of possibilities that were open to the rich allowed them to construct more private spaces and relationships with more women (as well as, of course, more commercial and labor market relationships with more men). Further, after emancipation only Trinidad, Guyana, and Cuba were really sugar frontiers where one might well make a fortune, so the masses of bachelor planters tended to disappear from the Caribbean; most of the (many fewer) men who had mistresses after emancipation were settler planters with wives.

The combination of the change from slave to free for colored and black women and the lower demand for alternative households by planters and other rich men must have decreased the frequency of such liaisons. But no doubt the best of the relations of white planters to their slave mistresses were less oppressive than the worst of the relations of those planters to their free colored and free black mistresses.

The general point here is that the legal standing of the parties in a domestic relation, even an illegitimate one, was an important, but not the only, determinant of how much benefit they got from each other. This was shown among other things by the fact that planters often gave up the difference in their legal standing by freeing their slave mistresses and their children.

A roughly similar analysis applies to labor relations during slavery and after emancipation. The worst labor relations from the workers' point of view were still mostly on plantations, and plantations made the most use of the monopolies in the labor market that allowed them to simulate slavery with free workers. The analysis of Chapter 5 of the slope of approximations to free status among slaves as we move from field plantation labor to urban domestics, slaves on small farms, slave mistresses, skilled workers, or commercial agents of the owners would be replicated by a dimension of autonomy and control of one's own fate in the free labor market in the same situations after emancipation. The possibilities for employers to monitor worker behavior, deny the worker access to alternative possibilities, and prevent informal organization remained in the same place, namely, in the sugar fields, for a long time. That dimension from more slave-like free labor to freer free labor started to break down in a substantial way only after unionization and political representation of field workers started to be important, first perhaps in about 1880–1900 in Guadeloupe and Martinique.

The sugar plantation gave its upper class a strong interest in repressive labor relations. The sugar planters wanted to penetrate deeper into the lives of workers, to root out potential freedoms so that work could be organized by coercion alone, so that none of slaves' rights would stand in the way. We argued in Chapter 3 that the wholesale merchants who organized overseas trade from cities in the imperial metropoles did not have that intense interest in destroying the freedom of their sailor workers. Shipping magnates could be oppressive when the occasion arose; in fact, the main reason it arose was that they were intensely interested in commercial relations with sugar planters, who at least believed that they in turn depended on repressive labor relations. But the maritime and commercial bourgeoisie put down revolutions in commercial cities, crushed sailors' trade unions, financed wars in the 18th and early 19th centuries on a scale rarely seen before in the history of the world, and otherwise used violence and coercion when it was convenient. But violence and coercion were not convenient to shipping magnates many times a day in their relation to sailors, the way they were on a sugar plantation.

Although a *hato* or cattle ranch in the Dominican Republic might well recruit its labor in slave markets, it was not convenient to monitor the slave all the time every day. Violence toward the worker, if pushed too far, could easily result in undetectable violence against the cattle. There was certainly a good deal of violence in Haiti and the Dominican Republic during the 19th century, but it did not have the systematic, enthusiastic-liberties-extinction character of violence in the neighboring slave societies. The extreme violence of the two civil wars in the last third of the 19th century in Cuba certainly must have killed more people outright than all the deliberate violence toward slaves in Caribbean history (probably more than half of that open violence against slaves, the actual killing and maiming, was in Haiti during the Revolution and war of independence), and destroyed nearly as many by disease as did all the "seasoning" of newly imported slaves in the Caribbean. But these wars were created by more or less free citizens organizing themselves to fight one another, rather than by an attempt to destroy all vestiges of freedom among slaves. It is hard to call dead people free in any significant sense, but the causes of that particular form of lack of liberty in late 19th century Cuba were different from the causes of coercion against slaves.

The coercion and violence prevalent in the non-slave societies in the Caribbean, then, had a more disorganized, episodic, unsystematic character than did the coercion and violence of slave societies. Trying to make sense in Chapter 11 of all the causes and conditions for the uses of coercion by various *caudillos* in the Dominican Republic, the eastern highlands of Cuba, and Haiti, I found them hard to write about except as one damn thing after another. On the other hand the continuity between the extraordinarily racist preamble to the slave code of Barbados and the nuances of the post-emancipation emigration regulations of Barbados or Antigua, which requires black workers to prove that they were leaving behind no one that they were obliged to support in order to be able to emigrate, was obvious. Both before and after emancipation, oppression involved the same white, rich people and the same dark, poor people making plantations profitable. The coercion of slavery was tied together over history by being part of the mode of production of sugar, a mode of production that continuously produced the sort of upper class that would be interested in as complete and systematic oppression as could be produced without completely destroying the labor force.

Thus while it is hard to build up much enthusiasm for the *caudillos* and dictators of The Dominican Republic or Haiti in the 19th century, I believe all of us would feel freer as workers on the land in those societies than as workers on the land in Barbados or Antigua, even after emancipation. The autonomous legislatures of Barbados or Jamaica could produce more consensus on oppression than any structure in The Dominican Republic or Haiti could produce on anything. But the slaves or ex-slaves were not in on that consensus. If anyone offers you a job on a sugar plantation, do not take it.

Freedom and Working Class Political Action

In mid-19th century England the supporters of emancipation and decent treatment for blacks took it as a matter of course that national welfare was increased if the poor had lower wages. The Jamaican and Trinidadian governments' taxing freed blacks to import indentured East Indian workers, which would lower wages, was understood to be taxing them to produce a public good. Perhaps nothing so thoroughly marks English liberal thought as bourgeois democracy as the fact that poverty was thought necessary to get the poor to work at low wages so as to procure competitive advantages for the English and to improve their own souls. That style of thought is back in fashion in the IMF in the 1980s and 1990s, so we need not feel too superior.

There was a left wing in the French revolutionary government of the 1870s that did not take the poverty of the poor as an unequivocal public good, and the Third Republic had a colonial policy that included some considerable commitment to universal suffrage even when blacks voted socialist and conducted strikes. But in England it was clearly an argument against universal suffrage that it might undermine the public policy of keeping wages down (Holt (1992) gives extensive evidence to this effect).

Using historical data to study the size of people's possibility set, to say whether Haitian anarchy and low productivity were more or less limiting to freedom than the systematic, hysterical, but productive and peaceful, racism of Barbados planters, is complicated by the fact that the many things not chosen are not apparent in the historical record. There is an inherent counterfactual nature to the concept of freedom. Even if I choose to write this book, and sometimes curse it, I am freer than most people in the world because I could choose to do a great many other things. But except for the last sentence, the alternatives that freedom consists of will not appear as a fact in the historical record, because I did not do the other things. But one can combine historical facts with socio-logical reasoning to make an argument that poorer black Haitians more likely to die by violence were freer than slightly richer and much more peaceful Barbados blacks. The counterfactual that does not appear in history appears as the experience of choice in the life experience of slave and free, of people who were oppressed and people who chose freely, though their alternatives were not lives we would choose over our own.

This book has been written with the conviction that this difficult sub-ject is worth battling with, though the central thing to be explained, freedom, is slippery conceptually, and the facts are not adequate to the purpose. I hope I have given the readers enough interesting facts and ideas about variations in the character of alternatives among which poor people in the Caribbean in the late 18th and early 19th century chose, so that this book seems to them to be a historical study of the sociology of freedom.

Bibliography

Acosta Saignes, Miguel. (1978) *Vida de los Esclavos Negros en Venezuela* (Life of black slaves in Venezuela). Havana: Casa de las Américas.

Alcindor, Émile. (1899) *Les antilles Françaises: Leur assimilation politique a la métropole* (The French Antilles: Their political assimilation to the metropole). Paris: V. Giard et E. Brière.

Amelunxen, C. P. (n.d.) *De Geschiedenis van Curaçao* (The history of Curaçao). Printed in Holland by Druk Firma H. Hamberg Jz.: Author.

Bangou, Henri. (1987a [1962];1) *La Guadeloupe 1492–1848, ou l'histoire de la colonisation de l'île liée a l'esclavage noir de ses débuts à sa disparition* (Guadeloupe 1492–1848, or the history of the colonization of the island tied to black slavery, from its beginnings to its disappearance), vol. 1. Paris: Éditions L'Harmattan [Éditions du Centre].

———. (1987b [1962];2) *La Guadeloupe: Les aspects de la colonisation 1840–1939* (Guadeloupe: Aspects of colonization 1840–1939), vol. 2. Paris: L'Harmattan.

———. (1989) *La revolution et l'esclavage à la Guadeloupe 1789–1802: Épopée noir et génocide* (The Revolution and slavery in Guadeloupe, 1789–1802: Black epic and genocide). Paris; Messidor/Éditions sociales.

Baretta, Silvio R. Duncan and John Markoff. (1978) "Civilization and Barbarism: Cattle Frontiers in Latin America." *Comparative Studies in Society and History*, **20**, 4 (October), pp. 587–620.

Barrow, Christine. (1983) "Ownership and Control of Resources in Barbados: 1834 to the Present," *Social and Economic Studies*, **32**, 3, 83–12.

Beckford, George L. (1972) "Peasant Movements & Agrarian Problems in the West Indies. Part II. Aspects of the Present Conflict between the Plantation and the Peasantry in the West Indies." *Caribbean Quarterly* **18**, 1, pp. 47–53 and 57–58.

Beckles, Hilary McD. (1990) *A History of Barbados from Amerindian Settlement to Nation-State*. Cambridge and New York: Cambridge University Press.

Bell, Daniel. (1993 [1954]) *The Racket-Ridden Longshoremen*. New York, NY: Irvington.

Bethell, Leslie, ed. (1985;3) *The Cambridge History of Latin America*, vol. 3. Cambridge: Cambridge University Press.

Bévotte, R. de. (1906) "Antilles Françaises" ("The French Antilles"). In Marseille Exposition Coloniale (1906) vol. 3, pp. 361–411.

Blerald, Alain-Philippe. (1986) *Histoire économique de la Guadeloupe et de la Martinique du XVIIᵉ siècle à nos jours* (Economic History of Guadeloupe and Martinique from the 17th century to our time). Paris: Karthala.

Boin, Jacqueline and José Serrule Ramúe. (1985 [1979]) *Proceso de Desarrollo del Capitalismo en la Republica Dominicana 1844–1930* (Process of development of capitalism in The Dominican Republic 1844–1930), 3d ed. Santo Domingo: Graniel.

Bonacich, Edna. (1972) "A Theory of Ethnic Antagonism: The Split Labor Market." *American Sociological Review*. **37**: pp. 547–59.

———. (1981) "Capitalism and Race Relations in South Africa: A Split Labor Market Analysis." In M. Zeitlin, ed., *Political Power and Social Theory*, 1981 volume. Greenwich, CT: JAI, pp. 239–77.

Borde, Pierre-Gustave-Louis. (1882;2) *Histoire de l'île de La Trinidad sous le gouvernement espagnol* (History of the island of Trinidad under the Spanish government), vol. 2. Paris. Maisonneuve et Cie.

Boswell, Terry E. (1986) "A Split Labor Market Analysis of Discrimination against Chinese Immigrants [in the United States]." *American Sociological Review*, **51**, (June) pp. 352–371.

——— and David Jorjani. (1988) "Uneven Development and the Origins of Split Labor Market Discrimination: A Comparison of Black, Chinese, and Mexican Immigrant Minorities in the United States." Pp. 169–185 in Smith et al., eds. (1988).

Boxer, C. R. (1988 [1965]) *The Dutch Seaborne Empire: 1600–1800*. Baltimore: Reprinted by Penguin Books [London: Hutchinson].

Braithwaite, Lloyd. (1975 [1953]) *Social Stratification in Trinidad: A Preliminary Analysis*. Kingston: Institution of Social and Economic Research; originally in *Social and Economic Studies*, **2**, 2 & 3.

Brandwein, Pamela. (1994) Sociology Dissertation, Northwestern University. "Reconstructing Reconstruction: The Supreme Court and the Production of Historical Knowledge."

Breen, Henry H. (1844) *St. Lucia: Historical, Statistical, and Descriptive*. London: Longman, Brown, Green, and Longmans.

Brereton, Bridget. (1981) *A History of Modern Trinidad 1783–1962*. Port of Spain and London: Heineman Educational Books.

———. (1983)"The Birthday of Our Race: A Social History of Emancipation Day in Trinidad, 1838–88." Higman, ed., (1983) pp. 69–83.

Breton, Raymond. (1964) "Institutional Completeness of Ethnic Communities and the Personal Relations of Immigrants [in Montreal]." *American Journal of Sociology* **70**, pp. 193–205.

Buffon, Alain. (1979) *Monnaie et crédit en économie coloniale: Contribution à l'histoire économique de la Guadeloupe 1635–1919* (Money and credit in the colonial economy: Contribution to the economic history of Guadeloupe 1635–1919). Basse-Terre: Société d'histoire de la Guadeloupe.

Butel, Paul. (1974) *Les négociants bordelais: l'Europe et les Iles au XVIIIᵉ siècle* (Bordeaux businessmen: Europe and the Islands in the 18th century). Paris: Aubier-Montaigne.

Campbell, Mavis Christine. (1976) *The Dynamics of Change in a Slave Society: A Sociopolitical History of the Free Colored of Jamaica: 1800–1865*. Rutherford, NJ: Associated Universities.

Carruthers, Bruce. (1989) "The Strength of Weak States: English Public Finance in the Early Eighteenth Century" (presented at the Midwest Sociological Society's meetings in St. Louis, MO).

Carter, Richard. (1987) "Public Amenities after Emancipation." In Marshall, ed. (1987) pp. 46–69.

Cauna, Jacques. (1987) *Au temps des isles à sucre: Histoire d'une plantation de Saint-Domingue au XVIIIe siècle* (In the time of the sugar islands: History of a plantation in Haiti in the 18th century). Paris: Éditions Karthala et A. C. C. T.

Centro de Investigaciones Históricas. (1978) *El Proceso Abolicionista en Puerto Rico: Proceso y Efectos de la Abolición: 1866–1896* (The abolitionist process in Puerto Rico: Process and effects of abolition: 1866–1896). San Juan: Universidad de Puerto Rico.

Chase, Jean, ed. (1987) *Geographie du capital marchand aux Ameriques 1760–1860* (Geography of merchant capital in the Americas 1760–1860). Paris: Éditions de l'École des hautes Études en Sciences Sociales.

Cohen, David W. and Jack P. Greene, eds. (1972a) *Neither Slave nor Free: The Freedman of African Descent in the Slave Societies of the New World*. Baltimore: Johns Hopkins University Press.

————. (1972b) "Introduction." In Cohen and Green (1972a) pp. 1–18.

Commons, John R. (1924) *Legal Foundations of Capitalism*. Madison: Univ. Wisconsin Press.

Constant, Fred. (1988) *La retraite aux flambeaux: Société et politique en Martinique* (Retreat with torches: Society and politics in Martinique). Paris: Éditions Caribéenes.

Conway, Jill Ker. (1990) *The Road from Coorain*. New York: Alfred A. Knopf.

Craton, Michael. (1978) *Searching for the Invisible Man: Slaves and Plantation Life in Jamaica*. Cambridge, MA: Harvard University Press. Cited in Higman, 1983.

————, and James Walvin. (1970) *A Jamaican Plantation: The History of Worthy Park 1670–1970*. University of Toronto Press.

Curtin, Philip. (1990) *The Rise and Fall of the Plantation Complex: Essays in Atlantic History*. Cambridge: Cambridge University Press.

David, B. (1974) *Les origines de la population Martiniquaise au fil des ans 1635–1902* (The origins of the Martinican population in the course of the years 1635–1902). Special issue of *Annales des Antilles*, Memoirs de la Société d'Histoire de la Martinique. Printed in Limoges, France.

Debien, Gabriel. (1953) *Les colons de Saint-Domingue et la Révolution: Essai sur le Club Massiac août 1789–août 1792* (The colonists of Haiti and the revolution: An essay on the Club Massiac from August 1789–August 1792) Paris: Librarie Armand Colin.

————. (1953–1954) "Les colons de Saint-Domingue réfugiés à Cuba (1793–1815)" ("Haitian colonists in refuge in Cuba (1793–1815)"). *Revista de Indias*, No. 54 (Oct.–Dec. 1953) pp. 559–605 and No. 55–56 (Jan.–June 1954) pp. 11–36.

————. (1974) *Les esclaves aux Antilles Françaises (XVIIᵉ–XVIIIᵉ siècles)* (Slaves in the French Antilles, 17th and 18th centuries). Basse-Terre and Fort-de-France: Société d'histoire de la Guadeloupe and Société d'histoire de la Martinique.

Dietz, James L. (1986) *Economic History of Puerto Rico: Institutional Change and Capitalist Development.* Princeton: Princeton University Press.

Drescher, Seymour. (1990a) "People and Parliament: The Rhetoric of the British Slave Trade." *Journal of Interdisciplinary History,* **20**, 4 (Spring) pp. 561–580.

———. (1990b) "Trends in der Historiographie des abolitionismus" ("Trends in the historiography of the abolition of the slave trade"). *Geschichte und Gesellschaft,* **16**, 2, pp. 187–211.

———. (1991) "British Way, French Way: Opinion Building and Revolution in the Second French Slave Emancipation." *American Historical Review,* **96**, 3 (June) pp. 709–734.

———. (1994a) "The Long Goodbye: Dutch Capitalism and Antislavery in Comparative Perspective." *American Historical Review,* **99**, 1 (February) pp. 44–69.

———. (1994b) "Whose Abolition? Popular Pressure and the Ending of the British Slave Trade." *Past and Present,* **143** (May) pp. 136–166.

Duffy, Michael. (1987). *Soldiers, Sugar, and Seapower: The British Expeditions to the West Indies and the War against Revolutionary France.* Oxford: Clarendon Press.

Dumaz, Bernard. (1986) *Guadeloupe: Économie agricole, le malaise à fleur de sable, étude de cas: la région basse-terrienne 1830–1980* (Guadeloupe: The agrarian economy, the "*malaise à fleur de sable,*" a case study: The region of Basse Terre 1830–1980). Paris: L'Harmattan.

DuPuy, Alex. (1989) *Haiti in the World Economy: Class, Race, and Underdevelopment since 1700.* Boulder: Westview Press.

Duverger, Maurice. (1959 [1951]) *Political Parties.* (tr. Barbara and Robert North) New York: Science Editions, John Wiley and Sons [Originally Paris: Armand Colin]. Pp. 206–254 are his analysis of the dependence of party structure on electoral laws.

Edwards, Bryan. (1801 [1793];2) *The History, Civil and Commercial, of the British Colonies in the West Indies.* vol. 2. London: J. Stockdale.

Ehrlich, Allen S. (1976) "Race and Ethnic Identity in Rural Jamaica: The East Indian Case." *Caribbean Quarterly* **22**, 1, pp. 19–27.

Elisabeth, Léo. (1972) "The French Antilles." In Cohen and Greene (1972a) pp. 134–171.

Esquemeling [Exquemelin]. (n.d. [1684 (English), 1678 (Dutch)]) *The Buccaneers of America.* Edited by William Swan Stallybrass. Reprinted "modernized in respect of punctuation and obsolete spellings and verbal and typographic eccentricities" London: George Routledge and Sons.

Fergus, Howard A. (1978) "The Early Laws of Montserrat (1668–1680): The Legal Schema of a Slave Society." *Caribbean Quarterly,* **24**, 1 & 2, pp. 34–43.

Finley, Moses I. (1960a [1959]) "Was Greek Civilization Based on Slave Labour?" In Finley (1960b) pp. 53–72 [Originally *Historia 8,* pp. 145–164].

———, ed. (1960b) *Slavery in Classical Antiquity: Views and Controversies.* Cambridge: Heffer, and New York: Barnes & Noble.

Frostin, Charles. (1975) *Les révoltes blanches à Saint-Domingue aux XVIIe et*

XVIIIe siècles (Haïti avant 1789) (White revolts in Saint Domingue in the 17th and 18th centuries (Haiti before 1789)) Paris: L'École.

Gallie, Duncan. (1983) *Social Inequality and Class Radicalism in France and Britain*. Cambridge: Cambridge University Press.

Geertz, Clifford. (1963) *Agricultural Involution: The Processes of Ecological Change in Indonesia*. Berkeley: University of California Press.

Geggus, David Patrick. (1982) *Slavery, War, and Revolution: The British Occupation of Saint Domingue 1793–1798*. Oxford: Clarendon Press.

Genovese, Eugene D. (1989 [1965]) *The Political Economy of Slavery: Studies in the Economy and Society of the Slave South*. Middletown: Wesleyan University Press.

————. (1969a) *The World the Slaveholders Made*. New York: Random House, Pantheon Books.

————. (1969b) "The American Slave Systems in World Perspective." In Genovese (1969a) pp. 3–150.

Gerth, Hans and C. Wright Mills, eds. (1946) *From Max Weber: Essays in Sociology* . New York: Oxford University Press.

Gibbs, Bentley. (1987) "The Establishment of the Tenantry System in Barbados." In Marshall, ed. (1987a) pp. 23–45.

Goffman, Erving. (1967a) "Where the Action Is." In Goffman (1987b), pp. 149–270.

————. (1967b) *Interaction Ritual: Essays on Face-to-Face Behavior*. Garden City, NY: Doubleday.

Goslinga, Cornelis Ch. (1979) *A Short History of the Netherlands Antilles and Surinam*. Den Haag: Martinus Nijhoff.

———— and Maria van Yperen. (1985) *The Dutch in the Caribbean and in the Guianas, 1680–1791*. Assen: Van Gorcum.

Goveia, Elsa F. (1980 [1965]) *Slave Society in the British Leeward Islands at the End of the Eighteenth Century*. Westport, CT: Greenwood Press [Originally, New Haven: Yale University Press].

Green, William A. (1976) *British Slave Emancipation: The Sugar Colonies and the Great Experiment 1830–1865*. Oxford: Clarendon Press.

Guerra y Sánchez, Ramiro. (1940) *La Industria Azucarera de Cuba* (The sugar industry of Cuba). Havana: Cultural S. A.

————. (1972) *Guerra de los 10 Años* (The Ten Years War [1868–1878]) Havana: Editorial de Ciencias Sociales.

Hall, Gwendolyn Midlo. (1972) "Saint Domingue." In Cohen and Greene (1972a) pp. 172–192.

Hall, Neville A. T. (1983) "Slavery in Three West Indian Towns [in the Danish Virgin Islands]." In Barry W. Higman, ed. (1983) pp. 17–38.

————. (1984) "The Victor Vanquished: Emancipation in St. Croix; Its Antecedents and Immediate Aftermath." *Niewe West-Indische Gids*, **58**, 1 & 2, pp. 3–36.

Halperin Donghi, Tulio. (1969) *Historia Contemporáneo de América Latina* (History of modern Latin America). Madrid: Alianza Editorial (El Libro del Bolsillo).

Hamilton, Bruce. (1956) *Barbados and the Confederation Question 1871–1885.* London: Government of Barbados and Crown Agents for Overseas Governments and Administrations.

Handler, Jerome S. (1974) *The Unappropriated People: Freedmen in the Slave Society of Barbados.* Baltimore: Johns Hopkins University Press.

Harding, Richard. (1991) *Amphibious Warfare in the 18th Century: The British Expedition to the West Indies 1740–42.* Rochester, NY: Bogdell Press [The Royal Historical Society].

Harrigan, Norwell and Pearl Varlack. (1991) "The Emergence of a Black Small-Holder Society in the British Virgin Islands." In Lisowski, ed. (1991) pp. 18–29.

Hayot, E. (1971) *Les Gens de Couleur Libres de Fort Royal 1679–1823* (Free people of color of Fort Royal [Martinique] 1679–1823). Paris: Société Française d'Histoire d'Outre-mer.

Heady, Earl Orel. (1952) *Economics of Agricultural Production and Resource Use.* New York: Prentice-Hall.

Heimer, Carol A. (1985) *Reactive Risk and Rational Action.* Berkeley: University of California Press.

———. (1986) "Producing Responsible Behavior in Order to Produce Oil: Bringing Obligations, Rights, Incentives, and Resources together in the Norwegian State Oil Company." Xerox, Næringsøkonomisk Institutt, Bergen Norway.

———. (1988) "Social Structure, Psychology, and the Estimation of Risk." *American Review of Sociology,* **14**, pp. 491–519.

Hein, Jeremy. (1992) *States and International Migrants: The Incorporation of Indochinese Refugees in the United States and France.* Boulder, CO: Westview Press.

Higman, Barry W. (1976) *Slave Population and Economy in Jamaica, 1807–1834.* Cambridge: Cambridge University Press.

———. (1983a) "Domestic Service in Jamaica, since 1750." In Higman (1983b) pp. 117–138.

———, ed. (1983b) *Trade Government and Society in Caribbean History 1700–1920.* Kingston: Heineman.

———. (1984) *Slave Populations of the British Caribbean 1807–1834.* Baltimore: Johns Hopkins University Press.

———. (1989) "The Internal Economy of Jamaican Pens, 1760–1890." *Social and Economic Studies,* **38**, 1: 61–86.

Hildebrand, Ingegerd. (1951) *Den Svenska Kolonin St. Barthélemy och Västindisk Kompaniet fram til 1796* (The Swedish colony St. Barthélemy and the West India Company up to 1796). Växjö (Lund): Smålandspostens Boktryckeri.

Hintzen, Percy C. (1985), "Ethnicity, Class, and International Capitalist Penetration in Guyana and Trinidad." *Social and Economic Studies,* **34**, 3 (September) pp. 107–163.

Hoetink, Harmannus. (1958) *Het Patroon van de oude Curaçaose Samenleving* (The pattern of the old society of Curaçao). Assen: van Gorcum.

————. (1972) "Surinam and Curaçao." In Cohen and Greene (1972a) pp. 59–83.

————. (1973) *Slavery and Race Relations in the Americas: Comparative Notes on their Nature and Nexus.* New York: Harper Torchbooks.

————. (1982 [1972]) *The Dominican [Republic] People 1850–1900: Notes for a Historical Sociology.* (tr. Stephen K. Ault) Baltimore: Johns Hopkins University Press.

Holt, Thomas C. (1992) *The Problem of Freedom: Race, Labor, and Politics in Jamaica and Britain, 1832–1938.* Baltimore: Johns Hopkins University Press.

Howarth, David, and Stephen Howarth. (1988) Lord Nelson: *The Immortal Memory.* Baltimore: Penguin Books.

Hoyos, F. A. (1978) *Barbados: A History from the Amerindians to Independence.* London: Macmillan Education Ltd. (Macmillan Caribbean).

Hull, David L. (1988) *Science as a Process: An Evolutionary Account of the Social and Conceptual Development of Science.* Chicago: University of Chicago Press.

James, Cyril L. R. (1963 [1938]) *The Black Jacobins: Toussaint L'Ouverture and the San Domingo Revolution,* 2d ed. New York: Vintage Books [Originally New York: Dial Press].

Jha, J. C. (1976) "The Hindu Sacraments (Rites de Passage) in Trinidad and Tobago." *Caribbean Quarterly,* **22,** 1, pp. 40–52.

Johnson, Howard. (1988) "Labour Systems in Postemancipation Bahamas." *Social and Economic Studies,* **37,** 1–2, pp. 181–201.

Jordan, Winthrop D. (1969 [1968, University of North Carolina Press]) *White over Black: American Attitudes toward the Negro 1550—1812.* Baltimore: Pelican Books.

Key, Valdimer Orlando, Jr., and Alexander Heard. (1949) *Southern Politics in State and Nation.* New York: Alfred A. Knopf.

Klein, Herbert S. (1967) *Slavery in the Americas: A Comparative Study of Virginia and Cuba.* Chicago: University of Chicago Press.

Knight, Franklin W. (1970). *Slave Society in Cuba during the Nineteenth Century.* Madison: University of Wisconsin Press.

————. (1990 [1978]) *The Caribbean: The Genesis of a Fragmented Nationalism,* 2d ed. New York: Oxford University Press.

Kuethe, Allan J. (1986) *Cuba, 1753–1815: Crown, Military, and Society.* Knoxville: University of Tennessee Press.

Labat, Jean Baptiste [Père Labat]. (1722) *Nouveau voyages aux isles de l'Amerique* (New travels to the islands of America). Paris: P. F. Giffart.

Lang, James. (1975) *Conquest and Commerce: Spain and England in the Americas.* Orlando [New York]: Academic Press.

Larson, Magali Sarfatti. (1966) *Spanish Bureaucratic-Patrimonialism in America.* Berkeley, CA: Institute of International Studies.

Laurence, K. O. (1971) "Review of Judith Ann Weller, East Indian Indenture in Trinidad." *Caribbean Quarterly* (March) pp. 34–47.

————. (1983) "Tobago and British Imperial Authority, 1793–1802." In Higman (1983b), pp. 39–56.

Lazarus-Black, Mindie. (1994) *Legitimate Acts and Illegal Encounters: Law and*

Society in Antigua and Barbuda. Washington, DC: Smithsonian Institution Press.

Léger, Abel-Nicolas. (1930) *Histoire diplomatique d'Haiti: Tome premier 1804–1859* (Diplomatic history of Haiti: first volume, 1804–1859). Port-au-Prince: Imprimerie Aug. A. Héraux.

Leger, Jacques Nicolas. (1907), *Haiti: Her History and Her Detractors*. New York and Washington, DC: The Neale Publishing Company.

Lémery, Henry. (1936) *La révolution française à la Martinique* (The French Revolution in Martinique). Paris: Larose.

Leon, Rulx. (1974) *Propos d'histoire d'Haiti* (Sketch of a history of Haiti), vol. 2. Port-au-Prince: Imprimerie La Phalange.

Lévi-Strauss, Claude. (1966a [1962]) "The Science of the Concrete." In Lévi-Strauss (1966b [1962]) pp. 1–33.

———. (1966b [1962]) *The Savage Mind*. Chicago: University of Chicago Press [Originally Paris: Librarie Plon].

Lewis, Matthew Gregory. (1929) *Journal of a West India [Jamaican] Planter 1815–1817*. Boston: Houghton Mifflin.

Lipset, Seymour Martin, Martin Trow, and James S. Coleman. (1956) *Union Democracy: The Internal Politics of the International Typographical Union*. New York: Free Press.

Lisowski, Joseph, ed. (1991) *Caribbean Perspectives: The Social Structure of a Region*, vol. 1 [The British Virgin Islands]. New Brunswick, NJ: Transaction Publishers.

Lloyd, Christopher. (1970 [c.1968]) *The British Seaman, 1200–1860: A Social Survey*. Rutherford, NJ: Farleigh Dickinson University Press.

Luperón, Gregorio. (1939 [1895–1896];1, 2, or 3) *Notas Autobiográficas y Apuntes Históricos*. (Autobiographical notes and historical pieces, 2d ed., vols. 1–3. Santiago, D. R.: Editorial el Diario.

MacNeill, John Robert. (1985) *Atlantic Empires of France and Spain: Louisbourg and Havana, 1700–1763*. Chapel Hill: University of North Carolina Press.

Marrero, Levi. (1978; 7 , 8, or 9) *Cuba: Economía y Sociedad*. Vol. 7, *Del Monopolio Hacia la Libertad Comercial (1701–1763)*. *II*; Vol. 8, *Del Monopolio Hacia la Libertad Comercial (1701–1763)*. *III*; Vol. 9, *Azucar, Ilustración y Conciencia (1763–1868)*. *I* (Cuba: Economy and society. Vols. 7 and 8, From monopoly to commercial liberty (1701–1763), part II and part III; Vol. 9, Sugar, enlightenment, and conscience (1763–1868), part I). Madrid: Editorial Playor.

Marseille Exposition Coloniale. (1906) *Les Colonies françaises au debut du XXe siècle: Cinq ans de progrès (1900–1905)* (The French colonies at the beginning of the 20th century: five years of progress (1900–1905)) Marseille: Barbatier.

Marshall, Bernard. (1982) "Social Stratification and the Free Coloured in the Slave Society of the British Windward Islands." *Social and Economic Studies*, **31**, 1, pp. 1–39.

Marshall, Thomas Henry. (1992 [1950]) *Citizenship and Social Class*. London: Pluto Press.

Marshall, Woodville K. (1972) "Peasant Movements & Agrarian Problems in the West Indies. Part I: Aspects of the Development of the Peasantry." *Caribbean Quarterly*. **18**, 1, pp. 30–46 and 53–57.

———, ed. (1987a) *Emancipation II: Aspects of the Post-Slavery Experience in Barbados*. Bridgetown: Department of History, University of the West Indies, Cave Hill, Barbados.

———. (1987b) "19th Century Crisis in the Barbadian Sugar Industry." In Marshall, ed. (1987a) pp. 85–101.

Martineau, Alfred and L.-Ph. May. (1935) *Trois siècles d'histoire antillaise: Martinique et Guadeloupe de 1635 a nos jours* (Three centuries of the history of the Antilles: Martinique and Guadeloupe from 1635 to our time) Paris: Société de l'histoire des colonies françaises et Librarie Leroux.

Martinez-Alier, Verena. (1974) *Marriage, Class, and Colour in Nineteenth Century Cuba*. London: Cambridge University Press.

Mathieson, William Law. (1967) *British Slave Emancipation 1838–1849*. New York: Octagon Books.

Maza, Sarah. (1993) *Private Lives and Public Affairs: The Causes Célèbres of Prevolutionary France*. Berkeley: University of California Press.

Mejía Ricart, Gustavo Adolfo. (1980) *Biografía del Caudillo Pedro Santana* (Biography of the Caudillo Pedro Santana). Santo Domingo: Fundación Mejía Ricart—Guzmán Boom.

Mentze, Ernst. (1966) *Dansk Vestindien* (The Danish West Indies). Copenhagen: Carit Andersens Forlag.

Merrien [de Fréminville], Jean. (1964). *La vie quotidienne des marins au temps du roi soleil* (Daily life of sailors in the time of Louis XIV). Paris: Hachette.

———. (1970) *La course et la flibuste des origines à leur interdiction* (The hunt for ships and privateering from their origins to their prohibition). Paris: Éditions Rencontre.

Miller, Elinor, and Eugene D. Genovese, (1974) *Plantation, Town, and County; Essays on the Local History of American Slave Society*. Urbana: University of Illinois Press.

Millette, James. (1985 [1970]) *Society and Politics in Colonial Trinidad*. Curepe, Trinidad: Omega Bookshop and London: Zed Books.

Mintz, Sidney W., ed. (1974a) *Caribbean Transformations*. Chicago: Aldine.

———(1974 [1958]) "Historical Sociology of Jamaican Villages." In Mintz (1974a) 157–179.

———(1974b). "Caribbean Peasantries." In Mintz (1974a) pp. 131–145.

———(1974 [1960]), "The Origin of the Jamaican Market System." In Mintz (1974a) pp. 180–213.

———(1974 [1961]) "The Origins of Reconstituted Peasanties." In Mintz (1974a) pp. 146–156.

Monclus, Miguel Angel. (1983) *El Caudillismo en la República Dominicana (Cuarta Edición)* ("Caudillismo" in The Dominican Republic), 4th ed. Santo Domingo: Publicaciones de la Universidad CETEC.

Moreno Fraginals, Manuel. (1976 [1964]) *The Sugarmill: The Socioeconomic Complex of Sugar in Cuba 1760–1860*. (tr. Cedric Belfrage) New York: Monthly Review Press [Originally Comisión Nacional Cubana de la UNESCO].

Naipaul, V. S. (1984 [1969]) *The Loss of El-Dorado: A History.* New York: Vintage Books, Random House [originally published by Knopf].

Oakes, James. (1991) *Slavery and Freedom: An Interpretation of the Old South.* New York: Vintage Books.

Olson, Mancur. (1982) *The Rise and Decline of Nations: Economic Growth, Stagflation, and Social Rigidities.* New Haven: Yale University Press.

Oostindie, Gert J. (1988) "Cuban Railroads, 1830–1868: Origins and Effects of 'Progressive Entrepreneurialism.'" *Caribbean Studies,* **20**, 3–4, pp. 24–39.

Ortega, Juan A. 1981. *Conflicto Ango-Español por el Dominio Oceánico* (The English-Spanish conflict for dominion of the oceans). Mexico City: Universidad Nacional Autónoma de México.

Ortiz Fernández, Fernando. (1947 [1940]) *Cuban Counterpoint: Tobacco and Sugar.* (tr. Harriet de Onís) New York: Alfred A. Knopf [Originally Havana: Jesús Montrero].

Ott, Thomas O. (1973) *The Haitian Revolution 1789–1804.* Knoxville: University of Tennessee.

Page, Benjamin and Robert Y. Shapiro. (1992) *The Rational Public: Fifty Years of Trends in Americans' Policy Preferences.* Chicago: University of Chicago Press.

Pares, Richard. (1950) *A West-India Fortune.* London: Longmans, Green.

Patterson, Orlando. (1967) *The Sociology of Slavery: An Analysis of the Origins, Development, and Structure of Negro Slave Society in Jamaica,* London: MacGibbon and Kee.

————. (1991; 1) *Freedom Volume I: Freedom in the Making of Western Culture.* No place given: Basic Books.

Paturau, J. Maurice. (n.d.) *Histoire Économique de île Maurice* (Economic History of Mauritius). Les Pailles, Île Maurice [Mauritius]: Henry & Cie.

Pérez-Mallaína Bueno, Pablo Emilio. (1982) *Política Naval Española en el Atlántico 1700–1715* (Spanish Naval Policy in the Atlantic 1700–1715). Sevilla: Escuela de Estudios Hispano-Americanos de Sevilla.

Pérotin-Dumon, Anne. (1985) *Être patriote sous les tropiques: La Guadeloupe, la colonisation, et la Révolution 1789–1794* (To be a supporter of the Revolution in the tropics: Guadeloupe, colonization, and the Revolution). Basse-Terre: Société d'Histoire de la Guadeloupe.

————. (1988) "Les Jacobins des Antilles ou l'Esprit de Liberté dans les Iles-du-Vent" ("The Jacobins of the Antilles, or the spirit of liberty in the French windward islands"). *Revue d'histoire moderne et contemporaine* (July) pp. 275–304.

————. (1989a) "Révolutionnaires françaises et royalists espagnols dan les antilles" ("French revolutionaries and Spanish royalists in the Antilles"). *Revue française d'histoire d'outre-mer,* **76**, 282–283, pp. 125–158.

————. (1989b) "Guerre et Révolution dans les Petites antilles: Le Prix du Sucre ou de la Liberté?" ("War and Revolution in the small Antilles: The price of sugar or of liberty). *Revue française d'histoire d'outre-mer,* **76**, 282–283, pp. 239–245.

Peterson, Mendel. (1975) *The Funnel of Gold.* Boston: Little, Brown.

Petitjean-Roget, Jacques. (1966) *La Gaoulé: La révolte de la Martinique en 1717*

("The Gaoulé": The revolt of Martinique in 1717). Fort de France: Société d' histoire de la Martinique.

Peytraud, Lucien. (1897) *L'Esclavage aux antilles Françaises avant 1789* (Slavery in the French Antilles before 1789). Paris: Hachette.

Polsby, Nelson W. and Fred I. Greenstein, eds. (1975) *Handbook of Political Science*, vol. 3. Reading, MA: Addison-Wesley.

Postma, Johannes M. (1990) *The Dutch in the Atlantic Slave Trade 1600–1815*. Cambridge: Cambridge University Press.

Poyer, John. (1971 [1808]) *The History of Barbados*, London: Frank Cass & Co.

Pred, Alan. (1987) "Structuration, Biography Formation, and Knowledge: Observations on Port Growth during the Late Mercantile Period." In Chase (1987) pp. 269–298.

Price-Mars, Jean. (1953;1 or 2) *La République d'Haiti et La République Dominicaine: Les aspects divers d'un problème d'histoire, de géographie et de ethnologie* (The Republic of Haiti and the Dominican Republic: Various aspects of a problem of history, of geography, and of ethnology), vols. 1 and 2. Port-au-Prince: publisher unknown.

Ramesar, Marianne. (1976) "The Impact of Indian Immigrants on Colonial Trinidad Society." *Caribbean Quarterly*, **22**, 1, pp. 5–17.

Rediker, Marcus. (1987) *Between the Devil and the Deep Blue Sea: Merchant Seamen, Pirates, and the Anglo-American Maritime World, 1700–1750.* (Cambridge and New York: Cambridge University Press)

Riverend, Julio le. (1972) *Historia Económica de Cuba* (Economic History of Cuba). Barcelona: Ediciones Ariel.

Rodríguez Demorizi, Emilio. (1981) *Documentos para la Historia de la República Dominicana* (Documents for the history of The Dominican Republic), vol. 52. Santo Domingo: Editorial del Caribe.

Roemer, John. (1982) *A General Theory of Exploitation and Class*. Cambridge, MA: Harvard University Press.

Royal Commission. (1884) *Report of the Royal Commission to Enquire into the Public Revenues (P.P., 1884, C-3840)*, vol. 1.

Rubin, Vera and Arthur Tuden. (1977) *Comparative Perspectives on Slavery in New World Plantation Societies*. Published as Vol. **292** of *Annals of the New York Academy of Sciences*.

Safford, Frank. (1985) "Politics, Ideology and Society in Post-Independence Spanish America." In Bethell (1985) pp. 347–421.

Sarfatti [Larson], Magali. (see Larson)

Scheppele, Kim Lane. (1988) *Legal Secrets: Equality and Efficiency in the Common Law*. Chicago: University of Chicago Press.

Scherer, André. (1974 [1965]) *Histoire de la Réunion* (History of Reunion Island). Paris: Presses Universitaires de France [Que sais-je?].

Scherer, Frederic M. (1980) *Industrial Market Structure and Economic Performance*. Boston: Houghton Mifflin.

Schnakenbourg, Christian. (1980; 1) *Histoire de l'industrie sucrière en Guadeloupe aux XIXe et XXe siècles*. Tome 1, *La crise du système esclavagiste (1835–1847)* (History of the sugar industry in Guadeloupe in the 19th and 20th centuries. Vol. l, The crisis of the slave system,1835–1847). Paris: Éditions L'Harmattan.

Schumpeter, Joseph A. (1950 [1942]) *Capitalism, Socialism, and Democracy.* New York: Harper & Brothers.

————. (1954) *History of Economic Analysis.* Edited by Elizabeth Boody Schumpeter. New York: Oxford University Press.

Scott, Rebecca Jarvis. (1985) *Slave Emancipation in Cuba: The Transition to Free Labor 1860–1899.* Princeton: Princeton University Press.

Serrano Mangas, Fernando. (1985) *Los Galeones de la Carrera de Indias 1650–1700* (The galleons of the fleet of the Indies 1650–1700). Sevilla: Escuela de Estudios Hispano-Ameriocanos de Sevilla.

Shepard, Charles. (1831) *An Historical Account of the Island of St. Vincent.* London: W. Nicol.

Simon, Herbert A. and Bonini, Charles. (1958) "On The Size Distribution of Business Firms." *American Economic Review.* **48** (September) pp. 607–17.

Sirmans, M. Eugene. (1962) "The Legal Status of the Slave in South Carolina, 1670–1740." *Journal Southern History,* **28**, 462–66.

Skocpol, Theda. (1979) *States and Social Revolution: A Comparative Analysis of France, Russia, and China.* Cambridge: Cambridge University Press.

Smith, Adam. (1976 [1776]) *An Inquiry into the Nature and Causes of the Wealth of Nations.* R. H. Campbell, A. S. Skinner, and W. B. Todd, eds. Oxford: Oxford University Press.

Smith, Joan, J. Collins, T. Hopkins, and A. Mohammad, eds. (1988) *Racism, Sexism, and the World System.* New York: Greenwood Press.

Smith, Michael Garfield. (1962) *Kinship and Community in Carriacou.* New Haven: Yale University Press.

————. (1965a) *Stratification in Grenada.* Berkeley: University of California Press.

————. (1965b) *The Plural Society in the British West Indies.* Berkeley: University of California Press.

————. (1965 [1953]) "Some Aspects of Social Structure in the British Caribbean [St. Vincent and Jamaica] about 1920." In Smith (1965b) pp. 92–115 [originally *Social and Economic Studies,* **1**, 4].

————. (1965 [1957]) "Ethnic and Cultural Pluralism in the British Caribbean." In Smith (1965b) pp. 10–17 [originally in *Ethnic and Cultural Pluralism in Intertropical Countries* (Brussels: International Institute of Differing Civilizations)].

————. (1965c) "A Framework for Caribbean Studies." In Smith (1965b) pp. 18–74.

————. (1965 [1960]), "Social and Cultural Pluralism." In Smith (1965b) pp. 75–91.

Steele, Beverley. (1976) "East Indian Indenture and the Work of the Presbyterian Church among the Indians in Grenada." *Caribbean Quarterly,* **22**, 1, pp. 28–39.

Stinchcombe, Arthur L. (1987 [1968]) *Constructing Social Theories.* Chicago: University of Chicago Press.

———. (1975) "Social Structure and Politics." In Polsby and Greenstein, eds. (1975) pp. 557–622.

———. (1978) *Theoretical Methods in Social History.* Orlando: Academic Press.

Tannenbaum, Frank. (1946) *Slave and Citizen: The Negro in the Americas.* New York: Vintage (Knopf).

Tarrade, Jean. (1972; I or II) *Le commerce colonial de la France à la fin de l'Ancien Régime: L'évolution du régime de "l'exclusif" de 1763 à 1789* (The colonial commerce of France at the end of the *Ancien Régime*: The evolution of the regime of imperial preference from 1763 to 1789), vol. 1 or 2. Paris: Presses universitaires de France.

Thomas, Robert J. (1985). *Citizenship, Gender, and Work: Social Organization of Industrial Agriculture.* Berkeley: University of California Press.

Thome, James A. and J. Horace Kimball. (1969 [1838]) *Emancipation in the West Indies [The Anti-Slavery Crusade in America].* New York: Arno Press [originally published by the American Anti-Slavery Society].

Tilly, Charles. (1990). *Coercion, Capital, and European States, AD 990–1990.* Cambridge, MA and Oxford: Basil Blackwell.

———. (1993) *European Revolutions, 1492–1992.* Oxford and Cambridge, MA: Blackwell.

Tolentine Rojas, Vincente. (1944) *Historia de la Division Territorial 1494–1943: Documentos y Estudios Históricos* (History of the territorial division between Haiti and the Dominican Republic 1794–1943: Documents and historical studies), vol. 3. Santiago, Dominican Republic: Editorial El Diario.

Trotsky, Leon. (1960 [1932]; 1, 2, or 3) *History of the Russian Revolution.* (tr. Max Eastman) Ann Arbor: University of Michigan Press. Reprinted in one volume with the original 3-volume pagination.

———. (1973 [1939]) *Their Morals and Ours.* New York: Pathfinder Press. The title essay is pp. 13–52.

Trouillot, Michel-Rolph. (1988) *Peasants and Capital: Dominica in the World Economy.* Baltimore: Johns Hopkins University Press.

Tuchman, Barbara W. (1988) *The First Salute: A View of the American Revolution.* New York: Knopf.

van Soest, Jaap. (1977) "Curaçao and Its Economy at the Turn of the [20th] Century." *Social and Economic Studies,* 26, 1, pp. 38–61.

Verna, Paul. (1980 [1969]) *Pétion y Bolívar: Cuarenta años (1790–1830) de relaciones haitiano-venezolanos y su aporte a la emancipación de Hispanoamérica* (Pétion and Bolívar: Forty years (1790–1830) of Haitian-Venezuelan relations and their contribution to the emancipation of Hispanic America). Caracas: Ediciones de la Presidencia [Originally Oficina Central de Información].

Veyne, Paul. (1976) *Le pain et le cirque: Sociologie historique d'un pluralisme politique* (Bread and circuses: Historical sociology of a political pluralism). Paris: Éditions du Seuil [Univers Historique].

Watts, David. (1987) *The West Indies: Patterns of Development, Culture, and Environmental Change since 1492.* Cambridge: Cambridge University Press.

Weber, Max. (1924 [1889]) "Zur Geschichte der Handelsgesellschaften im

Mittelalter nach südeuropäischen Quellen" (On the history of business societies in the Middle Ages according to southern European Sources). Reprinted in his *Gesammelte Aufsätze zur Sozial- und Wirtschaftsgeschichte*. Tübingen: G.C.B. Mohr (Paul Siebeck) pp. 312–443; Abhandlungen, Stuttgart: Ferdinand Enke.

———. (1946 [1919). "Politics as a Vocation." In Gerth and Mills (1946) pp. 77–128.

Welles, Sumner. (1928) *Naboth's Vinyard: The Dominican Republic 1844–1924*. New York: Payson and Clarke.

Wessel, G. A. and S. Leacock. (1957) *Barbados and George Washington*. Barbados: Advocate Co.

Westergaard, Waldemar. (1917) *The Danish West Indies under Company Rule 1671–1754 with a Supplementary Chapter 1755–1917*. New York: Macmillan.

Williams, Eric. (1962) *History of the People of Trinidad and Tobago*. Port of Spain: PNM Publishing Co.

———. (1964 [1944]) *Capitalism and Slavery*. London: Andre Deutsch.

Williamson, Oliver E. (1975) *Markets and Hierarchies, Analysis and Antitrust Implications: A Study in the Economics of Internal Organization*. New York: Free Press.

Wilson, Edmund. (1956 [1949]) *Red, Black, Blond and Olive, Studies in Four Civilizations: Zuñi, Haiti, Soviet Russia, Israel*, New York: Oxford University Press.

Woodward, C. Vann. (1957 [1955]) *The Strange Career of Jim Crow: A Brief Account of Segregation*. New York: Oxford University Press.

Zablocki, Benjamin. (1980) *Alienation and Charisma: A Study of Contemporary American Communes*. New York: Free Press.

Zeitlin, Maurice, ed. (1981) *Political Power and Social Theory*. Greenwich, CT: JAI Press.

Map Sources

Couper, Alastair, ed. (1983) *The Times Atlas of the Oceans*. New York: Van Nostrand Reinhold. Dominant winds and currents in the Atlantic, pp. 44–45; more detail on winds, including the Pacific and Indian oceans, p. 46; moisture content of the winds over the oceans, p. 47; Madagascar-Réunion-Mauritius place in the South Indian Ocean system, p. 49; hurricane zones in the Caribbean, Phillipines-South-China, and Madagascar regions, pp. 54–56.

Higman, Barry W. (1984) *Slave Population of the British Caribbean 1807–1834*. Outline maps with political subdivisions and cities pp. xxvi-xxxiii for the British islands of the period.

James, Preston E. (1959) *Latin America*, 3d ed. New York: Oddyssey Press. Landforms of various parts of the Caribbean are presented in different maps. Map 2.1 in Chapter 2 is based on these maps.

Nelles Maps. (n.d.) *Caribbean Islands 1: Bermuda, Bahamas, Greater Antilles 1/250,000; Caribbean Islands 2: Lesser Antilles 1/250,000; Special Maps of All Larger Islands*. Müchen: Nelles Verlag.

Rand McNally. (1987) *Universal World Atlas.* Chicago: Rand McNally. Political maps of the Caribbean, its coasts, and its islands, pp. 62–65, 76–77—highest peaks on pp. 64–65; populations and areas of islands or island groups can
  be extracted from pp. 225–228.
Watts, David. (1987) *The West Indies: Patterns of Development, Culture, and
  Environmental Change since 1492.* Cambridge: Cambridge University Press—
  many detailed overview maps of social and economic history, all empires.
  Highest peaks are in a table.

Index

About the Author

ARTHUR L. STINCHCOMBE is Professor of Sociology at Northwestern University. His works include *Information and Organizations, Constructing Social Theories, Economic Sociology,* and *Theoretical Methods in Social History.*